W9-APJ-355

Illinois

Illinois

Crystal Yednak
with photographs by the author

The Countryman Press ✳ Woodstock, Vermont

Explorer's Guide Illinois
978-0-88150-925-0

Interior photographs by the author unless otherwise specified
Maps by Erin Greb Cartography, © The Countryman Press
Book design by Bodenweber Design
Composition by PerfecType, Nashville, TN

Published by The Countryman Press, P.O. Box 748, Woodstock, VT 05091

Distributed by W. W. Norton & Company, Inc., 500 Fifth Avenue, New York, NY 10110

Printed in the United States of America

10 9 8 7 6 5 4 3 2 1

To Rob, Harry, and Max

EXPLORE WITH US!

Welcome to the first edition of *Illinois: An Explorer's Guide*. I spent two years driving around the state—hiking, biking, swimming, eating, and taking in grand museums and parks (rough life, I know). Here, I've laid out the best of the state. The book encompasses the entire state of Illinois, from dynamic Chicago to quaint historic towns to some of the most remote natural areas you'll find in the Midwest. If you're a longtime Illinois resident seeking a fun weekend trip, a traveler looking for places to stop on your road trip through Illinois, or a visitor looking to extend a visit to a major destination like Chicago, this book is for you. *Illinois: An Explorer's Guide* is based on my own travels, thoughts, and experiences. No paid ads or deals here. In most cases, I surprised the hosts with a visit so I could experience each place as you, my dear reader, are likely to. This is not a listing of every single tourist attraction in every single city in the state. Instead, I've gone deeper into the areas I believe will truly lead to fun explorations. I've structured the book in regional sections so you can easily build your own itineraries. I hope you enjoy.

WHAT'S WHERE

From Abe Lincoln to Zion, this alphabetical listing in the beginning of the book provides an overview of some useful terms. It also gives you an idea of what to expect during your travels.

PRICES

I took great care to make sure the prices listed in the book were accurate as of press time, but restaurants close, change their hours, and raise their prices without notifying me first. (The nerve!) So please be aware that the information is not static.

You should also know that Illinois has a statewide 6 percent tax on lodging. Then the picture gets confusing, as local governments can add their own additional taxes on top of that, so the total tax varies by city. The total hotel tax in Chicago is 15.4 percent. In Quincy, it's about 14 percent, Galena 11 percent. So you see the confusion. Meal taxes also vary by municipality.

SMOKING

Illinois has a statewide ban on smoking in most public places and workplaces, including bars and restaurants.

KEY TO SYMBOLS

♂ The wedding-rings symbol appears beside facilities that frequently serve as venues for weddings and civil unions.

🏵 The special-value symbol appears next to lodging and restaurants that combine high quality and moderate prices.

🏄 The kids-friendly symbol appears next to lodging, restaurants, activities, and shops of special appeal to youngsters.

🐾 The dog-paw symbol appears next to lodging that accepts pets (usually with a reservation and deposit) as of press time.

♿ The wheelchair symbol appears next to lodging, restaurants, and attractions that are partially or fully handicapped-accessible.

((ᵖ)) The broadcast signal appears next to listings where there is WiFi access, free or for a small fee.

⊷ The leaf symbol appears next to lodgings, restaurants, and attractions that are eco-friendly.

Y The martini glass indicates a destination is a bar or nightspot.

☂ The rainy-day activity symbol indicates a good place to go when the weather is foul.

LODGING

I've tried to avoid the chain hotels, because they tend to be the same everywhere. But there are a few areas where I've included one, especially if the chain hotel had a really great location or something that was difficult to find elsewhere. Each entry includes a range of prices for a standard, double occupancy room.

$ = Less than $100 per night
$$ = $100–200
$$$ = $200–300
$$$$ = Over $300

RESTAURANTS

Establishments in the Eating Out section are generally less expensive than those in the Dining Out section. Eating Out is for grabbing a quick bite or sampling some high-quality local fare in a very casual space. Dining Out restaurants are a little bit more expensive. Look to Dining Out if you're planning a fun night out and want to sit and enjoy your meal without hurrying. The prices in this category range from $15 entrees up to gourmet experiences that may cost you a couple hundred dollars. Each entry includes a range of prices for main dishes.

$ = $0–10
$$ = $10–20
$$$ = $20–30
$$$$ = Over $30

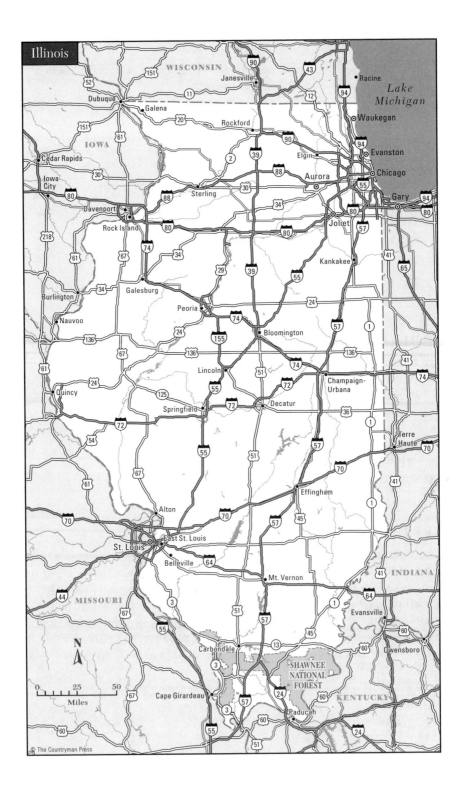

CONTENTS

Maps

ACKNOWLEDGMENTS

Many helpful people reinforced the stereotype that Midwesterners are genuinely nice, and in this case, I could not be more grateful to them for filling that role. To all of the friendly tourism folks, resort owners, tour guides, wait staff, and state park volunteers, thank you for taking the time to talk with me and answer my questions.

This project would have been impossible without my husband, Rob Kent, who hiked many a path alongside me, drove many, many miles, and gave many a pep talk. Now we can add navigator, proofreader, editor, and researcher to the long list of tasks at which you excel. I want to thank you and our two little adventure-seekers, Harry and Maxwell, for bringing even more fun than I thought possible to our road trips, and to my life.

To my sister and friend, Stephanie Yednak Norton, for listening, reading, and accompanying me on a grand adventure to the Mississippi River. I would not have been able to do this without your invaluable photographic advice.

To my parents, Steve and Linda Yednak, thanks for cheering me on as you always do, and for proofreading while doing so. My mother-in-law Carol Kent deserves special thanks for her support and editing. Thanks also to the rest of my excellent family for their help: Kathy and Jeff Knurek, Joe Norton, Angie and Aaron Pettis, Sue and Maggie Barney, and Bob and Phyllis Kent.

And to the amazing group of friends who listen, inspire, and are always there to tell me that I can do it: Jeannie Taylor, Beth Tidmarsh, Lara Flint, Mindy Johnston, and Heather Flett. Thank you. I'd also like to thank my good friends Shia Kapos and Peter Behle for connecting me with The Countryman Press, and Kim Grant, for sharing her wisdom.

Lastly, a special thanks to the countless friends who passed along recommendations, tips, and answered my questions about their hometowns and favorite places in the great state of Illinois. Thank you all!

INTRODUCTION

Deep roots and great heights—that's what you'll find in Illinois. The deep roots stretch across giant swaths of plains that yield new crops each year, thanks to a people proud of their long track record. Big thinkers have propelled the state and its cities skyward with dreams of tall buildings, industrial innovations, and creativity that knows no bounds.

Chicago is the big draw for travelers to Illinois, and rightly it should be, with its awe-inspiring cityscape, world-class museums, and premier cultural opportunities. This is where comic geniuses rise to the top, as do athletic superstars, literary giants, and future presidents.

But you would be ignoring many adventures if you did not venture beyond the city limits, toward the Mississippi River and its small river towns, through the land of Lincoln to trace the history of one of the nation's most revered presidents, and south to the Shawnee National Forest and the "Garden of the Gods." In between these diverse corners of the state, you'll find places where masterpieces were created as you tour the homes of great artists like Frank Lloyd Wright. You'll lose yourself in a drive through small towns with characters all their own, as you head toward state parks carved into works of art by rivers and glaciers. Step back in time when you tour the remaining mounds of a city built by tribes who long ago called Illinois home.

Illinois is often divided into two categories: Chicago, and everywhere else. Sweeping "everywhere else" into one giant "downstate" category overlooks the diversity of the natural beauty you will encounter here. Our western border, the Mississippi River, offers breathtaking views and excellent recreational opportunities. The Galena area is a must see. The Illinois River, which cuts through the heart of the state, will cajole you down past the canyons of Starved Rock State Park, to the riverside city of Peoria. Many of the state's smaller cities have embraced their riverside status and like Peoria, worked to revitalize areas near the water.

Great portions of the state are flat and devoted to agriculture, with field after field of soybeans and corn. But Illinois is so large, that as you continue driving, you'll hit valleys and lush woods, especially as you arrive at the state's southern tip, home to the Shawnee National Forest. Camp, canoe, swim, hike, fish, bike, sail—you can do it all as you move from Lake Michigan outward through the state's parks and preserves.

You can also meander the state's wine trails, a recent and welcome development as far as I'm concerned. In 1997 there were just 12 wineries in Illinois, now there are more than 70. With that growth, bed and breakfasts and other attractions have cropped up to complement the wineries, and help you to build great trips.

The wine trails were just one unexpected surprise in doing the research for this book. I've lived in Illinois most of my life, having grown up in a town outside Chicago. My parents took us to the state parks, to the beaches, and on longer trips to learn about Lincoln in Springfield. As a typical teenager, I tried hard to be bored on these trips, but I wasn't. I left the Midwest for a few years but realized how much I love Chicago, the lakefront, the energy, and the stories here. As a reporter and writer in Illinois for more than 15 years, I've traveled around the state talking to people and doing research for articles. I've played tour guide for friends, and taken trips to other Illinois destinations for fun. I thought I *knew* Illinois, but I discovered so much more about the state in my explorations for this book.

There are many different journeys you can take through Illinois. I enjoy days spent in museums, hiking, or on the water, followed up with a great dinner over a campfire or in a fantastic restaurant. At the end of the chapter, I've built a couple sample itineraries depending on what kind of trip you're looking for.

No matter where you go, make sure you take the time to listen to the stories of the people here. The people are much like the state itself—grounded but accustomed to stretching upward. For the most part you'll find friendliness, in small towns or on a Chicago street.

Undoubtedly, some of the stories you know. The most colorful come from our legendarily corrupt politicians, who never fail to shock and amaze. The nation's image of Illinois is often dominated with jokes about our politics, our tangled past with the Chicago mob, or our sports fans with their classic Midwestern accents. Yes, we are that.

But beyond the usual, there are many compelling Illinois stories to dive into. Retrace the steps of explorers like Jacques Marquette or Rene-Robert Cavelier de LaSalle, who saw the possibilities here. Or how about the fantastic adventures of Lewis and Clark? Their tale has an important chapter in Illinois. Walk where Abraham Lincoln, Ulysses S. Grant, Ronald Reagan, and Barack Obama did, to get a sense of what these presidents may have gleaned from their time living in Illinois. Wander through parks that reveal the beauty of the Midwest's plains, valleys, and rivers. Immerse yourself in museums that showcase the importance of Illinois to the worlds of art, music, agriculture, and architecture.

Welcome to Illinois. Be prepared to dig deep and stretch high.

WHAT'S WHERE IN ILLINOIS

ACCENTS In Chicago, we like to draw out our vowels here in a flat, nasally way. So instead of "Mom and Dad" it's "Mahhh-m and "D-aah-d." You will find some who cling to "youse guys" and to "dis" instead of "this." But for the most part, the Chicago/Illinois accent is not so over the top. As you travel south in the state, you may notice a more distinct Southern accent taking hold in some areas.

AQUARIUMS AND ANIMALS You must visit the Shedd Aquarium in Chicago. Truly world-class. My favorite zoo in all the world is Lincoln Park Zoo, just for the unique way it blends in with the lakefront and surrounding city neighborhoods. You are taking a city stroll, and look at that! There's a polar bear. Other cool places in Illinois to see wildlife up-close include the Shawnee National Forest and the Wildlife Prairie State Park outside of Peoria.

BALD EAGLES In the winter, you can observe the beautiful,

symbolic bird at Starved Rock State Park. The river waters near the dam remain unfrozen, enabling the eagles to continue catching fish. Every winter there is a bald eagle-watching weekend with all kinds of events centered around viewing the graceful creatures. Pere Marquette State Park and the Grafton area on the Mississippi River provide other good spots to view wintering eagles.

BEACHES With a lake as beautiful as Lake Michigan, Chicago has

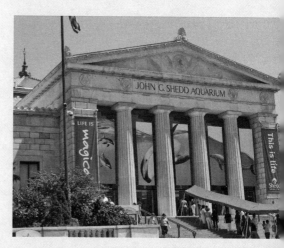

a number of great beaches. My favorite is Montrose Avenue beach because of the city views you can take in. Many people like Oak Street beach, but it's pretty packed on weekends. Evanston also has nice beaches worth exploring, although there is a fee to enter. A little farther north, you can find a less-populated beach at Illinois Beach State Park. But heed the swimming bans that are put into effect when the water levels are just not quite right.

CAMPING We like Starved Rock, Apple River Canyon, Giant City, and Pere Marquette. For a more unique camping experience, try Feather Down Farms in Northern Illinois, where you can stay in a tent/cabin on a working farm.

CORPORATE HEADQUARTERS With the railroad, airports, and interstate highways, Illinois has long made sense as the place to center business operations for

many companies. Boeing, United Airlines, John Deere, Playboy, Kraft, Sara Lee, Wrigley, Sears, McDonald's, Exelon, and Caterpillar all have their world headquarters in Illinois.

CORRUPTION It's not something that's good to be known for, but Illinois continues to attract national attention for the behavior of some of our elected officials. (Most recently, I speak of the jail time served by former Governor George Ryan. His successor, Rod Blagojevich livened things up with his hair, of course, but also when federal recordings of his conversations hit the news.) There always seems to be some political scandal unfolding in some level of government. The only thing I can say is that when Illinoisans do something well, they do it really well. Clout rules here.

DRIVES For scenic drives, we have the Meeting of the Great Rivers Scenic Byway through Alton and Grafton, which has really lovely views of the rivers. The stretch of road heading out toward Galena is excellent for its scenery as well. And of course, you have the famous Lake Shore Drive along Lake Michigan in Chicago.

EARTHQUAKES We do get them here, about once a year. The largest recorded quake registered a 5.4 on the Richter scale in 1968.

FARMS Illinois has roughly 76,000 farms spread out across almost 27 million acres. Farmland covers about 75 percent of the total land in the state. The prime crops are soybeans and corn.

FLOODS You will still see marks of some of the great floods that river communities have experienced. Near Alton, and Grafton—where the town was flooded for 195 days in 1993—you'll see buildings still marked with water levels from that flood that seem impossible. The Mississippi, Ohio, Illinois, Fox, and even the Chicago River, while great for recreation, can pose a threat when the rains are heavy.

FRANCHISES Sandwich shop entrepreneurs have been pretty successful in Illinois. You'll find the original Potbelly's, which got its start on Lincoln Avenue in Chicago and now stands at more than 200 shops in the Midwest, the mid-Atlantic, and Texas. Jimmy John's started in a garage in Charleston, Illinois, and is now at about 1,000 stores. While the first McDonald's opened in California in 1948, it took Ray Kroc to franchise the idea to turn it into the global empire it is today. See his first store in Des Plaines, Illinois, a suburb of Chicago, the first with those iconic yellow arches. Steak 'n Shake was founded in Normal in the 1930s and is now found across the country.

GRID SYSTEM Chicago's map is laid out on a grid. The intersection of State and Madison downtown is the zero point. All other addresses are figured as east or west, north or south, of this point. Each city block you travel, the address numbers should go up or down by about 100. Eight blocks, or 800 in addresses, equals about a mile. For example, Fullerton Parkway, which is 2400 North, is about 3 miles north of the downtown zero point. We also have a number of diagonal streets that cut across the city, some of which follow old Native American trails, but create chaotic six-way intersections. These include Elston, Lincoln, and Milwaukee avenues.

HISTORY World-class museums tell the story of Lincoln, great architects, important rivers, transportation innovations, titans of industry, and ancient peoples. Must-sees include the Field Museum in Chicago and the Abraham Lincoln Presidential Museum in Springfield.

HORSESHOE This Springfield dish is among many unique Illinois dining experiences that can range from the gourmet to the greasy (And I mean that in a good way). The Horseshoe consists of toast, topped with meat (it varies), smothered in a cheese sauce, and covered with fries.

HUMIDITY Our climate is humid, especially in the middle of July, so pack hair product or a hat.

ICE-SKATING Set against the backdrop of the cityscape, the ice-skating rink in Chicago's Millennium Park is an experience. Other places to try winter sports: Chestnut Mountain in Galena offers skiing and snowboarding. You'll also find cross-country skiing, ice-skating, and ice fishing at many of the state parks.

LINCOLN is everywhere. You can follow his life throughout the state, as there are preserved sites where he debated Douglas, where he stayed, where he ate, and where he lived. Springfield of course is a must, if you want to really know Lincoln, but other cities such as Vandalia bring chapters of his story to life.

LITTLE EGYPT is the nickname given to Southern Illinois.

MARATHON Every October, 45,000 runners arrive in Chicago, having spent months, sometimes years, working toward their dream of finishing the 26.2-mile race. Runners like the Chicago race because the course is relatively flat, the weather usually cool (though not always), and the crowd supportive. People line the course for most of the route, screaming, cheering, and playing music. It's awe-inspiring to see the runners pushing themselves that hard and to see all the people who care about watching someone achieve a dream. Chokes me up every time when strangers who've been cheering alongside me finally see *their* runner, whether it's Mom, Dad, Son, Daughter, Broth-

er, or best friend. It's an explosion of cheers, whoops, tears, applause, and whistles, emotion everywhere. I love it.

MOVIES The scenery here makes for good backdrops in movies. Among the titles that have been filmed in Illinois: *Transformers, High Fidelity, North By Northwest, My Bodyguard, The Blues Brothers, Risky Business, National Lampoon's Vacation, Sixteen Candles, Ferris Bueller's Day Off, About Last Night, Running Scared, The Untouchables, Adventures in Babysitting, Planes, Trains & Automobiles, Home Alone, Groundhog Day, The Fugitive, While You Were Sleeping, My Best Friend's Wedding, Never Been Kissed, Return to Me, Batman Begins, The Dark Knight,* and *Public Enemies.*

NUCLEAR Enrico Fermi and scientists at the University of Chicago achieved the first controlled, self-sustaining nuclear chain reaction on December 2, 1942, in the squash court below the university's stadium. The chain reaction was essential to the U.S. Army's top-secret Manhattan Project to develop an atomic bomb. You can see the site where it happened marked on the University of Chicago campus in Hyde Park, on South Ellis Avenue between 56th and 57th Streets.

OPRAH is an attraction all by herself, in Chicago. Her iconic TV show comes to a close in the fall of 2011, ending a favorite tourist activity—sitting in Oprah's audience. But there still will be the store, where you can buy Oprah's old clothes and her other favorite items.

PRESIDENTS Illinois can claim four presidents as residents at one time or another. There's Ulysses S. Grant, whose story you can hear more of in Galena, and Abraham Lincoln, of course. You can visit Ronald Reagan's childhood home in Dixon. Barack Obama made his adult home in Chicago, where he met wife, Michelle, and launched his political career. In addition, former First Lady and subsequent Secretary of State, Hillary Rodham Clinton, grew up in Park Ridge, a suburb of Chicago.

POPCORN The popcorn that people stand in line for hours to buy when they're in town for just a few hours: Garrett's. The store started out at 10 W. Madison Street but has nine locations throughout Chicago now, and one in New York. The selections are limited to plain, buttery, caramel crisp (with or without nuts), and cheese corn. Also, the first automated popcorn machine to pop corn in oil was invented in Chicago in the 1890s by Charles Cretors, and the family still makes the machines here.

PUBLIC ART From the iconic Picasso sculpture in Daley Plaza to the glass-blown magic of Dale Chihuly at the Garfield Park Conservatory, Chicago has great public art. We also frequently have special public art programs. Part of the reason for the collection of public art is that the city requires a percentage of the cost of constructing or renovating any municipal or public building to go toward public art. Other great pieces: *The Four Seasons* by Marc Chagall at 10 S. Dearborn Street, Alexander Calder's *Flamingo* at 50 W. Adams Street, and Buckingham Fountain in Grant Park.

QUOTABLE Carl Sandburg, Nelson Algren, Studs Terkel, Ernest Hemingway, Upton Sinclair, Mike Royko, Gwendolyn Brooks, and Saul Bellow, all brilliant writers connected to Illinois, either

through birth or the stories they found here.

RENAMING The park where the White Sox play used to be called Comiskey Park. Now it's U.S. Cellular Field. The tallest building in the U.S., the Sears Tower, is now Willis Tower. Marshall Field's is now Macy's. This is happening elsewhere, but Illinoisans cling to the old names. Five years after the name change, Marshall Field's fans were still staging protests. You'll still meet people who refer to Macy's as Field's on purpose, or who refuse to go at all. Personally, it will always be Field's, Comiskey Park, and the Sears Tower to me. You can't change city icons.

REVERSE THE RIVER In 1900, engineers in Chicago succeeded in a modern engineering feat: Reversing the flow of the Chicago River, which previously flowed into Lake Michigan, dragging all the river sewage with it. Once the project was complete, the river flowed toward the Chicago Sanitary and Ship Canal, improving life (and smells) in Chicago.

ROUTE 66 The famous highway popularized in songs and on TV starts in Chicago and cuts through the state for 421 miles on its way to California. For a nostalgic trip, try the Illinois Route 66 Scenic Byway. There are some signs marking the route, but if you want a detailed itinerary that will take you through the small towns and give you the proper flavor, call the byway office (217-525-9308; www.illinoisroute66.org). They'll also ship you a detailed map.

THE SECOND CITY The alum of the famous comedy, stage, and improvisation school include Dan Aykroyd, Jim and John Belushi, John Candy, Steve Carell, Dan Castellaneta, Stephen Colbert, Chris Farley, Tina Fey, Linda Lavin, Tim Meadows, Anne Meara, Bill Murray, Mike Myers, Gilda Radner, Joan Rivers, Horatio Sanz, Amy Sedaris, Nia Vardalos, and George Wendt. You can take in shows from the current crop of standouts in Chicago's Old Town neighborhood.

STREET FESTIVALS Chicago has many world-renowned festivals hosted at Grant Park or Millennium Park, from Jazz Fest to Blues Fest to Lollapalooza. Each year the festivals' fantastic lineups draw people from around the world to celebrate music at its best. But also, a little farther away from the city center, you'll find street festivals in the neighborhoods that attract excellent musicians. Consider the Old Town School of Folk Music's Folk and Roots Festival, or Pitchfork Music Festival. Beyond Chicago, there's the Burgoo festival in Utica—which centers around a pioneer stew cooked for 12 hours over a fire—and a number of sweet corn festivals.

SUPERHEROES Illinois has a few connections to superheroes.

Take the celebration of all that is Superman in Metropolis, at the state's far southern border. You can visit the Superman Museum and take part in a days-long celebration of the hero every year. In addition, the Batman film, *The Dark Knight,* was filmed in Chicago.

TRAILS Towns throughout the state have converted old railroad right-of-way into great bike trails, or just recognized the need to offer bike enthusiasts lanes or separate paths. Some fun trails to explore: The Vadalabene trail near Alton and Grafton, the Hennepin Canal Trail, and the Lakefront path in Chicago.

TRAINS Train buffs, Illinois has the Chicago Transit Authority (CTA) and Metra, with double-decker trains, subways, and elevated trains. The Chicago History Museum has the first "L" car and the first locomotive to serve Chicago. About an hour northwest of Chicago, you will definitely love the Illinois Railway Museum in Union, with giant warehouses of all kinds of trains. Many small towns have preserved their original train depots. The Chicago Botanic Garden has an excellent model train garden.

U-PICK FARMS In McHenry County and other northern Illinois areas, orchards abound. Stock up for your canning or pie-making needs. Great way to connect with nature.

VANDALIA The state's second capital was located in Vandalia. You can tour the building and other Lincoln sites in this south-central Illinois city.

WEATHER It is coldest up north, but in general, Illinois gets hot, hot, hot in July and August, and cold, cold, cold from about November to March. We have some violent storms in the spring. We do get tornadoes through the state from about April through August, so stay connected to weather reports where you can. In most areas, sirens are activated if there is a tornado warning, which means a tornado has been spotted on the ground or on the radar, and you need to seek shelter or get to an interior room away from windows.

ZION Illinois has drawn high-minded folks who believe seriously in their principles. For example, Bishop Hill in western Illinois was

founded as a Christian utopian community. Then in the far-north suburbs of Chicago, near the Wisconsin border, you have Zion. It was founded at the turn of the 20th century by a man looking to create a Christian society free of the evils of the world.

Chicago and Suburbs

DOWNTOWN AND LAKEFRONT

NEIGHBORHOODS

SUBURBS

DOWNTOWN AND LAKEFRONT

One day, Lake Michigan sparkles a turquoise blue, reflecting back a city gleaming in sunshine. The next day, choppy gray waves push against city blocks that are bustling and hard at work.

Chicago is known for its skyscrapers, the Loop, the sports teams, the museums—all wonderful man-made features of a truly fantastic city. But don't overlook the natural beauty that surrounds it—a lakefront that constantly changes its moods, and the city's with it, yet consistently offers new opportunities for those willing to explore.

A day spent walking north or south along the lakefront will give you a hint of the power of Lake Michigan for the people who live here. In the summer, the paths are filled with people running, biking, swimming, napping, picnicking, enjoying the beach, or just staring out from the shore. Walk far enough and you'll make the same discoveries made by many before as you stumble upon the city's free Lincoln Park Zoo, harbors filled with sailboats, or bird sanctuaries. You may also be stunned to find quiet areas along the lake as thousands of people whiz by you, just a few short blocks from the city center.

Without Lake Michigan, and the Chicago River that feeds into it, none of this would likely be here. With its excellent location for trading, the region attracted explorers such as Marquette and Joliet, who saw great possibility. The name Chicago is thought to have originated with the tribes of Native Americans who lived in the area, taken from the Algonquin word for wild onions. In the 1770s, Jean Baptiste Point DuSable, a free black man of French African descent, built the first permanent home on the area that would become Chicago. Fort Dearborn was established by the United States in the early 1800s—right near today's Michigan Avenue and Wacker Drive—both to protect the growing number of American settlers drawn by trade in the area, and to have a military post to counter British presence in the area. The fort was destroyed in 1812 in a conflict

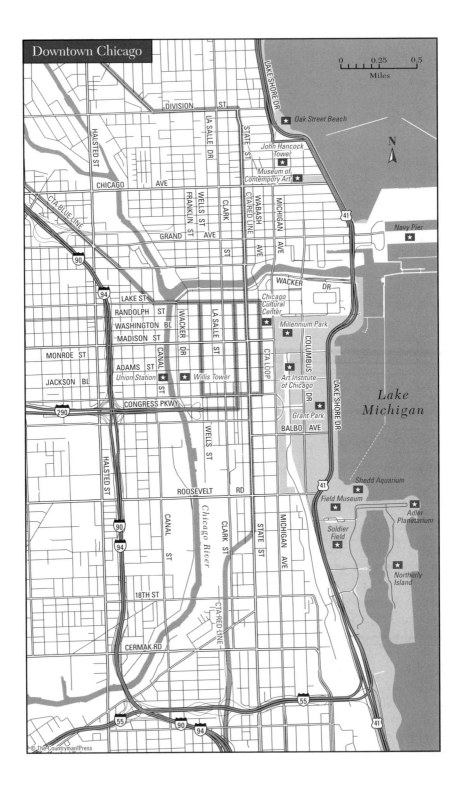

Downtown Chicago

with Native Americans and was later rebuilt. European Americans continued to settle in the area, and Chicago was officially incorporated in 1837. The completion of the canals linking the Great Lakes to the Mississippi River through Chicago, along with the designation of Chicago as the center of the national railroad system, propelled the city forward as a leader in industry and trade.

But most of the city was built of wood, right down to the street pavers, a decision that became disastrous when a fire started on the city's Southwest Side. The great Chicago Fire of 1871 wiped out thousands of buildings as it burned about 2,000 acres and displaced 100,000 people. But it didn't completely knock Chicago off its feet. The residents started over from scratch. Interestingly enough, the Chicago Fire Academy today stands on the site of the O'Leary property near the start of the fire. By the late 19th century, innovative buildings designed by visionary Chicago architects started sprouting skyward, laying the groundwork for the city scene today that includes some of the world's tallest and most well-known buildings, like the Sears Tower (recently renamed Willis Tower), which is the nation's tallest at 110 stories, and the John Hancock Center.

Manufacturing companies also took root, and the city became known for its iron and steel mills, its furniture making, and its meatpacking industry, which was centered in the Union Stock Yards on the Southwest Side.

With its industrial history, you must brush off a certain amount of grit when you look at the story of Chicago, but it is a grit that the people embrace. Many a family will proudly recount a story of earlier generations being drawn here for work in the city's industrial belt. They followed other European immigrants and joined African Americans who left the South in the early 20th century for new opportunities in Chicago. They settled in bungalows throughout the city, creating the ethnic neighborhoods that the city celebrates today.

Contrast the grit with one of the great features of Chicago: The abundance of parkland and green space across the city, especially downtown along the lakefront. The beautification of the city began as far back as 1893, when Chicago hosted the World's Columbian Exposition, creating the famed "White City" and the naturally landscaped Jackson Park. The Exposition also introduced the city to its first "L" car, which was used to transport visitors. The stretch of open lakefront we know today was the vision and work of Daniel Burnham, an architect who created the famous "1909 Plan of Chicago," sketching out the open green spaces like Grant Park and leaving the lakefront "free and clear" from private development. What is today the Museum Campus, Navy Pier, and Northerly Island all started in his imagination. These features make Chicago a unique urban center and draw residents and tourists every day to the "Urbs in Horto" as the city's motto goes, or "city in a garden."

SUGGESTED ITINERARIES

Summer in the City: Start with breakfast at any number of spots, then take a ride on the Chicago Architecture Foundation boat tour. You'll get your bearings and some great views in a relatively easy way. Book in advance though, these boats fill up fast. Afterward, walk over to Millennium Park to take in all the art—take a picture of your reflection in the Bean, take off your shoes and splash through the Crown Fountain, then study Frank Gehry's designs in the band shell. Lunchtime: For convenience sake, grab a table at the Park Grill at the plaza or the Gage across the street, so you can just walk across the street to the Art Institute of Chicago. Cool off in the sleek new modern wing, or in any of the other institutions in the Museum Campus. Walk through the campus, near the harbor, and enjoy the view of the skyline from the Adler Planetarium. For dinner, if you're a planner, you should secure a Frontera reservation a few months in advance. If you haven't gotten a reservation beforehand, in that nice way of his, Chef Rick Bayless sets aside some tables every night for walk-ins, but get there right when it opens; have a margarita while you wait. If you're with a big group, head to Café Iberico for tapas. The communal dining at Avec and the fascinatingly tasty menu make for a fun night. For a slightly more upscale experience, try Naha or Chef Art Smith's Table Fifty-Two.

Winter in the City: Start the day at the Museum of Science and Industry. For lunch, try a Chicago-style deep-dish pizza at Pizano's or Pizzeria Uno. Then bundle up and head to Millennium Park to ice skate with the breathtaking views of the city skyline surrounding you. Warm up at another of the fine museums, such as the Art Institute, Shedd Aquarium, or the Field Museum. End the day with the inviting comfort food of the West Town Tavern.

Chicago Neighborhoods: Start out at Lincoln Park Zoo, then head to the lakefront to rent bikes. For lunch, try Penny's Noodles in Lakeview and then some shopping. In the afternoon, head back to Lincoln Park and the Chicago History Museum to learn more about the city's people and places. Or, head south, for dim sum in Chinatown, and the National Museum of Mexican Art in Pilsen. You could go any number of ways with your dinner choice—beautiful artisanal plates at Nightwood in Pilsen, amazing Indian cuisine on Devon Avenue, beers and burgers in Wrigleyville. If you get a second wind, check out the music offerings for the evening or grab a cocktail and some jazz at the Green Mill.

Outdoor Illinois: One of my favorite trips to recommend to people who haven't been to Southern Illinois is a few days exploring the Shawnee National Forest, which is filled with many impressive sights and peaceful places. Combine it with a stop at the "Streets" of Giant City State Park, and a ride through the Shawnee Wine Trail. Another great nature itinerary is Starved Rock, with its canyons and waterfalls.

Historic Towns: Galena, a historic town in northwest Illinois, is definitely worth at least a weekend trip to take in the downtown, the green valley around it, and the great shopping and restaurants. Plus there are fantastic places to stay. Bishop Hill and Nauvoo are both intriguing, picturesque places in their own right—historic, preserved communities with compelling backstories.

After a century of rebuilding following the Fire, Chicago had a rough
go in the 1970s and 1980s, when it was pounded by the loss of industry
that formed one of the pillars of the local economy. Chicago again worked
hard to dust itself off. The downtown beautification efforts, the creation of
Millennium Park, and reinvestment in the Loop have paid off. Today,
about 2.8 million people call the city home, and roughly 40 million people
visit the city each year, for the museums, parks, theater, and architecture,
enjoying many different "Chicagos."

There's no better place to begin your exploration of Chicago than the
city's downtown and lakefront, where you can experience magical public art,
first-class museums, stellar park space, sandy beaches, scenic bike paths,
and the energy of a brilliant city. The food—from the classic deep-dish
Chicago pizza to impressive plates cooked up by gourmet giants—is enough
of a draw for many. The city's famous chefs—Rick Bayless, Grant Achatz,
Charlie Trotter, Art Smith—attract the attention of the culinary world for
their innovations. Make reservations ahead of time to get into these places.

Of course, weather plays a big role in the Chicago you'll see when you
get here. The winters can be brutal, but beautiful. There's still much to
see and do indoors at our many cultural institutions, and there's nothing
like ice-skating against the backdrop of skyscrapers at the Millennium
Park ice rink. A winter trip to Chicago can be very enjoyable, as long as
you pack many layers of clothing. Every year, tourists who packed light,
but fashionable clothing end up freezing when they get to the Magnificent
Mile, where the winds off the lake make the temperatures even more
unforgiving. If the thermometer says 20 degrees, be prepared for it to feel
much colder from the winds off the lake, especially on the Museum Campus. This is not a scientific study, but I find the point near the Adler Planetarium and the Shedd Aquarium to be the coldest in the city. Trust me,
dress warmly and your trip will be much more enjoyable.

The summer opens up endless outdoor opportunities along miles of
lakefront. Every weekend brings another fantastic music and food festival.
Head to the large music festivals in Grant Park that boast well-known
artists, or to the smaller festivals where you can grab a beer, sit in the sunshine, and listen to folk, country, rock, or blues.

This first section covers the main downtown attractions and includes
the Loop, Museum Campus, Lakefront area, River North, and Magnificent Mile area. After that, we'll get into Chicago neighborhoods and the
towns outside the city limits.

AREA CODES The area code for downtown Chicago is **312**. Attractions
along the lakefront north and south of downtown carry a **773** area code.

GUIDANCE The Chicago Office of Tourism (877-244-2246; www.explore
chicago.org) runs two visitor information centers, the Water Works loca-

tion at 163 E. Pearson Street, and another at the Chicago Cultural Center,
77 E. Randolph Street. Both locations are open 8–7 Monday through
Thursday, 8–6 Friday, 9–6 Saturday, and 10–6 Sunday. You could easily get
overwhelmed by the choices in a city as large as Chicago, but the tourism
center helps you sort out options. The stately cultural center, with its
bright stained-glass dome, is always filled with activity. In the tourism center, you'll find Chicago greeters who can help you devise the best itinerary, and tables where you can pore over brochures or plan your own day.
Greeters will also direct you to the best shows, performers, and special
events that might be visiting the city when you are. There's always something special happening, whether it's Blues Fest or a touring production of
a top Broadway show. You'll find free events as well as those that will have
you opening up your wallet. You can also pick up maps, neighborhood
scavenger hunt itineraries, and other suggestions. The Water Works Visitor Center also has a Hot Tix outpost that offers half-price tickets on local
shows. (There's also a Hot Tix site across the street from the Cultural Center on Randolph Street.) The Cultural Center location has a culinary
concierge to help you navigate the staggering number of dining options in
Chicago. Also check out the Chicago Convention and Tourism Bureau
(www.choosechicago.com) for more ideas of things to do.

GETTING THERE *By auto:* A web of interstates intersects in Chicago,
shuttling travelers from Wisconsin, Michigan, and Indiana along different
sections of I-90 and I-94. Traffic is a big headache as you get closer to
Chicago, so try to time your arrival during the non-rush hours. Otherwise,
a 10-minute drive can take an hour and get you off to a stressful start. For
example, if you are traveling between 7:30–10 AM or 3:30–7:30 PM on any
Chicago expressway, you want to check the traffic report (WBBM 780 AM
has traffic reports every 10 minutes on the "eights"). The code names
you'll hear for the various expressways are as follows: South of downtown,
I-94 is the Dan Ryan. West and north of downtown, joining with I-90, I-94
is the Kennedy. Farther north of the city I-94 is the Edens, heading to the
North Shore. If you're heading to the western suburbs, you'll likely take I-
290, also known as the Eisenhower. To get southwest, there's I-55, which
heads toward Midway Airport and is known as the Stevenson. I-294, or
the Tri-State Tollway, curves around the outer edges of the city. Beware
that some stretches of the interstates just outside the city and into the
suburbs are toll roads, where you'll pay anywhere from 80 cents to more
than $3 per toll. Also note: Chicagoans are known for their friendly ways,
but all bets are off when they get behind the wheel.

By air: **O'Hare International Airport** (800-832-6352; www.flychicago
.com) A major hub for the nation's and the world's major carriers, such as
United, American, US Airways, British Airways, Lufthansa, and Japan Airlines, O'Hare is located just northwest of the city limits. Once you exit

your plane, follow the signs for "Trains to the City" to hop on the CTA Blue Line train all the way downtown. Another option is to grab a taxi. Many have set prices for the ride from the airport to downtown, which may run about $35–40. Just 10 miles southwest of downtown is **Midway International Airport** (773-838-0600; www.flychicago.com), 5700 S. Cicero Avenue. Midway hosts major airlines such as Southwest and Delta. The CTA's Orange Line train will get you downtown to the Loop, and a taxi is always an option as well.

By train: (ᵞ) **Amtrak** (800-872-7245; www.amtrak.com), 225 S. Canal Street. Station is open 5:30 AM–11:59 PM daily. Several Amtrak routes from surrounding Midwest states will drop you into Chicago's Union Station on Canal Street.

By bus: **Greyhound** (800-231-2222; www.greyhound.com), 630 W. Harrison Street. Chicago's downtown station for the nationwide bus carrier.

(ᵞ) ⅏ **Megabus** (877-462-6342; http://us.megabus.com) This newer carrier has a bus stop on Canal Street just south of Jackson (south of Union Station), with routes to Chicago from many Midwest states including Michigan, Ohio, Indiana, Iowa, Missouri, Wisconsin, and Minnesota. You can book online and if the timing is right, you might be able to snag a cheap ticket. (They start at $1.)

GETTING AROUND *By auto:* If you're concentrating on downtown attractions, it's best to rely on public transportation or your feet. Save for some traffic jam, one of the quickest and most scenic ways to get north-south in Chicago is to take Lake Shore Drive, which runs along the eastern edge of the city from about 63rd Street all the way up to the northern city limits.

By public transportation: The best way to see Chicago is to hop on our famous "L" train. The "L," Chicago's elevated train system, easily lets you see many different "Chicagos" without the stress of a potential accident. The Chicago Transit Authority, or CTA, (888-968-7282; www.transitchicago .com) runs a comprehensive network of trains and buses across the city. If you're using public transportation, it's best to purchase a fare card at one of the CTA stations. Your fare for the bus or train will be automatically deducted. Train rides are $2.25, buses are $2 with a fare card, and the first transfer made within two hours of the first ride is 25 cents. Consider buying a one- or three-day pass, which will save you money if you're planning multiple rides. Passes are available online, at certain stations (like the Chicago Avenue Red Line station), currency exchanges, select Jewel and Dominick grocery stores, the Chicago Cultural Center, and the Water Tower Visitor Center.

As for CTA trains, the city's famous "L" runs throughout the downtown area as well. The Red Line will take you north and south along State

PARKING

Parking, and driving for that matter, can be a nightmare for visitors. Not to mention expensive. Parking rates can run as high as $25 for just an hour visit. Meter parking is available on certain streets, but difficult to come by. If you are considering driving, one of the most convenient choices downtown is the Grant Park North lot (888-692-0839; www.millenniumgarages.com). The entrance is on North Michigan Avenue between Randolph and Monroe Streets, which will put you in close proximity to Millennium Park, the Art Institute, and the Magnificent Mile. The garage costs between $5–29 depending on the length of your stay. There is also parking available in the Museum Campus lots. It's $16 for the first four hours. For street parking, look to the sidewalk for signs about parking. Instead of individual coin meters, the city has installed pay boxes on the sidewalks, so you may need to walk a few cars up to find a machine. Once you do, feed in your credit card or quarters, wait for a printed receipt, then place that on your dashboard. Rates vary. Downtown is of course more expensive than some neighborhood shopping districts. Do not ignore No PARKING signs; they will tow you, and it will be a very expensive and inconvenient experience.

Street, while the Brown, Orange, and Pink Lines make a circuit around the city's "loop," thus the name, before heading back out to the neighborhoods. The Blue Line will take you northwest out to O'Hare or west to the suburbs, while the Orange Line heads southwest out to Midway. Trains generally run every 5 to 15 minutes, but during rush hour, they may be more frequent.

Buses dominate the right-hand lane of most downtown streets. Bus stops are located every block or so, and marked by a white sign that lists the bus routes that will stop at your location. The signs provide a short description of the route, but for better information, plot out your trip on www.transitchicago.com. That way you'll know what bus number to take. You can also access www.ctabustracker.com to see how long it will be until your bus arrives. You can pay with cash on the bus, but it can be unnerving to do so if there's a long line of people, so it's better to get a fare card.

MEDICAL EMERGENCIES (ᵗᵖ) **Northwestern Memorial Hospital** (312-926-2000; www.nmh.org), 251 E. Huron Street. Located downtown, Northwestern Memorial is a premier academic medical center with 854 beds and just about every specialty imaginable. And most importantly, they have a top notch Emergency Department.

✳ Wandering Around

EXPLORING BY CAR Head east toward water and hop on Lake Shore Drive, which parallels the lakefront and offers breathtaking views of the waterfront and downtown area. The Drive will take you all the way up to the northernmost beaches of the city or south all the way toward Indiana. You can explore the neighborhoods by car, but you'll want to get an "L" pass or hop in a cab to take in the downtown sites.

EXPLORING BY FOOT The best way to see downtown is by foot, so you can truly gander at the architecture, the people, and public artwork. The best places to start: Michigan Avenue, the Museum Campus, or Millennium Park. There's much to see within several blocks in the city center. But be sure to dress in layers. It is often several degrees colder near the lake, and the wind can be rough off the lake, or as it plows through the tunnels created by city skyscrapers. Wear good walking shoes.

EXPLORING BY TROLLEY Chicago Trolley and Double Decker Co. (773-648-5000; www.chicagotrolley.com) You'll see these red double-decker buses throughout downtown. With a ticket, you can hop on and off the buses at the company's 15 stops all day. The company also leads a North neighborhoods tour past Wrigley Field and other sites, a South tour through President Barack Obama's neighborhood and around the Museum of Science and Industry, and a West neighborhoods tour of Chinatown, Little Italy, and the Oprah store. Tickets: $35 adult, $17 child, $24 senior/military. Get a 10 percent discount if you purchase online. Tickets can also be purchased in person at stops along routes.

Chicago Tours (888-881-3284; www.chicagotours.us) Tours depart every hour from 10–4 Wednesday through Sunday from mid-April through November. Another choice for trolley rides is this San Francisco-type car that makes stops at 13 destinations. The whole tour is about 90 minutes uninterrupted, but you can hop on and off at the designated stops. Tickets: $29.95 adults, $13.75 children 5 to 14.

EXPLORING BY BOAT ♿ **Chicago Architecture River Cruises** (312-922-3432; www.architecture.org) Dock for the boat cruise is at the southeast corner of the Michigan Avenue bridge at Wacker Drive. Tours run daily May through late November. This is one of the best ways to get your bearings in the city. The 90-minute architecture riverboat trip winds you by some architectural giants along the Chicago River, and the informed docents can relate just why they are important. You'll also learn the history of the city through this fantastic tour. Cost: $32.

Chicago Water Taxi (312-337-1446; www.chicagowatertaxi.com) Buy tickets on board the taxi (cash only) or at the kiosks at the Madison Street or Michigan Avenue dock near the Trump Tower. The bright yellow boats run from about 6:30 AM–7:15 PM weekdays, 9:30–7:30 weekends. Closed during the winter. This water taxi route is operated by the Wendella Boat Co., founded in 1935 by a Swedish immigrant, and now operated by the third generation of the family, who definitely know what they're doing when it comes to showing off the city. The route stops at Michigan Avenue, LaSalle and Clark, Madison Street, and Chinatown along the Chicago River. Fares: $2 for a one-way trip, $4 to reach the Chinatown stop. You can also purchase all-day passes for $6. Wendella also does a 75-minute Chicago River architecture tour. Tickets: $25 adults, $23 seniors, $12 children under 12.

Shoreline Sightseeing (312-222-9328; www.shorelinesightseeing.com) Main ticket booth for water taxis is on Navy Pier. Operates from Memorial Day through Labor Day. Taxis generally start runs between 9:30–10 depending on the route you're taking, and operate until 9–10, although some stop service earlier. Tours run at least every 20 minutes. Call ahead to check. Water taxi routes include stops at Navy Pier, Buckingham Fountain, the Museum Campus on the lakefront, and a river taxi that will take

BOAT RIDES ON THE CHICAGO RIVER

you between Navy Pier, the Michigan Avenue bridge, and near Sears/Willis Tower. Fares range from $4–7 for adults, $2–4 children under 13. You can also purchase all-day passes: $24 adult and $12 for children under 13.

✳ To See

MUSEUMS The admission fees can add up, especially for Chicago's top museums, but you can save some money through the **Chicago City Pass** (www.citypass.com/city/chicago.html). A pass will get you into five Chicago attractions—all good ones at that. You'll have nine days to see the Shedd Aquarium, the Field Museum, the Adler Planetarium, the Museum of Science & Industry, and either the Hancock Observatory or the Willis Tower. And instead of spending $130 or more on admissions, you can get admission to all five for $69, $59 for children 3 to 11. Also be sure to check each museum for its free days.

THE ART INSTITUTE OF CHICAGO

& ↑ ✎ ♂ **The Art Institute of Chicago** (312-443-3600; www .artic.edu/aic), 111 S. Michigan Avenue. Open 10:30–5 Monday through Wednesday, 10:30–8 Thursday through Friday, 10:30–5 Saturday and Sunday. This exquisite building guarded by the city's two iconic lions contains some of the world's most famous pieces of art. Even if you're not an art aficionado, you are likely to recognize some of the works here. Stand in front of Georges Seurat's *A Sunday on La Grande Jatte* and get lost in the tiny dots of color. Grant Wood's *American Gothic* and Edward Hopper's *Nighthawks* are also here. Plan some time so you can explore the photography, paintings, sculpture, and other excellent works. Wander through the permanent collections or the new Modern Wing, which opened in May 2009 to bring the total square footage of the museum to 1 million and provide an impressive new home for the modern collection,

architecture and design, and photography. The Modern Wing, designed by
architect Renzo Piano, is made of Indiana limestone similar to the original
building and has stunning walls of glass. You'll also find temporary exhibitions that are not to miss. But because they're so good, you often need a
special ticket to get in. Check before you arrive to be sure you don't miss
out. Admission: $18 adults, $12 students, seniors. Children under 14 are
free. Check the schedule for the museum's free days.

   ⚥ ⬆ ✄ ♂ **The Field Museum** (312-922-9410; www.fieldmuseum.org),
1400 S. Lake Shore Drive. Open 9–5 daily. The museum was originally
founded to house the biological and anthropological collections for the
1893 World's Columbian Exposition. Today, the museum has amassed an
astounding collection of 20 million artifacts and specimens from around
the world, documenting the planet's rich human and natural history. The
museum continues to build on its collection, such as through the addition
of "Sue," the largest and best-preserved T. rex. This is not a plastic model,
but the fossilized skeleton of the dinosaur. A newly opened DNA discovery center takes you inside the work of genetic researchers. The museum
has updated quite a few of its exhibits, making it a must-see. Admission:
$15 adults, $12 seniors, students, $10 children 3 to 11. Extra fees apply for
IMAX movies and special exhibitions.

   ⚥ ✄ ⬆ ♂ **Shedd Aquarium** (312-939-2438; www.sheddaquarium.org),
1200 S. Lake Shore Drive. Open 9–5 weekdays, 9–6 weekends Labor Day
through Memorial Day. From Memorial Day through Labor Day, open
9–6 daily. A large glass wall on the eastern edge of the building incorpo-
rates Lake Michigan as part of the museum, and the Beluga whales in the
gorgeous "reimagined" Oceanarium appear to be swimming near the lake.
But you'll also be able to explore aquatic environments around the world.
Walk through the Caribbean reef and you'll feel as if you're underwater
yourself. Plan ahead so you can score a seat for one of the regular shows
where highly skilled trainers truly impress with their cast of whales, dol-
phins, and penguins. The 4-D Theater shows movies where you may be
sprayed with a mist of water, feel the wind, or smell a fragrance. A general
admission Shedd Pass for adults will get you into all the exhibits and the
Oceanarium for $27; it's $20 for children 3 to 11. Entrance to the aquatic
show will add $2 to the ticket price. Buy ahead of time to avoid long lines
that snake around the aquarium like an eel, on summer days. If it's winter,
plan your travel to avoid outside exposure, as the winds off the lake in this
area can be brutal.

   ⚥ ⬆ ♂ **Museum of Contemporary Art** (312-280-2660; www.mca
chicago.org), 220 E. Chicago Avenue. 10–8 Tuesday, 10–5 Wednesday
through Sunday. If you need something to talk about over dinner, head
here beforehand. Since 1945, the out-of-the-ordinary collections and exhibitions at MCA have been stirring up conversation. The museum presents

contemporary painting, sculpture, photography, video, film, and performance. The permanent collection focuses on surrealism, minimalism, conceptual photography, and work by Chicago-based artists. In 1969, the artist Christo did his first draping of an entire building in the United States at the MCA. For a different way to see the collections, the museum hosts "First Friday" events where you can see the museum exhibits while sipping on wine and mingling. Admission: $12 adults, $7 students, seniors. Free, children 12 and under. Free on Tuesday.

  Chicago Children's Museum (312-527-1000; www.chicago childrensmuseum.org), 700 E. Grand Avenue at Navy Pier. Open 10–5 Monday through Wednesday, and Friday through Sunday, 10–8 Thursday. Tucked into Navy Pier, the children's museum offers plenty for the little members of your crew. Check the schedule when you arrive for special daily activities that will get the kids moving or creating. A firehouse, dinosaur expedition, lab, tree house, and water area are among the permanent exhibits. In kids' town, they can drive a CTA bus, shop in a grocery store, or take on other neighborhood roles. But be prepared, to get to the museum you have to pass many Navy Pier goodie stands and stores that may entice the kids, so bring extra cash if you plan to indulge. Admission: $10 adults and children; $9 seniors; free, children under 1 year. Free admission Thursday 5–8.

  Adler Planetarium (312-922-7827; www.adlerplanetarium .org), 1300 S. Lake Shore Drive. Open 10–4 weekdays, 10–4:30 weekends. Extended hours during summer. With a space theater, sky theater, and 3D theater, the planetarium offers top-notch astronomy shows. These shows do cost more, but you'll definitely want to see at least one, so build the time into your plans. In addition to the sky shows, the museum has exhibitions with cool items such as the Gemini 12 spacecraft flown by Jim Lovell. Kids will absolutely love the "Planet Explorers" exhibit, where they can suit up like an astronaut, blast off in a rocket simulator, and work in a space station. Every third Thursday, the Adler hosts an "after dark" evening from 6–10 for the over 21 crowd, offering cocktails while you take in the skyline. It's the only chance to peek through the largest telescope in the Midwest that the public can access. The patio here offers one of the most stunning views of the city's skyline. Great for photos. Admission: $10 adults, $8 seniors, $6 children 3 to 14.

  Driehaus Museum (312-932-8665; www.driehausmuseum.org), 50 E. Erie Street. One-hour guided tours depart at 10, 1, and 3 Tuesday, Wednesday, and Saturday. You can also take self-guided tours from 10–4 Thursday and Friday. The museum is located in the Samuel Nickerson mansion, a house commissioned in 1879 and designed by one of the city's earliest professional architects. Nickerson spent $450,000 on the "marble palace," the city's largest private residence of its time. The building passed through

several private hands before being donated to the American College of
Surgeons, which owned it until 2003. The museum opened its doors in the
restored mansion in 2008. Founder Richard Driehaus, a philanthropist
with a heavy interest in architecture, design, and fine arts, wanted to create a place that showcased the design philosophies of the late 19th century
and early 20th century. The gorgeous rooms are filled with pieces that will
impress and may deepen your appreciation for European and American
decorative and fine arts. The Driehaus collection is also one of the leading
private collections of works by American decorative designer Louis Comfort Tiffany. Admission with guided tour: $25 adults, $17.50 seniors,
$12.50 children age 12 to 16, students. Admission for self-guided tour:
$17.50.

&. ↑ **Loyola University Museum of Art** (312-915-7600; www.luc.edu
/luma), 820 N. Michigan Avenue, Chicago. Open 11–8 Tuesday, 11–6
Wednesday through Sunday. Located in a 1926 Gothic Revival building
right on the Magnificent Mile, the exhibits and collections showcase religious art from around the world. Admission: $6 adults, $5 seniors. Free on
Tuesday, and daily for students under 25, military families, and clergy.

&. ↑ ♂ **Spertus** (312-322-1700; www.spertus.edu/museum), 610 S.
Michigan Avenue. Open 10–5 Sunday through Thursday. Spertus, a center
for Jewish learning and culture, spotlights the history of Chicago Jewish
life through a rotating exhibit on its ground floor. The center also has a
full calendar of programming. Free.

&. ↑ **Museum of Contemporary Photography** (312-663-5554; www
.mocp.org), 600 S. Michigan Avenue. Open 10–5 Monday through
Wednesday, Friday, and Saturday, 10–8 Thursday, noon–5 Sunday. The
visual arts-focused Columbia College hosts this small museum with changing exhibitions of compelling photography. Free.

HISTORIC SITES Chicago Water Tower 806 N. Michigan Avenue.
Open 10–6:30 Monday through Saturday, 10–5 Sunday. This historic
structure is located in the heart of the Magnificent Mile. The Water
Tower was built between 1867 and 1869 and was one of the few survivors
of the 1871 Great Chicago Fire. While the tower hasn't functioned in over
100 years, inside the Water Tower you'll find a gallery for art exhibitions.
The original water works building across the street is now home to the
Lookingglass Theatre. Free.

CULTURAL SITES ↑ &. **Chicago Cultural Center** (312-744-6630;
www.chicagoculturalcenter.org), 78 E. Washington Street. Open 8–7 Monday through Thursday, 8–6 Friday, 9–6 Saturday, 10–6 Sunday. With the
recently restored Tiffany stained-glass dome, the world's largest, you
should at least take a walk through this beautiful building. Built in 1897 as

the city's main library, the center is home to free music, dance, theater, films, lectures, art shows, and other community events year-round. Free.

✳ To Do

BEACHES All beaches managed by the Chicago Park District have rest room-beach house facilities, concessions, and lifeguards, who are on duty from 11–7. Open Memorial Day through Labor Day. You'll want to check before you go to make sure there is no swim ban in effect, which occurs at times based on weather or water quality. Dog-friendly beaches are located at Belmont Harbor, Montrose Beach, and Foster Beach. Aside from North Avenue and Oak Street beach, you may be able to score parking on the inner drives that wind through the lakefront parks. If not, there are also pay lots with low hourly rates. Admission to the beaches is free (312-742-5121; www.chicagoparkdistrict.com).

ART EVERYWHERE

The city of Chicago has more than 700 public art pieces across the city. Of course, the new installations at Millennium Park have garnered a lot of attention, but there are others you may want to consider. As you leave McCormick Place and head south, you'll notice a giant bronze figure greeting you. This statue is Alison Saar's *Monument to the Great Northern Migration*, which honors the African American families who moved to Chicago in the 20th century from the South in hope of a better life (Martin Luther King Drive and 26th Place). There are the lions of the Art Institute of Chicago, created by artist Edward Kemeys, whose plaster animal sculptures were featured in the World's Columbian Exposition. And our most famous piece of public art is called simply *The Picasso*. At 50 feet tall, it hardly goes unnoticed, and has also become a city mascot, bearing hats and banners according to various sports teams wins. In 1963, the architects of the Daley Center commissioned Picasso to create a monument for the plaza. His work, which deviated from the traditional sculptures of historical figures, created a stir. It's made of the same steel as the building it fronts, and was created at the U.S. Steel Co. in Gary, Indiana. Picasso never explained what it should represent (50 W. Washington in Daley Plaza). Its bookend seems to be Alexander Calder's *Flamingo,* the large red steel curve that pops against the backdrop of the Federal Plaza buildings designed by Ludwig Mies van der Rohe (50 W. Adams Street).

Oak Street Beach, 1000 N. Lake Shore Drive. This is the most fashionable of all the beaches, located in the Gold Coast, just north of the Magnificent Mile. Also Oak Street Beachstro (312-915-4100; www.oakstreet beachstro.com) has a good selection for breakfast, lunch, and dinner, as well as wines, but expect to pay a bit more for the location in one of Chicago's most elite zip codes. Open May through September, 11–11 weekdays, 8–11 weekends.

North Avenue Beach and Beach House, 1600 N. Lake Shore Drive. Another popular beach because of its proximity to the downtown attractions, North Avenue beach also has volleyball and a beach house that looks like an ocean liner with a bar and grill, concessions, showers, rest rooms, and volleyball equipment rental. If you're staying farther north, consider Montrose Beach (4400 N. Lake Shore Drive.), or Foster Avenue Beach, 5200 N. Lake Shore Drive. For a South Side beach, you have 63rd Street Beach (6300 S. Lake Shore Drive) in Jackson Park, which has a restored beach house, or 12th Street Beach (1200 S. Lynn White Drive) on Northerly Island.

BICYCLING There are plenty of options to rent bikes along the lakefront, but think twice about renting one of the quadracycles for the lakefront path. The four-wheel cycle takes up the whole bike lane and can be a little stressful to navigate through congested areas of the path. Better to try a tandem bike.

Bike and Roll Chicago (888-245-3929; www.bikeandroll.com/chicago), Millennium Park, 239 E. Randolph Street. Summer hours: 6:30 AM–8 PM

63RD STREET BEACH

weekdays, 8–8 weekends. Spring and fall: 6:30–7 weekdays, 9–7 weekends. Winter: 6:30–6:30 weekdays, closed weekends. Rent a beach cruiser, mountain bike, or tandem bike at this bike rental center in Millennium Park, then take in the sights along the lakefront. From the bike center, head either north or south for equally breathtaking views as you breeze past beaches and harbors. But keep your wits about you. The path tends to be crowded during good weather, especially the stretch from the Museum Campus to North Avenue Beach. Bike prices range from $30–59 for a half-day rental or $35–69 for a full-day rental. Kids' bikes and seats also available. Guided tours of the lakefront and city also available from Bike and Roll Chicago at this location. Bike and Roll runs nine rental locations total, including those at Navy Pier, North Avenue Beach, and the DuSable Museum.

Bobby's Bike Hike Chicago (312-915-0995; www.bobbysbikehike.com) Two rental and tour locations: 465 N. McClurg Court (8:30–7 Sunday through Friday, 8–8 Saturday, April through October) and 141 W. Diversey Parkway (open 9–5 daily June through Labor Day). The 5020 S. Cornell (Hyde Park Art Center) location offers Hyde Park tours only. Tour the lakefront neighborhoods, see city lights at night, or the sites important to President Obama's life in Chicago. The bicycle tours last two to three hours and are run at a relaxed pace. Tickets: $35 adults; $25 seniors, students, and military; $20 children under 12. Kids under 4 can ride along for $5 in a seat or trailer. You can also rent bikes and gear for solo trips. Half-day bike rentals run $20–40 and full-day rentals are $30–55. Save 10 percent if you reserve online.

Lakeshore Bike (630-886-6188, 847-712-6776; www.lakeshorebike.com), 3650 N. Recreation Drive (at the Waveland Park Tennis Courts). Open 11–7 daily May through September, weekends only in fall and spring, hours may vary depending on weather. If you have some trouble along the lakefront bike path, you can get your flat fixed or bike tuned up at this small booth. Tune-ups are $45. You can also rent bikes a bit more cheaply than the centrally located bike centers, $30 for a full day on weekdays, $8 hourly, and $40 for a full day on weekends, $10 hourly.

BOATING & **Seadog Cruises** (888-636-7737; www.seadogcruises.com), Board at Navy Pier. Cruises depart hourly 11–7 April through October. If you'd like a fast tour of the lake, try the 30-minute speedboat lake tour that races you past Navy Pier to the Museum Campus. There's also an extreme thrill ride on a boat that is 30 percent faster than their other boats, reaching 45 mph. Also some spins included. Tickets: $20 for speedboat, $29 for extreme thrill ride. Make reservations online or by phone 24 hours in advance. There is a height restriction on the extreme ride, kids must be at least 48 inches tall. Extreme ride not encouraged for people with health issues.

Tall Ship *Windy* (312-595-5555; www.tallshipwindy.com) Departs from Navy Pier several times daily. With its giant white sails, this tall ship relies on the wind to steer its course along the Lake Michigan shore. As a passenger, you can help raise and trim the sails. Rides are 60 to 90 minutes long, and the schedule includes some themed rides, such as a pirate sail and a Chicago maritime history ride. Tickets: $24–30, $10–20 children, $20–25 seniors and students. Purchase tickets online or at the booth near the ship.

Wateriders (312-953-9287; www.wateriders.com), 950 N. Kingsbury Street. Kayak tours given at 10 and 2:30 daily during the summer. Cost is $60 per person for an over two-hour ride infused with history about Chicago writers, mobsters, and other famed residents. There's also a tour that investigates the supposed haunted spots on the river. On Wednesday and Saturday, try the fireworks paddle that gives you a different view of the Navy Pier fireworks. You can also rent kayaks for $15 per hour. You must book ahead on Monday and Tuesday. Otherwise rentals available 1–6 Wednesday through Thursday, 11–6 Friday, 9–6 weekends.

Kayak Chicago (630-336-7245; www.kayakchicago.com), 1501 N. Magnolia Avenue on the Chicago River. Open 10–7 Wednesday through Sunday from May through October. Also has locations at Montrose and North Avenue beaches that are open Memorial Day through Labor Day, weather permitting. There are no rentals after 6, and boats must be back by 7. Architectural tours, a lakefront paddle from beach to beach, and a river tour are offered as well as a nighttime paddle. Best to book online so you can reserve your spot for the tours. Tours are $50, $25 for kids under 8. Rent a kayak for $15 per hour or $60 per day, tandem is $25 per hour or $100 per day. Kids 12 and older can paddle by themselves, under 12 needs to ride in tandem kayak.

FISHING You will see people fishing in the harbors and lagoons on the lakefront path, but to fish Lake Michigan by boat you can charter one through **Captain Al's Charters** (312-565-0104; www.captainalscharters .com), open April through October. No age restrictions. Captain Al has decades of experience in these waters. He's located in Burnham Harbor, 19th Street and Lake Shore Drive. Cost: $155 per person for five hours, with fishing equipment provided.

FOR FAMILIES ♿ ✐ ☂ **Navy Pier** (312-595-7437, 800-595-7437; www.navypier.com), 600 E. Grand Avenue. Open 10–10 Sunday through Thursday, 10 AM–midnight Friday and Saturday, May through August. Offseason, the pier closes at 8 PM Sunday through Thursday. Head toward the giant Ferris wheel on the lakefront and you'll find Navy Pier, a bright, lively (especially in summer) stretch of shopping, restaurants, bars, museums, theater, live entertainment, miniature golf, boat rides, a carousel, a funhouse maze, IMAX theater, and games. The indoor part of the pier is like a giant mall, only with the Chicago Children's Museum and gems like the Chicago Shakespeare Theater inside. The pier is also home to a large food court and the Smith Museum of Stained Glass Windows. Many tours depart from the pier. The pier opened in 1916 and has served as a naval training base, a college campus, and shipping facility. A massive redevelopment effort in the 1990s overhauled the site, and the 15-story Ferris wheel was added. Parking is available on site, and several bus routes will take you to the Pier. Free admission, but good luck getting out without spending some money!

GOLF The Green at Grant Park (312-540-9013; www.thegreenonline .com), 352 E. Monroe Street. Located between Columbus Drive and Lake Shore Drive. Open daily spring through mid-October weather permitting; 11–11 weekdays, 10 AM–11 PM weekends. Just steps away from skyscrapers you'll find this challenging, foliage-rich 18-hole putting course tucked in Grant Park. The course boasts sand traps and dramatic shifts in elevation. There's also a restaurant with outdoor patio seating, featuring salads, sandwiches, and burgers. Fees: $12 adults, $6 children.

NAVY PIER

SEGWAY These tours are not for everyone, as the Segway can take some getting used to. But there are several companies that will train you on the device then help you see the sites. There are age and weight limits for these tours, so check the company Web sites for guidelines.

Chicago Segway Tours (312-890-3701; www.chicagosegwaytour .com), 505 N. Lake Shore Drive, Chicago. Tours operate daily year-round, departing at 8:45, 11:30, 2:30, 5:30, and 8:30. Glide past the main attractions, the beaches, harbors, Museum Campus, and other sites on this Segway tour. A two-hour tour is $55 in the morning and a slightly longer tour is $65 in the afternoon. The 8:30 Glide at Night tour is two hours and will run you $75, but includes fireworks on some nights.

Steve's Segway Tours (312-946-9467; http://stevessegwaytours.com), Northeast corner of Monroe Street and Columbus Drive. Take the stairs underground for the East Monroe Garage Entrance, and you'll see a sign for Steve's Segway Tours. The door is opposite the sign. Open year-round, but reservations required during the spring, fall, and winter months. A three-hour morning or afternoon tour winds through the Museum Campus and some of the major sites. You can also take an architecture or neighborhood tour. Tickets: $70–85 depending on the tour, with private tours available for $100.

TOURS Chicago Architecture Foundation (312-922-3432; www .architecture.org), 224 S. Michigan Avenue. In addition to its fabulous river cruise, the Chicago Architecture Foundation also leads detailed tours about Chicago's structures and neighborhoods. Some are walking tours, some by bus. The menu of options includes "The Devil in the White City" tour, built around the best-selling book about a mass murderer on the hunt in Chicago during the World's Fair. Other tours focus on the works of architect Frank Lloyd Wright, or Chicago neighborhoods such as Beverly and Hyde Park. You can also tour Chicago's famous Loop by train. Some tours are free; others carry a charge.

&. **Willis Tower and Skydeck Chicago** (312-875-9447; www.thesky deck.com), 233 S. Wacker Drive, Chicago. Open 9 AM–10 PM daily April through September, 10–8 October through March. Take a trip near the top of what once was called the Sears Tower and is still, at 110 stories, the tallest building in the U.S. Look down at your feet from the tower's 103rd floor, and see the ground 1,353 feet below you. "The Ledge," a glass box that extends out from the building, with a clear floor, is a definite thrill, or panic inducing, depending on how you feel about heights. But the views are unparalleled. There will be some in every group who want to study up on exactly how this box is supported, since the supports are nearly invisible. The boxes are made of three layers of half-inch thick glass, and are made to retract so they can be cleaned and maintained. You can also absorb more about Chicago's important role in the world of architecture through exhibits on the building and city. If you want to avoid the crowds, try visiting after 5 PM. Tickets: $15.95 adults, $11 children 3 to 11, which includes a walk onto The Ledge.

&. **John Hancock Tower and Observatory** (888-875-8439; www .hancockobservatory.com), 875 N. Michigan Avenue. Open 9 AM–11 PM daily. While not as tall as the Willis Tower, you're still high—94 stories— but the difference here is you can also feel the breeze thanks to the open-air Skywalk. A multimedia tour is narrated by actor David Schwimmer of *Friends* fame, who co-founded the Lookingglass Theatre. Admission: $15 adults, $10 children 3 to 11. If you'd like to take in the view in a less touristy way, have a drink or dinner with spectacular views at the Signature Room or Signature Lounge on the 95th and 96th floors (312-787-9596; www.signatureroom.com). You'll avoid the admission fees, but the drinks are in the double digits. A recent addition for winter visitors is an ice-skating rink on the 94th floor.

Chicago Film Tour (312-593-4455; www.chicagofilmtour.com) Tours depart at 10:30, 12:30 Thursday through Sunday, April to early December. Board from the west side of Clark Street between Ontario and Ohio Streets. This motorcoach tour focuses on the dozens of famous movies filmed on the city streets, from *The Dark Knight* to *The Break-Up.* Tickets: $30 adults, $20 children. Book online or call to purchase.

✹ Green Space

& ✑ **Millennium Park** (312-742-1168; www.millenniumpark.org), 201 E. Randolph Street. Open daily 6 AM–11 PM. The city certainly aimed high when planning this latest addition to the downtown cultural scene, and the results are most impressive. As you meander down Michigan Avenue, you will notice the twisted curls of steel that form the Jay Pritzker Pavilion, an outdoor concert venue designed by acclaimed architect Frank Gehry. The

"THE BEAN" AT MILLENNIUM PARK

pavilion was designed so the audience perched on the sloping grassy lawn in the back would hear the same sounds as those sitting in front-row seats. Nearby skyscrapers and the lake only enhance the scenery, creating a truly remarkable venue. Throughout the summer, you can catch performances of all types, or you may find a giant group yoga class. When there aren't events scheduled, it's become a place for office workers and tourists to lounge. Mr. Gehry also designed the BP Bridge, a winding elevated path through the park that showcases amazing views of the Chicago skyline and Lake Michigan. One of the most popular attractions is the *Cloud Gate* sculpture, better known as "The Bean." You'll see why it's called that as you approach the highly polished steel sculpture that reflects the city skyline. It's everyone's favorite Chicago backdrop for photos. The kids will love the *Crown Fountain,* two 50-foot glass-block towers that project video images of giant faces. The mouths on the faces spurt water at regular intervals, freshening the reflecting pool where kids splash and play. Be sure to dress so you can easily roll up your pants and slip off your shoes to wade through it. During the winter, take a spin around the ice-skating rink. And the best part about the 24.5-acre park? It's all free. Everything except for skate rentals, which run $10 a pair.

Grant Park (312-742-7648; www.chicagoparkdistrict.com) Stretches between Michigan Avenue and Lake Shore Drive, and Randolph Street south to Roosevelt Road. The city's "front yard," Grant Park is home to the Museum Campus and Buckingham Fountain. It's named after Ulysses S. Grant and also is home to the sculptural installation *Agora* by artist Magdalena Abakanowicz. She has created 106 haunting cast-iron figures that each stand about 9 feet tall. The park also has baseball fields, a dog-friendly park, playgrounds, a skate park, and tennis courts. This is also the location for the annual Taste of Chicago, and the city's big music festivals.

Lakefront Path (312-742-7648; www.chicagoparkdistrict.com) This is one of my absolute favorite things about Chicago. Run, walk, bike, or lounge along 20-plus miles of path—gravel, crushed rock, and paved—along the beautiful lakefront. There are numerous spots to stop as well, to shoot a picture, camp out with a book, view wildlife, or play chess. At Montrose, check out the bird sanctuary, a nature path that winds through a dune. In the 1990s as the lake level dropped, dunes began to form and native wetland plants sprouted. Today the sanctuary beckons to 150 bird species and has been designated as an important bird area by the National Audubon Society. Butterflies, rabbits, and foxes can also be spotted here. At Montrose, there's a fishing pier and giant concrete steps that offer great skyline shots of the city. But note that the path dead-ends at the harbor, so you'll have to walk all the way back to Montrose Beach to continue on the path. A nearby tackle shop, at the intersection of Montrose and Montrose Harbor Trail, is open 4 AM–8 PM daily. Just south of

BUCKINGHAM FOUNTAIN

North Avenue beach is a cement pavilion with chess boards built into the concrete.

✷ Lodging

Chicago offers a plethora of hotels at every price point, though the downtown options can get pretty pricey. If location is your priority, you will want to book ahead. Frequent conventions and festivals help keep hotel rooms filled throughout the year, so get a jump-start. But if you haven't planned ahead, you still may be able to bid on a last-minute vacancy on various travel Web sites. Note that parking fees can add to your bill significantly, so be sure to inquire about that if you're driving into the city.

⚤ ((ψ)) 🐾 ♿ **Hotel Allegro** (800-643-1500; www.allegrochicago.com), 171 W. Randolph Street. For a location closer to the downtown theaters, the Hotel Allegro has 480 rooms with pewter, blues, and browns merging in a modern-looking room that is heavy on graphic elements. The rooms have flat-screen TVs, iHome docking stations with alarm clocks, safes, and Aveda bath products. You can get WiFi throughout for $10. The staff rolls out Wii for guests and kids during the wine reception. $$–$$$.

((ψ)) ♿ 🐾 **The James Hotel** (312-337-1000; www.jameshotels.com), 55 E. Ontario Street. Great location for shopping on the Magnificent Mile. Sleek and modern with natural accents, the gallery lobby has works by local artists. Standard rooms are all white and minimalist, with dark wood platform beds, flat-screen TVs, and Kiehl's bath products. There's turndown service each night, robes on the bed, ice in the bucket, and sweets from the steakhouse downstairs. The hotel has a fitness center, full spa, and offers free bikes, helmets, and maps to the lakefront. Downstairs, you'll find JBar and David Burke Primehouse. $$$–$$$$.

The Allerton Hotel (312-440-1500; www.theallertonhotel.com), 701 N. Michigan Avenue. The hotel was one of the first high rises on Michigan Avenue in the 1920s. To find it on today's cityscape, look for the illuminated TIP TOP TAP sign, first turned on in the 1940s. Today it's a historic landmark. Standard rooms come with marble bathrooms, iHome docking stations, Bath & Body Works toiletries, upholstered headboards, flat-screen TVs, and safes. The décor features warm yellow walls and white and blue bedding. There is a $10 a day charge for wireless in the room but there is complimentary WiFi in the lobby. The hotel also has the M Avenue Restaurant and Lounge and a fitness center. $$–$$$$.

W Hotel (312-943-9200; http://whotelsofchicago.com), 644 N. Lake Shore Drive, Chicago. If you want a view of the lake from your hotel room, try this modern hotel with a spa, rooftop lounge, and restaurant. Standard rooms have a king or two double beds, flat-screen TVs, robes, bath products from Bliss, and safes. But you'll need to score a "spectacular" room, as it's classified here, if you want the Lake Michigan view. There is free WiFi in the main areas, but you'll have to pay extra for access in guest rooms. Hotel also has a fitness center, outdoor deck, and an indoor pool with views of the lake and Navy Pier. $$$–$$$$.

THE JAMES HOTEL

  🏃 ⌀ 🐾 ⚥ (((•))) **Palmer House Hilton** (312-726-7500; www .palmerhousehiltonhotel.com), 17 E. Monroe Street. The Palmer House was built in 1871, a wedding gift from businessman Potter Palmer to his wife, Bertha. But just 13 days after opening, the Great Chicago Fire hit. Potter Palmer rebuilt and reopened the grand hotel two years later, across the street from the original location. You can still see Bertha's touch throughout the hotel in its emphasis on art. The lobby features ceiling frescoes by French artist Louis Pierre Rigal, and Tiffany 24-karat gold chandeliers. The legendary Palmer House has hosted presidents and numerous stars, and word is the chefs here invented the dessert we know as the brownie. Rooms have been remodeled in the past few years, and feature iPod alarm/docking stations, and WiFi access in rooms for a fee. The hotel has a lounge, restaurant, fitness center, pool, and spa. $$–$$$.

  🏃 (((•))) 🐾 ⌀ **The Drake Hotel** (312-787-2200; www.thedrake hotel.com), 140 E. Walton Place. Located in a curve of Lake Shore Drive, the Drake has an iconic presence on the city's skyline. Today, the 535 rooms include flat-screen TVs, clock radios with iPod connections, safes, and marble bathrooms. The hotel also has a fitness center. $$$–$$$$.

✳ Where to Eat

EATING OUT ⌀ **Lou Mitchell's** (312-939-3111; www.loumitchells restaurant.com), 565 W. Jackson Boulevard. Open 5:30 AM–3 PM Monday through Saturday, 7–3 Sunday. Opened in 1923 at the start of Route 66, this is a place that many native Chicagoans like to take out-of-town guests. Ladies and children can expect a box of Milk Duds (the owner of Milk Duds was a friend and customer) and everyone can look forward to donut holes. Pancakes are a popular option here, but the menu also has omelets, burgers, salads, and other diner fare. Cash only, but there is an ATM in the building. $–$$.

Xoco (312-334-3688; www.rick bayless.com), 449 N. Clark Street. Open 8 AM–9 PM Tuesday through Thursday, 8 AM–10 PM Friday and Saturday. Rick Bayless is a culinary superstar who is known for taking Mexican food to new levels, with his own line of products in grocery stores. He wrote his first Mexican cookbook with his wife Deann, while living in Mexico. He continued writing cookbooks and started his TV show *Mexico One Plate at a Time*. In 1987, he opened Frontera Grill, and the fancier, fine-dining Mexican restaurant Topolobampo followed in 1989. Xoco is the most casual member of the Bayless family of restaurants. When you walk into the restaurant you see the cooks at work, and that's on purpose. It's as if you were ordering from a street vendor, only this vendor is one of the best Mexican chefs around.

Order tortas from the wood-burning oven, fresh soups, or breakfast empanadas. You can also get freshly whipped hot chocolate. Churros are available all day long. Breakfast: $, Lunch/Dinner $–$$.

Billy Goat Tavern Original (312-222-1525; www.billygoat tavern.com), 430 N. Michigan Avenue, Lower Level. Open 6 AM–2 AM weekdays, 10 AM–3 AM Saturday, 10–2 Sunday. You have to go beneath Michigan Avenue to get to this Chicago institution (stairs and signs are located on Michigan Avenue in front of the Tribune Tower and Wrigley Building). Yes, this is the place of CHEEZBORGER, CHEEZBORGER, NO FRIES, CHEEPS! NO COKE, PEPSI! made famous by John Belushi on *Saturday Night Live*. This is dive bar at its finest, with tables like you had in your high school cafeteria. You'll find tourist groups in here and a number of reporters, as it's been a longtime hangout of journalists from the two local papers back to the days of Mike Royko. (Notice all the memorabilia on the walls.) By the way, the burgers really are great. $.

& **Gold Coast Dogs** (312-917-1677; www.goldcoastdogs.net), 159 N. Wabash Avenue. Open 10–8 weekdays, 10–6 Saturday, 11–5 Sunday. As with pizza, there are many hot dog stands where you can find Chicago-style dogs. Gold Coast has multiple locations, but serves up Vienna Beef dogs, steam or char grilled in a poppy seed bun, with your choice of toppings, if you want to make it a tra-

ditional Chicago-style dog: yellow mustard, onions, tomato, sweet pickle relish, dill pickle spear, sport peppers, and fresh tomatoes. You can also get bratwurst, corn dogs, sandwiches, and burgers. $.

& **Foodlife** (312-335-3663; www .foodlifechicago.com), 835 N. Michigan Avenue. Open 8–8 Sunday through Thursday, 8–8:30 Friday and Saturday. Located in Water Tower Place, this is a good stop if you're on a shopping marathon along the Magnificent Mile. Everyone can choose their own cuisine, from make-your-own stir-fry to fried chicken, pizza, Chinese by Big Bowl, burritos, or burgers. Pick up a card when you walk in, peruse the offerings, hand the card to the kitchen staff helping you, then pay as you exit. $–$$.

Star of Siam (312-670-0100; www.starofsiamchicago.com), 11 E. Illinois Street. Open 11–10 Sunday through Thursday, 11–11 Friday and Saturday. Excellent, inexpensive Thai food just off Michigan Avenue. This restaurant with its bustling dining room is a local favorite. Cashew chicken and pad see-ew are especially good. $.

& **Sopraffina Marketcaffe** (312-984-0044; www.sopraffina.com), 10 N. Dearborn Avenue, is the original location, but there are other Sopraffinas downtown, at 111 E. Wacker Drive (312-861-0200); 200 E. Randolph Street, lower level in the AON Center (312-729-9200); 175 W. Jackson Boulevard (312-583-1100); and

CHICAGO PIZZA

It's impossible to narrow down the pizza restaurants and I'm likely to start heated arguments with neighbors and family if I leave out some of the classic deep-dish pizza creators. And to be honest, you need a couple to choose from because the lines at these places can stretch on. To begin, we should first review what makes a Chicago deep-dish pizza: It has a thick crust, is stuffed with cheese, really stuffed, and maybe sausage or spinach, then topped with a chunky tomato sauce. One piece will likely fill you up, but finding yourself with a whole beautiful pizza in front of you, it will be difficult to stop. That is how Chicago-style pizza works, so don't plan on going swimming afterward or putting on a bikini. The original locations for these pizza places downtown do tend to feel pretty touristy and there are long waits, so you may want to check out some of the less central locations if you're pressed for time. The deep-dish pizzas take at least 35 minutes cooking time once ordered.

Pizano's (312-751-1766; www.pizanoschicago.com) Original location at 864 N. State Street. Open 11 AM–2 AM weekdays, Sunday; 11 AM–3 AM Saturday. Also a location at 61 E. Madison Street. Opened in 1991 by the son of pizza pioneer Rudy Malnati, the thin butter crust is also a favorite of many here. $–$$.

& **Giordano's** (312-951-0747; www.giordanos.com), 730 N. Rush Street, Chicago. Open 11–11:30 daily. Opened in 1974 by two sons using their mother's recipe from Italy, Giordano's is now a pizza empire serving deep-dish at 12 city locations, 27 in the suburbs, and 6 in Florida. I actually really like their thin crust too, a family favorite for delivery. Scandalous, I know. $–$$.

& **Lou Malnati's Pizzeria** (312-828-9800; www.loumalnatis.com), 439 N. Wells Street, Chicago. Open 11–11 Monday through Thursday, 11–midnight Friday and Saturday, noon–11 Sunday. This is the River North location, but you can also find Malnati's in Lincoln Park, the South Loop, Lawndale, and Bucktown. Lou passed in 1978 but the pizza love is continued by his family, who serve up buttery crusts and lovely fresh tomato sauce with chunks of tomatoes. You can get an individual pizza or one that will serve your group. $–$$.

♿ **Gino's East** (312-266-3337), 162 E. Superior Street. Open 11–10 Monday through Thursday, 11–11 Friday and Saturday, noon–10 Sunday. Opened in 1966, Gino's has 12 locations in the city and Illinois suburbs, but the original is on Superior, with layers of customers' writing on the walls. This pizza is all about the golden crust. $–$$.

♿ **Pizzeria Uno** (312-321-1000; www.unos.com), 29 E. Ohio Street. Open 11 AM–1 AM weekdays, 11–2 Saturday, 11–11 Sunday. This original location at Ohio Street and Wabash Avenue is a very popular spot to sample the Chicago-style deep-dish. They started making it here in 1943, updating a recipe from Italy that became a Chicago staple. $–$$.

LOU MALNATI'S PIZZA

222 W. Adams Street in the AT&T/USG building (312-726-4800). The Dearborn location is open 11–4 weekdays for lunch, but other locations serve breakfast starting as early as 6. For a quick, casual, but fresh and good bite to eat, head to a Sopraffina cafe. You can get a fresh pizza, homemade pasta, focaccia sandwiches (The Caprese . . . yum), and a salad tossed with dressing. Also order antipasti and other salads from the deli cases. $.

& **The Gage** (312-372-4243; www.thegagechicago.com), 24 S. Michigan Avenue. Kitchen is open 11–11 weekdays, 10 AM–midnight Saturday, 10 AM–10 PM Sunday. Brunch served on weekends until 2:30. Bar stays open later on weekends. Located in an 1890 building that has the touch of master architect Louis Sullivan, this gastropub is directly across from Millennium Park and offers an excellent, wide-ranging menu that covers just about everything you could want, from risotto to elk to halibut and locally made sausages. The owners have termed their approach "refined rusticity." Brunch, which includes a traditional Irish breakfast, and lunch are also served, as is a long list of beers and other libations. $$–$$$$.

DINING OUT & **Park Grill** (312-521-7275; http://park-grillchicago.com), 11 N. Michigan Avenue. Open 11–9:30 Monday through Thursday, 11–10:30 Friday, 10–10:30 Saturday, 10–9:30

Sunday. An especially convenient option if you're checking out Millennium Park or the museums, the restaurant offers a broad, upscale menu that includes steaks, homemade raviolis, and seafood. A great combination in winter is to go ice-skating, then get a bite to eat here. Lunch: $$, Dinner: $$–$$$. But in the summer, I prefer **The Plaza at Park Grill**, same hours as Park Grill but opens at 11 on weekends. Plaza is only open mid-May to October. The giant outdoor dining area allows you to continue to enjoy the skyline and offers a menu of appetizers such as hummus, pork sliders, or kabobs created with seasonal market items. You can also order salads, burgers and sandwiches, or drinks.

& **The Purple Pig** (312-464-1744; www.thepurplepigchicago .com), 500 N. Michigan Avenue. Open 11:30 AM–midnight Sunday through Thursday, 11:30 AM–1 AM Friday and Saturday. Put together the chefs behind three famous Chicago restaurants—Spiaggia, Mia Francesca, and Heaven on Seven—and you get another great trio of things through the Purple Pig's focus on "cheese, wine and swine." The entryway to the restaurant is through an arch off Michigan Avenue. There's a robust wine selection, cheese sampler dish, interesting fried pig ear dish, and excellent chorizo-stuffed fried olives. The staff is very good with wine pairings in an unpretentious way. Head there when you're in a friendly mood, as the tables are communal. Outdoor seating is also available during pleasant weather. $$.

& **Café Iberico** (312-573-1510; www.cafeiberico.com), 739 N. LaSalle Drive. Open 11 AM–midnight Sunday through Thursday, 11 AM–1:30 AM Friday and Saturday. Lively and so good, this is a great place to take groups and sample some fantastic tapas and sangria. (The *queso de cabra,* baked goat cheese with a bright tomato basil sauce over it, is always a pleaser.) I recommend ordering in phases, starting with a few dishes, and holding onto a menu so you can order additional dishes later, otherwise the table gets too full and you may not get to taste everything! $$.

& **Reza's Restaurant** (312-664-4500; www.rezasrestaurant.com), 432 W. Ontario Street, Chicago. Open 11–10 daily. Persian, Middle Eastern, and Mediterranean food served in large portions. This is another good place for groups. Many of the meats are cooked over an open fire so they have a nice char to them, as do the vegetables. The vegetarian sampler gives you a taste of a wonderful array of appetizers: falafel, dolmeh, hummus, and tabbouli. Entrees are served with fresh Persian bread, soup, and choice of a Mediterranean couscous dish, dill rice, or white rice. Also a location at 5255 N. Clark Street in the Andersonville neighborhood. $$–$$$.

& **Spiaggia** (312-280-2750; www.spiaggiarestaurant.com), 980 N. Michigan Avenue, Level Two. Dinner service starts at 6 Sunday through Thursday, 5:30 Friday and Saturday. Opened in 1984, Chef Tony Mantuano's authentic, fine-dining approach to Italian cuisine has attracted droves of local fans for the high-quality ingredients in the antipasti, fresh made pastas, and wood-grilled entrees. Jackets are required. $$$–$$$$.

You can get a slightly less expensive experience with Chef Mantuano's food in a more casual setting at **Café Spiaggia**. Open for lunch 11:30–2:30 daily. Dinner: 5:30–9:30 Monday through Thursday, 5:30–10:30 Friday and Saturday, 5:30–9 Sunday. The menu includes salads, pastas, and entrees like steak, fish, or pork shoulder. $$–$$$.

& **Naha** (312-321-6242; www.naha-chicago.com), 500 N. Clark Street. Open for lunch 11:30–2 weekdays. Dinner: 5:30–9:30 Monday through Thursday, 5:30–10 Friday and Saturday. Chef Carrie Nahabedian blends her Armenian background with her experiences as a chef in California to produce a menu that is seasonal with Mediterranean influences. Seafood, duck breast, squab, and quail are among the stars of the menu of entrees. More than 30 wines are available by the glass. $$$$.

& **Morton's** (312-266-4820; www.mortons.com), 1050 N. State Street, Chicago. Open 5:30–11

Monday through Saturday, 5–9:30 Sunday. Even though you can find 75 Morton's across the country, the original steakhouse is here in this popular basement restaurant in Chicago. The place has an old-school romance about it and high-quality steaks. Business or dressy attire recommended, no T-shirts, shorts. $$$$.

& **Graham Elliot** (312-624-9975; www.grahamelliot.com), 217 W. Huron Street. Open 5–10 Monday through Saturday. The term the chef uses to describe this hip and fun restaurant is "bistronomic," as he seeks to present fine cuisine with a touch of humor. No dress codes or white tablecloths. This is contemporary American food as seen through the eyes of Chef Graham Elliot Bowles, who has won honors as best new chef and

NAHA

become a TV personality in cooking competition shows. How about a deconstructed caesar salad complete with brioche Twinkie and parmesan fluff? You'll find seafood, steak, and poultry dishes to choose from, presented in an artful way. $$$–$$$$.

& **Frontera Grill** (312-661-1434; www.rickbayless.com), 445 N. Clark Street, Chicago. Open for lunch 11:30–2:30 Tuesday through Friday; brunch: 10:30–2 Saturday; dinner: 5:20–10 Tuesday, 5–10 Wednesday and Thursday, 5–11 Friday and Saturday. How I love this food, with Chef Rick Bayless always pushing to make favorite Mexican dishes a little more special. You can taste the extra steps that are taken to ensure quality here, I swear. You will find the mole stellar. The menu changes monthly, but usually reflects Mr. Bayless's focus on quality ingredients and supporting local farmers. Most of the tables are first-come, first serve, so plan on a wait. They do set aside a small number of tables for reservations but you have to call way in advance to score one of those. Arrive right when they open if you want to cut down on your wait. $$–$$$.

Attached is the more upscale **Topolobampo** (312-661-1434), which takes a slightly more elegant but still authentic approach, offering up wild game, less well-known regional dishes, and traditional flavors in a fine dining room with museum-quality art. Open for lunch 11:30–2 Tuesday

FRONTERA GRILL AND TOPOLOBAMPO

Elm Street, Chicago. Open 5–10 Monday through Saturday, 4–10 Sunday. Chef Art Smith, who specializes in Southern cooking, offers the public a taste of the food that wowed Oprah when he was her personal chef. The dining rooms cover two stories of the Biggs Mansion, which survived the Great Chicago Fire. Start out with shrimp and grits or fried green tomatoes before moving onto a wood-fired pizza or salad. Entrees include dishes like Frogmore stew (which blends crawfish, lobster broth, fingerling potatoes, and andouille sausage), duo of gnocchi, or a beef short rib. The menu of sides, of course, includes a three-cheese mac, and fried pickles, served with roasted garlic aioli. $$$$.

& **Tru** (312-202-0001; www.tru restaurant.com), 676 N. St. Clair

through Friday; dinner: 5:30–9:30 Tuesday through Thursday, 5:30–10:30 Friday and Saturday. $$$$.

& **Table Fifty-two** (312-573-4000; www.tablefifty-two.com), 52 W.

TABLE FIFTY-TWO

Street. Open 6–10 Monday through Thursday, 5:30–11 Friday, 5–11 Saturday. A four-star restaurant that includes famed pastry chef and cookbook author, Gale Gand, as a partner, and offers French cuisine through a three-course fixed menu with a choice of appetizer, entree, and dessert. There's also a tasting menu of six to nine courses. It will not be a cheap evening, but you're not likely to leave disappointed. Three-course menu: $95 per person.

BUDDY GUY'S LEGENDS

Tasting menu: $110–145. Dessert: $15–40.

✳ Entertainment

LIVE MUSIC ♿ **Buddy Guy's Legends** (312-427-1190; www .buddyguys.com), 700 S. Wabash Avenue. Music starts at 9:30 Sunday through Thursday. On Friday, an acoustic set is from 5:30–8, followed by the opening band around 9 and headliner around 10:30. On Saturday, the acoustic set runs from 6–8 and the headliner starts at 11. When designing this new venue, Mr. Guy ordered that it not be too sparkly looking, telling architects that a blues club should look kind of old and funky. But what matters here is not the décor but the blues music that fills the rooms each night. If you want to see Buddy, the Chicago legend plays every January, but his club books a calendar of worthy blues artists. Note for families wanting to show the kids some Chicago history: It's 21 and over after 8 PM but there is a free lunch-time performance noon–2 on weekdays, as well as the earlier evening acoustic sets that run until 8. There are no advance tickets, just pay the cover at the door, which is $10 Sunday through Thursday, $20 Friday and Saturday; bigger name acts may cost more.

♿ **Charter One Pavilion at Northerly Island** (www.live nation.com/Charter-One-Pavilion -at-Northerly-Island-tickets -Chicago/venue/33036), 1300 S. Lynn White Drive. One of my favorite stories about Mayor Richard M. Daley ever: In the middle of the night, Daley sent crews out to the former Meigs Field airport to carve giant Xs into the airstrip, rendering it useless as an airport and setting it on a path to becoming a municipal park, as he always wanted it to be. Today there is a 7,500-seat concert pavilion there, right on the lakefront, which makes for an excellent outdoor music venue (as long as the weather cooperates.) It's now run by Live Nation.

MOVIES & **Siskel Film Center** (312-846-2800; www.siskelfilm center.org), 164 N. State Street. Box office open 5–9 weekdays, 2–9 Saturday, 2–6 Sunday. The film center named in honor of the well-respected and -liked film critic, Gene Siskel, lines up independent, foreign, and classic films. Also hosts several festivals through the year. Tickets: $9 adults.

& **AMC River East 21** (312-596-0333; www.amcentertainment .com/RiverEast/), 322 E. Illinois Street. This giant movie complex halfway in between the Lake and Michigan Avenue hosts red-carpet events. It features stadium seating and 3D movies as well. Tickets: $11.50 adults, $8.50 children, $10.50 seniors. Matinees: $9.50 before 4 PM for adults. All seats before noon are $6. An extra $3 charge applies for 3D films.

SPORTS & **Soldier Field** (312-235-7000; www.soldierfield.net; www.chicagobears.com), 1410 S.

Museum Campus Drive. Opened in 1924, the field was the site of many historic sporting events, such as the Dempsey-Tunney fight. In 2003, Soldier Field underwent a controversial overhaul that resulted in the strangest mesh of architectural styles. It appears as if a spaceship has landed in the historic stadium. But the field is supposed to be more fan friendly now, as it has been home of the Chicago Bears since 1971. Tickets for games available through Ticketmaster range from $68–365. Soldier Field occasionally hosts concerts and other special events.

THEATER AND PERFORMANCE Check **Hot Tix** (www.hottix.org) for half-price deals from the League of Chicago Theaters. You must buy online or in person. There are two Hot Tix locations downtown: 72 E. Randolph and 163 E. Pearson. Open 10–6 Tuesday through Saturday, 11–4 Sunday. If you're interested in a Broadway show, such as a *Rent* or *Shrek the Musical*, I'd suggest starting with **Broadway in Chicago** (800-775-2000; www .broadwayinchicago.com), which will provide a good overview of what's in town when you're planning a trip. Broadway in Chicago represents several downtown theaters that host those productions, including the Cadillac Palace Theater and the Ford Center for the Performing Arts Oriental Theater. You can buy tickets through Ticketmaster, or at the individual theater box office. Call 312-977-1700 for the box office hours that week.

&. **Theater on the Lake** (312-742-7994; www.chicagoparkdistrict.com/theateronthelake), right on the lakefront at Fullerton. Performances at 7:30 Wednesday through Saturday, 6:30 Sunday, from mid-June through mid-August. This theater that is true to its name has a rotating schedule of Chicago theater groups presenting works. Tickets: $17.50.

&. **Auditorium Theatre** (312-922-2110; http://auditoriumtheatre.org), 50 E. Congress Parkway. Box office open noon–6 weekdays. Designed by architects Louis Sullivan and Dankmar Adler, this is a beautiful, artful backdrop for any performance. The Joffrey Ballet and other dance companies perform here as do occasional musical acts. Tours of the building are $10 and start at 10:30 and noon Monday, 10:30 Thursday. Tickets for performances are available through Ticketmaster.

&. **Goodman Theatre** (312-443-3800; www.goodmantheatre.org), 170 N. Dearborn Street. Box office is open 10–5 weekdays, noon–5 weekends. Another Chicago theater recognized nationwide, the Goodman, under the leadership of artistic director Robert Falls, has attracted such well-known names as William Petersen, Rip Torn, and Frank Galati. A partnership between Falls and the actor Brian Dennehy resulted in Tony Award-winning presentations

in New York. The theater, established in 1922, also hosted Tennessee Williams's last produced play and has premiered several David Mamet plays.

&. **Chicago Theatre** (312-462-6300; www.thechicagotheatre.com), 175 N. State Street. Box office open noon–6 weekdays. With its famous marquee sign outside, the Chicago Theater has welcomed many great artists and wowed audience members throughout its history. Opened in 1921, the theater was the first large movie "palace" of its kind in the country. When designing it, the owners adopted grand design ideas from around the world, from the replica of the Arc de Triomphe above the sign to the murals painted on the ceilings. The auditorium has 3,600 seats and is 7 stories high. The theater draws names from the full spectrum of musical genres, and is also a popular venue for comedians.

Joffrey Ballet (312-922-2110; www.joffrey.com), 50 E. Congress Parkway. The company founded by Robert Joffrey continues to delight today. The schedule of performances usually includes retold masterpieces and new works. Performances and box office are at the Auditorium Theater. Box office is open noon–6 weekdays.

&. **Harris Theater** (312-334-7777; www.harristheaterchicago.org), 205 E. Randolph Street. Box office open noon–6 weekdays, 10–4 Saturday, open until curtain

CHICAGO THEATRE

on performance days. Part of Millennium Park, the Harris gives dance groups and musicians from around the city a space to shine, while also hosting artists from around the world. Among the companies who call it home is Hubbard Street Dance (312-850-9744; http://hubbardstreetdance.com). If you drive to the Harris, you can get parking validation for the Millennium Park Garages that cuts the price by a couple dollars.

& **Lyric Opera of Chicago** (312-332-2244, x5600 for ticket info; www.lyricopera.org), 20 N. Wacker Drive. Buy tickets noon–6 Monday through Saturday or until curtain on performance days. The Lyric has eight operas during a season that runs from October through late March in the gorgeous Civic Opera House. To find out more about the opera you're about to see, you can sit in on a lecture one hour prior to the curtain's opening.

& ♪ **Chicago Shakespeare Theater** (312-595-5600; www. chicagoshakes.com), 800 E. Grand Avenue. Box office hours extended on performance days, but generally open noon–5 Tuesday through Saturday, noon–4 Sunday. Recently awarded a Tony for regional theater, the Chicago Shakespeare Theater on Navy Pier has an intimate stage inspired by the Royal Shakespeare Company's Swan Theater, with seating on three sides of the stage. Considered one of the city's top cultural institutions under artistic director

Barbara Gaines, the theater also has programming for children.

✹ Selective Shopping

Magnificent Mile (312-409-5560; www.themagnificentmile .com), North Michigan Avenue. One of the world's most famous shopping districts, the Magnificent Mile presents classic department stores, chic boutiques, and plenty of great people-watching. Even if you're not planning to buy, it's still an experience. Some of these shops may be found in your local mall, but those likely won't be as grand as the incarnations you see here, as many companies make their Michigan Avenue locations flagship destinations.

Water Tower Place (www.shop watertower.com), 835 N. Michigan Avenue. Open 10–9 Monday through Saturday, 11–6 Sunday. American Girl Place is here, on two levels, as is Macy's and 100 other stores. If you want a bite to eat, try Foodlife on the mezzanine level, where you can find just about anything you want to eat from the 14 different kitchens.

State Street from Monroe to Randolph You'll find the big department stores of Macy's (although the building still has the marks of Marshall Field's), Carson Pirie Scott, and Sears, as well as the Old Navy and Urban Outfitters of the world.

River North Art Galleries A collection of dozens of art galleries concentrated between Chicago Avenue and Huron Street, and LaSalle Boulevard and Orleans Street.

French Market (312-575-0306; www.frenchmarketchicago.com), 131 N. Clinton. Open year-round, 7:30–7:30 weekdays, 8:30–6 Saturday. This West Loop indoor marketplace provides a home for local vendors who have a passion for making things by hand. Reminiscent of European fresh markets, vendors sell fresh produce, breads, cheeses, wines, meats, and seafood. You can pick up prepared foods for a snack or meal outside. Free parking with $20 purchase.

✱ Special Events

June: **Chicago Blues Festival** (www.chicagobluesfestival.us), Grant Park. Three-day festival in mid-June that celebrates the genre that made Chicago famous around the world. The schedule pays homage to the creators of the music while also welcoming some new performers to the stage each year as well.

Taste of Chicago (www.tasteof chicago.us) Starts in late June and runs until July 4. This famous festival of food is definitely worth a visit, for the frozen chocolate bananas, the slices of deep-dish pizza, and the tastes of cuisines from just about every ethnicity. But for some reason, it always seems to be 104 degrees during the festival, meaning one can only eat so much fried food with the sun beating down. Best to swing through during your lunch and dinner hours, then take a break in nearby Millennium Park or an air-conditioned museum. The city has booked an impressive line of national and local musical acts at the Petrillo Music Shell in past years, but has been considering making changes to save money. Be sure to check the schedule.

August: **Lollapalooza** (www.lolla palooza.com) When organizers revived this 1990s alternative music festival, they chose Grant Park to host, and it exploded into one of the best music festivals in the country. With several stages, you may have The Strokes and Lady Gaga playing at the same time, or Arcade Fire playing while Soundgarden is on at the opposite end of the park. Fans can float from stage to stage, taking in the vendors, foods, and other attractions. Pack a refillable water bottle. There is a full lineup of programming for kids during the day.

Chicago Air and Water Show (www.chicagoairandwatershow.us) Centered off North Avenue Beach (1600 N. Lake Shore Drive). Every year, I forget this show is coming and am shocked to see the military jets fly very low over the skyline. Then, the pilots do some fancy maneuvers and I remember OH, YES, AIR AND WATER SHOW TIME. See the U.S. Navy Blue Angels, parachute teams, and there are also some cool celebrity surprises. The best place to see it is from the lakefront, as that's where the action is centered.

September: **Chicago Jazz Festival** (www.chicagojazzfestival.us) Performances at Millennium Park, Grant Park, and the Chicago Cultural Center during early September showcase the best from the city's jazz scene and beyond. Free.

October: **Chicago Marathon** (312-904-9800; www.chicago marathon.com) Race starts at 7:30 AM on a Sunday. This excellent marathon winds throughout the city, with spectators lining the route. Many streets are closed off for the race, so think about taking the CTA to get around to various spots.

November: **The Magnificent Mile Lights Festival** (http://magnificentmilelightsfestival.com), North Michigan Avenue. In late November, Mickey Mouse leads the procession down Michigan Avenue to turn on all the twinkling lights for the holiday season. The festival brings other Disney characters, celebrities, bands, and tons of families to the downtown area.

NEIGHBORHOODS

Y ou will need many storytellers to grasp what Chicago is truly about and to appreciate the beauty, adventure, and experience it offers. Michigan Avenue and the downtown area offer one portrait of the city painted especially for tourists. Venture out from the city center to see Chicago through a different lens.

Take the train or a drive from the Loop, and as you emerge from the man-made cavern created by the skyscrapers that surround it, you'll discover historic neighborhoods, sports stadiums, universities, museums, and restaurants. Many of the neighborhoods here would stand up against a medium-sized city in terms of what they offer in nightlife, dining, and things to do.

North Side/South Side is perhaps the easiest division to make when looking at the map, one that also plays into the Cubs fan/Sox fan rivalry. (I descend from a long line of South Side Sox fans.) But the city's neighborhoods are a patchwork of dozens of individual communities imprinted by cultures a world away.

If we head South first, you have the South Loop, which is just west of the Museum Campus. There's been much activity over the past decade in constructing new high-rises, townhomes, college dorms, and restaurants for a neighborhood where the lights used to go out after 5 PM. Nearby, there's the Blues District of Bronzeville, where you are greeted by the Great Migration statue recognizing the movement of millions of African Americans to Chicago looking for a better opportunity in the early 20th century. There's academic Hyde Park, home to the University of Chicago, and nearby Kenwood, which is home to President Obama. Chinatown transports you across the globe as you pass beneath the large red and green Chinatown gate. Just west is Pilsen, a vibrant Mexican American community where art and food intersect in an interesting way. North of Pilsen is Little Italy and Greektown, where you can sample some of the best of those cuisines at restaurants built by immigrants who arrived in

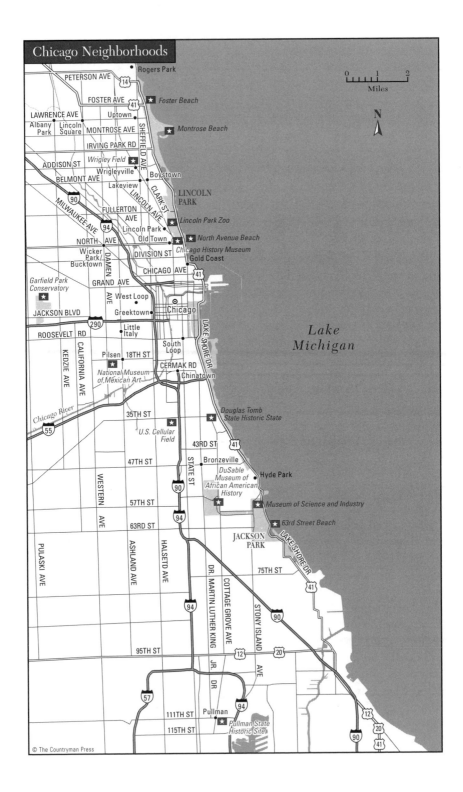

Chicago Neighborhoods

Rogers Park

PETERSON AVE — 14

FOSTER AVE — 41 · Foster Beach

LAWRENCE AVE · Uptown
Albany Park · Lincoln Square · MONTROSE AVE · Montrose Beach

IRVING PARK RD

ADDISON ST · Wrigley Field
Wrigleyville · Boystown
BELMONT AVE · Lakeview

LINCOLN PARK

FULLERTON AVE · Lincoln Park Zoo
Lincoln Park · Old Town
NORTH AVE · North Avenue Beach
Wicker Park / Bucktown · DIVISION ST · Chicago History Museum
Gold Coast

CHICAGO AVE — 41

Garfield Park Conservatory
GRAND AVE · West Loop · Chicago
JACKSON BLVD · Greektown

ROOSEVELT RD · Little Italy
South Loop
Pilsen · 18TH ST
CERMAK RD
National Museum of Mexican Art · Chinatown

Chicago River

35TH ST · Douglas Tomb State Historic State
55
U.S. Cellular Field

43RD ST — 41
47TH ST · Bronzeville
DuSable Museum of African American History · Hyde Park
57TH ST · Museum of Science and Industry
63RD ST · 63rd Street Beach

JACKSON PARK

75TH ST — 41

95TH ST

57
111TH ST · Pullman — 94
115TH ST · Pullman State Historic Site

MILWAUKEE AVE · 90 · 94 · DAMEN AVE · LINCOLN AVE · CLARK ST · SHEFFIELD AVE · LAKE SHORE DR

KEDZIE AVE · CALIFORNIA AVE · 290

PULASKI AVE · ASHLAND AVE · HALSTED AVE · WESTERN AVE · STATE ST · DR. MARTIN LUTHER KING JR. DR · COTTAGE GROVE AVE · STONY ISLAND AVE · LAKE SHORE DR

90 · 94 · 12 · 20

Lake Michigan

0 — 1 — 2
Miles

N

© The Countryman Press

LINCOLN SQUARE NEIGHBORHOOD

Chicago a couple generations ago. Continue on to discover the West Loop and its cadre of hip restaurants, bars, galleries, and condos.

If we head north from the Loop, you have historic Old Town, which has brick streets and architecture that give it a turn-of-the-century quaintness. Adjacent to the lakefront, you have the neighborhood of Lincoln Park, with the Chicago History Museum, zoo, upscale shopping districts, and restaurants. Housing is not inexpensive in these parts, and many neighborhoods are worth a stroll. North of Lincoln Park is Lakeview, which seems to be a point of entry to the city for many college grads, with the bars and nightlife around Belmont Avenue and Wrigleyville (named of course for Wrigley Field.) Wicker Park/Bucktown has a great late-night scene, as well as commitment to art, but you just may see artists rolling their eyes at the high-end shoppers they feel have invaded the neighborhood. Boystown is the center for the gay community in Chicago, and is located around of Belmont and Halsted streets. It's marked by the rainbow flags and has some seriously great restaurants. Farther north, Andersonville is a neighborhood proud of its Swedish roots, with excellent pubs and dining. To the far Northwest there's Lincoln Square, a welcoming, easily strollable strip of stores and restaurants in a neighborhood with strong German ties, and Albany Park, one the city's most diverse neighborhoods. Devon Avenue is the center of the Indian community in Chicago.

You may get the picture that Chicago is a city of fabulous neighborhoods, which is true, but it's also a very segregated city when it comes to where people live. The diversity here, though, has resulted in an amazing infrastructure of restaurants. We have some serious culinary superstars like Charlie Trotter's, and Grant Achatz's Alinea. But away from the glare of the spotlight shown on establishments like that is a world of restaurants in the city's neighborhoods that offer up tastes of the world's best cuisines. And don't forget classic Chicago establishments that promise the best Chicago-style hot dog or pizza.

Now we can dig a little deeper into what the neighborhoods can offer. I've arranged the listings by geographic area.

GETTING AROUND *By auto:* Lake Shore Drive is a pleasant route to take north or south, and provides access to many of the neighborhoods if you just head west, away from the Lake. If you are driving through the neighborhoods, be prepared for stress at the city's six-way intersections that some will avoid at any cost.

By bus: Chicago Transit Authority buses service most of the sites you'll want to take in. See the downtown Getting Around section for more tips on riding Chicago public transportation.

By train: The "L" is a great way to get to and see the neighborhoods. The Brown Line to Kimball will take you to River North, Old Town, Roscoe Village, Lincoln Square, and Albany Park. The Red Line stretches north to south. If you take the Red Line from downtown and head north to Howard, you can access the Gold Coast, Lincoln Park, Lakeview, Wrigleyville, and Uptown. The Red Line train headed to 95th Street will take you to Printers Row, the South Loop, Chinatown, and U.S. Cellular Field. The Blue Line heading out to O'Hare will make stops in the Bucktown/Wicker Park area and Logan Square. The Pink Line will take you to Pilsen at the 18th street stop.

MEDICAL EMERGENCIES University of Chicago Medical Center (773-702-1000; www.uchospitals.edu), 5841 S. Maryland Avenue. Located in Hyde Park on the South Side of the city, the adult and children's hospitals offer cutting-edge care as well as a Level I trauma center for pediatrics.

Advocate Illinois Masonic Medical Center (773-975-1600; www .advocatehealth.com/immc), 836 W. Wellington Avenue. A Level I trauma center in Chicago's Lakeview neighborhood, this hospital also has many specialists.

✱ Wandering Around

EXPLORING BY FOOT The shoppers of the bunch will love to explore boutiques and other unique shops along Armitage Avenue, Damen

Avenue in Wicker Park/Bucktown, or Southport Avenue near Addison. Take the Brown Line to the Western Avenue stop and you'll find the charming Lincoln Square neighborhood, with great restaurants, cafés, a fountain square, and shops. If you'd like to take in some impressive homes, take a stroll around the Gold Coast, or head up to Wrigleyville to the Alta Vista Terrace District (located between Grace and Byron streets).

✳ To See

MUSEUMS, NORTH ⟨symbols⟩ **Chicago History Museum** (312-642-4600; www.chicagohistory.org), 1601 N. Clark Street. Open 9:30–4:30 Monday through Saturday, noon–5 Sunday. The backstory to the Chicago you see today is quite fascinating, as told at this museum in Lincoln Park. The "Chicago: Crossroads of America" permanent exhibition includes the city's first "L" car that also took people to the World's Fair of 1893. There are also melted items from the Chicago Fire and a helmet from the 1968 Democratic National Convention riot. Kids especially like the historic dioramas that illustrate key moments of the city's past. With an extensive costume collection, there are often remarkable costume displays as well as exhibits that detail the stories of specific neighborhoods. A new permanent exhibit called "Facing Freedom" looks at American history through the museum's collection. The museum offers historic tours around the city including history pub-crawls, and The *Devil in the White City* tour that stops at locations featured in the bestselling book. Admission with audio tour: $14 adults; $12 seniors, students; free children 12 and under. Free

DUSABLE MUSEUM OF AFRICAN AMERICAN HISTORY

on Monday. Reduced parking is available across the street, 1 block north, at Clark and LaSalle, off Stockton Drive.

⇗ ↑ ✐ ♿ ♂ **The Peggy Notebaert Nature Museum** (773-755-5100; www.naturemuseum.org), 2430 N. Cannon Drive. Open 9–4:30 weekdays, 10–5 weekends. On a cold day, this is a wonderful haven, with more than 75 species of butterflies in a large glass greenhouse, as well as re-created prairies and dunes. Exhibits also teach about wetlands, waterways, the work of naturalists, and green living. The children's area is filled with activities that will get them moving. Admission: $9 adults, $7 students and seniors, $6 children 3 to 12.

MUSEUMS, SOUTH ♿ ✐ ↑ ♂ **Museum of Science and Industry** (773-684-1414; www.msichicago.org), 57th Street and Lake Shore Drive in the Hyde Park neighborhood on the city's South Side. Open 9:30–4 daily. Extended hours from 9:30–5:30 daily during the summer months and some other holiday periods. Of the many fascinating parts in the largest science museum in the Western Hemisphere is the U-505 that was captured during World War II, one of a handful still in existence and the only enemy ship boarded and captured on the high seas by the U.S. Navy since the War of 1812. Listen closely, because you'll hear how important this catch was (it put German codebooks into U.S. hands), and how the captain, a Chicago native, saved it and brought it home to Chicago. Elsewhere in the museum, the kids will love the model train display of the city, Yesterday's Main Street (which depicts a main street from 1910), and the Fairy Castle dollhouse. The Science Storms exhibit allows you to stand beside a 40-foot tornado and investigate the causes of lightning, tsunamis, and avalanches. The temporary exhibits that come through are phenomenal as well. The museum is housed in the former Palace of Fine Arts, which was built for the 1893 World's Columbian Exposition. The museum opened in 1933, with the interactive coal-mine exhibit that you can still visit today. General admission, which also gets you into the submarine exhibit, but not an onboard tour, is $15 adults, $14 seniors, $10 children. There are days, sometimes weeks, when general admission is free, so check the calendar. A guided tour of the U-505 submarine is $8 for adults and seniors, $6 for children. Omnimax theater tickets (a 5-story domed wraparound movie screen): $8 adults, $7 seniors, $6 children. Note that parking in the underground garage at the museum is $18.

♿ ↑ ♂ **Smart Museum of Art** (773-702-0200; http://smartmuseum .uchicago.edu), 5550 S. Greenwood Avenue. Open 10–4 Tuesday through Friday, 11–5 weekends. This museum on the University of Chicago campus in Hyde Park usually has great exhibitions pulled from a superb collection of modern art, Asian and European art, and contemporary art. Some of the highlights of the collection: prints from Francisco de Goya's

The Disasters of War series, paintings by Walter Kuhn and Mark Rothko, dining room furniture designed by Frank Lloyd Wright for the Robie House, and a Ming dynasty Buddha sculpture. Free.

& ↑ **Oriental Institute** (773-702-9514; http://oi.uchicago.edu/museum), 1155 E. 58th Street. Open 10–6 Tuesday, and Thursday through Saturday, 10–8:30 Wednesday, noon–6 Sunday. Housed in a gorgeous University of Chicago building, the institute is devoted to the history, art, and archaeology of the ancient Near East. What's especially unique is that most of what's here was uncovered by the Institute itself, through excavations in ancient Egypt, Persia, and Mesopotamia. Peruse pottery, tablets, and vessels of what may have been the world's first urban civilization, or study a 17-foot tall statue of King Tutankhamun dug up by the institute in 1930. Suggested donation: $7 adults, $4 children.

& ↑ **DuSable Museum of African American History** (773-947-0600; www.dusablemuseum.org), 740 E. 56th Place, in the Hyde Park neighborhood. Open 10–5 Tuesday through Saturday, noon–5 Sunday. With a mission to preserve the history and culture of African Americans, this museum is named after Jean Baptiste Pointe DuSable, Chicago's first permanent settler and a French Canadian of Haitian descent. The museum's permanent exhibitions include the story of Harold Washington, Chicago's first black mayor, and the march on Washington. It also features paintings, sculptures, and African works of art. Rotating traveling exhibitions round out the story told here. Admission: $10 adults, $7 students and seniors, $3 children 6 to 11 years.

& ↑ **National Museum of Mexican Art** (312-738-1503; www.national museumofmexicanart.org), 1852 W. 19th Street, in the Pilsen neighborhood Open 10–5 Tuesday through Sunday. The largest Latino arts center in America presents exhibitions and events centered around Mexican art,

NATIONAL MUSEUM OF MEXICAN ART

history, and culture. The works span borders, with pieces from the U.S. and Mexico, and mediums, from multimedia pieces to traditional religious paintings. Free.

&. ↑ **Jane Addams-Hull House Museum** (312-413-5353; www.uic.edu /jaddams/hull), 800 S. Halsted Street. Open 10–4 Tuesday through Friday, noon–4 Sunday. Social reformer Jane Addams, the first American woman to be honored with the Nobel Peace Prize, co-founded the Hull House on the Near West Side in 1889 as a social settlement to help poor immigrant neighbors. She also worked to advance public policy in the arenas of public health, education, and immigrants' rights, among others. A recent renovation project opened up the second floor of the Hull House to the public, including the personal living space of Jane Addams. The museum details the lives of Ida B. Wells, W. E. B. DuBois, and many others who were affiliated with the house.

♂ **Glessner House Museum** (312-326-1480; www.glessnerhouse.org), 1800 S. Prairie Avenue. Tours depart at 1 and 3, Wednesday through Sunday. Tour center opens at 11:30. Peek into the lifestyle of the exclusive Prairie Avenue that was home to Marshall Field, Philip Armour, and George Pullman, among other Chicago business and civic leaders. This home was completed for John and Frances Glessner in 1887. Glessner was a partner in a farm machinery company that later merged with others to form International Harvester. The couple helped found the Chicago Symphony Orchestra. Tours: $10 adults, $9 seniors and students, $6 children 5 to 12. You can purchase a combined ticket that also gets you into the Clarke House and saves $5 on adult entry. Free on Wednesday but it's crowded, so space is limited.

&. **Clarke House Museum** (312-326-1480; www.clarkehousemuseum .org), 1827 S. Indiana Avenue. Tours are given at 12 and 2, Wednesday through Sunday, and depart from the visitor center at the Glessner House on 18th Street between Indiana and Prairie Avenues. This white house fronted by large pillars is Chicago's oldest surviving domestic structure, built in 1836. Henry and Caroline Clarke moved their family from New York to a 20-acre site where they could see Native American campfires in the distance. Mr. Clarke served as city clerk. The house has been moved around, and its current site is near the original build site. This home and the nearby Glessner House are part of the Prairie Avenue Historic District, where Chicago's wealthiest residents built their palaces. Tours: $10 adults, $9 seniors and students, $5 for children 5 to 12 years. You can purchase a combined ticket with the Glessner House tours and save $5 on adult entry. Tours are free on Wednesday.

&. ↑ **National Veterans Art Museum** (312-326-0270; www.nvam.org), 1801 S. Indiana Avenue, in the Prairie Avenue Historic District on the Near South Side. Open 10–5 Tuesday through Saturday. Originally created

CLARKE HOUSE MUSEUM

to showcase the art created by veterans of the Vietnam War who sought healing through their work, the museum now has expanded to cover all wars. The museum features everything from exhibitions of combat photography from current conflicts, to an exhibition of *The Things They Carried* inspired by Tim O'Brien's book about the items soldiers bring into battle. The goal is to show the real impact of war, through art created by veterans or influenced by war. Admission: $10 general, $7 seniors, students. Free active military.

HISTORIC SITES, NORTH Graceland Cemetery (773-525-1105; www.gracelandcemetery.org), 4001 N. Clark Street. Open 8:30–4:30 daily. Stroll through the cemetery of architects, where brilliant artists like Louis Sullivan and Ludwig Mies van der Rohe are buried. Other notable Chicagoans who rest at this North Side cemetery: Daniel Burnham, Potter Palmer, and Marshall Field.

HISTORIC SITES, SOUTH Historic Pullman Foundation (773-785-8901; www.pullmanil.org), 11141 S. Cottage Grove Avenue, on the city's South Side. Visitor Center open 11–3 Tuesday through Sunday. The story of the Pullman factory is one of wealth and the working man. From 1880–84, George Pullman built an entire planned community for his workers at Pullman's Palace Car Company on Chicago's South Side. Roughly 1,000 row houses still exist, and the ones immediately surrounding the hotel and visitors center are being restored by private owners. The squat visitor center is not the prettiest building, but features an exhibit, a 15-minute film, and self-guided maps to start your own tour. You can see the ruins of the old factory buildings and the administration building with its clock tower. Bonus fact for those following the story of Lincoln through Illinois: His son, Robert Todd Lincoln, was president of the company after George Pullman died in 1897. By 1907, the town was sold off to private owners. By 1960, it was declared a blighted area, and a decade later the Historic Pullman Foundation was created to work on preservation efforts. Guided walking tours of the neighborhood are given the first Sunday of every month at 1:30, May through October. Note: if the building appears locked, be sure to hit the doorbell. Suggested donation: $5.

The Pullman State Historic Site (773-660-2341; www.pullman-museum.org), 11111 S. Forrestville Avenue. Open 11–3 daily, but call ahead as hours are reduced according to demand. Also, a renovation is planned at the Hotel Florence, which may result in it closing for a period. After the Hotel Florence was saved by the Historic Pullman Foundation, the Illinois Historic Preservation Agency took over the hotel and the clock tower administration building, as well as the factory buildings. The Hotel Florence is a Queen Anne–style hotel George Pullman built to impress the guests and businessmen coming to the factory. Group tours of factory grounds must be arranged in advance. Free. The **Bronzeville Historical Society** (773-291-9115; www.bronzevillehistorical society.com) also has a rotating exhibit space in the Hotel Florence.

HOTEL FLORENCE AT THE PULLMAN STATE HISTORIC SITE

Oak Woods Cemetery (773-288-3800), 1035 E. 67th Street. Open 8:30–4:15 daily. Jesse Owens, Ida B. Wells, Harold Washington, Mayor Big Bill Thompson, and Enrico Fermi are buried at this South Side cemetery. There also is a memorial to 6,000 Confederate prisoners who died at Camp Douglas.

Stephen A. Douglas Tomb and Memorial (312-225-2620; www
.state.il.us/hpa/hs/douglas_tomb.htm), 636 E. 35th Street. Open daily 9–5.
Short in stature during his life, Stephen Douglas towers high above everyone in this memorial that pays homage to his historic career. Douglas
moved to Chicago in 1847 to a lakeside property called Oakenwald,
intending to build a grand estate, but his work in Washington required too
much attention, so he only had a cottage built. He died in Chicago in 1861
at the age of 48. His estate was used to train troops during the Civil War
and eventually became a camp for Confederate prisoners of war.

CULTURAL SITES, SOUTH ⅙ ↑ **Robie House** (312-994-4000; www
.gowright.org), 5757 S. Woodlawn Avenue. Museum shop open 9–4 Thursday through Monday. Various tours available 11–5. With spectacular art
glass, overhangs that seem—impossibly—to float, exquisite design, and
respect for the natural environment, the Robie House near the University
of Chicago has been named one of the top 10 most significant structures
of the 20th century. The Robie also hosts events such as "After Hours,"
where you can have a drink at the home, or a "Geek's Guide to the Robie
House," that provides a more detailed discussion of the architectural concepts used in the home. A guided interior tour is offered from 11–2
Thursday through Monday: $15 adults, $12 youth, seniors. Self-guided
tour is available from 3–4 Thursday through Monday. Audio tour of the
surrounding neighborhood: $15.

Willie Dixon's Blues Heaven Foundation (312-808-1286;
http://bluesheaven.com), 2120 S. Michigan Avenue. Open noon–4 weekdays, noon–3 Saturday, but call
ahead. Real blues lovers, can tour
the offices of Chess Records, the
main studio where Muddy Waters,
Chuck Berry, and many others
recorded, with Willie Dixon often
producing, arranging, and playing
bass. Other Chess Artists include
Buddy Guy, Etta James, Aretha
Franklin, and John Lee Hooker.
The Rolling Stones also recorded a
blues instrumental piece here.
Admission: $10.

ROBIE HOUSE

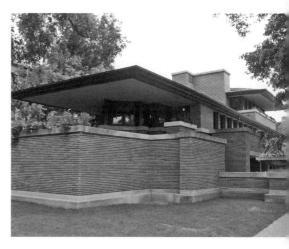

GALLERIES, NORTH/WEST
Woman Made Gallery (312-738-
0400; www.womanmade.org), 685
N. Milwaukee Avenue. The gallery

is open noon–7 Wednesday through Friday, noon–4 weekends. Dedicated to getting the work of female artists before more eyes, this nonprofit hosts juried group exhibitions, and solo exhibitions at its River West location throughout the year.

& **Flatiron Building** (708-415-6370; www.flatironartists.com), 1579 N. Milwaukee Avenue. The Flatiron building, a local landmark of the Wicker Park-Bucktown area, is home to dozens of working artists who open up the studio space for monthly First Friday art shows, from 6–10 on the first Friday of every month. Also hosts other events throughout the year.

GALLERIES, SOUTH Gallery Guichard (773-373-8000), 3521 S. Martin Luther King Drive. Open 10–6 Monday through Saturday, 2–4 Sunday. Located in a historic building in the Bronzeville neighborhood, the gallery focuses on the art of the African Diaspora, showcasing the works of owner, Andre Guichard, and more than 30 others.

& **Hyde Park Art Center** (773-324-5520; www.hydeparkart.org), 5020 S. Cornell Avenue. Open 9–8 Monday through Thursday, 9–5 Friday and Saturday, noon–5 Sunday. The oldest "alternative" space in the city, the vibrant art center has a full calendar of exhibitions featuring Chicago area artists, as well as gallery talks, poetry readings, and music performances.

Chicago Arts District (http://chicagoartsdistrict.org), 1821 S. Halsted Street. From 6–10 on the second Friday of the month, galleries in the Pilsen area open to the public. In the 1960s, artists started converting empty buildings in Pilsen into artists' lofts and studios, laying the foundation for the Chicago Arts District that exists today. Pick up a map at the information center at the address above and start exploring, while meeting the artists themselves.

✳ To Do

BOATING Chicago River Canoe and Kayak (773-704-2663; http://chicagoriverpaddle.com), 3400 N. Rockwell Avenue, on the North Side. There are also suburban launch sites in Skokie and Winnetka. Open late May through October, 1–6 weekdays, 9–6 weekends. The river hasn't always had a reputation as a waterway you want to explore, because of pollution, but several groups have been working hard to clean it up, so now you'll regularly see canoes and kayaks out on the waters. Rates: $15 per hour for single canoe or kayak, $20 for tandem kayak. Tours of river and downtown can run $35–50 per person depending on tour, and if you get a single kayak, tandem, or canoe.

BOWLING Southport Lanes (773-472-6600; www.sparetimechicago .com), 3325 N. Southport Avenue, on the North Side. Open noon–2 AM weekdays, noon–3 AM Saturday, noon–1 AM Sunday. Bowling starts after 5:30 on weekdays. Test out one of the last remaining hand-set bowling alleys in the country at this bowling/billiards/bar and grill establishment in the Lakeview neighborhood. $15 per hour per lane Monday through Thursday. On weekends, the rate goes up to $20, although Sunday bowling is $10. Shoes are $3. Note that because of the bar, you must be 21 to enter.

GOLF The Chicago Park District has several golf courses throughout city neighborhoods, including **Sydney R. Marovitz Golf Course** (312-742-7930; www.cpdgolf.com), 3600 N. Recreation Drive, on the North Side. Bounded by the lakeshore on one end and the lakefront running/biking path on the other, the location provides great scenery for this 9-hole, par 36 course. Fees: $22–25 for 9 holes, carts are $9 per person.

Jackson Park Golf Course (773-667-0524; www.cpdgolf.com), 6401 S. Richards Drive, on the South Side. Historic Jackson Park offers this 18-hole, par 70 golf course with driving range. Fees: $24–27 for 18 holes. Carts are $16 per person.

South Shore Golf Course (773-256-0986; www.cpdgolf.com), 7059 S. Shore Drive. Opened as the South Shore Country Club in 1905, today the former private club is a public course and has a gorgeous cultural center that hosts many community arts events; it was also the site of the wedding reception for Barack and Michelle Obama. The 9-hole golf course is a par 33 along Lake Michigan. Fees: $16–18 for 9 holes, $9 for carts.

TOURS & **Chicago Neighborhood Tours** (312-742-1190; www.chicago neighborhoodtours.com) Depart from the Chicago Cultural Center at 77 E. Randolph Street at 10 on Saturday from late February through early December, with some weekday tours available Memorial Day through Labor Day. Tour a specific neighborhood like Wicker Park or South Chicago, or learn about a specific topic on special interest tours like "The White City," "Daniel Burnham's Chicago," or "Greek Chicago." You'll have to walk some but will also ride on a motor coach. Tours: $30–50 adults, $25–45 for seniors, students, and children.

ZOOS & **Lincoln Park Zoo** (312-742-2000; www.lpzoo.org), 2400 N. Cannon Drive, for east entrance and parking. Additional entrances located on west side of zoo off Stockton Drive, on the city's North Side. Open 10–5 weekdays, 10–6:30 weekends Memorial Day through Labor Day. Daily 10–5 April through May, September through October; 10–4:30 November through March. Nothing like walking through a city and stumbling across an African elephant or polar bears on the lakefront. Take the Regenstein African Journey, watch penguins jump

GARDENS AT LINCOLN PARK ZOO

into the water, check out the bat exhibit, or ride an old-fashioned carousel. At the farm in the zoo, kids will enjoy feeding cows, and petting other animals. The climbing opportunities in the children's zoo are also pretty cool.

BIKE TOUR IN LINCOLN PARK

Keeping with the conservation and earth-friendly themes supported throughout the zoo, the Café at Wild Things! offers a menu of all organic or local foods, and sustainable servingware. Also explore the nature boardwalk along the pond on the south end of the zoo.

✳ Green Space

Lincoln Park (312-742-7648; www.chicagoparkdistrict.com) Lincoln Park is a ribbon of green that stretches along the west side of Lake Shore Drive from North Avenue all the way to the far North Side of the city. A wonderful place to wander, with playgrounds, benches, and paths stretching across the lakefront. Named after Abraham Lincoln following his assassination, today it stretches 1,028 acres, and includes the Lincoln Park Conservatory and Lincoln Park Zoo.

Jackson Park (312-742-7648; www.chicagoparkdistrict.com) Located between 57th and 67th Streets, Lake Shore Drive and Stony Island Avenue. This 600-acre South Side park was the site of the 1893 World's Columbian Exposition and the center of the book *The Devil in the White City.* The designer of New York's Central Park, Frederick Law Olmsted, laid out this park and with planner, Daniel H. Burnham, designed the fairgrounds. After the World's Fair, it was converted into a park. You can see the *Golden Lady* sculpture, which is a smaller version of the statue that originally greeted people. From the park, you also have nice views of the former Fine Arts Palace, now the Museum of Science and Industry. The large park has baseball fields, a golf course, paths for jogging or biking, tennis courts, and is home to the Osaka Japanese Garden and Wooded Island. To get to Japanese Garden, from Lake Shore Drive turn onto Science Drive just south of 57th and follow the signs.

 ♿ ✿ ♈ **Garfield Park Conservatory** (312-746-5100; www.garfield-conservatory.org), 300 N. Central Park Avenue. Open 9–5 daily year-round, with extended hours on Wednesday until 8. This greenhouse wonderland is a favorite urban oasis of many Chicago residents, especially during the winter, when it's also a great place to feel a little bit of nature without braving the cold. It's kid friendly even outside of the children's garden area. The greenhouses and outdoor spaces stretch over 4.5 acres. The conservatory often has cool art exhibits and other events, evidenced

OSAKA GARDEN

by the Dale Chihuly glass pieces in the Aroid House, which were purchased by the conservatory alliance after the success of a giant show featuring the artist's works nestled into plants in the greenhouses. Free.

✴ Lodging

BED AND BREAKFASTS ⟨ᵧ⟩

City Scene B&B (773-549-1743; www.cityscenebb.com), 2101 N. Clifton Avenue. This is a great base to explore the city's North Side neighborhoods. This Victorian four-flat was built just after the Chicago Fire and is located in the Sheffield Historic District of Lincoln Park. Take a walk in any direction and you'll happen upon great restaurants, bars, and coffee shops. You'll also see some stunning Chicago mansions. Suites come with a full kitchen, bath, and sitting area. No pets. $$–$$$.

⟨ᵧ⟩ **Gold Coast Guest House Bed & Breakfast** (312-337-0361; www.bbchicago.com), 113 W. Elm Street. Just a short walk from Michigan Avenue shopping and Lake Michigan, this bed and breakfast will put you right in the heart of the Gold Coast. There are no signs on this 3-story house, so look for the red front door. The house has four rooms with private baths, flat-screen TVs, and DVD players. The rooms have a modern yet comfortable décor, accented with vintage Chicago travel posters. A beautiful two-level lush garden and sitting area in back provides a peaceful escape to relax after a day of sightseeing. Tight spiral stairs will take you to the upper levels, where the dining room table overlooks the garden.

Breakfast is served each morning, with beverages and snacks available throughout the day in the open kitchen. There's a computer for guests to use in the common area, and free use of beach chairs and umbrellas for venturing out to Oak Street Beach or into the city on a rainy day. Children 10 and older are welcome. $$.

⟨ᵧ⟩ **Wicker Park Inn** (773-645-9827; www.wickerparkinn.com),

GOLD COAST GUEST HOUSE INN

1329 N. Wicker Park Avenue. Stay on a lovely residential street in the artsy Wicker Park neighborhood on the city's North Side. The owners have the main inn and apartments in a building across the street, all nicely decorated. Rooms come with private bath, satellite TV, and free parking. The apartment rooms have access to a full kitchen, so breakfast is not provided. Note that a three-night stay is required on weekends during the peak season. $$–$$$.

HOTELS, NORTH ♿ 🛜 **Belden-Stratford Hotel** (800-800-8301; www.beldenstratfordhotel.com), 2300 Lincoln Park West. This is an excellent location just across from Lincoln Park Zoo, within walking distance to the lake and great restaurants. Rooms have 9-foot ceilings, Queen Anne–style furniture, and come with a microwave, range, refrigerator, dishwasher, Jacuzzi bathtub, and TV. The studio rooms are also nicely sized, with good options for families. You can head up to the rooftop sundeck for great views. The historic hotel also has a fitness center, valet parking, a spa, and two restaurants on site—L20 and Mon Ami Gabi. $$–$$$.

🛜 **The Willows Hotel** (800-787-3108; www.willowshotelchicago .com), 555 W. Surf Street. This historic landmark building, just a couple blocks from the lake in the Lakeview neighborhood, is an option for those who want quarters on the North Side. The 55 rooms are French Country and come with cable TVs, hair dryers, irons, and extras like free afternoon cookies. You have access to a Bally's fitness center with your stay. $$–$$$$.

HOTELS, SOUTH 🛜 **Wheeler Mansion** (312-945-2020; www .wheelermansion.com), 2020 S. Calumet Avenue. Located in the Prairie District in the South Loop, this small hotel has 11 guest rooms, all decorated differently but handsomely with a few antiques, and modern baths. Close to the Museum Campus, the Wheeler Mansion was built in 1870 as part of the wealthy Prairie Avenue District where all the city's business leaders flocked. The building survived the Great Chicago Fire the next year. Built for Calvin Wheeler, president of the Chicago Board of Trade, the property later ended up being used by

BELDEN-STRATFORD HOTEL

a publishing company and as a distribution warehouse. It was renovated and restored in 1999 as a hotel. Rooms have private baths and cable TVs. Free parking included. $$$.

((ŋ)) & ♥ **The Wyndham Blake Chicago** (312-986-1234; www.hotelblake.com), 500 S. Dearborn Street. This South Loop hotel has 165 rooms with king or two queen beds, alarm clock/iPod stereo systems, and hair dryers. Some rooms come with floor-to-ceiling windows looking out onto downtown. The hotel is attached to the Custom House Tavern. $$–$$$$.

✳ Where to Eat

EATING OUT

UIC/Greektown/Little Italy
Jim's Original (312-733-7820; www.jimsoriginal.com), 1250 S. Union Avenue. Located near the University of Illinois at Chicago campus, and having the distinction of being open 24 hours a day, this hot dog stand comes with a little history, as it started at the famous Maxwell Street Market. In the 1940s, "Jim" or "Jimmy," a new immigrant from Yugoslavia, bought his aunt's hot dog stand and started selling Polish sausage sandwiches with sweet caramelized grilled onions and mustard. The restaurant has been moved from the original location, but still serves up those Polish sausage sandwiches. Sandwiches come with free fries. Menu also includes a Vienna Beef hot dog, hamburgers, and pork chop sandwiches. $.

Manny's Cafeteria and Delicatessen (312-939-2855; www.mannysdeli.com), 1141 S. Jefferson Avenue. Open 5 AM–8 PM Monday through Saturday. Family-run cafeteria-style joint that is a Chicago institution, often frequented by politicians. The menu of lunch dishes rotates throughout the week, so you may have a choice of stuffed cabbage and roasted tongue one day, Salisbury steak and spaghetti another. Sides include potato pancakes, knish, or herring with bread. A whole list of sandwiches round out the menu. For dinner, there's skirt steak, turkey meatloaf, and several other comfort food cafeteria servings. $–$$.

& ♛ **Pompei** (312-421-5179; www.pompeipizza.com), 1531 W. Taylor Street. Open 10–10 Monday through Saturday, 10–9 Sunday. There are also locations throughout the city, luckily. Pompei has been a favorite discovery of many Chicagoans and tourists since it was founded in 1909. Since then the popular casual Italian spot has expanded into several neighborhoods and the 'burbs. The cafeteria-style setting is a great, economical choice when you're on the go but still want to experience great Chicago food. Specialties include the pizza strudel, a rectangular slice of stuffed pizza that can be filled with everything from turkey to steak fajitas. You can also get a classic slice of thin or stuffed pizza. If you go for the stuffed, there is no tomato sauce, so be sure to ask for a side of their wonderfully rich marinara for dipping. If you're looking for something lighter, Pompei's bright, fresh salads are large enough to serve as a full meal. Handmade pasta dishes are created fresh daily. Don't forget to save room for a lemon knot or cannoli. $.

Chinatown

♿ **Phoenix** (312-328-0848; www .chinatownphoenix.com), 2131 S. Archer Avenue. Dim sum daily 9–3 weekdays, 8–3 weekends. Dinner: 5–9:30 Sunday through Thursday, 5–10:30 weekends. Chinese food as you would experience in Hong Kong or Shanghai, as that's where the chefs trained. Phoenix has a giant menu of 50 kinds of dim sum—Chinese small plates that are steamed, baked, or fried. Dumplings, filled buns, noodles and other bite-size dishes are pushed through on a cart and you flag the waiter when you see something you like. The dinner menu is expansive. $–$$.

♿ **Joy Yee Noodles** (312-328-0001; http://joyyee.com), 2139 S. China Place in Chinatown Square Mall. Open 11–10:30 daily. Besides the Chinatown Square Mall location, Joy Yee also has restaurants in Evanston, Naperville, and near UIC. True to the name, Joy Yee has a long list of noodle soups, chow mein, and other noodle dishes. The menu blends Asian cooking styles that

CHINATOWN

please the diners that crowd into the small dining room and onto the outdoor patio. Also serves bubble teas and fruit freezes. $–$$.

Hyde Park

(((•))) & **Medici on 57th** (773-667-7394; www.medici57.com), 1327 E. 57th Street. Open 9 AM–11 PM Monday through Thursday, and Sunday, 9 AM–midnight Friday and Saturday. Bakery opens at 7 am. Popular Hyde Park restaurant, with a lengthy menu, outdoor patio, and floors of dining space. The Medici is known for its Chicago-style pizza but the menu also covers Moroccan ragout, burgers, salads, and other dishes. There's also a bakery with breads, pastries, and cookies. BYOB. $$.

& **Zaleski & Horvath Market-Café** (773-538-7372; www.zh marketcafe.com), 1126 E. 47th Street and 1323 E. 57th Street. Open 7–7 weekdays, 8–6 weekends. If you're in Hyde Park or Kenwood, this is a nice café with a focus on local and regional produce that has offerings of sandwiches and interesting homemade soups, like chicken cilantro lime or rustic garlic. While you're there, you can shop in the market for ingredients for dinner. $.

Old Town/Lincoln Park

& **Pequod's** (773-327-1512; www.pequodspizza.com), 2207 N. Clybourn Avenue. Open 11 AM–2 AM Monday through Saturday, 11 AM–midnight Sunday. Pequod's serves just all-over awesome pizza. When I found out we moved out of the delivery area, I reconsidered the move for a moment. We now drive quite a ways to pick up the pizza. The dining room is not all that, kind of dark, with expensive beers, but you'll find a great Chicago thin-crust pizza and a thick-crust pan pizza with signature caramelized crust. $–$$.

Old Jerusalem Restaurant (312-944-0459; www.oldjerusalem restaurant.com), 1411 N. Wells Street. Open 11–11 daily. Inexpensive but tasty Middle Eastern dishes in Old Town. The restaurant has an especially good sandwich menu, with shawarma, kefta kabob, and shish kabob. For entrees you can opt for grilled meats or spiced meat patties with grilled vegetables, rice pilaf, salad, and Lebanese bread. If the weather's nice, you can sit outside on the sidewalk patio. $–$$.

& **Bacino's** (773-472-7400; www.bacinos.com), 2204 N. Lincoln Avenue. Open 11–9 Monday, 11–10 Tuesday through Thursday Sunday, 11–11 Friday and Saturday. Also a West Loop location (312-876-1188) at 118 S. Clinton Street, open 11–3 weekdays. Starting out on Lincoln Avenue, founder Dan Bacin wanted to find a way to win in the competitive Chicago pizza market. He decided to use fresh everything and make pizza sauce from scratch. When discussing Chicago-style pizza, the term heart-healthy rarely comes up, but Bacino's boasts a heart-healthy stuffed spinach pizza, which is a big player at the Taste of Chicago. The menu also includes poached pear and gorgonzola salads, and extra thin and extra crispy pizzas with traditional ingredients from Italy, like prosciutto di parma, arugula, fresh mozzarella, and olive oil. $–$$.

Orange (773-549-7833; www .orangerestaurantchicago.com), 2413 N. Clark Street. There are also locations in Roscoe Village, River North, and River West. Open 8–3 daily. Orange has a brunch with pancake flights and frushi (fruit sushi). The pancake dishes include cinnamon roll pancakes, jelly doughnut, and "boring cakes" that are just regular old buttermilk cakes. You'll also find

omelets and free-range egg dishes, like Green Eggs and Ham that come scrambled with basil pesto, ham, roasted tomatoes, and mozzarella. A kids' menu and lunch offerings of grilled cheese and veggie sandwiches are also available. And of course, like the name suggests, you can get freshly squeezed orange juice and other fruit juice combinations as well. $–$$.

♿ **Goose Island Brewpub** (312-915-0071; www.gooseisland.com), 1800 N. Clybourn Avenue. Open 11–midnight daily, bar menu after 10 PM. Goose Island started producing its craft beers in 1988, and now has a second location for microbrews on Clark Street. The brewpubs have drafts on tap that

ORANGE IN LINCOLN PARK

you can't find at the store, with over 20 beers available every day, and offerings that change throughout year. The pub has a menu of steaks, seafood, and the popular Stilton burger. On Sundays you can do a tour of the brewery, and have a tasting. $$.

Lakeview
&. **Penny's Noodles** (773-281-8448; www.pennysnoodleshop.com), 950 W. Diversey Street. Open 11–10 Sunday through Thursday, 11–10:30 Friday and Saturday. A combination of Vietnamese, Japanese, and Thai, this is an inexpensive, great fresh option, with locations in Wicker Park (1542 N. Damen Avenue) and Wrigleyville (3400 N. Sheffield Avenue) as well. Try the Gyoza, Vietnamese Spring Rolls, hot soups, and my personal favorite dish, Sliced Chicken, which features thin rice vermicelli noodles with an awesome sweet soy sauce piled with bean sprouts, green onion, cilantro, peanuts, and chicken. The menu also features dishes like pad Thai, Lad Nar, curry, and pepper beef. $.

Wicker Park/Bucktown
&. **Irazu** (773-252-5687; www.irazuchicago.com), 1865 N. Milwaukee Avenue. Open 11:30–9:30 Monday through Saturday. Costa Rican. This is another restaurant that I took for granted, until I left Chicago for a few years and searched for a replacement that could make a similar sandwich in my new state. These kinds of

sandwiches are not found just anywhere. The one I sought out had French bread, black beans, cheese, lettuce, tomato, avocado, and the special Lizano sauce. The rest of the menu is great too, with appetizers that include ceviche, black bean dip, and fried green plantains. Sample an authentic Costa Rican dinner of thin meat with veggies, rice, black beans, plantains, an over-easy egg, and cabbage salad. Vegetarians will be pleased with a lengthy list of veggie-centered dishes. Irazu is named after a volcano in Costa Rica, from where the owner's family originates. No reservations and cash only. $–$$.

City Northwest
Hot Doug's (773-279-9550; www.hotdougs.com), 3324 N. California Avenue. Open 10:30–4 Monday through Saturday. A bit west of Roscoe Village, you'll find Hot Doug's, which has the traditional Chicago-style dog, but goes beyond with boar sausage, other specialty sausages, and foie gras. For a little something extra special, try the duck fat fries served on Friday and Saturday only. There's the Elvis, which is a Polish sausage, "smoked and savory just like the king." Then there are the truly "hot" dogs, named after the hot actress of the day. The name changes, but the dog is always hot. Cash only. $.

Smoque (773-545-7427; www.smoquebbq.com), 3800 N. Pulaski. Open 11–9 Tuesday through Thursday, Sunday, 11–10 Friday and Saturday. A group of five friends who love good barbecue opened Smoque, and it seems like every other person I meet in Chicago is calling this one of their favorite barbecue places. They combine hardwood smoke, spicy rubs, and sweet sauces, serving up brisket, pulled pork, chicken, and ribs. And these guys have really thought about how they want to prepare these dishes, as proven through their four-page manifesto about barbecue. The restaurant is usually pretty busy, as it's a local favorite for takeout. BYOB. $–$$.

Far North-Andersonville/Uptown/West Rogers Park
♧ **Thai Pastry** (773-784-5399; www.thaipastry.com), 4925 N. Broadway Avenue. Open 11–10 Sunday through Thursday, 11–11 Friday and Saturday. Hands down, this is my favorite casual Thai restaurant in Chicago. You can dine BYOB at the unassuming storefront on Broadway in Uptown, which is a decent space to eat, although I must admit I am under the spell of the food when I visit. Start with the spring rolls and baby egg rolls, which my husband will travel miles and miles in city traffic to pick up. The popular basic noodle dishes like Pad Thai and Pad See-ew are really well done here, as are rice and curries. The specialty entrees include a number of fish and seafood dishes like eel. $–$$.

♧ ♿ **Hopleaf** (773-334-9851; http://hopleaf.com), 5148 N. Clark Street. Kitchen open 5–11 Monday through Thursday, 5–midnight Friday and Saturday, 4–10 Sunday. The bar has longer hours. This Andersonville institution has the most comprehensive selection of Belgian beers on tap. It's also usually packed, and a place for a pretty good dinner too. We're not just talking regular burgers and pub fare. How about the tilapia sandwich with lemon pickles, or the CB&J—house-made cashew butter, fig jam, and cheese? The menu also includes seafood, steaks, and salads. No children allowed because it's a bar. $$–$$$.

♧ **M Henry** (773-561-1600; www.mhenry.net), 5707 N. Clark Street. Open 7–2:30 Tuesday through Friday, 8–3 weekends. For brunch, this is the place. Located in Andersonville, with a focus on locally produced and organic ingredients, M Henry entices with brioche French toast, drunken eggs, and pancakes smothered with fresh fruit. It's BYOB and there are no reservations, so be prepared for a wait. $–$$.

♧ **Indian Garden** (773-338-2929; www.indiangardendevon.com), 2546 W. Devon Street. Open 11:30–3, 5–9:30 Monday through Thursday, 11:30–3, 5–10:30 Friday and Saturday. This traditional Indian restaurant on Devon churns out wonderful dishes that have been prepared in their clay oven. Try the samosa, wonderful naan, and soups. $–$$$.

South Shore/Hyde Park

&. **The Parrot Cage** (773-602-5333; http://kennedyking.ccc.edu/washburne/parrot_cage), 7059 S. Shore Drive. Open 5–9 Wednesday through Saturday, 11–3 Sunday. The Washburne Culinary Institute runs this upscale restaurant located in the fantastic South Shore Cultural Center, with lake views and a menu of steak with wine reductions, seared salmon, lamb shank, and chicken and shrimp etouffee. The name of the restaurant is derived from the local Monk Parakeets, a type of wild parrot found in Hyde Park and South Shore neighborhoods. You can bring your own wine, but there is a corkage fee. Brunch is also served on Sundays. $$–$$$.

&. **Le Petite Folie** (773-493-1394; http://lapetitefolie.com), 1504 E. 55th Street. Open for lunch 11:30–2 Tuesday through Friday, dinner begins at 5 Tuesday through Sunday. This upscale Hyde Park restaurant tucked away in a shopping center focuses on classical French food, and has built an extensive French wine list to accompany it. $$$$.

Greektown/Little Italy

&. **RoSal's Italian Cucina** (312-243-2357; www.rosals.com), 1154 W. Taylor Street. Open 4–9 Monday through Thursday, 4–11 Friday and Saturday. This is Sicilian food as dreamed up by Roseanne and Salvatore (whose names combine to form RoSal's), whom you will see pictured on the walls. They have created a comprehensive menu out of their family cookbook, offering pastas, veal dishes, seafood, chicken, and beef. $$–$$$.

Pegasus Restaurant and Taverna (312-226-3377; www.pegasus chicago.com), 130 S. Halsted Street. Open during the summer 11–11 Monday through Thursday, 11 AM–midnight Friday, noon–midnight Saturday, noon–11 Sunday. The rooftop deck beckons during the summer, as do the methzethes, (Greek-style tapas). Of course, you can dive into a whole host of full entrees, with a menu of Greek specialties like spanakopita and pastitsio. The combination platters give you a tour of Greek cuisine. $$.

&. **Athena Greek Restaurant** (312-655-0000; www.athenares taurantchicago.com), 212 S. Halsted Street. Open 11–midnight daily. A favorite for its outdoor patio, the water flowing in the fountain and Greek columns add to the feel that you've traveled across the globe. The kitchen does a good job here with traditional Greek items like the lamb dishes, keftedes (Greek spiced meatballs), tirokafteri (spicy feta cheese spread), and shrimp opaa (shrimp, tomatoes, onions, green and red pepper, and feta cheese flamed in brandy). $$.

Pilsen

&. **Nightwood** (312-526-3385; http://nightwoodrestaurant.com),

2119 S. Halsted Street. Open 5:30–11 Monday through Saturday, 9–2:30 Sunday. This Pilsen restaurant opened by the same folks behind Lula in Logan Square focuses on local, sustainable, artisanal products. Their focus on handmade items and simplicity can be seen throughout, in the room and in menus written by hand according to what the farmers and markets are offering that day. A sample menu may feature pasta with roasted chicken thigh, goat cheese, and broccoli puree. Entrees may also include roasted duck leg with sweet corn, black beans, and cilantro. Brunch is served on Sundays, and there's a nice outdoor dining space. $$–$$$.

Mundial Cocina Mestiza (312-491-9908; www.mundialcocina mestiza.com), 1640 W. 18th Street. Open for lunch 11–3 Tuesday through Sunday, dinner : 4:30–10:30. Upscale Mexican served in a modest dining room with muted blue Mexican tiles, golden brown walls, and plenty of art. But expect the dishes to include influences from around the world. $$–$$$.

Nuevo Leon Restaurant (312-421-1517; http://nuevoleonrestaurant.com), 1515 W. 18th Street. Open 7 AM–11 PM daily. For big portions and good Mexican at a decent price, try this family-owned restaurant. The Gutierrez family has expanded from the small taco stand they bought in 1962, creating the lively destination here today, with brightly painted murals on the wall and food that pleases the crowds who pack in. $$.

Chinatown
Lao Sze Chuan (312-326-5040), 2172 S. Archer Avenue. In Chinatown Square Mall on the south end. Open 10:30–midnight daily. This is a favorite of Chicagoans seeking out an authentic Chinese meal. Chef Tony Hu does not shy away from the spice either, and travels to China annually to freshen his menu with new ideas and spices from the Szechuan province. $–$$.

West Loop
&. **Avec** (312-377-2002; www.avecrestaurant.com), 615 W. Randolph Street. Open 3:30–midnight Sunday through Thursday, 3:30–1 AM Friday and Saturday. Bar is open later. If you're feeling very social, head to the Mediterranean-inspired Avec and its communal dining tables. Get to know your neighbors and share a special focaccia or a plate of roasted artichoke crostini with caramelized onion. The focus here is on the food and the company. Simple elegance is their goal and you'll see that carried out, from the beautiful long wooden dining table to the plates, which showcase the fresh ingredients used in each dish. A must try is the chorizo-stuffed dates with smoked bacon and piquillo pepper-tomato sauce. Other favorites include octopus

and wood-roasted chicken thigh. $$–$$$.

Old Town/Lincoln Park

& **Twin Anchors** (312-266-1616; www.twinanchorsribs.com), 1655 N. Sedgwick Street. Open 5–11 Monday through Thursday, 5–midnight Friday, noon–midnight Saturday, noon–10:30 Sunday. Established in 1932, Frank Sinatra visited this rib restaurant many a time and even had the ribs shipped to him on the road. A large portion of the film *Return to Me* was shot here. As for the food that lured them in, there's the slow-cooked, baby back ribs served with a choice of sauce, or steaks, slow-roasted chicken, and a fish fry. $$$.

& **Charlie Trotter's** (773-248-6228; www.charlietrotters.com), 816 W. Armitage Avenue. Open for dinner Tuesday through Saturday, reservations required. This Lincoln Park institution has three daily tasting menus—the grand menu, vegetable menu, and kitchen table menu that change daily. The inspired creations of the famed Mr. Trotter may include sashimi or honey-glazed duck with spring garlic, lavender, and thyme. If you opt for the kitchen table menu, you can watch the chef go to work on the fresh ingredients and see why the honors have piled up for him. $$$$.

& **Alinea** (312-867-0110; www.alinea-restaurant.com), 1723 N. Halsted Street. Open 5:30–9:30 Wednesday through Friday, 5–9:30 weekends. Owner, Grant Achatz, has quite the resume: He worked at the French Laundry in Napa Valley, under top-notch chefs, and as the executive chef at Trio, where he was named one of the best new chefs in the country. With the opening of Alinea, the accolades have continued. The food here is not like you are used to it being served, as a piece of art, a thought-provoking, imaginative plate. Achatz is considered a leader in progressive American cooking and the restaurant is considered by some the best in Chica-

CHARLIE TROTTER'S

go and in the country. Plan to spend hours and serious money here if you secure a reservation. $$$$.

Lakeview

& **El Tapatio Café** (773-598-5578), 3400 N. Ashland Avenue. Open 10–10 Monday through Thursday, 9 AM–midnight Friday, 10 AM–11 PM weekends. This Lakeview Mexican restaurant has been family owned for more than 30 years. If it's summer, arrive early to score a patio spot, with the lights twinkling above you. The salsa is hot. The entrees are awesome, especially the tacos al pastor. And oh my, the margaritas. (Read: Strong!) The interior dining room is bright and cozy. In my experience, the staff has been very attentive, even bringing out non-spicy versions of their salsa for toddler mouths that can't quite handle the heat. $$.

Hearty Restaurant (773-868-9866; www.heartyboys.com), 3819 N. Broadway Avenue. Open 5–10 Wednesday through Thursday, 5–11 Friday and Saturday, 5–9 Sunday, 9 AM–2 PM Sunday for brunch. The Hearty Boys, Dan Smith and Steve McDonagh, like to freshen up the old standbys at this Lakeview restaurant. The menu changes throughout the year according to the season. You may start with a corn dog, only this one is made of rabbit sausage, wrapped in honey-mustard corn batter, and served with spicy apple slaw. The Southern Fried Chicken

is made with a cornflake crust and served with creamy Dijon potato salad. Tuna Noodle Casserole is made with panko-crusted ahi and saffron cream egg noodles. You can also order sandwiches and salads if you're not up for a full entree. I seriously would save room for the frozen hot chocolate, though. You may recognize the Hearty Boys from the Food Network. The two beat out thousands for a shot at their own cooking show, and have their own cookbook as well. Keeping with their philosophy to serve food that you could re-create at home, the wine list is accessible, as is the beer list, with many local craft beers and Schlitz as well. You'll also find some creative cocktails. $$–$$$.

Lincoln Square/Albany Park

& **Pizza D.O.C.** (773-784-8777; www.mypizzadoc.com), 2251 W. Lawrence Avenue. Open 5–10 Tuesday through Thursday, noon–11 Friday and Saturday, 11:30–10 Sunday. For authentic pizza as it is served in Italy, this is the place. Start with rice balls stuffed with fresh mozzarella and deep-fried. Or maybe bruschetta, and antipasto misto. Pizzas are extremely thin crust, in the traditional Italian way, with simple fresh combinations of ingredients, like prosciutto, mozzarella, mushrooms, and tomato sauce. They are then cooked in a brick oven. The menu also covers the straightforward pasta dishes like Bolognese. The room is busy, with lots of conversation bouncing off the exposed brick walls, and kept warm by the brick ovens. $$–$$$.

✆ & **Café Selmarie** (773-989-5595; www.cafeselmarie.com), 4729 N. Lincoln Avenue. Open 11–3 Monday, 8 AM–9 PM Tuesday through Thursday, 8 AM–10 PM Friday and Saturday, 9 AM–8 PM Sunday. Located on the square in Lincoln Square. A small bakery with glass cases of beautiful pastries, cakes, and cookies greets you before you walk into the larger dining room. In the summer, the dining space doubles with the opening of the lovely outdoor

CAFÉ SELMARIE IN LINCOLN SQUARE

patio in the plaza. For breakfast, the quiche of the day is usually a good bet, as is the breakfast burrito. For lunch, the croque monsieur, smoked turkey and brie sandwich, or chopped salad are great. For dinner, you'll find a few comfort foods—chicken pot pie and macaroni and cheese—as well as salmon and steak. A nice wine and craft beer list caps off the experience. A good place for families. $–$$.

Noon O Kabab (773-279-9309; http://noonokabab.com), 4661 N. Kedzie Avenue. Open 11–10 Monday through Thursday, 11–11 Friday and Saturday, 11–9 Sunday. North of the Kedzie Brown Line stop. For excellent, filling, and healthy Persian food, try this Albany Park restaurant. The family opened the restaurant in 1997 and has continued to expand as people responded to their authentic dishes. If you dine in, notice the elaborate Persian tiles on the wall. My favorite dish is the Adass Polo with Koubideh, a blend of lentils, raisins, caramelized onions, saffron, and Persian barberry with rice that is slightly sweet to complement the Persian-spiced ground beef. Of course, you also must sample the fantastic appetizers, which include hummus, dolmeh, and baba ghannouj. $$.

& **Semiramis** (773-279-8900; www.semiramisrestaurant.com), 4639-41 N. Kedzie Avenue. Open 11–10 Monday through Thursday, 11–11 Friday and Saturday. This is a great BYOB restaurant in Albany

Park that focuses on Lebanese cuisine and puts out phenomenal falafel. The sandwiches are generous portions of fresh produce and grilled meats. One interesting menu feature: French fries with sumac and a garlic mousse. We like to get the vegetarian plate as an appetizer so we can sample all the wonderful dips and falafel. $$.

& **Jaafer Sweets** (773-463-3933; www.jaafer.com), 4825 N. Kedzie Avenue. Open 10 AM–11 PM daily. After your meal at Noon O Kabab or Semiramis, consider stopping into Jaafer Sweets for Middle Eastern desserts.

Arun's (773-539-1909; www.arunsthai.com), 4156 N. Kedzie Avenue. Seatings between 5–8 Tuesday through Sunday. Reservations preferred, so call well in advance. For an upscale Thai experience, Arun's is the place. Chef Arun Sampanthavivat designs a 12-course prix fixe tasting menu keeping in mind your preferences and how adventurous you are as a diner. So if you like spice or don't, the dishes can be calibrated just for you. The entrees are served family style. But it is not inexpensive, at $85 per person, so it's definitely a special night out. $$$$.

Ukrainian Village/Bucktown

& **West Town Tavern** (312-666-6175; www.westtowntavern.com), 1329 W. Chicago Avenue. 5–10 Monday through Saturday. The exposed brick walls, cozy lighting,

and oak bar create an inviting atmosphere for settling in with a glass of wine and some comfort food. Start out with tavern potato chips or antipasto before moving onto a zinfandel-braised pot roast with garlic mashed potatoes and a Pennsylvania Dutch black vinegar sauce that will instantly warm your spirits. Entrees like pasta, fish, pork, and duck fill out the menu. $$–$$$.

& **Takashi** (773-772-6170; www.takashichicago.com), 1952 N. Damen Avenue. Open 5:30–10 Tuesday through Friday, 5:30–10:30 Saturday, 5–10:30 Sunday. Brunch is served 11:30–3 Sunday. The food here is French American with a Japanese influence. Owner and chef, Takashi Yagihashi, has blended the feel of fine dining with that of a neighborhood tavern to create a welcoming Bucktown space. The seafood here is sustainable and the dishes excellent, especially the soba gnocchi with scallops. $$$.

& **Green Zebra** (312-243-7100; www.greenzebrachicago.com), 1460 W. Chicago Avenue. Open 5:30–10 Monday through Thursday, 5–11 Friday and Saturday, 10:30–2 for brunch and 5–9 for dinner Sunday. This high-end, inventive vegetarian restaurant by star chef Shawn McClain presents small plates of food that show how inspired this type of cuisine can be. A tasting menu is also available. $$$$.

Logan Square

& **Lula** (773-489-9554; www.lula cafe.com), 2537 N. Kedzie Boulevard. Open 9 AM–10 PM Monday, Wednesday through Friday, 9 AM–11 PM Saturday and Sunday. Vegetarians will love this place, but there's plenty of meat on the menu to please all kinds of diners. The mission is to use seasonal, organic, locally grown produce, wild-caught fish, and naturally raised meats and poultry. That translates into dishes like homemade orrecchiette with a ragu of farm veal, heirloom tomatoes, capers, and artichokes. You can also get breakfast, lunch, and brunch. $$–$$$.

Y **Longman & Eagle** (773-276-7110; www.longmanandeagle.com), 2657 N. Kedzie Avenue. Open 11 AM–2 AM weekdays, Sunday, 10 AM–3 AM Saturday. Brunch served until 3 PM, dinner menu available after 5. No reservations accepted. This newcomer to the scene has generated quite a bit of buzz, but the changing creations of Chef Jared Wentworth deliver. $$-$$$.

✳ Entertainment

LIVE MUSIC Y **Lee's Unleaded Blues Club** (773-493-3477; www.leesunleadedblues.com), 7401 S. Chicago Avenue. The music starts at 9 or 10 Friday through Sunday. Doors open at 8. For blues, head to this unassuming South Side music club where the focus is on the music. Cover: $5.

Y **Reggie's** (312-949-0121; www.reggieslive.com), 2105-2109 S. State Street. Open 11 AM–2 AM Sunday through Friday, 11 AM–3 AM Saturday. Reggie's has the rock club, which books 17-and-over shows, and the Music Joint, which is a 21-and-over bar and grill with a calendar of live music.

Y **Metro** (773-549-0203; www.metrochicago.com), 3730 N. Clark Street. A medium-sized concert venue, the Metro is north of Wrigley Field on Clark Street, with a calendar of punk, ska, indie rock, heavy metal, and whatever else strikes their fancy. Downstairs, Smart Bar has DJs and dancing. Save service fees by buying tickets in person at the Metro store box office.

Y **Schubas** (773-525-2508; www.schubas.com), 3159 N. Southport Avenue. Bar opens at 11:30 AM, show times vary. Schubas is the place to see the best in alt-country and indie rock. Located in the Lakeview neighborhood, the place also has a pretty good restaurant attached in the Harmony Grill, which also has an outdoor patio.

& Y **Lincoln Hall** (773-525-2501; www.lincolnhallchicago.com), 2424 N. Lincoln Avenue. Bar opens 5 PM weekdays, noon weekends. One of the newer venues on the Chicago music scene, Lincoln Hall is housed in the old 3 Penny Cinema building and features a roster of excellent acts throughout the year. Note that all tickets are will-call, you won't have an actual ticket, your name will be at the ticket booth.

☿ **The Hideout** (773-227-4433; www.hideoutchicago.com), 1354 W. Wabansia Street. You will think that you got the address wrong when you head down a drive in an industrial district to the Hideout. But there is indeed a great bar tucked away there. In the back, you'll find a music space that regularly welcomes skilled performers. The bar puts on the fantastic Hideout Block Party every year, assembling a lineup of impressive acts, from alt-country to indie rock.

☿ **Kingston Mines** (773-477-4646; www.kingstonmines.com), 2548 N. Halsted Street. Doors open at 7, although the time varies. Music begins at 9:30 usually and runs until 4 AM Sunday through Friday, 5 AM Saturday. Located in Lincoln Park, this is a good place to hear great blues. Established in 1968, its location exposed a whole new audience, including tourists, to Chicago blues.

♿ ☿ **Empty Bottle** (773-276-3600; www.emptybottle.com), 1035 N. Western Avenue. Open 5 PM–2 AM Monday through Wednesday, 3 PM–2 Thursday through Friday, noon–3 AM Saturday, noon–2 AM Sunday. Indie rock venue that also books experimental and jazz. Usually, everyone who is cool plays here first long before they are discovered by the masses.

☿ **Green Mill** (773-878-5552; www.greenmilljazz.com), 4802 N. Broadway Avenue. Open noon–4 AM Sunday through Friday, noon–5 AM Saturday. Cover charge ranges from nothing to $8. If you're looking for an early evening cocktail or just catching your second wind late at night, the Green Mill is most definitely worth a stop. All kinds of jazz are played here, and all kinds of people are drawn here—from suited businesspeople to young hipsters. With the art deco décor and attitude inside, you'll feel like you've stepped back in time into the 1940s. Opened in 1907, the club has since hosted many jazz greats and built quite a history. Check out the famous booth where Al Capone's henchmen would keep an eye on the door.

♿ **Old Town School of Folk Music** (773-728-6000; www.old townschool.org), 4544 N. Lincoln Avenue. This space has an intimate feel, which is great for the lineup of artists who perform here each year, usually the type who don't need any extras, just a guitar and their voice. The school also has festivals and other free concerts at Millennium Park through the summer.

MOVIES Brew and View at the Vic (www.brewview.com), 3145 N. Sheffield Avenue. The Vic is a music venue that hosts big name acts. When there isn't a show booked, they pull out tables and chairs onto the floor and serve up beer. The movies are usually second-run double features and best when seen while drinking.

Music Box Theatre (773-871-6604; www.musicboxtheatre.com), 3733 N. Southport Avenue. Art house cinema with the movies you'll never find in the blockbuster theaters. Sometimes, a performer plays the old organ before the show starts. The Music Box also books a number of fun events, like *Grease* sing-a-longs, the *Rocky Horror Picture Show*, and film festivals.

BARS/NIGHTCLUBS Chicago's nightlife scene spans from great, casual dive bars to exclusive dance clubs with lines wrapped around the block.

Y **Old Town Ale House** (www.oldtownalehouse.net), 219 W. North Avenue. Open noon–4 AM Sunday through Friday, 11 AM–5 AM Saturday. This Old Town institution is an authentic-feeling place with a jazz juke box and all kinds of beer. The bar has drawn attention for some of the nude paintings of politicians on the walls.

Y **Map Room** (773-252-7636; www.maproom.com), 1949 W. Hoyne Avenue. Open 6:30 AM–2 AM Monday through Friday, 7:30 AM–3 AM Saturday, 11 AM–2 AM Sunday. Bar opens at 11 AM. Intelligentsia coffee and pastries are served in the morning, sandwiches later in the day. This Bucktown bar has a great beer selection, and a welcoming space.

Y **The Pump Room** (312-787-7200; www.pumproom.com), 1301 N. State Parkway, in the Gold Coast neighborhood. Lounge is open 5–11 Sunday through Thursday, 11 AM–1 AM Friday and Saturday. Bar menu served from 5–10. This is where all the legends hung out. To experience a piece of Chicago bar history, visit the elegant, old school Pump Room lounge in the Ambassador East Hotel.

Y **The Tasting Room** (312-942-1313; www.thetastingroomchicago.com), 1415 W. Randolph Street. Open 5–1 weekdays, 5–2 Saturday. This West Loop lounge and restaurant aims for an attitude-free wine-drinking experience. They have hundreds of wines by the glass, and also offer flights.

Y **Enclave** (312-654-0234; www.enclavechicago.com) 220 W. Chicago Avenue on the Near North Side. Open 9–2 Friday, 9–3 Saturday. To dance with pretty people and possibly mix with celebrities, you may want to try Enclave, which also has DJs and table service.

SPORTS & ∅ **U.S. Cellular Field** (866-769-4263; http://chicago.whitesox.mlb.com), 333 W. 35th Street, on the city's South Side. The Red Line will drop you off right near the stadium at 35th Street. Home of the Chicago White Sox. If you're a Chicago native, this will always be Comiskey Park, even though that was torn down years ago and replaced with this modern and fan-friendly stadium in Bridgeport complete with an exploding scoreboard. It's a great place to take kids to see a game as it also has batting cages, base running, and practice pitching areas. Tickets range in price from $10 for upper reserved to $68 or more for prime seats, depending on the game.

&. ✎ **Wrigley Field** (800-843-2827; http://chicago.cubs.mlb.com), 1060 W. Addison Street. Red Line will drop you off just south of the stadium at Addison, on the city's North Side. Built in 1914, this historic stadium started hosting the Cubs in 1916. It was named Wrigley Field in 1926 after the team's owner at the time. It's a great place to see a game (although it can be freezing in the upper decks on a seemingly warm day.) Games often sell out on weekends and nice days, but you can take your chances with scalpers. For a closer look at this historic park, tour the famed "Friendly Confines," through a 90-minute guided visit that will take you to the clubhouse, press box, bleachers, dugouts, and maybe even the on-deck circles, depending on whether there's a game or not. The tours are given on scheduled dates from May through early October. Tour Tickets: $25. As for games, the tickets range from $8 for upper deck seats on the coldest, least-popular game days to $315 for the box behind the dugouts.

&. **United Center** (312-455-4500; www.unitedcenter.com), 1901 W. Madison Street. This West Side arena hosts the Chicago Blackhawks for hockey season and the Chicago Bulls for basketball. (A bronze statue of Michael Jordan greets guests in front of the center.) In addition to sports, it welcomes big-time concerts and shows.

WRIGLEY FIELD

THEATER ⅇ **Chicago Dramatists** (312-633-0630; www.chicago dramatists.org), 1105 W. Chicago Avenue. This group known as the "playwrights' theater" has gained national attention recently, after its production of *A Steady Rain*, by resident playwright Keith Huff, went on to Broadway. The theater group is focused on discovering and developing new plays and has a stable of resident playwrights with whom it works. Tickets: $20–32.

ⅇ **Redmoon Theater** (312-850-8440, x111; http://redmoon.org), 1463 W. Hubbard Street. Since 1990, this theater group has launched site-specific productions throughout the city showing what pageantry is all about. Their performances sometimes involve puppetry, sometimes acrobatics, as they strive to push your imagination. Redmoon has performed at the White House for the Obamas as well.

ⅇ **Blue Man Group** (773-348-4000; www.blueman.com), 3133 N. Halsted Street. At the Briar Street Theatre. This intense multimedia show starring three bald, blue men who don't speak still intrigues after years in Chicago. The show lasts about 105 minutes and includes a drumbeat that moves you. Children under 5 not permitted. Tickets: $49–69.

ⅇ **Steppenwolf Theatre** (312-335-1650; www.steppenwolf.org), 1650 N. Halsted Street. Gary Sinise, Jeff Perry, and Terry Kinney co-founded this famed theater collective in 1974, with the original membership including Laurie Metcalf and John Malkovich. Steppenwolf today has a complex of theaters near North Avenue and Halsted Street and more than 40 actors, directors, and playwrights working together as an ensemble, including Tom Irwin, John Mahoney, and Joan Allen.

ⅇ **The Second City** (312-337-3992; www.secondcity.com), 1616 N. Wells Street. Shows run at 8 Tuesday through Thursday 8, 11 PM Friday and Saturday, 7 PM Sunday. This comedy institution has given rise to the careers of Steve Carell, Stephen Colbert, Tina Fey, and many, many others, so it's worth a trip just so you can say you saw the next big stars before they hit it big. The resident troupe guarantees an original revue that is likely to reflect on the latest absurdity in the world of politics or pop culture. You can also try Second City e.t.c., which is located next door to the main stage. Tickets: $20–25.

✳ Selective Shopping

Chinatown Square (312-225-1088) Between Archer Avenue and China Place, west of Wentworth and north of Cermak. This Chinatown retail center has herbal shops, Chinese grocery stores with interesting ingredients, restaurants, and statues of the 12 animals of the Chinese zodiac calendar.

57th Street Books (773-684-1300; www.semcoop.indiebound .com), 1301 E. 57th Street. Open

GREEN CITY MARKET

10–8 daily. Independent bookstore near University of Chicago in Hyde Park.

Green City Market (773-435-0280, 773-880-1266; www.chicago greencitymarket.org) From May through October, open from 7–1 PM every Wednesday, Saturday at the south end of Lincoln Park. From November through April, it moves inside to the Peggy Note-baert Nature Museum, 2430 N. Cannon Drive, and is held 8–1 PM every other Saturday. You're head-ed in the right direction when you start seeing smiling people emerg-ing with cloth shopping bags filled with fresh flowers and beautiful produce. With the slogan KNOW YOUR FOOD . . . KNOW YOUR FARMER, Chicago's year-round farmers' market offers high-quali-ty, locally farmed, sustainably, or organically produced foods. Food-ies love it, and many of the city's

top chefs offer cooking demon-strations here. Sample the best of local breads, cheeses, pastries, honey, meats, and of course, pro-duce.

Damen Avenue From North Avenue to Armitage Avenue in Wicker Park, you'll find this strip of high-end home stores, cutting-edge fashion boutiques, and unique gift stores. Peruse the lat-est fashions at P.45, an upscale women's clothing boutique. Finish out your trip by picking up a more unusual snack at The Goddess and Grocer, a gourmet deli.

Lincoln Square Along Lincoln Avenue, you'll find this stretch of fun shops, including the culi-nary-focused **Chopping Block** (773-472-6700; www.the choppingblock.net) at 4747 N. Lincoln Avenue. There's also the independent record store **Laurie's Planet of Sound** (773-

271-3569; www.lauriesplanetof sound.com), at 4639 N. Lincoln Avenue, and the **Book Cellar** (773-293-2665; www.bookcellar inc.com), 4736-38 N. Lincoln Avenue. And, kids of all ages will love the independent **Timeless Toys** (773-334-4445; www.time lesstoyschicago.com) 4749 N. Lincoln Avenue.

If you're looking for a special piece for your home, wander **into Architectural Artifacts** (773-348-0622; www.architecturalarti facts.com), 4325 N. Ravenswood. There's also **Salvage One** (773-733-0098; http://salvageone.com), 1840 W. Hubbard Street. Open 11–6 Friday, 9–5 Saturday, noon–5 Sunday.

✳ Special Events

June: **Printer's Row Lit Fest** Located in the historic Printers Row neighborhood, along Dearborn Street from Congress to Polk. This free outdoor literary festival attracts big name authors and lit-loving fans from throughout the Midwest who want to browse the offerings and hear from the speakers at various stages.

Old Town Art Fair (312-337-1938; www.oldtowntriangle.com) Every June for more than 60 years, the Old Town neighborhood has been the backdrop for this juried art fair that includes children's activities, food, and music in one of the city's most charming neighborhoods.

57th Street Art Fair (773-493-3247; www.57thstreetartfair.org) June also brings out art-minded folks to Hyde Park for this juried art fair that has been in operation for more than 60 years. You'll find it on 57th Street between Kenwood and Kimbark.

July: **Chicago Folk & Roots Festival** (773-728-6000; www .chicagofolkandroots.org) Lincoln Square is home to this festival put on by the Old Town School of Folk Music that showcases all kinds of music from around the world. Includes great children's activities.

Pitchfork Music Festival (www .pitchforkmusicfestival.com) is an annual celebration of indie music over three days in Union Park, usually during the hottest part of the summer.

SUBURBS

The greater Chicago area is a web of hundreds of communities inter-connected by history and highways. Many Chicago suburbs offer fine dining, entertainment options, and historic downtown squares and other attractions. But here, I try to focus on a few day-trips that you can take from the Chicago area that will be worth your while.

One such trip is a drive up Lake Shore Drive to the northern suburbs. Lake Shore Drive turns into Sheridan Road on the north side of the city, and if you continue to follow Sheridan north, you will ride past amazing, jaw-dropping estates on pristine pieces of lakefront property. Just when you think you've seen a big house, keep driving north and you will see a bigger one. The communities that front Lake Michigan are known collec-tively as the "North Shore," a label that translates into tony shopping dis-tricts, heart-stopping real estate prices, and upscale restaurants. The Metra commuter train connects shoppers easily to the picturesque down-towns of Lake Forest or Highland Park.

You can also find a nice day-trip heading out to the Fox River towns of St. Charles, Geneva, and Batavia, also accessible by train. It's quite a drive out there, an hour plus from Chicago, but the shopping districts are quaint and friendly, set against the lovely backdrop of the Fox River.

You can say the same about Naperville, which has seen explosive popu-lation growth. Naperville's giant downtown retail district is walkable and pleasant. A visit to the living history museum, combined with good dining options add up to a day-trip.

Just west of the city you'll find the one and only Oak Park, with its ties to architecture and literary giants Frank Lloyd Wright and Ernest Hem-ingway. The housing stock is lovely and the people proud of the town's reputation for open-mindedness.

AREA CODES Not too long ago, we had just 708 for the suburban area code. But as the metropolis grows, we've added 847 and 224 for the com-

Chicago Suburbs

WISCONSIN

0   5   10
Miles

173
131
Zion
YORKHOUSE RD
Illinois Beach
State Park
41
31
Six Flags
Great America
137
Waukegan
Gurnee
120
BELVIDERE RD
GREEN BAY RD
120
60
Fox River
12
Lake
Michigan
45
21
94
TOWNLINE RD
14
Lake Forest
45
41
43
Highland Park
N
LAKE COOK   RD
Chicago Botanic Garden
Glencoe
294
SHERIDAN RD
59
WILLOW RD
12
Wilmette
Baha'i House
of Worship
90
Glenview
Illinois Holocaust Museum
20
290
DEMPSTER ST
Evanston
31
25
14
Skokie
TOUHY   AVE
O'Hare
International
Airport
94
Des Plaines River
90
355
290
294
43
50
St. Charles
64
NORTH   AVE
41
Geneva
Frank Lloyd Wright
Home and Studio
Oak
Park
Chicago
Batavia
38
290
59
53
88
Brookfield
34
Brookfield
Zoo
55
90
41
88
Naperville
Lisle
Downers
Grove
294
12
Midway
International
Airport
Naper
Settlement
34
355
55
50
94
© The Countryman Press

munities north of the city, and 630 for the western suburban area. 708 is
now reserved for some inner-ring suburbs and the southern suburbs.

GUIDANCE The following local tourism bureaus may be able to give you
more information:

Chicago's North Shore Convention and Visitors Bureau (866-369-
0011; www.visitchicagonorthshore.com), 8001 Lincoln Avenue, Skokie.
This office covers the suburbs north of Chicago.

Lake County Convention and Visitors Bureau (847-662-2700; www
.lakecounty.org), 5465 W. Grand Avenue, Suite 100, Gurnee. Lake County
is north of Chicago.

Oak Park Area Convention and Visitors Bureau (888-625-7275; www
.visitoakpark.com), 1010 Lake Street, Oak Park.

Naperville Convention and Visitors Bureau (630-305-7701; www.visit
naperville.com), 212 S. Webster Street, Suite 104, Naperville.

St. Charles Convention and Visitors Bureau (800-777-4373; www.visit
stcharles.com), 311 N. Second Street, Suite 100, St. Charles.

GETTING AROUND *By auto:* Lake Shore Drive is a great way to see the
North Shore. You can also take I-94, the Edens Expressway. To reach Oak
Park, take I-290, the Eisenhower Expressway, west to Austin Boulevard.
To access the Fox River towns of Geneva, Batavia and St. Charles, contin-
ue down the Eisenhower, then take I-88 toward Aurora to merge onto
Roosevelt Road. Continue on Roosevelt until you reach Geneva, or take
the I-355 tollway north to North Avenue, which you will follow into St.
Charles. IL 25 and 31 will transport you in between the three Fox River
towns on each side of the river. Naperville is about 31 miles southwest of
Chicago, and can be reached by taking I-88.

By train: **Metra** (312-836-7000; www.metrarail.com) The Metra commuter
rail will take you from downtown Chicago to the downtown districts of
many North Shore towns, out west to Geneva and southwest to Naperville.
You can purchase a ticket on the train, but if a station agent was on duty
where you boarded, you will be charged an additional $2 fee. One-way
tickets start at $2.25. The cost depends on how far you are traveling.

The **CTA**'s Yellow Line will take you to Skokie, and the Purple Line connects you to Evanston. To get to Oak Park by the "L," take the Green line;
jump off at the Oak Park or Harlem stop, and you'll be in the heart of the
shopping and restaurant district.

MEDICAL EMERGENCIES ((ᵩ)) **Evanston Hospital** (847-570-2000;
www.northshore.org), 2650 Ridge Avenue, Evanston. Level I trauma center for the northern suburbs.

Loyola University Hospital (888-LUHS-888; www.loyolamedicine.org),
2160 S. First Avenue, Maywood. This large teaching hospital in the western suburbs has 561 beds and a regional burn center. As a Level I trauma
center, the hospital is equipped to handle the most critical cases.

✳ Wandering Around

EXPLORING BY CAR Sheridan Road is a curvy but beautiful route to
take through the North Shore. Pay attention to signs, though, as the road
loses its Sheridan Road title for a few stretches. For the Fox River Valley
towns, IL 25 or 31 are pretty scenic and give you a taste of the riverfront
shopping areas and the larger shopping district in Geneva.

EXPLORING BY FOOT The Fox River Valley towns of Geneva, Batavia, and St. Charles, as well as the North Shore cities of Highland Park, Lake Forest, and Winnetka/Wilmette are all great places to wander on your feet, with pedestrian-friendly shopping districts.

✳ Towns and Villages

Evanston is north of Chicago and is connected to the city through the purple line CTA train and the Metra. Evanston is home to Northwestern University, situated on a gorgeous lakefront campus. The city, which was officially incorporated in 1863, is named after university founder John Evans. Historically, Evanston had quite a strict policy on alcohol, prohibiting the sale of it in the city limits until the 1970s. Today, with 78,000 people, Evanston has wonderful beaches, parks, and shopping districts.

Skokie Just west of Evanston, Skokie has a strong Jewish heritage, as more than 7,000 Holocaust survivors relocated here after the war. You can see more of that story at the world-class and emotionally haunting Illinois Holocaust museum. Today, Skokie is a very diverse community of 66,000 just north of Chicago, with a nice sculpture park along the river, the North Shore Center for Performing Arts, and the sprawling Old Orchard Mall. Located at Chicago's northern border, Skokie is also connected to the city through the Skokie Swift Yellow Line train.

Highland Park This city of about 31,000 was incorporated in 1869 and is positioned on the shores of Lake Michigan. Highland Park is home to Ravinia, which hosts a full calendar of performances at its historic outdoor music venue, where people can pack picnics and sprawl out on the lawn to listen to concerts.

Lake Forest Founded in 1861, about 21,000 people call this beautiful city home, drawn by its market square and amazing parks.

St. Charles is situated along the picturesque Fox River and has a nice shopping district with restaurants near the river. It was originally called Charleston but had to change its name after the townsfolk discovered another Charleston existed in the state. At one time, it was known as the pickle capital of the world, even though there was not a big pickle manufacturer here.

Oak Park has a number of notable former residents, including Ernest Hemingway, Edward Rice Burroughs, and Frank Lloyd Wright. Wright built his home in the village in 1889, but Oak Park did not officially come into existence until 1902. Today you can visit his home and studio, and the birthplace of Hemingway. About 53,000 people call Oak Park home today, with its Harrison Arts District and close connection to downtown Chicago via the CTA.

Naperville is a large city of about 143,000 people that makes national lists of the best places to live. With a riverwalk dressed up with public art and lots of activity, the city also has a busy downtown shopping district.

✷ To See

MUSEUMS

North Shore

♿ ☂ **Illinois Holocaust Museum and Education Center** (847-967-4800; www.ilholocaustmuseum.org), 9603 Woods Drive, Skokie. Open 10–5 weekdays with extended hours until 8 on Thursday, 11–4 weekends. Opened in 2009, this museum tells the horrific story of Nazism and the Holocaust through amazing exhibits, designed in a way to make you feel this story to your core. The exterior of the building is industrial looking, as is the dark lobby of exposed ductwork and concrete. The idea is to start from a place of darkness and move into the light, like the story of the Jewish people since the war. The story begins with framed family photos and heirlooms from local families that are used to discuss Jewish culture. As you move through the exhibit, you see how the Nazis began working to unravel these families and destroy a whole people. Video testimonies of survivors are used throughout the building. For the Kristallnacht section of the exhibit that details the night the Nazis burned synagogues, books, and destroyed Jewish businesses, you walk into a room with a floor that appears to be made of broken glass. A replica synagogue is featured on one wall, with a giant framed photograph of a Jewish businessman cleaning up from the night of destruction. You can walk inside a freight-train car like the ones used to transport the Jews to death camps, to see how dark and suffocating it must have been, packed with people. Other arresting artifacts: A child's shoe that belonged to a victim of Auschwitz-Birkenau, an inmate uniform, and models of the concentration camps made by survivors. You also learn about the group of neo-Nazis who wanted to march through Skokie, where 7,000 Holocaust survivors lived, in the 1970s, waking efforts to educate the world about the story of what happened. Those efforts ultimately led to this museum. The exhibition ends in a bright white room where you see a 10-minute film that shows that the world has yet to learn its lesson about genocide, with continued horror in countries throughout the world, in places like Rwanda and Bosnia. The room includes a line that one veteran camp survivor would share with newcomers: I HAVE TOLD YOU THIS STORY NOT TO WEAKEN YOU BUT TO STRENGTHEN YOU, NOW IT IS UP TO YOU. Because of the grim subject matter, the museum is not recommended for children under 12. Allow at least two hours to take in this compelling institution. There are temporary exhibits as well. Admission: $12 adults, $8 seniors, students.

ILLINOIS HOLOCAUST MUSEUM

  ⚡ **Mary and Leigh Block Museum of Art** (847-491-4000; www.block museum.northwestern.edu), 40 Arts Circle Drive, Evanston. Arts Circle Drive is just north of the bend in Sheridan Road near the Medill School of Journalism. Open 10–5 Tuesday and weekends 10–8 Wednesday through Friday. Call ahead as the museum closes to change exhibitions and has reduced hours in the summer. A fine-arts museum located on the campus of Northwestern University, the Block attracts thought-provoking exhibitions and events, from the Polaroids of Robert Mapplethorpe to the sculpture of Polish artist Magdalena Abakanowicz, whose sculptures can be seen in Millennium Park. The permanent collection, of mostly prints and photographs, focuses on art that can be reproduced. The museum also screens films and hosts lectures. You need a $7 parking permit to park in the nearby lot until 4. In the evening and on weekends, parking is free. Free.

  ⚡ **Mitchell Museum of the American Indian** (847-475-1030; www .mitchellmuseum.org) 3001 Central Street, Evanston. Open 10–5 Tuesday through Saturday, with later hours on Thursday, until 8, noon–4 Sunday. If you've traveled Illinois much, you've heard lots of mention of the Native American cultures that settlers found when they arrived, but this museum fills in the blanks, focusing on the art and culture of the tribes in the U.S. and Canada. The bulk of the collection came from the Mitchells, who were interested in Native American art and culture. The permanent exhibit includes models of an Iroquois house, a wigwam, a canoe made of birch bark, and pottery from southwestern U.S. tribes, among other items. The museum brings in several temporary exhibits a year. Admission: $5 adults, $2.50 children, seniors, and students.

 & ↑ **Ernest Hemingway Birthplace & Museum** (708-848-2222; www
.ehfop.org) The museum is located at 200 N. Oak Park Avenue, Oak Park.
The birthplace is at 339 N. Oak Park Avenue. Open 1–5 Sunday through
Friday, 10–5 Saturday. Ernest Hemingway was born in 1899, in the area
that would later become Oak Park. You can see the house where the bril-
liant novelist lived until he was 6 years old with his parents, siblings, and
grandfather. He went to school in Oak Park, writing for the Oak Park-
River Forest High School newspaper and literary magazine. Inside the
Oak Park Arts Center, you can learn what happened to Ernest after he left
Oak Park and set about becoming one of the world's most famous writers.
(If you're interested in seeing the home where he spent his high school
years, it is located at 600 N. Kenilworth Avenue, but is not open to the
public.) The museum offers more of a glimpse into the life of the writer
through his childhood diary, photos, letters, and early writings from gram-
mar school. It includes the letter from Agnes von Kurowsky ending their
engagement, which is also played out in *A Farewell to Arms*. Admission:
$10 adults, $8 seniors and youth. Under 5 years free. Admission price gets
you into both the museum and birthplace.

Naperville
 ♂ & **Naper Settlement** (630-420-6010; www.napersettlement.org), 523
S. Webster Street, Naperville. The buildings are open April through Octo-

HEMINGWAY BIRTHPLACE

HEMINGWAY MUSEUM

ber Tuesday through Saturday 10–4, Sunday 1–4. From November
through March, the buildings are closed but you can tour the village
grounds and visitor center from 10–4 Tuesday through Friday. Costumed
villagers and a recreated historic village transport you back to the 19th
century. Naperville's own story is explained through an exhibit in the visitors center. The settlement also has changing exhibits and a children's
area, where they can try on pioneer clothing. Summer admission: $9
adults, $8 seniors, $6.50 youth. Winter admission: $5.25 adults, $4.75 seniors, $4 youth.

HISTORIC SITES

North Shore

Grosse Point Lighthouse (847-328-6961; www.grossepointlighthouse
.net), 2601 Sheridan Road, Evanston. Open June through September for
guided tours at 2, 3, 4 on weekends. Closed October through May and
holiday weekends. The cream-colored building looks like another mansion
on Lake Michigan, then you see the towering lighthouse behind it. Built
in 1873 by the government to prevent any further shipwrecks, it stands
113 feet tall. The light from the top could be seen from 21 miles away
over the lake on a good day. On summer weekends you can tour a museum in the keeper's quarters and climb 141 steps to the top of the light
tower. Admission: $5 adults, $3 children 8 to 12 years.

Historical Society of Oak Park & River Forest (708-848-6755; www
.oprfhistory.org), 217 S. Home Avenue, Oak Park. Tours 12:30, 1:30, and
2:30 Thursday through Sunday, March through November, no 2:30 tour
December through February. The society puts together exhibits on the
interesting local history and Edgar Rice Burroughs, who created Tarzan.
You can find it on the second floor of the Pleasant Home. **Pleasant
Home** (708-383-2654; www.pleasanthome.org) Designed by architect
George W. Maher, another prairie-style architect, this 1897 house has
been designated a National Historic Landmark. Admission: $5 adult, $3
student.

CULTURAL SITES

North Shore

& $\mathcal{O}$ **Baha'i House of Worship** (847-853-2325), 100 Linden Avenue,
Wilmette. The auditorium is open to the public 6 AM–10 PM daily, and the
visitor center is open 10–5 daily.
The white domed building with
intricate carvings, one of seven
Baha'i houses of worship in the
world, stands out even in the picturesque town of Wilmette. The
cornerstone for the building was
laid by the son of the religion's
founder in 1912, but it was not
built until 1953. Inside, the deli-
cately carved dome is impressive.
Note that there are services at
12:30, and no cameras are allowed
in the auditorium. Free.

GROSSE POINT LIGHTHOUSE

Oak Park

& ♛ **Frank Lloyd Wright Home
& Studio** (708-848-1976; www.go
wright.org), 951 Chicago Avenue,
Oak Park. Open daily 11–4. Museum shop open 10-5 daily. The
famed architect spent the first
phase of his career here, from
1889 to 1909, at his private residence and workplace, where he
experimented with design concepts. He and first wife Catherine

BAHA'I TEMPLE

Tobin raised six children here. He eventually added the studio, where he and his team created the Prairie Style of architecture that you can see throughout the Chicago area. Guided tours of the home start every 20 minutes. A guided tour of the home and studio is $15 adults, $12 youth and seniors. Walking tours of the historic neighborhood are $15. A combination ticket for both the interior tour and historic walking district tour is $25 for adults, $20 for children. Purchase tour tickets in the museum shop. The home also offers other intriguing programs such as a design detectives family tour, designed to bring the concepts of design alive for children and families. The home is not wheelchair accessible, but the studio is. Another Wright design to see nearby: The **Unity Temple** (www .unitytemple-utrf.org), 875 Lake Street, Oak Park. Tour the Unitarian Universalist church designed by the master architect. Services are still held every Sunday. Open 10–4:30 weekdays, 10–2 Saturday, 1–4 Sunday. Admission $9, $7 seniors and students. Children 5 and under free.

Fox River Towns

Fabyan Villa Museum and Japanese Garden (630-377-6424; www .ppfv.org/fabyan.htm) Located in the Fabyan Forest Preserve, on the east side of IL 31, Geneva. Open mid-May through mid-October 1–4 Wednesday, 1–4:30 on weekends. During the summer, also open Thursday 1–4. Frank Lloyd Wright redesigned and enlarged the home of George and

Nelle Fabyan in 1907, transforming it from a farmhouse to a prairie-style home with a low roof, new verandas, and other features that help it merge with the natural surroundings. Across the way, you can also wander through the Japanese gardens with the river as a backdrop. The museum inside has items from the intriguing couple who lived here. Suggested donation: $2 adults, $1 children.

✳ To Do

BEACHES

North Shore
♂ ♿ **Evanston Beaches** (www.cityofevanston.org/parks-recreation /beaches/) Open mid-June through Labor Day, 10:30–7:30 daily. Evanston has some mighty fine sandy lakefront beaches, which anyone can access for an entrance fee. Lighthouse Beach is at Central Street and Sheridan Road. Greenwood Street Beach and South Boulevard Beach are both located at the street in their title right at the lakefront. The Lighthouse Landing Park next to the Grosse Point lighthouse has a large playground and a bike platform right at the beach. Lifeguards are on duty during swimming hours. Greenwood and Lighthouse beaches are handicap accessible. Call ahead to 847-859-7822 to make sure swimming is allowed that day. A daily pass is $8, $6 for children 1 to 11 years.

FRANK LLOYD WRIGHT HOME & STUDIO

CHICAGO AND SUBURBS

North Shore

Lakefront You can continue to bike the lakefront north from the city proper, but it moves onto Sheridan Road for a bit in Evanston. From about Lee Street to Northwestern University, there is a bike path along the lakefront. The university has a lakefront path, but it basically loops around campus, so if you want to go farther north you may have to figure out a different route. As you go farther north, some of the North Shore towns have more bike-friendly approaches than others, some with bike lanes, some not.

Turin Bicycle (847-864-7660; www.turinbicycle.com), 1027 Davis Street, Evanston. Open 11–8 Monday through Thursday, 11–6 Friday, 10–6 Saturday, noon–5 Sunday. This bike shop just west of the Metra tracks rents Bianchi Milano hybrid bikes for $8 an hour or $32 per day. Rentals are first-come, first-served. Helmets and a lock are included.

EVANSTON BEACHFRONT

Fox River Towns

Fox River Bike Trail (www .northernfoxrivervalley.com /visitors-biketrail.cfm) This bike path has more than 30 miles of trail for biking, hiking, and cross-country skiing. The path connects to northern towns and counties along the Fox River. You'll find entry points in various towns along the way, including through St. Charles and Geneva.

Great Western Trail (630-232-5980; www.kaneforest.com), 37W370 Dean Street, St. Charles, at the LeRoy Oakes Forest Preserve You'll find about 14 miles of limestone trail for hiking and biking with rest areas along the way. The trail runs along an abandoned railway from St. Charles to the DeKalb County line.

Mill Race Cyclery (630-232-2833; http://millrace.com), 11 E. State
Street, Geneva. Open 10–7 weekdays, 10–5 Saturday, 11–5 Sunday. Hours
reduced in winter. Rent all kinds of bikes, tandems, child trailers, and
recumbent bikes. Bikes and trailers are $7 per hour, tandems are $15 per
hour.

Bike Shop on the Fox (630-587-5335; www.thebikeshopsc.com), 1 W.
Illinois, Suite 180, St. Charles. Open 10–6 weekdays with extended hours
until 8 on Thursday, 10–5 Saturday, 10–4 Sunday. Reduced winter hours.
Just off the Fox River Trail, this bike shop rents hybrid bikes and trailers.
Helmets free. $6 per hour.

BOATING

North Shore
Kayak/Sailboat rental (847-866-4167) The Evanston parks department
rents sailboats and kayaks from the Dempster Street Beach from mid-
June through Labor Day. Open 3:30–7:30 weekdays, 11–7 weekends.
Kayaks are $35 per hour. Sailboats: $40 per hour.

Fox River Towns
Geneva Kayak Center (630-232-0320; http://genevakayak.com) Open
June through August, 10–6 weekdays, 7–5 Saturday, noon–5 Sunday. Offseason: noon–6 Tuesday through Friday, 8–5 Saturday, noon–5 Sunday.
Explore the lower Fox River with an experienced guide, on a 7.5-mile trip
from Yorkville through Silver Springs State Park. Cost: $65, lunch is
included. A 15-mile trip is $99. Trips also available on Lake Michigan and
the Chicago River. You can rent a kayak for $30 for two hours.

St. Charles Paddlewheel Riverboats (630-584-2334; www.stcriver
boats.com), 2 North Avenue, St. Charles. From June through August, trips
depart at 3:30 weekdays, and hourly from 2–4 Saturday, and 2–5 Sunday.
During May and September, there are no weekday trips, and trips depart
hourly 2–4 weekends. Relax on the Fox River on a paddlewheel riverboat,
a replica of steamboats that traveled the same waters 100 years ago. Board
just north of Pottawatomie Park. Tickets: $7.50 adults, $6 children 15
years and younger.

FOR FAMILIES ᵼ ⌀ ⚓ **DuPage Children's Museum** (630-637-8000;
www.dupagechildrensmuseum.org), 301 N. Washington Street, Naperville.
From June through August open 9–4 weekdays, 9–5 Saturday, noon–5
Sunday. Reduced hours offseason. Behind the giant red door, you'll find
three bright floors of exhibits for playing, including a tool bench where
kids can build projects, a wind tunnel, water area filled with toys, and an
art studio. Admission: $8.50, $7.50 seniors.

&. ◊ ☂ **Kohl Children's Museum** (847-832-6600; www.kohlchildrens museum.org), 2100 Patriot Boulevard, Glenview. Open 9:30–noon Monday, 9:30–5 Tuesday through Saturday, noon–5 Sunday. During the summer, hours on Monday are extended until 5. Toddlers and children up to age 8 will have plenty to fan the imagination at this museum. The exhibits include a large water-play area, music section, Chicago area with a replica CTA train, and a house they can build on their own. The kid-sized Main Street has a sandwich shop, car repair shop, doll day care, and grocery store. Generally, you'll always find a fun temporary exhibit as well. Admission: $8.50 adults and children over 1; $7.50 seniors.

◊ **Six Flags Great America and Hurricane Harbor** (847-249-4636; www.sixflags.com/greatAmerica), 542 N. IL 21, Gurnee. During the height of summer, the amusement park is open 10–10, the water park 11–7. But hours are reduced according to the season, check before going. The water park operates Memorial Day through Labor Day, the amusement park from May through October. With admission you get access to both Great America and the water park at Hurricane Harbor. Great America has a number of roller coasters, such as the inverted, outside-looping Batman, the classic wooden American Eagle, the stand-up looping Iron Wolf, and the Superman that you ride head first to simulate flight. There are also plenty of rides that don't involve hanging upside down or vomiting. Hurricane Harbor has 26 waterslides, a wave pool, and water playground. Single ticket: $57, child under 48 inches tall $37. But save yourself $20 by buying online, as everyone pays the child price. You can use the savings toward parking, which costs $20 a day. Also save time by buying a "flash pass" that electronically holds your place in line so you don't waste half the day waiting. But it's not cheap, passes start at $35 for one person and go up from there.

GOLF ◊ **Cog Hill Golf and Country Club** (866-264-4455; www.coghill golf.com), 12294 Archer Avenue, Lemont. A premier golf course in the southwest suburbs that hosts PGA tournaments, Cog Hill has the famed "Dubsdread" course that makes many best-of lists. Fees for Dubsdread are $155. You can play courses 1 and 3 for $37–45. Course 2, the Ravines, will cost you $57.

ZOOS &. ◊ ◊ **Brookfield Zoo** (708-688-8000; www.czs.org), First Avenue and 31 Street, Brookfield. Summer hours 9:30–6 weekdays, Saturday, 9:30–7:30 Sunday. Winter hours 10–5 daily. From the Great Bear Wilderness with grizzlies, polar bears, and eagles to the Seven Seas "dive into ocean life" environments, Brookfield really takes you for a tour around the world. There's a lot of walking involved, so plan accordingly. Admission: $13.50, $9.50 seniors, children 3 to 11. Parking is another $9, and there is also a fee for the play zoo, which is designed for infants up to age 10. $3.50 for adults, $2.50 for children. The children's zoo is $2 adults, $1 for seniors, children. Also fees for dolphin shows and other special exhibits.

✳ Green Space

North Shore

&. ♪ ⚙ **Chicago Botanic Garden** (847-835-5440; www.ohwow.org), 1000 Lake Cook Road, Glencoe. Open 8–sunset daily. During the summer, hours extended from 7 AM–9 PM. I've not met one person who has visited the gardens and not been impressed by the nine islands, 24 display gardens, and four natural areas. They've earned their Web site name of ohwow.org, but note that although Chicago is in the name it's not actually in the city, but in north suburban Glencoe. A great way to make a night of it is to take advantage of the evening events, where you can get a drink on the esplanade or learn to dance amid the gardens. From May through October, the kids will love the model railroad garden, with miniature trains that run on tracks past Wrigley Field, Napa Valley, Hollywood, San Francisco, and the White House. The garden café serves breakfast, lunch, and dinner. Several bike trails also lead to the park. Admission is free, but parking is $20. There is a fee for the railroad garden as well.

Illinois Beach State Park (847-662-4811; http://dnr.state.il.us/lands /landmgt/parks/r2/ilbeach.htm), Lakefront, Zion. If you want a quieter

CHICAGO BOTANIC GARDEN

ILLINOIS BEACH STATE PARK

beach experience, the state park offers that, with stretches of lakefront open to explore. In a slightly strange way, a nuclear power plant divides the park into north and south sections. But there are miles of trails winding through the dunes and through woods nearby. Sand Pond on the north end of the park is stocked with rainbow trout for fishing, and there are boat launch facilities at the North Point Marina, which has 1,500 boat slips. There are a few beaches, but no lifeguards on duty. No pets allowed on beach.

Western Suburbs

& ✿ ♂ **Morton Arboretum** (630-968-0074; www.mortonarb.org), 4100 IL 53, Lisle. Located at I-88 and IL 53 in west suburban Lisle, open 7–sunset daily. The stats here are stunning: 1,700 acres with a collection of 186,000 trees and plants. To help you take it all in, the arboretum has 16 miles of paved or wood-chipped trails for you to hike, like the Heritage Trail that tells the story of the land dating back thousands of years. Other highlights: A 250-year old tree, ponds and marshes, and a maze garden that you can view from a 12-foot high platform. If you don't feel like hiking, there are 9 miles of roads for driving or biking. The arboretum has a great calendar of year-round events, including big-name concerts. The children's garden has playground equipment and many things to climb and explore. No pets. Admission: $11 adults, $10 seniors, $8 youth 2 to 17. Discounts on Wednesday.

✳ Lodging

BED AND BREAKFASTS

North Shore

((ᵖ)) **The Margarita European Inn** (847-869-2273; www.margarita inn.com), 1566 Oak Avenue, Evanston. Walk up to the Grand Parlor of this inn and you know you're in a place with serious character. In 1927, the inn was opened as the Margarita Club for Working Women, to host young businesswomen. It is named Margarita in honor of the first female resident of Evanston. The current owner has tried to retain the character, running it as a European-style inn. Each room has a different look, with antiques and carpet, many with flowery bedspreads and curtains. Some have shared baths. The inn also has a rooftop deck, an Italian restaurant on the first floor, and a library of rich dark woods and ruby reds. $–$$.

((ᵖ)) **The Homestead** (847-475-3300; www.thehomestead.net), 1625 Hinman Avenue, Evanston. Located close to campus, you can relax on the large, white-columned porch. All 90 rooms, which are pretty standard, have cable TV. The Homestead is also home to Quince restaurant. $$.

Oak Park

((ᵖ)) **Under the Ginkgo Tree Bed & Breakfast** (708-524-2327; www .undertheginkgotreebb.com), 300 N. Kenilworth, Oak Park. This bed and breakfast is located in an 1890 restored home that has original woodwork and stained glass. The dark but beautiful entryway has a mix of sculpture and painting and a lovely wood staircase to the second floor. There are five rooms, two with private bath; three share two baths. Rooms have king, queen, or twin beds. Breakfast is served on the veranda or in the dining room depending on weather. $.

✶ ✱ ((ᵖ)) **The Write Inn** (708-383-4800; www.writeinn.com), 211 N. Oak Park Avenue, Oak Park. Located within walking distance to the historic sites, restaurants, and shopping on Oak Park Avenue and Marion, the inn is located in a 1926 building with an inviting lobby. Rooms are small but comfortable with a sitting area, refrigerator, microwave, and desk. $–$$$.

INNS

Fox River Towns

✶ ((ᵖ)) 🐾 **Herrington Inn and Spa** (630-208-7433; www.herring toninn.com), 15 S. River Lane, Geneva. Located directly on the Fox River, in an old creamery building, the lovely Herrington has 61 rooms and suites, some with fireplace and whirlpool tubs. As a nod to its past as a creamery, the staff leaves chilled milk and freshly made cookies in each room. Try to score a river view room, which literally places you on the river. In addition to the rooms, the hotel has a full spa and **Atwater's** restaurant with an outdoor patio. $$–$$$.

North Shore

&. (((•))) ♂ ☀ **Hilton Orrington** (847-866-8700; www.hotelorring ton.com), 1710 Orrington Avenue, Evanston. Located just south of Northwestern University's campus, this is a popular choice for visiting parents. Rooms have safes, radio alarms with CD players, coffeemakers, and flat-screen TVs with cable. A fitness center and business center also are on site. $$.

&. (((•))) ♂ **Illinois Beach Resort and Conference Center** (847-625-7300; 866-452-3224; http://ilresorts.com), 1 Lake Front Drive, Zion. Located on the shore of Lake Michigan, this is a good home base for a beachy getaway at the state park. The resort is a little worn on the outside, but the guest rooms and suites are decent, comfortable rooms. They are handsomely designed with greens and tans, mission-style furniture, and clean white bedding. Request a room overlooking the lakefront instead of the "park," which can have some unsightly views of the pool roof. The hotel has a fitness center, pool, restaurant, lounge, and Jacuzzi. Rooms have a microwave, a small patio, and a TV. $$.

Fox River Towns

&. (((•))) **Hotel Baker** (630-584-2100; www.hotelbaker.com), 100 W. Main Street, St. Charles. The walls breathe history at this gorgeous hotel on the Fox River. You enter a 2-story foyer and walk into a marble lobby with carved wood beams on the ceilings. The front desk has old-time mail slots. The five floors are filled with unique rooms of varying size and feature photos of "Colonel" Baker around the halls. (You can also see him with his straw hat sitting on a bench outside). Rooms come with flat-screen TVs, and are nicely decorated with leather headboards, and gold linens in some rooms. You can have your lunch on the waterfront patio, accessible through the ROX City Grille. $$.

CAMPING

North Shore

&. **Illinois Beach State Park** (847-662-4811; http://dnr.state.il .us/lands/landmgt/parks/r2/ilbeach .htm) Located on lakefront, Zion. Open April through October. These sites are located behind a sand dune, in very close walking distance to the beach. The 240 camping sites in the southern portion of the park have access to showers and electricity. There is also biking and hiking nearby. Sites 248 to 257 are popular because they are under a grove of pine trees. Also note that the southeast end of the campground has an alcohol ban in effect. Reservations can be made at www.reserveamerica.com. Fees: $25 per night.

Western Suburbs

Blackwell Forest Preserve (630-933-7248; www.dupageforest

.com/Conservation/ForestPreserves /Blackwell.html) Near Butterfield and Winfield Road, Warrenville. Open weekends May through September. For a camping option just southeast of Batavia, you'll find 60 spots for tents, trailers, or motor homes. The campground has rest rooms, showers, electric hookups, and a dump station on site. The greater preserve covers 1,300 acres and also offers biking, fishing, boating, hiking, and horse- back riding. Fee: $25–30.

✳ Where to Eat

EATING OUT

North Shore

& ⌓ **Lulu's Dim Sum** (847-869- 4343; www.lulusdimsum.com), 804 Davis Street, Evanston. Open 11:30–10 daily. The Asian noodle dishes, dumplings, and other plates blend Japanese, Chinese, and Thai cooking. Dishes include pad Thai, Japanese miso, Szechuan chicken pao. The sesame noodles are yum. A collec- tion of Godzilla toys may keep the kids busy while you wait for the food. $–$$.

& **Hecky's Barbecue** (847-492- 1182; www.heckys.com), 1902 Green Bay Road, Evanston. Open 11–9 Monday through Thursday, 11–10 Friday and Saturday, 2–8 Sunday. Legendary barbecue joint serves up a sauce made from a family Creole recipe that is deli- cious on everything from pulled pork to baby back ribs. It's not the greatest for atmosphere, but if you want a quick bite or takeout for good barbecue, here's your place. $.

& **Dave's Italian Kitchen** (847- 864-6000; www.davesik.com), 1635 Chicago Avenue, Evanston. Open 4–10 Sunday through Thursday, 4–11 Friday and Satur- day. As the restaurant's autobiog- raphy explains, it's intentional that the kitchen is larger than the din- ing room because that's where the focus should be—on preparing the food, not on fancy walls. You can choose your pasta, then whether you'd like meat sauce, marinara, or butter and garlic sauce on top. There's also a brown rice risotto for those trying to avoid gluten, dairy, or meat. You'll find tradi- tional Italian entrees like veal parmesan and fettuccine alfredo, as well as pizzas, calzones, and sal- ads. The kitchen also makes its own bread. $–$$.

Walker Bros. Original Pancake House (847-251-6000; www .walkerbros.net), 153 Green Bay Road, Wilmette. Open 6:30 AM–10 PM daily. The Walker Brothers opened this location in 1960, serv- ing up the famous apple pancake. Besides all kinds of pancakes, you can order waffles, omelets, egg dishes, and lunch fare. $.

& ⚘ **Pita Inn** (847-677-0211; http://pita-inn.com), 3910 Demp- ster Street, Skokie. Open 11–11 Sunday through Thursday, 11 AM–midnight Friday and Satur- day. For quality, fresh Mediter- ranean food, try the Pita Inn, which has been packing in diners since 1982. Dishes include fabulous appetizers, shish kabob, kifta kabob, shawarma sandwiches, and entrees served with rice pilaf, salad, and pita. It's all very, very good. $.

Oak Park
& *ℐ* **Buzz Café** (708-524-2899; www.thebuzzcafe.com), 905 S. Lombard Avenue, Oak Park. Open 6 AM–9 PM weekdays, 7 AM–9 PM Saturday, 8–2 Sunday. In the Oak Park Arts District along Harrison, you will find this café with a menu of organic and vegetarian options for breakfast, lunch, and dinner. It's a great option for kids. The menu also features pizzas, sandwiches, wraps and salads, pastries and of course, coffee. Brunch served on Sundays. Local art featured on the wall, and local musicians are brought into play as well. $.

Fox River Towns
& **Il Giardino del Dolce** (630-443-2497; www.ilgiardinodel dolce.com), 131 S. 1st Street, St. Charles. Open 8–4 Sunday and Monday, 8–6 Tuesday through Saturday. Reduced winter hours. Giant glass cases of colorful desserts, including amaretti cookies, biscotti, tiramisu, and cannoli, reel you into this riverfront satellite location for a popular Chicago bakery. You can also pick up gelato, or fresh homemade loaves of rustic bread. $.

Town House Books and Café (630-584-8603 for cafe; www.town housebooks.com), 105 N. 2nd

THE BUZZ CAFÉ IN OAK PARK

Avenue, St. Charles. Open 9–5 Monday through Saturday, 10:30–4 Sunday for brunch. The café and attached bookstore are a great place to lose yourself in a book. The bookstore is like wandering through an old house, with separate rooms to investigate. The café has good food in the form of homemade soups and interesting sandwiches. Dine indoors in the small inviting dining room or in the cute outdoor patio area. $.

DINING OUT

North Shore
Oceanique (847-864-3435; www.oceanique.com), 505 Main Street, Evanston. Open for dinner at 5:30 Monday through Saturday. This fine-dining seafood restaurant with a French American flair is a favorite of many local foodies. The seafood comes from sustainable sources and is presented beautifully. A lengthy and interesting wine list also pleases. $$$$.

&. **The Stained Glass Bistro** (847-864-8600; www.thestained glass.com), 1735 Benson Avenue, Evanston. Open 5–9 Sunday through Thursday, 5–10 Friday, Saturday. Here you will find contemporary New American cuisine that pairs well with the wine list, which includes 32 wines by the glass or half-glass samplers. The focus is on the wine throughout this bistro, with wine bottles lining the walls. Dishes include filet mignon with potato galette and shallot cabernet butter, or a Scottish salmon with miso glaze. $$$.

&. **Convito Café and Market** (847-251-3654; www.convitocafe andmarket.com), 1515 Sheridan Road, Wilmette. Open 11:30 Monday through Thursday with the last seating at 9 PM. On Friday and Saturday the last seating is at 10 PM. Sunday brunch is from 11–3, and the café is open until 8:30. The Convito Café blends the dishes of the French and Italian countryside. Dine indoors or take a seat at the outdoor café for lunch, brunch, a glass of wine, or dinner. Lunch menu includes pastas, salads, and bistro sandwiches. Dinner menu includes more pasta selections and seafood dishes. A food and wine market is connected, with a wide selection of gourmet foodie items. $$–$$$.

Oak Park
&. **Hemmingway's Bistro** (708-524-0806; www.hemmingways

TOWN HOUSE BOOKS IN ST. CHARLES

bistro.com), 211 N. Oak Park Avenue, Oak Park. Open daily 7–3 for breakfast and lunch, 4–10 for dinner (until 11 on Friday and Saturday). There's also a champagne brunch on Sunday. The bistro has a straightforward dining room with terrazzo floor and white tablecloths, plus a full bar in the center of the room. You'll find French bistro food and a seafood bar, with dishes like duck a l'orange, beef Wellington, and steak frites. Seafood delivered fresh daily from the East Coast. $$–$$$.

New Rebozo (708-445-0370; www.newrebozo.com), 1116 Madison Street, Oak Park. Open for lunch: 11–3 Thursday through Saturday, dinner 4–10 Monday through Saturday. On a busy street a bit south of downtown Oak Park, the food in this colorful and wel-

coming restaurant is worth the trip. You'll find a range of enchiladas, meat entrees, and seafood off the grill. The mole also drives people here. $$–$$$.

✧ **Marion Street Cheese Market** (708-725-7200; www. marionstreetcheesemarket.com), 100 S. Marion Street, Oak Park. This environmentally friendly establishment, with tables made from sustainable cherry wood and chairs with webbing made from recycled seat belts, has a modern but warm décor with a brick fireplace and wood walls. On one side is the market, the other the bistro. Market side offers cheese, charcuterie, select wines, and more. Bistro side offers pastries and coffee starting at 9, lunch 11–3 weekdays, dinner at 5 and brunch on the weekends. The bistro menu

THE WRITE INN AND HEMMINGWAY'S BISTRO

focuses on locally and organically grown ingredients, with cheese and charcuterie flights, creative sandwiches for lunch, and eclectic meat and pasta dishes for dinner. In addition to the unique wines, they also offer a selection of craft beers. Live jazz music on Thursday. $–$$.

Fox River Towns
& **Francesca's by the River** (630-587-8221; www.miafrancesca.com), 200 S. 2nd Street, St. Charles. Open 11:30–9:30 Monday through Thursday, 11:30–10:30 Friday and Saturday, 4:30–9 Sunday. This popular Chicago restaurant chain presents authentic Italian cuisine in downtown St. Charles as well. The menu changes every two weeks, but you're likely to find excellent pasta dishes, pizzas, and entrees, and of course, wonderful Italian wines. $$.

& **Bien Trucha** (630-232-2665; www.bientrucha.com), 410 W. State Street, Geneva. Open for lunch: 11–3 Tuesday through Friday, noon–3 Saturday; dinner: 5–9 Tuesday through Thursday, 5–10 Friday and Saturday. Mexican street food dances and shines at this fantastic Mexican restaurant. The restaurant is modern, simple yet urban in feel; the menu is the same. For example, the tacos a la diabla entail sautéed shrimp, butter mojo de ajo, chipotle lime, and avocado. These dishes are designed to be shared. $–$$.

Naperville

& ♂ **Meson Sabika** (630-983-3000; www.mesonsabika.com), 1025 Aurora Avenue, Naperville. This tapas restaurant is housed in some pretty cool quarters, the 1847 Willoway Mansion near downtown. The menu features hot or cold Spanish tapas, paella, sangria, cocktails, and wine. Dine outdoors on the brick patio or inside the mansion. $$–$$$.

❋ **Entertainment**

LIVE MUSIC & **Ravinia** (847-266-5100; www.ravinia.org), 418 Sheridan Road, Highland Park. Open June through September. For a casually elegant evening, pack up a blanket and a picnic and hop on the Metra to hear music in a beautiful outdoor setting at Ravinia. The lawn is usually covered with groups enjoying the music under the stars, but you can also purchase seats in the pavilion if you want a covered seat. Every year the lineup includes classical music, Broadway productions, and big names performing in the unique setting.

THEATER

North Shore
Piven Theatre Workshop (847-866-8049; www.piventheatre.org), 927 Noyes Street, Evanston. Housed at the Noyes Cultural Center, this theater company was founded by Byrne and Joyce Piven in the 1970s and puts forth a full calendar of creative shows each

year, from classics to new works. They also run a noted training center, whose alums include the founders' son, Jeremy Piven, Rosanna Arquette, Lara Flynn Boyle, the Cusacks, Hope Davis, Aidan Quinn, and Lili Taylor.

& **North Shore Center for the Performing Arts** (847-673-6300; www.northshorecenter.org), 9501 Skokie Boulevard, Skokie. With two theaters, the center is home to the Northlight Theatre and Skokie Valley Symphony Orchestra. The North Shore also welcomes dance companies and big names in comedy and music.

Fox River Towns
Arcada Theatre (630-962-7000; www.thearcada.com), 105 E. Main Street, St. Charles. Still with its original pipe organ, this 1926 theater is being used as an entertainment venue once again, welcoming bands and comedians to its historic stage throughout the year.

✳ Selective Shopping

Lake Forest A mix of independent boutiques, restaurants, and upscale chain stores are located near the Metra train station in a lovely setting. Stores include Talbots, J Crew, Williams-Sonoma, the Lake Forest Bookstore, and many others.

Highland Park A larger retail district also located around the train station includes Paper Source, Perfect Blend, She, Style

Shack, Baby Dreams, and numerous restaurants.

Oak Park has unique and boutique shops along Lake Street and Marion Street. The Arts District on Harrison Street between Austin and Ridgeland has studios, galleries, and personal health establishments.

St. Charles East of the Fox River and just north of IL 64, you'll find this quaint historic shopping district called **Century Corners,** which includes **Stonehouse on Cedar** (630-762-0762; www.stone houseoncedar.com), 201 Cedar Avenue, St. Charles. The stonehouse shop covers two floors of this 1840s building and features cool handmade artisanal items. You'll find rugs, baskets, candles, jewelry. Also check out the sales "porch."

Geneva has a unique, high-end shopping area of beautiful boutiques centered around 3rd Street. Check out Artemisia, Persimmon Tree, Past Basket, and Graham's Chocolates if you need an ice cream break.

Naperville's downtown has dozens of specialty shops, restaurants, and clothing stores. You'll find a mix of chain and independent shops in this area.

Gurnee Mills (www.simon.com), 6170 W. Grand Avenue, Gurnee. Right off I-94. Open 10–9 weekdays, 10–9:30 Saturday, 11–7 Sunday. If you're near Six Flags and roller coasters aren't your thing, try the outlet malls in Gurnee Mills, which has more than 200 stores.

✳ Special Events

July: **Ribfest** (www.ribfest.net) in Naperville attracts some big headliners to the four-day festival each year. The festival also features a carnival, giant inflatables, and other family events. The organizers recruit rib makers from across the country to cook up ribs for the crowds. Admission: $12.

August: **Evanston Lakeshore Arts Festival** (www.cityof evanston.org), Dawes Park, Sheridan Road and Church Street. Since 1973, Evanston has invited artists to set up shop at Dawes Park for this lakefront festival. There's also live jazz and classical music, food from local restaurants and children's crafts. Free.

Up North 2

BOONE, MCHENRY, AND
WINNEBAGO COUNTIES

BOONE, MCHENRY, AND WINNEBAGO COUNTIES

F ar from the illuminated city, you can look up to the sky and see stars. These northern Illinois counties are still connected to the Chicago metro area, but disconnected just enough to offer a different experience.

By "Up North," I mean the counties of McHenry, Boone, and Winnebago that border Wisconsin. On fantastic drives past lush green fields, you'll find U-Pick farms, great parks, campgrounds, and . . . quiet.

The town of Woodstock in McHenry County is a destination unto itself, with a lovely historic square. So picture-perfect is it that it was the backdrop for the film *Groundhog Day.* In honor of that fact, each year the town celebrates "Groundhog Days." This is also a place that has hosted weekly family-friendly band concerts in the park, a tradition that dates back a century.

Woodstock, like nearby Crystal Lake, is linked to Chicago by commuter train (about an hour's ride), and more and more people have felt the draw of the town. Over the past couple decades, Chicagoans have moved in droves from the city and inner suburbs to McHenry County, looking for more land and a slower way of life. The influx of people has made some towns a little less slow. Preservationists have awakened and are positioned to keep what is beautiful and special about this area intact. So far they've done a good job, leaving a nice mix of quiet spaces and bustling activity for travelers to explore.

The urban center of this Northern Illinois region is the city of Rockford, which has some spots worth visiting if you're passing through. For one, the museum complex on the riverfront has a great children's museum, a small but impressive art museum, and the Burpee Museum of Natural History, which is also great for families. I'd also work in time to peruse the few blocks of fun restaurants that are part of revitalization efforts along the river.

Rockford's slogan is REAL. ORIGINAL. ROCKFORD, and the city certainly

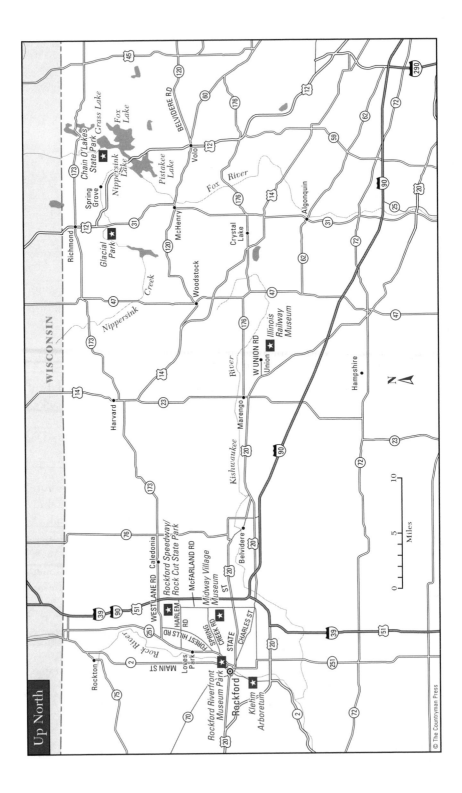

Up North

WISCONSIN

Chain O'Lakes State Park
Grass Lake
Fox Lake
Pistakee Lake
Nippersink Lake
Spring Grove
Richmond
Glacial Park
McHenry
Volo
Crystal Lake
Algonquin
Fox River
Woodstock
Nippersink Creek
Harvard
Marengo
Union
Illinois Railway Museum
Kishwaukee River
Hampshire
W UNION RD
BELVIDERE RD

N

Rockton
Rock River
Loves Park
Caledonia
Rockford Speedway/ Rock Cut State Park
WESTLANE RD
HARLEM RD
Midway Village Museum
FOREST HILLS RD
SPRING CREEK RD
MAIN ST
STATE
CHARLES ST
Rockford Riverfront Museum Park
Rockford
Klehm Arboretum
McFARLAND RD
Belvidere

0   5   10
Miles

© The Countryman Press

WOODSTOCK TOWN SQUARE

has that sense of realness that comes only from experiencing life with all of its ups and downs. Rockford's story starts in the 1830s when three men came from Galena to settle on the Rock River. They formed a community that became known as Midway because it was halfway between Chicago and Galena. Soon after, the railway powered through, fueling Rockford's growth into an industrial city. The city has solid Swedish roots, which you can see reflected in the town's museums, historical sites, and restaurants. Baseball was also important to the city. In the 1940s, Rockford was home to the Rockford Peaches, an all-female professional baseball team featured in *A League of Their Own*. But when the manufacturing industry withered in the 1970s and 1980s so did Rockford's economy. The city has worked hard to right the path, with several big projects like the new conservatory and other revitalization efforts prettying up the scene. Also of note in Rockford: It is the home of the band Cheap Trick and of *Symbol*, the 30-ton sculpture along the banks of the Rock River created by a Russian artist in recognition of Rockford's industrial ties.

Farther out from the cities and towns found up north, you'll find grand open spaces, roadside farmstands, and excellent parks. Chain O'Lakes and Rock Cut State Parks both are worth an escape from the city.

GUIDANCE & **McHenry County Convention and Visitors Bureau** (815-363-6177; 888-363-6177; www.visitmchenrycounty.com), 5435 Bull Valley Road, McHenry. Open 9–5 weekdays.

(((•))) & ✎ ↝ **McHenry County Conservation District's Lost Valley Visitor Center** (815-678-4532; www.mccdistrict.org), 7210 Keystone Road, Richmond. Located in Glacial Park. Open 8–6 daily April through October. In the offseason, open 8–4:30 weekdays, 9–4 weekends. If you'd like to do more exploring of the land here, the conservation district has created several of the best open spaces around and can provide more information on biking, hiking, and camping at this visitor center.

Rockford Area Convention & Visitors Bureau (815-209-2495; 800-521-0849; www.gorockford.com), 7801 E. State Street, Rockford. Open 5 AM–2 weekdays, 8–noon Saturday. If you approach the city on I-90 from the east, you'll see the clock tower off the side of the expressway. At the clock tower visitors center, you can pick up all the reference material you need and talk to a staff member who will help you figure out where to go.

GETTING THERE *By auto:* From Chicago, I-90 West will get you to McHenry County and Rockford. To get to Woodstock, exit the expressway at IL 47 heading north until you reach Lake Street. Turn left onto Lake, which will take you toward the downtown. Rockford is farther west on I-90. About where I-90 meets I-39, take US 20 West to the downtown area.

By bus: **Greyhound** (815-964-8671; www.greyhound.com), 542 N. Lyford Road, Rockford.

By air: Your best bet would be to fly into **O'Hare International Airport** (www.ohare.com), and drive out to the area on I-90 unless you're coming from one of the destinations serviced by the airlines at Chicago **Rockford International Airport** (815-969-4000; www.flyrfd.com), 60 Airport Road,

CHAIN O'LAKES PRAIRIE

Rockford. Allegiant and Direct Air operate out of Rockford, flying to and from Florida, Las Vegas, and Phoenix. Free parking.

By train: **Metra** connects Chicago with the McHenry County towns of Cary, Crystal Lake, Woodstock, McHenry, and Harvard (815-836-7000; www.metrarail.com). Tickets range from $6.50–8.50 depending on where you board and depart.

GETTING AROUND *By auto:* You'll pretty much have to drive out here. IL 47 cuts McHenry County in half and is a main road through Woodstock. US 14 moves diagonally across the county linking Woodstock to Harvard. US 20 links McHenry towns with the Rockford area.

By bus: In Rockford, you'll have the option of bus service through the **Rockford Mass Transit District** (815-961-9000; www.rmtd.org). Fares: $1.50 adults, 75 cents children 5 to 11 years, students. In McHenry County, there are limited routes through the **Pace** suburban bus service (847-364-7223; www.pacebus.com). Bus fare is $1.75 for adults.

MEDICAL EMERGENCIES **Centegra Hospital Woodstock** (815-338-2500; www.centegra.org), 3701 Doty Road, Woodstock. This Level II trauma center provides emergency care with round-the-clock emergency physicians. The health system also has a hospital in McHenry and two immediate care centers.

Rockford Memorial Hospital (815-971-5000; www.rhsnet.org), 2400 N. Rockton Avenue, Rockford. This hospital has roughly 400 beds, a pediatric intensive care unit, brain and spine center, and an emergency department licensed to handle the most critical cases.

✳ Wandering Around

EXPLORING BY CAR Head north outside the Rockford city limits toward Rockton, and its main street of antique shops, the homemade ice cream store, and the nearby re-created pioneer village. Elsewhere the farm country of McHenry makes for an enjoyable scenic drive.

EXPLORING BY BIKE **Prairie Trail Bike Path** (815-338-6223; www.mccdistrict.org) From Algonquin to the Wisconsin border, this 26-mile path follows the old Chicago and Northwestern Railway line while passing through Glacial Park and other peaceful pastures. You can access it at Algonquin Road just north of Meyer Drive, at Petersen Park in McHenry, or at Glacial Park in Ringwood. The path is paved in parts and gravel in others, and you will encounter hills in Crystal Lake.

♿ **Rock River Recreation Path** (815-987-8858; www.rockfordpark district.org) A 10-mile path along the Rock River through downtown Rockford connects to the Sinnissippi Gardens, and winds past the twisted red *Symbol statue*. You can access the path at Davis Park and Sinnissippi Gardens.

&. **Long Prairie Trail** (815-547-7935; www.boonecountyconservation district.org) A 14.2-mile paved trail through Northern Boone County prairie, woods, and the towns of Capron, Poplar Grove, and Caledonia. Parking lots are available in each town and on County Line Road in Capron. Rent bikes for the whole family at **Side by Side Cycle** (815-569-2472; www.sidebysidecycle.com), 142 W. Main Street, Capron. Rates: $6–8 per hour, $30–40 per day.

EXPLORING BY TROLLEY Trolley Car 36 (815-987-1685; www.rock fordparkdistrict.org), 324 N. Madison Street, Rockford. Operates from early June through August. Rides depart hourly from noon–4 Thursday, Saturday, Sunday. Take in the Rock River and the Sinnissippi Gardens from this refurbished trolley that leaves from Riverview Park. Tickets: $4 adults, $3.50 youth age 5 to 17 years.

✳ Towns and Villages

You will find a number of larger suburbs in McHenry County, as well as interesting small towns in the areas in between.

Crystal Lake Centered around a 230-acre lake, Crystal Lake has a Metra station that connects it to downtown Chicago, an active retail and dining district, and the Spanish Mission–style 1929 Raue Center for the Arts. The town was first settled in 1836, with a log cabin inn playing host to various stage coaches passing through. Today, it's one of many McHenry County towns that have seen population explosions as people move outward from the older Chicago suburbs.

Woodstock In 1990, Woodstock had just 14,000 people. At last count in 2009, it was 24,000. With the historic courthouse square, well-preserved downtown, historic homes, and areas where you can still find a quiet life, Woodstock continues to beckon to people. It's a great day-trip from the city, as you can take the train right downtown, and worthy of an overnight stay.

Richmond This small town was incorporated in 1872. As the town lore goes, there was a climbing contest held, with the agreement that whoever could climb to the top first would get to name the new settlement. The man who climbed the highest named the small town after his hometown of Richmond, Vermont. The shopping district here is charming, and I don't mean that in a "you'll have to overlook a bunch of stuff" way. The downtown is pretty and feels authentic with a sense of sophistication about it. In the residential area, you'll find Sears catalog homes and Victorians. Located near Glacial Park and Chain O' Lakes State Park, it'd be a good place for a break while exploring the parks or to get away.

Rockton Nestled in farm country, but still a short drive from Rockford, this small town has a nice shopping strip that is home to a few antique shops, including one that has a sign out front that reads: CLOSED MONDAY TO WASH OUR PIG. The Dairyhaus has great ice cream during the summer. The Rock River, of course, runs through it, offering a good spot for fishing.

✳ To See

To make it easier to navigate, I've grouped most of the attractions into two areas: McHenry County and Rockford.

MUSEUMS

McHenry County Area
✎ ♿ **Illinois Railway Museum** (815-923-4000; www.irm.org), 7000 Olson Road, Union. From I-90, exit US 20/Marengo. Take US 20 northwest about 6 miles to S. Union Road, Follow S. Union Road north through the town of Union. Be sure to keep your eye on the signs directing you to the museum as some people (myself) have gotten lost heading out for a visit. Open 10:30–5 weekends, 11–4 weekdays June through August. During the spring and fall, check for dates as the museum is open on some weekends. Check the schedule for the train operations as the museum offers rides on diesel trains, steam trains, and others. The museum itself is a giant swath of land with 5 miles of tracks running throughout. Large warehouse buildings hold rows and rows of electric cars, passenger cars, steam trains, diesel trains, and trolleys, including many historic trains from throughout the country. It also has an old Chicago "L" station. Part of the attraction is getting to ride on old trains, like an old Pullman observation car. The volunteers

RICHMOND

here are knowledgeable and friendly, happy to share their interest in trains with the groups coming out to this museum. You'll have to walk outdoors between the buildings and while waiting for the trains, so dress appropriately. Admission: $8–12 adults, $4–8 children. Family tickets maximum are $25–45.

✔ & **Volo Auto Museum** (815-385-3644; www.volocars.com), 27582 Volo Village Road, Volo. Open 10–5 daily. The showrooms here will be a hit with any car lovers. You can see the Batmobile built for the TV series, *Doc Hudson* from the Pixar film *Cars,* KITT from *Knight Rider,* and cars from the *Dukes of Hazzard* and *The Blues Brothers.* It also has a giant antique mall on site, and an armed forces exhibit. Admission: $10 adults, $8 seniors, $6 children.

Rockford Area

The Riverfront Museum Park is home to the **Burpee Museum of Natural History, the Rockford Art Museum, and the Discovery Center Museum**, all conveniently connected.

& ♈ **Rockford Art Museum** (815-968-2787; www.rockfordartmuseum .org), 711 N. Main Street, Rockford. Open 10–5 Monday through Saturday, noon–5 Sunday. The museum is small but welcomes some interesting temporary exhibits to its upstairs gallery, while the creamy white walls downstairs display some highlights of the permanent collection, which

RIVERFRONT MUSEUM PARK

includes more than 1,500 pieces with a special focus on local and Chicago artists. A very cool small gift shop has bright glassware, toys, books, cards, and dishes. Admission: $7 adults, $3 seniors, students, Children under 12 years free. Tuesday is free to all.

♿ ✎ ☂ **Discovery Center Museum** (815-963-6769; http://discoverycentermuseum.org), 711 N. Main Street, Rockford. Open 10–5 Monday through Saturday, noon–5 Sunday. During the summer, Thursday hours are extended until 7. Excellent children's science museum that offers kids a wide range of experiences—from standing inside a body-sized bubble to working a giant crane to building their own creature. The bright and lively museum has a tot spot for the tiniest ones of your set, as well as a pretty cool playhouse. And instead of stairs, kids can climb tunnels up to the second floor. My inner 5-year-old found it awesome. Admission: $7, free under 2.

♿ ✎ ☂ **The Burpee Museum of Natural History** (815-965-3433; www .burpee.org), 737 N. Main Street, Rockford. Open 10–5 daily. Here, you can investigate and identify fossils, learning how to tell the difference between the fossil of a saber-toothed cat and a mountain lion. Walk into a 2-story forest with cross-sections revealing the layers of the earth. The centerpiece of the museum is Jane, a half-grown T. rex who stands 21 feet tall. She was discovered in southeastern Montana in 2001. An intriguing extra dimension is added by stations where you can hear from the scientists who found Jane. Another exhibit delves into geology by making local connections to the science, teaching the concepts through a look at ancient Rockford. Admission: $7 adults, children 3 to 17 years. This is a great museum for kids, especially combined with the children's museum. Save $1 at the children's museum if you visit the Burpee the same day.

♿ ✎ **Midway Village Museum** (815-397-9112; www.midwayvillage.com), 6799 Guilford Road, Rockford. Open 10–4 Tuesday through Friday, 10:30–4 weekends from May through August. During the offseason, museum center open 10–4 Tuesday through Friday, 10:30–4 Saturday (Historic Village not open). This museum introduces you to the story of Rockford from the 1830s when the first settlers arrived and the first homes were built, then allows you to walk through the story yourself, through a re-creation of a typical Northern Illinois town at the turn of the 20th century. There's the general store, print shop, bank, hotel, and barber shop among 26 historical buildings. Interpreters in period clothing will lead you through the village. The indoor museum also recounts the story of the sock monkey here in Rockford and the Rockford Peaches (a team of the all-American Girls Professional Baseball League started during World War II, while men were in the Army). Admission: $6 adults, $4 children.

✎ **Tinker Swiss Cottage Museum** (815- 964-2424; http://tinkercottage.com), 411 Kent Street, Rockford. Tours given at 1, 2, 3 Tuesday

TINKER HOUSE COTTAGE

through Sunday, March through December. Inspired by Swiss architecture, this cottage was built in 1865 by Robert Hall Tinker, who later became mayor of Rockford. The ornate brown home overlooks Kent Creek and contains original furnishings, artwork, and a 2-story library with spiral staircase. Admission: $6 adults, $5 seniors, $3 kids 5 to 17 years.

HISTORIC SITES

McHenry County Area

♂ **Old Court House Arts Center** (815-338-4525; www.oldcourthouse artscenter.com), 101 N. Johnson, Woodstock. Open 11–5 Thursday through Saturday, 1–5 Sunday. Now used as an art gallery space, you can peruse the work of regional artists and see their pottery, jewelry, glass, sculpture, and paintings. The historic building has a small exhibit detailing the town's most famous prisoner, Eugene V. Debs. The early labor leader was jailed here for ignoring a federal injunction obtained by President Grover Cleveland during the labor war between railroad workers and the Pullman Co. Authorities feared for his safety in Chicago, so Mr. Debs was moved here and visited by the famous newswoman Nellie Bly. Free.

CULTURAL SITES ♿ ♂ **Woodstock Opera House** (815-338-4212; www.woodstockoperahouse.com), 121 W. Van Buren Street, Woodstock. Box office open 9–5 weekdays, 1–5 Saturday. Tours by appointment. Built in 1889, this gorgeous theater in the town square of Woodstock boasts some famous alums. Orson Welles starred in a play on stage here as a young student. The opera house brings in national acts while also providing a home for local performers. The building's supporters have worked to keep pace with the times by installing contemporary sound and lighting, but preserving historically significant features. The interior is similar to showboats from the time. Fun fact: The Opera House appeared as the Pennsylvanian Hotel in *Groundhog Day.* Be sure to browse through the lobby, where you can see original photos and programs from the early days, including one that shows Paul Newman starring as "Brian Strange" in *Mr. Pim Passes By.* The play counted Tom Bosley as the stage manager.

✻ To Do

BOATING

McHenry County Area

Tip A Canoe (262-342-1012; www.tipacanoellc.com) Schedule is dependent on water and weather conditions. This company is based out of Wisconsin, but operates canoe trips in Illinois on the Fox River and Nippersink Creek. What's your limit—two hours? A couple days; 3 miles; 40 miles? Tip A Canoe offers trips for these distances. Call ahead to make your reservation and they'll meet you at the launch site with your equipment. Cost: $55 per boat, which includes delivery and pickup, shuttle service for driver of the party, equipment, and launch assistance.

Flatwater Canoe & Kayak Rental (815-353-7333; www.flatwaterrentals.com/), 8621 US 12, Richmond. Open May through early October with trips departing at 9, 10:30, 12:30, and 2:30 weekends. Canoe the Nippersink, a Class A-rated creek, with these outfitters. The trip takes about three hours. Boaters follow Flatwater to the end of the route, park their cars, then are transported out to the launch. Cost: $40 for single kayak, $60 for tandem kayak, $60 for two-person canoe. Reservations recommended.

WOODSTOCK OPERA HOUSE

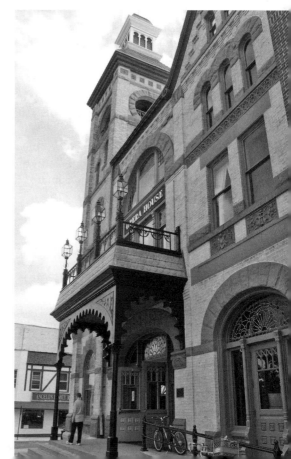

Rockford Area

Larsen's Landing Outfitters (815-505-3466; www.canoethekish.com), 1951 New Milford School Road, Rockford. These outfitters can get you ready for a day on the Kishwaukee River, which gets a top rating from the Illinois Department of Natural Resources for water quality. Cost: $60 for one-day-trip in two-person canoe, $45 for one-day kayak trip.

& *Forest City Queen* **Riverboat** (815-987-1685; www.rockfordpark district.org), 324 N. Madison Street, Rockford. Trips depart at 2, 3, 4 Wednesday, Friday, and hourly from noon–4 on the weekends from June through August. The city park district hosts cruises on the Rock River, providing a narrated history of the river and great views of some of the riverfront houses. Purchase tickets at the Trolley Station in Riverview Park. Admission: $5 adults, $4 kids 5 to 17 years, free for 4 and under.

FOR FAMILIES

McHenry County Area

🐾 & ✿ **Richardson Corn Maze** (815-675-9729; www.richardsonfarm .com), 9407 Richardson Road, Spring Grove. Open August through October, 3–10 Wednesday through Thursday, 3–11 Friday, 10 AM–11 PM Saturday, noon–10 Sunday. The corn maze is part of a farm entertainment complex. The maze itself is giant, with 33 acres of fields involved. Take it all in from a 50-feet high observation tower. The farm also has a giant slide, campfires, and other rides. Bring your own picnic. Admission: $12.95 adults, $9.95 kids.

& **Donley's Wild West Town** (815-923-9000; www.wildwesttown.com), US 20 and S. Union Road, Union. Open 10–6 daily late May through late August. Weekends only in September, October. A bit touristy, but kids may get a kick out of it. You can pan for gold, ride ponies and trains, learn cowboy roping skills, and take in the Wild West shows, which are given at noon, 2, and 4:30. See gunslingers in action, some cool stunts, and watch a bank robbery. Admission: $15.

Rockford Area

⛅ ✂ **CoCo Key Water Park** (815-398-6000; www.cocokeywaterresort .com), 7801 E. State Street, Rockford. Open 10–9 Saturday, 10–8 Sunday with hours varying during the week depending on school vacations. Accepting that this is Northern Illinois and half of the year we are inside, this indoor water park stays a warm 84 degrees year-round and has three waterslides, a water playground for younger kids, a tube ride, whirlpools, and a pool where you can watch movies. It's located at the Clock Tower Resort, which has lodging. Admission: $20–25, but if you are planning to stay, book together with your hotel room to save money.

FRUIT AND VEGETABLE PICKING & 🐾 **Susie's Garden Patch**
(815-597-3011; www.susiesgardenpatch.com), 10258 US 20, Garden
Prairie. Located west of Marengo. Open May through October, 9–6:30
Monday through Saturday, noon–5 Sunday. Pick your own strawberries,
okra, tomatoes, pumpkins, eggplants, cucumbers, and zucchini at this family-run farm. Selection depends on what's ripened. Bring bug spray, wear
appropriate clothing for farm work, and bring containers. Also has a playground and farm animals.

& 🍃 **All Seasons Orchard** (815-338-5637; www.allseasonfarm.com/new
/orchard.php), 14510 IL 176, Woodstock. Open late August to early
November, 10–5 daily. Pick your own apples from some of the 11,000
trees at this apple orchard and farm that carries 12 different kinds of
apples. There is also a corn maze, farm tour, and activities for kids. Admission: $5–8 adults, $3 seniors.

Prairie Sky Orchard (815-923-4834; www.prairieskyorchard.com), 4914
N. Union Road, Union. Open September and October. Pick your own
apples and raspberries. You can also buy pumpkins on this family-run farm
that has a shop with jams, salsas, and gourmet foods. Free admission, pay
for what you're taking home.

GOLF

McHenry County Area

Oak Grove Golf Course (815-648-2550; www.oakgrovegolfcourse.com),
16914 Oak Grove Road, Harvard. This highly rated course in Harvard
promises a challenge. With five tees on every hole, the course aims to
serve every level of golfer. Also has a driving range on site. Fees: $25–69
depending on the time of play.

Plum Tree National Golf Club (815-943-7474; www.plumtreegolf.com),
19511 Lembcke Road, Harvard. Open March to November. A picturesque
area in McHenry County, this par-72 course is open to the public. Fees:
$47–65 for 18 holes with cart.

Rockford Area

The Ledges (815-389-0979; www.wcfpd.org/golf) Located off McCurry
Road, 2 miles east of IL 251 near Roscoe. Open April through October.
A par-72 course with water on 10 holes, a putting green, and pro shop.
Designed as a private course, the Ledges was later purchased by the
Winnebago County Forest Preserve District. Fees: $21–25 for 18 holes,
carts: $22.

Aldeen Golf Club (815-282-4653; www.aldeengolfclub.com), 1902 Reid
Farm Road, Rockford. Open March through November, 7–7 daily. From
May through September, course opens at 6 AM on weekends. The Aldeen

family donated the money to make this upscale golf course available to working men and women, thus the course earns recognition for its value. Some call it the best municipal course in Illinois. It features 18 holes with water on 12 holes and 62 sand bunkers. Fee: $40–45, carts $30.

HORSEBACK RIDING Chain O'Lakes State Park Riding Stable (815-675-6532; www.chainolakesstable.com), 8916 Wilmot Road, Spring Grove. Open January through October. Ride through the state park on horseback, with a guide. Cost: $25 for 40 minutes, $32 for one hour. If you have a group, you may also book an old-fashioned wagon ride. Children 7 and older can try the trail ride. Those 6 years and younger can do pony rides, which run $7 for 7 minutes.

RACING Rockford Speedway (815-633-1500; www.rockfordspeedway .com), 9572 Forest Hills Road, Loves Park. NASCAR-sanctioned speedway has a calendar of racing April through October. You'll also find family events and monster trucks. Ticket prices vary by event.

TOURS & *Groundhog Day* **Movie Tour** (815-338-4483; www.wood stockgroundhog.org), Woodstock. Tour the locations where the movie *Groundhog Day* was filmed in the spring of 1992. You may notice plaques around town designating "Bill Murray's Puddle" and other sites seen in the film. The town has an annual festival for Groundhog Day with socials, free showings of the movie, chili cook-offs, walking tours of the locations, and pancake breakfasts. Pick up or print out a map from the Web site above and take the walking tour. Free.

✳ Green Space

McHenry County Area
McHenry County Conservation District (815-678-4532; www.mcc district.org),has several fine recreational areas to explore, preserving over 23,000 acres of country in an area of the state that is butting heads with developers in some parts. There's hiking, fishing on rivers and ponds, camping, horseback trails, and picnic areas.

Glacial Park, 6316 Harts Road, Ringwood. Located off IL 31 between the cities of McHenry and Richmond, the park has restored prairies, woods, the Kettle bog, and the Lost Valley Marsh. You'll find great hiking along the 6 miles of trails, places to fish, a canoe launch, a sledding hill, and wild turkeys.

Chain O'Lakes State Park (847-587-5512; http://dnr.state.il.us/lands /landmgt/parks/r2/chaino.htm), 8916 Wilmot Road, Spring Grove. Summer hours: 6 AM–9 PM. Winter hours: 8 AM–sunset. The park stretches across 6,000 acres, in the center of Illinois' largest concentration of natural lakes. In fact, three lakes border the park and the Fox River runs through it. The park offers camping, hiking, bike trails, and horseback riding. The popular Goldfinch and Badger trails take you up on a bluff overlooking the expanse of prairie and the Fox River. No swimming, but you can fish, canoe, and kayak.

Rockford Area

Sinnissippi Gardens (815-987-8858; www.rockfordparkdistrict.org), 1300 N. 2nd Street, Rockford. These gardens pretty up the area along the Rock River, with 2,000 roses and a flower clock. As of press time, the park district was expecting to open the gleaming new **Nicholas Conservatory & Gardens** (815-987-1689; www.rockfordparkdistrict.org) **Due to open** in fall 2011. The glass-encased tropical forest will have 21,000 square feet of tropical trees, plants, and flowers.

&. ♂ **Anderson Japanese Gardens** (815-229-9390; www.andersongardens.org), 318 Spring Creek Road, Rockford. Open 9–sunset weekdays, 9–4 Saturday, 10–4 Sunday, May through October. From November through April, open 11–3 Tuesday through Saturday, 10–2 Sunday. These acres of impressive gardens take you past pools, streams, pagodas, and waterfalls. There's also a gift shop and restaurant, Seasons in the Gardens. Admission: $7 adults, $6 seniors, $5 students. Children 4 years and younger free.

KLEHM BOTANIC GARDEN

& ☀ ♂ **Klehm Arboretum and Botanic Garden** (815-965-8146; www
.klehm.org), 2715 S. Main Street, Rockford. Open 9–4 Sunday through
Thursday, 9–6 Friday and Saturday, April through October. Offseason
hours: 9–4 Tuesday through Saturday. Wander through colorful, beautiful
flower gardens then duck into forested areas where the air feels 10
degrees cooler. This 150-acre nature-filled wonderland is a great place to
find quiet in the city, through the butterfly garden, prehistoric garden,
daylily garden, and children's garden. Admission: $6 adults, $3 seniors,
students, children. Children 2 and under free. Entry is free on Monday.

& ☀ **Rock Cut State Park** (815-885-3311; http://dnr.state.il.us/lands
/landmgt/parks/r1/rockcut.htm), 7318 Harlem Road, Loves Park. Anglers
like the 162-acre Pierce Lake while swimmers head to the smaller Olson
Lake, where there is a shower building. For hikers, there are more than
40 miles of trails winding through the park. Mountain bikers have 23
miles of trail and horseback enthusiasts have 14.

✳ Lodging

BED AND BREAKFASTS

McHenry County Area

((ᵠ)) **Muirhead Farmhouse Bed &
Breakfast** (847-464-5224; www
.muirheadfarmhouse.com),
42W814 Rohrsen Road, Hampshire. For those who have been
drinking in all the Frank Lloyd
Wright designs throughout Northern Illinois, here's a chance to stay
in a farmhouse that he designed in
Hampshire. There's a master suite
with queen bed, private bath, and
outdoor patio, DVD/CD player,
and other furniture designed by
Wright. You can read through the
letters the Muirheads exchanged
with Wright while he was designing their farmhouse, and will also
receive a tour of the home. $$.

((ᵠ)) **Morning Glory B&B** (815-
943-1633), 8701 N. IL 14, Har-
vard. If you've always wished you
had a laid-back aunt and uncle
with a farmhouse where you could

stay, you might get that feel at this
bed and breakfast on a rural high-
way north of Harvard. The sign for
the bed and breakfast also advertis-
es the farm-fresh eggs and flowers
that Harold and Linda Vierck grow
in the back. Linda will prepare
those farm-fresh eggs anyway you
like. The Viercks have a sitting
room with hardwood floors and gas
stove, a long dining table with a
bay window, and two guest rooms
upstairs. They built the place
themselves, but it's not the usual
vintage bed and breakfast. The
rooms are straightforward, clean,
comfortable, and reasonably
priced. They come with private
baths, TVs, and Jacuzzi tubs. The
road has gotten pretty busy so you
can hear the traffic at times. But if
you go out back you can stare out
over their 5 acres of fields, take a

FARM ANIMALS AT MORNING GLORY B&B

swim in their pool, check out the llama, donkey, and chickens that Harold keeps in the barn, or sit around the bonfire pit. $.

((y)) **Alexandria House B&B** (815-206-5000; www.alexandriabnb .com), 315 Dean Street, Woodstock. Just a few blocks from the Woodstock town square, this 1865 house is run by a chef and former restaurateur who satisfies her love of cooking by serving guests breakfast of tomato Provencal, fruit with fresh cream, or eggs baked in asiago cheese bread with parmesan and rosemary sprinkled on top. Breakfast is served either in a sun-filled breakfast nook or the more formal and dark dining room. The cookie jar is usually filled with

cookies. The house has two common rooms on the main floor that can be separated by pocket doors and is decorated with pieces the owner has picked up from her world travels. All rooms have private bath. One queen room has an adjacent twin room that is a good option for families. $–$$.

((y)) **Bundling Board Inn** (815-338-7054, www.bundlingboard .com), 220 E. South Street, Woodstock. Just 3 blocks from the square, the owners have added many details to make you feel as if you've stepped back in time in their 1910 Queen Anne inn, with beds that have quilts from as far back as 1870. The inn's name comes from an old courting practice that dates back to when suitors had to travel quite a ways to meet their ladies. Because the men would have to stay the night, parents would put a board between the young couple and bundle them to it. The linens are hand-ironed for an extra touch and fresh flowers are put in every room. Every room has a basket with old magazines, such as *Life* magazines from the 1940s or *Click* magazine from 1939. In the parlor/breakfast room, guests will find a Woodstock typewriter, homage to the time when about half of the world's typewriters were manufactured in Woodstock. In the evening, guests can find hot water for tea and homemade baked goods, as well as juices and drinks in the refrigerator. No children or pets. $$.

HOTELS AND INNS

McHenry County Area
Town Square Inn (815-337-4677; www.townsquareinn.com), 112½ Cass Street, Woodstock. The inn is on the second floor of a building in the historic town square. The seven rooms were decorated by owner, Bethany Souza, who appears on HGTV's *Designed to Sell,* and has created different themes in each room. One is English manor, one a traveler's room. All have nice, modern baths. Two large suites have sweeping views of the square. The family suite with a large kitchen features a king master bedroom and twin-bed alcove. There's also a two-bedroom, two-bath suite. Rooms come with flat-screen TVs, bathrobes, refrigerators, CD players, central air, history books on Woodstock, and of course,

ALEXANDRIA HOUSE B&B

Groundhog Day DVDs in all the rooms. Guests have 24-hour access and can walk down a back stairway directly into the Woodstock Public House. $–$$.

Rockford Area

♂ **Copperstone Inn** (815-629-9999; www.copperstoneinn.com), 6702 Yale Bridge Road, Rockton. This is a definite getaway. On 130 acres, this lovely limestone inn is perched up on a hill. The property is a nice drive from Rockford, just several miles outside of small Rockton. The individually designed rooms come with private bath, TV, Jacuzzi tub, fireplace, and balcony. Some have beautiful woodwork and stone fireplaces or features, with luxury bathrooms. There are also walking trails, gardens, and outdoor areas plus a mini-spa on site where you can get massages. No children or pets. $$–$$$$.

& ♂ **Best Western Clock Tower Resort & CoCo Key Water Park** (815-398-6000; www.clock towerresort.com), 7801 E. State Street, Rockford. The exterior looks a little worn on this 1970s-era hotel, but the rooms have a somewhat updated look with exposed brick walls, gold and maroon décor, and standard all-white bedding. Rooms include desk, TV, granite counter kitchen area, very old-school hairdryer, and pinky peach tile in the bathroom. Good for families going to the water park. Rooms have a glass door going out to a little patio and outdoor pool. Hotel has

the Sundial restaurant and bar, and a coffee shop. $$.

& 🐾 (ᵞ) ♂ **Cliffbreakers Riverside Resort** (815-282-3033; www.cliffbreakers.com), 700 W. Riverside Boulevard, Rockford. The lobby has rich wood detailing, leather couches, a fireplace, fountain, and giant paintings. The guest rooms are a little more low-key, designed with rose bedspreads and framed gold pictures to match. Rooms have private baths, with refrigerators, microwaves, and coffeemakers. There are also bikes available for rent in front. Ask for a riverfront view if available. $–$$.

BUNDLING BOARD B&B

COPPERSTONE INN

CAMPING

McHenry County Area
McHenry County Conservation District (815-338-6223; www.mcc district.org) has several group campgrounds throughout the county. You can rent individual sites at Thomas Woods in Marengo Ridge, 3100 N. Route 23, Marengo, from May through October. Fees: $15–30.

Chain O'Lakes State Park (847-587-5512), 8916 Wilmot Road, Spring Grove. Campground open April through October. This state park has 150 Class-A sites, with electricity, flush toilets, and shower houses, plus a total of 87 Class-B sites that have access to showers and vault toilets. Three cabins are

available for $50 per night. They are small log cabins, but right along the waterfront. Honey Suckle Hollow campground has nice campsites along the lake as well. Electric sites: $25 per night, $35 per night on holiday weekends; non-electric sites: $12.

Rockford Area
♿ 🐾 **Hononegah Campground** (815-877-6100; www.wcfpd.org), 80 Hononegah Road, Rockton. Open mid-April to mid-November. This Winnebago County Forest Preserve campground just outside Rockton has 62 sites, electric hookups, water, and outhouses. The preserve itself fronts the Rock River. Fees: $8–15 per night.

Rock Cut State Park (815-885-3311; http://dnr.state.il.us/lands /landmgt/parks/r1/rockcut.htm), 7318 Harlem Road, Loves Park. Open year-round, this park has a giant campground with 215 Class-A sites and 60 Class B. To round out your stay, you'll find water, electricity, dump stations, a decent shower house, toilets, boat launch, and playground. There's also a store. If you'd like to be closer to the lake, keep driving deeper into the campground. You'll also find a primitive cabin available for rent there. Reservations can be made at www.reserveamerica.com. Fees: $12–35.

&. **Feather Down Farms at Kinnikinnick Farm** (512-524-1817; http://featherdown.com), 21123 Grade School Road, Caledonia. Available May through October.

For a gourmet camping experience, try a stay at Feather Down Farms' Kinnikinnick Farm location. This is one of the first of this company's forays into the US. You stay in an upgraded tent that is really more like a cabin on this family-owned working organic farm in Caledonia. You can participate in farm work or just relax among the peaceful spread of prairie, woods, and farm. There are activities for the kids—ropes to climb, sandbox, swings, bikes to ride. There are chickens and other farm animals to get to know, and you can pick up some of the farm's produce in the "Honesty Shop." (You'll add up all you've taken from the Honesty Shop at the end of the week and settle up with the farmer.) The sunsets truly are great from here, and the host

CHAIN O'LAKES STATE PARK

MACKTOWN SETTLEMENT IN ROCKTON

farmers, David and Susan Clever-
don, really nice people to know.
The tent has a master bedroom, a
bunk bedroom, flushing toilet,
cold water in the kitchen, wood-
burning cooking stove, dining
area, cooler chest, and a nook with
a canopy bed. It's outfitted with
kitchen gear and you rent linens.
There's no electricity, just candles
and oil lamps, and in the mornings
you can pull back the tent fabric
to open up the place to the farm
around you. $$–$$$.

✳ Where to Eat

EATING OUT

McHenry County Area
☥ **Doyle's Pub** (815-678-3623;
www.doylespubrocks.com), 5604
Mill Street, Richmond. Open 11–9
Tuesday through Thursday, 11–10

Friday and Saturday, 11–8 Sunday.
The bar is open later, but winter
hours may vary. In cute downtown
Richmond this pub has a full
menu of burgers, salads, ribs, pizzas, and a Friday fish fry with
beer-battered fish. Reubens and
hot wings are favorites here. The
pub is housed in the second oldest
building in town, and has a wrap-
around deck for outside dining.
Live music too. $–$$.

Jenapea's (815-206-5732; www
.jenapeas.com), 109 E. Van Buren,
Woodstock. Open 8–4 weekdays,
9–4 Saturday. The owners have
put some thought into their menu,
offering a lengthy menu of creative sandwiches. Try the Chive
Turkey with cranberry-horseradish
cream cheese, fresh chives, tomato, scallions, and lettuce on whole
grain bread. The Maple Chicken

includes maple cream cheese, maple smoked-chicken breast, raisins, red onions, and lettuce. There is also a line of paninis and grilled cheese sandwiches that get the same creative treatment. Veggie sandwiches, salads, soups, and wraps round out the menu. Outdoor seating on the historic Woodstock square available during the summer. $.

&. **The Heritage House Restaurant** (815-943-6153; www.the heritagehouserestaurant.com), 21225 E. US 14, Harvard. Open 4–9 Wednesday and Thursday, 4–10 Friday and Saturday, noon–8 Sunday. Inside this chalet-looking building with stone front and chocolate brown trim, you'll find a German-influenced menu. All dinners include soup or salad. Inside, the dark wood of the room is lightened up by the colorful stained-glass windows depicting scenes like Paul Revere's ride. $$–$$$.

((ϕ)) **Expressly Leslie Vegetarian Specialties** (815-338-2833; www .expresslyleslie.com), 110 S. Johnson Street, Woodstock. Open 11–4 Tuesday through Saturday. For a veggie-centric but tasty lunch, try this small café specializing in vegetarian, all-natural, and Middle Eastern foods. Dishes include falafel, hummus, soups, salads, and smoothies. $.

Richmond Dog N Suds (815-678-7011; www.richmonddogn suds.com), 11015 US 12, Richmond. Open 11–10 daily April through October. This nostalgic restaurant serves up an old-fashioned drive-in experience alongside its Coney dogs, corn dogs, burgers, and other sandwiches. Car hops deliver your food. And you must top off any order with a classic Dog N Suds root beer in a frosty mug that will take you back to those times when these drive-ins were everywhere. You also can get ice cream, chocolate-dipped frozen bananas, and funnel cakes. $.

Rockford Area
Dairyhaus (815-624-6100), 113 E. Main Street, Rockton. Open noon–10 daily April through October. Since 1983, this homemade ice cream shop has been pleasing passersby of this adorable limestone building on Rockton's Main Street. Hard to choose a favorite here, although many swear by the

RICHMOND DOG N SUDS

wedding cake ice cream, which indeed tastes exactly like a wedding cake. $.

& **Stockholm Inn** (815-397-3534; www.stockholminn.com), 2420 Charles Street, Rockford. Open 6 AM–8 PM weekdays and Saturday, 7–2 Sunday. Many consider this a Rockford institution for the Swedish pancakes, which are served all day long. The cooks also serve up salads, sandwiches, soups, and other Swedish specialties. Expect long lines on weekends. $.

& **Carlyle Brewing Company** (815-963-2739; www.carlylebrew ing.com), 215 E. State Street, Rockford. Open Monday 3–10:30, Tuesday and Wednesday 3–11, Thursday 3–midnight, Friday 3–2, Saturday 3–2 AM. This local brewery has a wide variety of beers on tap, and a great atmosphere with high ceilings and exposed brick. The menu is straightforward pub fare. $.

DINING OUT

McHenry County Area
((ŋ)) & **Pirro's Restaurante** (815-337-9100; www.pirrosrestaurante .com), 228 Main Street, Woodstock. Open 11–9 Tuesday through Thursday, 11–10 Friday and Saturday, 4–9 Sunday. Owner, Terry Pirro, took family recipes and ideas from his travels to create the dishes at this Italian restaurant. The dining room has exposed brick, red velvet curtains, hardwood floors, and minimalist wooden tables and chairs. You'll find

osso buco, veal marsala, fresh fish dishes, and the staples like lasagna and pizzas. Live music on Fridays and Saturdays. $$–$$$.

((ŋ)) **Woodstock Public House** (815-337-6060; http://wphdine .com), 201 Main Street, Woodstock. Open 11–10 Monday through Thursday, 11–10:30 Friday and Saturday, 11–9 Sunday. Bar is open later. *Cheers*-like in its setup, patrons walk downstairs on a side-street entrance to enter the public house in this historic building on the square. Stone walls and dark red paint warm the place. Entrees include the bleu-cheese rib eye with smashed potatoes and veggies, or jumbo prawns stuffed with crab meat and a lemon sauce. Main dishes are accompanied by soup or salad. The menu offers a little bit of everything from fajitas to gorgonzola-stuffed gnocchi for an Italian touch. Sandwiches, burgers, and salads also available. $$–$$$.

La Petite Creperie and Bistrot (815-337-0765; www.lapetite creperie.net), 115 N. Johnson Street, Woodstock. Open for lunch 11–2:30 weekdays, Saturday. Dinner: 5–9 Monday through Thursday, 5–9:30 Friday and Saturday. Breakfast: 9–2 Sunday. The location in the historic downtown square is great, especially if you are able to sit on the outdoor brick patio. The menu is French bistro fare. For dinner, choose from roasted duck with orange sauce, fish of the day, or braised lamb-shank bourguignon. The savory crepes are also available for dinner, and come with a salad. $$.

♿ **Paisano's on Broadway** (815-678-4500; www.paisanosonbroadway.com), 5614 Broadway, Richmond. Dinner service starts at 5 Tuesday through Friday, 4 weekends. Off the Main Street in Richmond, you'll find this unexpected but lovely bistro with paintings of Italian scenes and a menu of pastas, steaks, chops, and seafood. Make a reservation in advance. $$–$$$.

Rockford Area

♿ ♿ **Brio Restaurant** (815-968-9463; www.briorockford.com), 515 E. State Street, Rockford. Open 5–10 Monday through Thursday, 5–midnight Friday and Saturday. Bar is open later each night. Located among a bustling strip of restaurants in Rockford's River District, Brio is for those who are looking for a more creative approach to their food, which you will find in these small plates. You can also order flatbreads, and from an extensive wine list and drink menu. There's a cool bar with a lovely stone fireplace and a garden patio with vine-covered walls, where you should definitely sit if the weather is nice. $$–$$$.

♿ **Octane** (815-965-4012; www.octane.net), 124 N. Main Street, Rockford. Lunch: 11:30–3, dinner 5–10:30 weeknights, 5–11 weekends. A neat space, with bright walls, a wall of windows, and a swerve of a cement bar greets you at Octane. A menu of craft beers and martinis encourages you to settle in for a while. The burgers and sandwiches get their names

BRIO IN ROCKFORD

from old TV shows, like the *Father Knows Best* or the Ricky Ricardo Cuban sandwich. Menu also covers pastas, quesadillas, and small plates. The café is open serving coffee at 8 AM each day. Located in Rockford's River District, Octane also has outdoor seating. $–$$.

✷ Entertainment

BARS ♿ 🍸 **Cliffbreakers Riverside Resort** (815-282-3033; www.cliffbreakers.com), 700 W. Riverside Boulevard, Rockford. Bar open 11 AM–1 AM Sunday through Thursday, 11 AM–2 AM Friday and Saturday. With the riverside location, the views are great from the Cliffbreakers restaurant, but I'd recommend a drink in the Fauerbach Brewery Beer Hall. The taproom was built as part of the 1848 Fauerbach brewery in Madison, Wisconsin. With Prohibition and other problems, the brewery fell on hard times, and eventually, the taproom landed here. It's a cool room, with live music on Saturday. The Fauerbach grandchildren now make beer again, and sometimes you can sample it from the tap.

LIVE MUSIC/THEATER ♿ 🍸 **Kryptonite Music Lounge** (815-965-0931; www.kryptonitebar.com), 308 W. State Street, Rockford. Open 5 PM–2 AM weekdays, 8–2 Saturday. In downtown Rockford, look for the green kryptonite hanging outside the building and you've found this 200-person music venue, with live music five nights a week from local and nationally known bands. Occasionally they host outdoor music events downtown.

♿ **MetroCentre** (815-968-5222; www.metrocentre.com), 300 Elm Street, Rockford. Box office open noon–5 weekdays. With 10,000 seats, this arena in downtown Rockford welcomes hockey, soccer, and big-name concerts throughout the year.

Coronado Performing Arts Center (815-968-2722; www.coronadopac.org), 314 N. Main Street, Rockford. The Rockford Symphony Orchestra, Rockford Dance Co., and other performing arts organizations liven the stage of this historic theater, which also hosts Broadway shows, comedians, and musicians. The theater dates back to 1927.

♿ **Raue Center for Performing Arts** (815.356.9212; www.rauecenter.org), 26 N. Williams Street, Crystal Lake. Box office open noon–4 Monday, Wednesday through Saturday. Broadway shows and other performers can be seen at the 800-seat Raue Center, a 1920s historic theater in downtown Crystal Lake, where you'll find bars and restaurants too.

MOVIES McHenry Outdoor Theatre (815-385-0144; www.cyouatthemovies.com/theatres/mchenryoutdoortheatre.html), 1510 N. Chapel Hill Road, McHenry. Open Friday and Saturday seasonally. Drive-in theater

CORONADO

that programs fun older movies. Cash only. Admission:$7 adults, $4 seniors, children 11 and under.

✳ Selective Shopping

McHenry County Area
Woodstock Historic Square is a great place for shopping, centered around the quaint and charming park in the center. You'll find home interiors at Designs by Maida and Peg & Co. Cobblestones on the Square offers ice cream and coffee drinks, while Tarts & Truffles has culinary items and gorgeous miniature tartlets. Read Between the Lynes is a friendly book store, while Green Box Boutique stocks eco-friendly home furnishings, gifts, and children's items. Browse through the racks in the pink and sherbet-colored Lulu's on Benton Boutique, which mixes new items with consignment and stocks all sizes from XS to 3X.

Richmond Antique District is another nice place to browse. Located at IL 12 and Broadway, you'll find a number of decent shops and restaurants.

Rockford Area
♂ **McEachran Homestead** (815-978-5120; www.mceachran homestead.com), 1917 Wyman School Road, Caledonia. Open 9–5 Wednesday through Friday, 11–3 Saturday. Visit a sesquicentennial farm at the McEachran Homestead, which was originally settled in 1857 by the great-great-grandfather of the current owner. Today it is a 285-acre farm with corn, soybeans, garden produce, grapes, and raspberries. The family also makes its own wines from its 1 acre of vineyard, and jams, jellies and juices, which you can purchase at the farm. They will also provide a wine tasting for you.

Rockton For an enjoyable small-town shopping experience, I'd recommend the Main Street of

RICHMOND

Rockton. Eccentricities offers home interiors and you'll also find a couple antique stores to wander, like Main Street Antique Mall.

Chocolat by Daniel (815-969-7990; www.chocolatbydaniel.com), 211 E. State Street, Rockford. Open noon–9 weekdays, noon–10 Friday and Saturday. The gorgeously crafted chocolates at this shop in downtown Rockford are made by Daniel Nelson, who learned from Valrhona's L'Ecole du Grand Chocolat in France.

JR Kortman Center for Design (815-968-0123; www.jrkortman .com), 107 N. Main Street, Rockford. Open 10–6 Monday through Saturday. Downstairs, you'll find art glass, jewelry, and many modern pieces in this design-focused

shop. Upstairs is a gallery with a rotating exhibit space.

CherryVale Mall (815-332-2440; www.shopcherryvalemall.com), 7200 Harrison Avenue, Rockford. Open 10–9 Monday through Saturday, 11–6 Sunday. More than 130 stores, including all the big names.

✳ Special Events

June: **Milk Days** (815-943-4614; www.milkdays.com) First weekend in June. This annual festival in Harvard celebrates the town's dairy-farming heritage with food, parades, performances, bed races, and pageants where kids are dressed in costumes made out of crepe paper, a tradition initiated about 50 years ago.

September: **On the Waterfront** (815-964-4388; www.onthewaterfront.com) Downtown Rockford. Four-day music festival over 25 city blocks that brings performers, children's music, food vendors, a carnival, and arts and crafts. There's also a 5K run.

The Mississippi River 3

GALENA

This was once the western frontier. With a well-preserved downtown and historic places that seem very much alive, Galena can transport you back to that time, just like it does for the 1.2 million people who visit here each year. When town governments try to create Main Streets nowadays, they ultimately want to achieve what Galena has: charming authenticity. Historical plaques mark some of the town's bigger moments, lending credibility. I counted just a couple illuminated signs on the main strip; all the rest were painted wooden signs that really create a peaceful streetscape, kind of like a small mountain town out West. One unusual feature about Galena's roads is the red shade of the concrete, which also lends to the attractiveness of the downtown area.

Even if "shopper" is not a word generally associated with your name, you still may find yourself entertained by the broad array of shops here. A shop for garlic? Why, of course. Knitting? Gourmet food products? Fine imported chocolates? Boutique baby wear? How about a shop that blends country crafts with Cubs paraphernalia? And within each shopping category, you'll find quite a range of styles, from country casual to sleek sophistication.

Then comes mealtime. There are so many options it can be difficult to narrow it down, but this is a good problem to have. I've tried to help you below in the Where to Eat section. Plan to spend some time—and money—here. The list of hotels, bed and breakfasts, inns, cabins, and resorts is equally lengthy. And Galena has a large number of private owners who put their homes up for vacation rentals through companies. The homes are a good option for families or groups of friends who want to pool their resources and rent a larger house as their home base for the vacation.

In short, Galena is worth the trip just for the inviting Main Street, restaurants, shops, and lodging. Now if you take this historic downtown and tuck it among the gorgeous hills and valleys of Jo Daviess County, then you truly have something extraordinary. As you drive into Galena, the

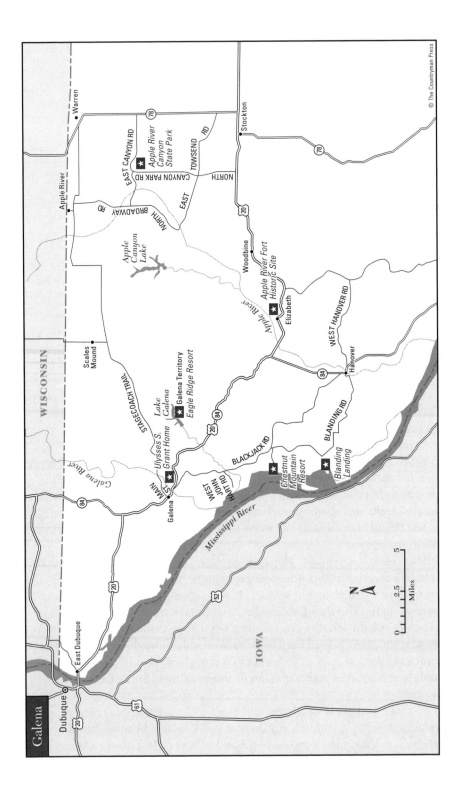

Galena

WISCONSIN

Warren

Apple River

Apple Canyon Lake

Scales Mound

STAGECOACH TRAIL

Galena River

East Dubuque

Dubuque

IOWA

Mississippi River

EAST CANYON RD
EAST CANYON PARK RD
Apple River Canyon State Park
NORTH BROADWAY RD
EAST CANYON RD
NORTH TOWSEND RD

Stockton

78

78

20

Woodbine

Apple River

Apple River Fort Historic Site

Elizabeth

WEST HANOVER RD

Hanover

84

Lake Galena

Galena Territory
Eagle Ridge Resort

Ulysses S. Grant Home

MAIN ST

Galena

WEST JOHN HART RD

BLACKJACK RD

Chestnut Mountain Resort

BLANDING RD

Blanding Landing

20

84

52

61

20

N

0   2.5   5
Miles

© The Countryman Press

view that greets you is of the white steeples of buildings stretching above the tree line. The town itself stretches up a hillside, so long staircases—with as many as 190 steps overall—have been built to get you from one street level up to the next one above it. A recreational trail snakes alongside the Galena River that cuts through the middle of town, perfect for biking, hiking, or running.

Galena was originally called La Pointe. With lead mines stretching across northwestern Illinois, workers were drawn to the area around Fever River, which is now the Galena River, in the 1820s. In 1826, the town name was changed to Galena (Latin for sulfide of lead.) With its river location and nearby mines, Galena's townspeople took full advantage of the river economy and built the town into a major steamboat stop, hauling out the lead and positioning itself as the major port north of St. Louis. As a town marker brags: GALENA BECAME A THRIVING CITY WHEN CHICAGO WAS STILL A SWAMP VILLAGE.

The 1840s brought the construction of some of the grand homes you'll find today. But the mining industry soon faltered because all the lead had been mined out. The river started to gather silt, further complicating things. The final nail in the coffin for the vibrant, bustling town came with the railroad. As more products were shipped by rail, the river commerce dried up along with the river. With the railroad, Chicago emerged as the transportation hub, leaping ahead of Galena.

GALENA STEPS

The river wreaked more havoc on the downtown through a devastating 1937 flood. Afterward, work began on a major flood-control project, the results of which were unveiled in 1948. You may notice flood-control gates as you enter the downtown area.

The downtown shriveled until artists and other history buffs discovered the area and were able to make others see beyond the crumbling facades of the buildings. In 1969, the historic district was

HISTORIC GALENA

added to the National Register of Historic Places. The historic district covers 85 percent of the city, and the buildings are maintained as they appeared in 1859.

In the 1980s, these energetic backers of Historic Galena also formed a foundation to support the town's ongoing restoration efforts. Today, downtown Galena is an example of successful revitalization and historic preservation efforts.

Beyond the boundaries of Galena, Jo Daviess County is also a great place to go for a drive. The rural roads sweep you through hilly terrain with stunning pastoral views. Today, those gorgeous green fields produce hay, dairy and beef cattle, oats, corns, beans, and pumpkins, making agriculture the second largest revenue-producing industry in the county and feeding the quaint farmers' markets and restaurants that focus on local produce.

Galena offers a variety of itineraries: An adventure weekend mixing river recreation and hiking with filling meals and some shopping, or you can flip the focus and plan a weekend of shopping as the main activity, with wineries, great meals, a short hike in the surrounding parks, or a long drive through the hilly countryside to sample the landscape.

GUIDANCE If you're near Main Street, pick up a pile of brochures or seek out advice at the historic **Market House**, 123 N. Commerce Street, Galena. Open 9–4:45 daily. On the other side of the river, try the **Galena/Jo Daviess County Convention & Visitors Bureau** (877-464-2536; www.galena.org), 101 Bouthillier Street, Galena. Open 9–5 Sunday through Thursday, 9–6 Friday and Saturday, from April through November. Hours reduced to 10–5 during the offseason.

GETTING THERE *By auto:* Driving is your best option for getting to this region. From Chicago take I-90 West towards Rockford. (It's a toll road so you will need either an I-PASS unit or plenty of change for tolls.) Exit US 20 West toward Freeport and Galena. US 20 is a four-lane highway that is separated by a grassy median, so traffic moves pretty quickly given there are no problems. The closer you get to Galena, the more amazing the view outside the car window. Whoever designed the roads in these parts selected a route along ridges and hilltops so that you have amazing views of the green-blanketed valleys below. On the way, you'll pass through small towns that are just a few storefronts.

By air: **Dubuque Regional Airport** (563-589-4127; www.flydbq.com) Located 6 miles south of Dubuque, Iowa, on US 61, this airport is about a 30-minute drive from Galena. American and American Eagle airlines operate flights out of this airport in neighboring Iowa.

GETTING AROUND *By auto:* US 20/IL 84 is a nice stretch to take to get to some of the other sites in Elizabeth and the Galena Territory. So is Stagecoach Trail, which you can access from downtown Galena by following Main to Meeker, taking a right and following the left curve around until it becomes Field Street. Field Street then becomes Stagecoach Trail and will take you up toward Apple Canyon Lake.

MEDICAL EMERGENCIES **Midwest Medical Center** (815-777-1340; www.galenahealth.org), One Medical Center Drive, Galena. From downtown Galena, head west on US 20 to Norris Lane, take a left and the drive will be on your right. Midwest offers round-the-clock emergency care by board-certified emergency physicians.

✳ Wandering Around

EXPLORING BY CAR Head in just about any direction from Galena and you will find a scenic drive. If you head south of Galena along Blackjack Road (accessed off 4th Street) you'll have a tour along a curvy, green route that takes you to many resorts and inns near the Mississippi River. You can take the road all the way to Hanover.

EXPLORING BY TROLLEY ♪ **Galena Trolley Tours** (815-777-1248; www.galenatrolleys.com), 314 S. Main Street, Galena. The company offers a one-hour narrated tour that covers downtown, mansions, generals' homes, and museums. The tour leaves daily every hour from 10–5 April through October. Call for hours from November through February. Tickets: $18 adults, half price for kids 12 and under. A longer two- to three-hour tour that includes a visit to the Grant Home, Dowling House, and Belvedere Mansion leaves at 11 and 2 daily. Tickets: $44, which includes admission to the sites. Note that the Grant Home is closed Monday and Tuesday. You can also take a haunted tour of Galena by trolley, which runs daily at 6:30 and 8 PM. Tickets: $25.

♿ **Tri State Trolley** (815-821-2402; www.tristatetravel.com) Tours depart at least five times a day from May through October, and on weekends in November. A 1940s-style San Francisco trolley takes you on a one-hour tour of the historic town, where the tour guide will tell you about lead mining, the Civil War, the steamboat era, and the merchants' homes on Prospect Hill. Tickets: $15 for adults, $10 children under 10.

EXPLORING BY FOOT Just start anywhere along Main Street and venture into the cafes, restaurants, and shops. You may want to investigate the town further by heading up to Bench Street, just west of Main (and a little above it), or farther up the hill to Prospect. But be prepared for the challenge of the stairs. Bench Street has a number of pretty churches and the history museum. If you want something a little more official, try the walking tours offered by the **Galena Historical Society** (815-777-9129; www.galenahistorymuseum.org). Knowledgeable guides lead a one-hour trip down Main Street on Saturdays from May through October. The guides are armed with tidbits of information and can point out buildings where U. S. Grant worked and where *Field of Dreams* was filmed. Tours start at 10 in the lobby of the DeSoto House Hotel, 230 S. Main Street. Cost: $5.

✳ Towns and Villages

Galena Territory You may notice a number of signs for Galena "Territory." This is a private resort community that encompasses Lake Galena. The sprawling resort and golf courses of Eagle Ridge are located here.

Elizabeth (www.elizabeth-il.com) With a population of just about 700, Elizabeth is a small street of shops located on a hill. The Apple River State Fort is on one corner, the railroad depot museum on the other. It's a decent place to pick up a coffee or have lunch while you're out exploring the countryside.

VIEW FROM APPLE RIVER FORT

❋ To See

MUSEUMS ⚓ **Chicago Great Western Railway Depot Museum**
(815-858-2343; www.elizabethhistoricalsociety.com), E. Myrtle Street,
Elizabeth. Open 11–3 weekends, May through October, call for an
appointment during offseason. A bright, shiny orange train car and the
maroon railroad depot make great backdrops for photos, but train lovers
will be intrigued by the collection of artifacts inside. Walk through the
restored Milwaukee Road caboose, and the depot, which was built in
1888. It's still on the original site and has a spot on the National Register
of Historic Places. The museum's collections are dedicated to preserving
the history of the Chicago Great Western Railway and other railroads of
Northwest Illinois, so you'll find things like an exhibit on the Winston tunnel, the longest railroad tunnel ever constructed in Illinois. The kids can
create their own railroad stories on a Lego table and most likely will enjoy
seeing the 10 operating model trains in the depot. Admission: $3 adults.

 ⚓ **Galena History Museum** (815-777-9129; www.galenahistory
museum.org), 211 S. Bench Street, Galena. Open daily 9–4:30 year-round.
For a small-town history museum, Galena has amassed an impressive collection of artifacts. You may want to start your day here to learn the backstory of this unique locale. It's a great foundation to have before moving
on to the other historic sites. Housed in the 1858 Daniel Barrows

CHICAGO GREAT WESTERN RAILWAY DEPOT MUSEUM

mansion, the museum includes exhibits on the Civil War, on important local industries like lead mining and steam boating, and on costumes and textiles from the 1830s–1930s. You can peer down an original 30-foot lead mine shaft from the 1830s to really get a sense for the cramped dark conditions area miners worked in. An old switchboard may be fun for a reminder of life before cell phones. The collections also include a banner from Ulysses S. Grant's 1868 presidential campaign, the famous *Peace in Union* painting of Lee surrendering to Grant, items from his family's leather store, Civil War records, Galena pottery, and a cigar butt that President Grant dropped after learning he lost the nomination for a third term in 1880. Admission: $7 adults, $6 seniors, $5 for youth 10 to 18 years, free under 10 years. Maximum family rate: $18.

✐ ↑ **Chicago Athenaeum Museum of Architecture and Design** (815-777-4444; www.chi-athenaeum.org), 601 S. Prospect Street, Galena. Open noon–5 Friday through Sunday year-round. Located in the old Fulton Brewery building, this museum is focused on promoting good design and has a collection of architectural models, drawings, and photographs as well as examples of graphic design and industrial design. Some highlights of the collection include a Herman Miller chair, Frank Lloyd Wright desk, and a model of the Skyneedle building proposed in Chicago that would have been taller than the Sears/Willis Tower but was never built. There are also revolving exhibitions. This is the western Illinois branch of the Chicago Athenaeum, which has other locations in Chicago and around the world. Free.

HISTORIC SITES Apple River Fort State Historic Site (815-858-2028; www.appleriverfort.org), 311 E. Myrtle Street, Elizabeth. Open 9–4 Wednesday through Sunday. Positioned on a hill overlooking the surrounding valley, the Apple River fort was attacked by the famous Native American warrior Black Hawk in June 1832. The settlers built a fort because they had been worried about an attack during the Black Hawk War. As the settlers started firing at the approaching Sauk and Fox warriors, Black Hawk assumed the settlers were well resourced and decided his followers should instead turn back, get what they could from the cabins nearby, and head out. A local historic foundation hired an archaeologist to locate the site. Once the site had been identified, work started on reconstructing the fort, even constructing it with the same tools and materials the settlers would have had. Tall upright logs form a perimeter fence that protects the site from the outside. You can view a film and a small exhibit that provides context for the story at the visitors center. Once there, you may find "settlers" in period clothing making food inside the fort or carrying out other chores.

Dowling House (815-777-1250), 220 Diagonal Street, Galena. Open 11–4 weekdays, 10–6 Saturday from mid-March through October. Open weekends in November. On a road veering off Main Street, you will see an old limestone structure up on a hillside. Built in 1826, the structure is considered the oldest home in Galena. It was originally constructed as a trading post with living quarters above. Only one piece of furniture has survived from that time period, a dry sink, but a fireplace and the plank floors upstairs are original. A 30-minute guided tour of the building is $9 adults, $4.50 for children ages 6 to 12. If you plan to check out the Belvedere House too, there is a combination ticket for $17 that will save a few dollars.

&. ⚲ **Elihu B. Washburne House State Historic Site** (815-777-3310; www.granthome.com), 908 Third Street, Galena. Open

APPLE RIVER FORT

BLACK HAWK

You'll find numerous references to the Native American warrior Black Hawk as you travel through Illinois, and his is an important story to understand. In 1804, leaders of the Sauk and Fox signed over some of their tribal land to the U.S. government for roughly $2,200. The government agreed to make $1,000 annual payments to the tribes. There was an agreement that the Sauk and Fox people could continue living on the land until it was sold. But when the tribes returned home from the winter hunt in 1829, and found new settlers living on their land, they were none too happy. After learning their land had been put up for sale, they started moving to the west side of the Mississippi River. But none of this sat well with Black Hawk, a warrior who had fought against the U.S. on behalf of the British in the War of 1812. He felt the land had been stolen from his people. In April 1832, he set out to take back the land, leading 500 warriors and 700 women, children, and old men up the Rock River. As the stories of this feared warrior preceded him, the governor called in the Illinois militia. Some settlers fled. There were a number of battles in the 15-week war, the last Indian war east of the Mississippi River. The war ended August 2, when the Sauk and Fox were trapped between a steamboat and Army troops. Of his followers, only 150 people survived. Black Hawk was eventually captured, sent to prison and released in 1833, only after being taken on a media tour of big cities. He was released into the custody of his arch political rival, a humiliating time for him. He died at the age of 71.

10–4 Friday, May through October. From the outside, this stately home could use a little love. A victim of state funding woes, the home is now only open one day a week. Knowledgeable volunteers give tours, which are well worth it. The story told through this important Galena family tells the history of the town itself. Elihu Washburne moved to Galena after graduating from Harvard Law. He had this Greek-Revival home built in 1844. The next year he married and in time had eight kids, one of whom became a mayor of the city of Chicago. Washburne was very active in politics, and represented the area in Congress. His three brothers also served in Congress, and together the family helped create the Republican Party. He became friends with U. S. Grant, even hosting Grant and others at his home in 1868 to await presidential election results. This night is represented in the home by a telegraph set up in the library, which is what they used to collect vote totals. Because of this, Grant was the first president to know he had won the presidency on Election Night. Washburne, who also advised Lincoln, became Secretary of State for just a few days before becoming ambassador to France. Washburne was known as a watchdog of the treasury as a congressman, so during the tour, you may notice small dog statues around the house, gifts given to him once that reputation spread. After his service in France, the family returned to Galena, but by that time the town was just a version of its former grand self, so Washburne moved to Chicago, where he was the president of the Chicago Historical Society. Only one other family lived in the home, which is just down the hill from Grant's home, until it was sold to the state in 1968. The house appeared in *Harper's* magazine in 1866, and drawings from that were used for the restoration of the house. Suggested donation: $3.

Old Market House State Historic Site (815-776-9200; www.granthome.com), 123 N. Commerce Street, Galena. Open 9–4:45 daily. The market house was set up downtown to provide a central place for vendors to show their wares. The building was constructed in 1846 and featured indoor stalls for the townspeople to set up shop. The market house carries on that tradition today with farmers' markets and other sales still held on the grounds. Inside, the site features small exhibits on Ulysses S. Grant and other subjects. This is a great place to pick up brochures or get advice about what to do in town. Suggested donation: $2.

The Old Blacksmith Shop (815-777-9129; www.galenahistory museum.org), 245 N. Commerce Street, Galena. Open 10–4 Friday through Monday, May through October. Wander into this 1897 blacksmith shop to see volunteers actually melding metals over an open fire. They know a lot about the subject and can fill you in on its importance to a town like Gale-

WASHBURNE HOUSE

na in its early years. This shop was built by Louis C. Readel and used for decades by other blacksmiths. Mr. Readel built it to be a full-service wagon shop, which is why there was a wheelwright and a farrier station, where you could have a blacksmith/veterinarian deal with any hoof issues your horse might have. Willard Richardson bought the shop in 1929 and worked as a blacksmith here for the next 50 years. His original tools are on display. The site also has a gift shop that includes a small exhibit on original blacksmith tools and demonstrations of blacksmithing. Some of the items they make on the forge are pressed with a Galena stamp and sold in the gift shop, such as bookmarks, planter stands, and fireplace sets. Suggested donation: $2.

 ♿ ⛜ **Ulysses S. Grant Home** (815-777-3310; www.granthome.com), 500 Bouthillier Street, Galena. Open 9–4:45 Wednesday through Sunday from April through October; 9–4 Wednesday through Sunday from November through March. Grant arrived in Galena to work with his family in a leather store on Main Street. While here, the Civil War broke out, and friends convinced him to return to the Army. Obviously, it was a good decision for his career. He returned a hero and soon became president. The local town leaders were so proud of Grant that they presented this home to the Union Civil War general in 1865 after his return from the war. Grant left for Washington, D.C., in 1869 to serve as president and maintained the home until his last visit in 1881. The house itself is perched up on a hill, and enjoys a stunning view of Galena. You can tour the home with a guide, who may point out the smoking stand that held the president's frequently smoked cigars. Most of the furniture is original, including the green velvet chair he took with him to the White House. The house has portraits of the family, including his wife, Julia, who didn't like to pose because she was self-conscious of her lazy eye. There are also paintings of the couple's parents. (Hers owned slaves; his were strict abolitionists, and therefore, did not attend the couple's wedding.) On the street next to the home you will find other structures that are being preserved by the state. They are not all original to the site, having been moved from other locations. Down the hill near the highway, there is an 1851 log house that was moved from its site about 10 miles east, in Elizabeth Township. The home, built by John and Mary Long, provides a glimpse of frontier life in the mid-1800s. The Longs had four kids here. A later couple, the Binns, who lived in the cabin from 1921 until as recently as 1970, had a brood of six. The grounds also feature a general store that you can peek inside. Suggested donation: $5.

CULTURAL SITES ♿ **Belvedere Mansion & Gardens** (815-777-0747; www.belvederemansionandgardens.com), 1008 Park Avenue, Galena. This grand Italianate 1857 mansion along the riverbank was the home of steamship owner, J. Russell Jones, who was also an ambassador to Belgium. Today, you can take tours of this privately owned home. The owners have filled the 22 rooms with antiques, although not all are from the period. But some exciting finds include drapes from the film *Gone with the Wind,* and a collection of Liberace's. From May through mid-November, half-hour tours start every 15 minutes, 11–3:30 Sunday through Friday, 11–5 Saturday. Admission: $12 adults, $6 children. You can purchase a combined ticket that will also get you into the Dowling House at a savings.

✳ To Do

BALLOONING Galena on the Fly (815-777-2747; 800-690-1287; www .buyaballoonride.com) Flights are offered daily at sunrise and a couple hours before sunset from early spring through October. They depart from the main inn at Eagle Ridge Resort. To see the green valleys and hills from above, a hot-air balloon flight offers a truly different perspective of Galena. You'll see parts of Iowa and Wisconsin too. The actual ride is about 45 minutes. Don't worry, it starts out at treetop level so you can get your bearings before the balloon rises to 3,000 or 4,000 feet. But you should set aside two to three hours for this venture. The balloons will land in a field somewhere, depending on the flight, and you'll be picked up by the company van and returned to Eagle Ridge. Riders must be 6 years and older. Cost: $175.

BOATING Fever River Outfitters (815-776-9425; www.feverriverout fitters.com), 525 S. Main Street, Galena. From Memorial Day through Labor Day, open 10–5 daily. Offseason: open 10–5 weekends. For canoeing or kayaking, check out this adventure-tour operation on Main Street in Galena. They'll get you out on the water for a paddle on the Fever River or on the Mississippi. You can also rent mountain bikes and scooters. The trip rates are $45 per person. A freestyle paddle is $26.

FOR FAMILIES Chestnut Mountain Alpine Slide (800-397-1320; www.chestnutmtn.com), 8700 W. Chestnut Mountain Road, Galena. The entrance road to the resort is located south of Galena off Blackjack Road. Opens Memorial Day, 10–8 weekends, call for weekday hours because they change throughout the summer. In the spring and fall, the slide is only open during weekends. In the summer, you can ride a sled down 2,050 feet of the alpine slide's track, down the mountain to the Mississippi River. A lift will take you back to the top. One sled ride is $8 for adults, $7 for children and seniors. You can buy discounted five-ride books or unlimited passes. The site also has miniature golf, mountain bike rentals, and Frisbee golf. You can also take the slide down to the waterfront to board a Mississippi Explorer cruise on the river. The trip is 90 minutes and costs $25 adults, $20 children 7 to 11, and $15 kids 3 to 6. Starting Memorial Day weekend, the cruises depart at 11, 1:30, and 3:30 weekends.

CHESTNUT MOUNTAIN RESORT

GOLF Apple Canyon Lake Golf Course (815-492-2477; www.apple canyonlake.org), 14A200 E. Apple Canyon Road, Apple River. For a scenic game, try this 9-hole golf course. Apple Canyon Lake is a private resort community but the course is open to the public. The course also has a pro shop, bar, and restaurant. Fees: $17–23 for 18 holes, $12–16 for 9 holes. Carts: $13–17 for 18 holes, $7–9 for 9 holes.

Eagle Ridge Resort & Spa (800-892-2269; www.eagleridge.com), 444 Eagle Ridge Drive, Galena. The North course is open year-round. The other courses are open mid-April to about late October, but all depend on the weather. Eagle Ridge offers four championship courses, including the award-winning The General, which opened in 1997. With its limestone cliffs and forests, the landscape is stunning. The elevation changes make for an interesting and challenging game. PGA professionals are on hand for instruction. The resort also has its original course, built in 1977, the North Course, as well as the South Course. The East Course is a 9-hole par-34 course. From late May to mid-October, the fees are $90–105 for the North and South, $110–125 for the General, and $35–45 for the East course. During the offseason, fees are $60–75 for the North and South courses, $85–95 for the General.

Galena Golf Club (815-777-3599), 11557 US 20 West, Galena. Open 7–7 daily April through October. Open to the public, this par-71 course offers a challenge and features a pro shop, bar and grill, and practice range. Fees: $30 for 18 holes, $40 for 18 holes with a cart.

HORSEBACK RIDING ✐ ❋ **Shenandoah Riding Center** (815-777-2373; www.shenandoahridingcenter.com), 200 N. Brodrecht Road, Galena. No matter your experience, the crew here promises a ride to fit your comfort level with these great beauties, all professionally trained. And the trails cut through some beautiful countryside, up hills, across streams, and into woods next to the Eagle Ridge Resort. Trail rides are available daily year-round at 9:30, 11:30, 1:30, and 3:30. There are longer rides available for intermediate riders. For children, those out for the first time can ride with a lead line. Riders must be 8 years old. Reservations required for the trail ride, which costs $40–75 per person depending on the trail.

✐ **Stage Coach Trails Livery** (815-594-2423), 5656 Stagecoach Trail, Apple River. If you are traveling in a group or can get one together, you may want to arrange for an authentic stagecoach ride. The cost is $125 for 6 to 8 adults to take an hour's ride down through scenic territory to a river bottom. Call several days in advance for reservations. In the winter, the operators also offer sleigh rides when weather permits.

SKIING ((•)) ✐ ❋ **Chestnut Mountain Resort** (815-777-1320/800-397-1320; www.chestnutmtn.com), 8700 W. Chestnut Mountain Road, Galena. With a 475-foot vertical drop, it may not exactly fit some people's definition of a mountain, but compared to the flatness otherwise seen throughout the Midwest, the word seems appropriate here. During the winter, the resort is all about skiing and snowboarding and accommodates those at all skill levels. The ski shop also offers equipment rental. Skis, boots, and poles can be rented for $30 per day. The resort's winter terrain park has 7 acres of quarter pipes, half pipes, rails, and box jumps for snowboarders. Weekend lift tickets: $45 adults, $35 children, seniors. Weekday tickets: $35 adults, $30 children, seniors.

TOURS **Annie Wiggins Ghost Tour**s (815-281-0408; www.ghostsof galena.com), 1004 Park Avenue, Galena. Tours depart from the Annie Wiggins Guest House every Friday and Saturday, May through October. Times vary. Not sure if this is *boo!* scary, but Annie Wiggins tries to show you a quieter Galena, walking past historic homes while she shares legends about the town. The tour guides are dressed in 1860s mourning wear. The walking tour runs about an hour and is designed to share the story of this town with you in an atypical way. Tickets: $10. Reservations required.

WINERIES **Galena Cellars Vineyard & Winery** (800-397-9463; www .galenacellars.com) Tasting Room is at 515 S. Main Street, Galena; Vineyard Tasting Room is at 4826 N. Ford Road, Galena. Three generations of the Lawlor family are involved in making more than 40 varieties of wine from local and imported grapes. The tasting room is located in an old vine-covered building when you first enter the downtown shopping area. Tastings in the Main Street tasting room are from 9–8 Monday through Saturday, 9–6 Sunday, from June through December. Hours are reduced in the offseason. At the vineyard, sample wines from noon–6 Monday through Thursday, noon–8 Friday through Sunday from June through October. Tours are given daily at 2 and 4. The first tasting is free. You can get six tastes for $3.

♂ **Rocky Waters Vineyard and Winery** (815-591-9706; www.rocky watersvineyard.net), 2003 W. Hanover Road, Hanover. Tasting room open 10–6 Monday through Saturday, noon–4 Sunday. The Spahn family transformed this property into a vine nursery in 1994. They kept the deer and cattle away from their beloved vines with an electric fence, but when it was removed one weekend for a repair, cows trampled the plantings, leaving just a portion remaining. The oldest grandchild in the

BLANDING LANDING

crew suggested the name Rocky Waters because of the rocky stream through the property, but it was also considered fitting for what the family considered a rocky start. The first grapes were sold to Galena Cellars in 2001, and the Spahns started making their own wine in 2004. Tastings in the cabin-like dark-wood-walled room are $5 per person, and include 5- to 6-ounce samples of everything from their dry Tower Red to a sweet Hillside Rosé.

✳ Green Space

Galena River Trail (815-777-9772; www.cityofgalena.org) To find nature very close to downtown, head over to the trailhead at Depot Park, just below the US 20 bridge. You'll find several miles of crushed limestone that is wonderful for biking, running, and hiking. In the winter, some use it for cross-country skiing. The trail hugs the Galena River, then heads through forests towards the Mississippi River. Parking is available along the river at the trailhead. There is also a boat launch.

&. **Apple River Canyon State Park** (815-745-3302; www.dnr.illinois .gov), 8763 E. Canyon Road, Apple River. Grounds open sunrise to sunset year-round. About 35–45 minutes outside Galena, this small but picturesque state park also has five trails, great for hiking or running. Primrose Trail is a 1-mile crushed rock path that runs parallel to the cliff, past white pine trees and red oaks marked by woodpeckers. Peer out through the trees, and you're overlooking a steep slope down to the river canyon below. Keep an eye out for mourning doves, great blue herons, or ruby-throated hummingbirds. The park also has a large green picnic area down on the riverfront. During the booming mining times, a town called Millville thrived here until it was bypassed by the railroad. A flood then virtually wiped it out in 1892. The original site of the town in the park has been added to the National Register of Historic Places. The 297-acre park also provides great fishing access, as the clear, cold water is stocked with trout every spring. No boating or swimming allowed.

Blanding Landing (www.mvr.usace.army.mil/missriver/Recreation /BlandingLanding.htm) Blanding is west of Hanover in Jo Daviess County. We felt a little lost on the drive to this park, but I mean that in a good way. The location is remote and off the beaten path. The U.S. Army Corps of Engineers manages this site, which includes a campground (see Lodging). Once you find the spot, there's a pier for fishing and a boat ramp on the Mississippi River.

✳ Lodging

There is no shortage of great places to stay in Galena. I've listed some of my favorite inns, bed and breakfasts, cabins, and resorts. There are also a number of chain hotels, but I've included just one in here because it's a good option for families traveling with small children. In addition, you'll find numerous private homes, cottages, and condos are available for rent. If you want to go that route, contact one of the vacation rental companies. All are open year-round unless otherwise indicated.

A+ Reservations by Dixie (888-801-3111; www.galenareservations .com) Choose from one- to five-bedroom homes throughout the area, including Apple Canyon Lake and Galena Territory. $$–$$$$.

Amber Creek (800-781-9530, 815-777-2713; www.ambercreek .com), 5148 US 20 West, Galena. Rent one- to six-bedroom homes in the Galena Territory and Galena.

BED AND BREAKFASTS ((p))
Annie Wiggins Guest House (815-777-0336; www.anniewiggins .com), 1004 Park Avenue, Galena.

On the east bank of the river next to the Belvedere Mansion, this beautiful 1846 mansion skillfully combines the feel of a bed and breakfast with modern comforts. The plum-colored bed and breakfast is just across the river from the downtown area and offers a wonderful view. The baths are modern and new, but their style helps them blend with the look of the rooms, furnished in 1860s antiques. The owners also run the Ryan Mansion bed and breakfast, and Annie herself (known in real life as Wendy Heiken) rotates

ANNIE WIGGINS GUEST HOUSE

pieces through the house to keep it interesting. During a recent visit, she had her daughter's wedding dress on a mannequin in a front sitting room. You may also want to listen if she shares any stories, as she runs Annie Wiggins's Ghost Tours as well. While staying here, you'll also have a nice outdoor space, with a small garden, fountain, and patio. All rooms have a private bath, queen beds, and come with a full breakfast. Some also have two-person tubs and fireplaces. $–$$$.

((•)) **Ryan Mansion Bed & Breakfast** (815-777-0336; www .ryanmansiongalena.com), 11373 US 20 West, Galena. Built in 1876, this large ornate mansion outside of downtown is open for tours or for a stay. In Minnie's room, sleep in a four-poster bed with sheer curtains draped around the bed. The rooms include private baths, queen beds, and a full breakfast. The garden cottage has a king bed and living area, and the grounds also feature 2 acres of gardens and a pergola. Rooms: $–$$$. Tours of the house are available about every 15 minutes in which "servants" are dressed up in period costumes. Open 10–3:30 Friday through Tuesday year-round. Tours: $10 adults, $5 children.

((•)) **The Steamboat House** (815-777-2317; www.thesteamboat house.com), 605 S. Prospect Street, Galena. For a bed and breakfast close to the historic downtown area, the Steamboat House sits on a hill in a residential section of town, just off Spring Street. Filled with antiques, the 1855 home also has a billiards room, central air, a screened gazebo porch, and gardens. The original owner was Daniel Smith Harris, who was a steamboat captain. The rooms will detail the story of his wife Sarah (interesting fact: She became a doctor at the age of 50) and their 10 children. The five guest rooms include fireplaces, queen beds, flat-screen TVs, and DVD players. "The Bess" room also has its own screened-in porch. The owners serve wine every evening. $$.

INNS ♿ (ᵞ) ♂ **Goldmoor Inn** (800-255-3925; www.goldmoor .com), 9001 Sand Hill Road, Galena. These rooms are a definite splurge, as the inn seems designed to make you feel like a guest at a castle. With granite countertops in the bath and kitchenette area, two-person tubs, complimentary beverages in the refrigerator, dark wood armoires, and special touches like mini chess sets and jeweled pillows, there are plenty of extras here. Many rooms also share in the stellar view of the Mississippi River below. The inn was fully remodeled four years ago and hosts many events and weddings. It also has lovely screened-in dining rooms overlooking the river and a patio with a view of the garden. Rooms include robes, heated towel bars, and a full breakfast in your room or in the dining room. Suites have dining areas with views. The inn has cottages and cabins also available with many of the same amenities as the rooms but with a screened-in porch. $$$–$$$$.

GOLDMOOR INN

((ᵀ)) **Abe's Spring Street Guest House** (815-777-0354; www.galenabedbreakfast.com), 414 Spring Street, Galena. Artist Charles Fach and wife, Sandy, are your hosts in this 1876 building near downtown Galena. The building has 27-inch thick limestone walls because it was constructed as an icehouse, to hold up to 800 tons of ice in the upstairs level. The couple also owns the former brewery next door and can fill you in on the history of the beer maker and the site. The two rooms have king beds, private baths, full breakfast, TVs, DVDs, central air, fireplaces, and private entrances. You will see Charles's artistic touch in the handmade tiles surrounding the fireplace and in a wrought-iron bed and other pieces around the rooms. There is a spa room next door at the Artists' Annex that you can use, and it comes with a sauna, hot tub, and a deck. No pets. $–$$.

Galena Cellars Lodging (800-397-9463; www.galenacellars.com), 4826 N. Ford Road, Galena. Just 10 minutes outside of town, you can tour the vineyard or stay in a cozy suite above the tasting room. The suite is located in a large house with a view of a quiet piece of the valley. The suite sleeps four, with a living room, kitchen, bedroom, 1.5 baths, a two-person whirlpool tub, and private deck. A more-plain looking 2-story farmhouse is also available with two bedrooms. $$.

((ᵀ)) ♂ ☙ **LeFevre Inn & Resort** (815-777-3929; www.lefevreinn.com), 9917 W. Deininger Lane, Galena. Perched high on a hill, LeFevre advertises "amazing views and unforgettable sunsets," and certainly delivers. The inn is spread across a few different buildings, but all 11 rooms in the inn have wood-burning fireplaces, small living areas with a sofa sleeper, flat-screen TVs, DVDs, refrigerators, and coffeemakers. The modern, clean, private baths include a standup shower and some have whirlpool tubs. All have decks or patios. The property also has a lake with a sand beach, a gazebo, and outdoor pool. A larger suite, which includes a full kitchen, and two-bedroom cottages are also available for rent. $$.

CABINS ♿ ☙ **Galena Log Cabin Getaway** (815-777-4200; www.galenalogcabins.com), 9401 W. Hart John Road, Galena. The log cabins offer an authentic experience on a 45-acre resort. I mean authentic because the cabins were made in the style of 1820 pioneers and constructed without the use of nails. Inside, you'll find one large room that covers 660 square feet with an open loft above that holds a second bedroom. The cabins also have a private bath with double whirlpool tub, heat, central air, refrigerator, gas fireplace, satellite TV, DVD, skylight, queen bed downstairs, and a double bed in the loft. The nearby alpaca farm adds an unusual but intriguing twist. The property also has more than 2 miles of trails and has trademarked itself as Galena's Dark-Sky Site, meaning that the rural location and lack of lights makes it so you can actually see many, many stars. Dogs are OK. $$.

RESORTS (ᵗᵖ) ♂ Chestnut Mountain Resort (815-777-1320/800-397-1320; www.chestnutmtn.com), 8700 W. Chestnut Mountain Road, Galena. Reminiscent of a Swiss lodge in the Alps, this resort is the logical place to stay if you're taking advantage of the skiing, alpine slide, or other recreational opportunities at the resort. With the relatively new restaurant, the Sunset Grille, and its patio overlooking the mountain below, you can ski, eat dinner with a lovely view, then head back to your room without having to travel anywhere. The rooms, while clean, are a bit dated, with key locks on the doors still. However, rates are affordable. $–$$.

(ᵗᵖ) ♂ & Eagle Ridge Resort & Spa (800-892-2269; www.eagleridge.com), 444 Eagle Ridge Drive, Galena. Eagle Ridge sprawls across a beautiful part of the valley, and with its fine dining, championship golf courses, and spa, it has a country club feel. (And some country club price tags.) But the resort offers a few different options for lodging that make it a good choice. For a couple or smaller group, choose from guest rooms in the 80-room inn. The inn has a café, store, bar, and restaurant with views of Lake Galena as well as an indoor pool,

steam room, and sauna. You can also rent a villa, which are townhomes spread throughout the Galena Territory that have anywhere from one to three bedrooms and come with full kitchens and views of the woods or golf course. There are also large homes available for rent throughout the territory as well. The homes, which feature from three to eight bedrooms, have full kitchens, gas grills, and fireplaces. I would consider the villas or homes if I had a large group. Both the villas and homes include daily housekeeping, grocery delivery, and shuttle service to the resort. You may be charged extra for pools, hot tubs, and pets. The resort does provide great activities such as biking, horseback riding, and cross-country skiing. Inn rooms: $$–$$$. Villas: $$–$$$. Homes: $$$$.

HOTELS & (ᵗᵖ) DeSoto House Hotel (815-777-0090, 800-343-6562; www.desotohouse.com), 230 S. Main Street, Galena. The DeSoto helps visitors imagine the Main Street of yesteryear. With the large block letters on the side, and flags draped over the balcony, you can see the carriages on the road and people visiting on their way to the frontier. Opened in April 1855 with 255 rooms, this was the largest luxury hotel in what was considered the northwest at the time. Abraham Lincoln and Stephen Douglas both spoke from its balcony at different points. But, as Galena faltered, so

DESOTO HOUSE HOTEL

did the hotel, and in 1880 the two upper floors were removed. You can learn more about the history of the hotel by viewing a short film played in the atrium library. The hotel also celebrates its historic roots in the current design, with the names of historic figures who visited Galena—such as the presidents and generals—hanging on each door. Today, the hotel has 55 guest rooms, decorated in Victorian style, with queen or king beds, TVs, hairdryers, and coffeemakers. Parking is included in the indoor garage. No pets. $–$$$.

✄ ᒼ (ꙩ) **Country Inn & Suites** (815-777-2400; www.countryinns .com/galenail), 11334 Oldenburg Lane, Galena. This is a good option for families as the hotel has an indoor pool with large water-slide. Younger children and toddlers who may not meet the height requirements for the water-slide may like the smaller, fenced-in children's pool that has a large frog slide in the center. And one nice feature about Galena is that even the chain hotels have great views. Here, many rooms overlook a green valley and feature queen or king beds, TVs, refrigerators, and coffeemakers. Breakfast, including some hot items, is served buffet style in the dining area. Larger one-bedroom suites are also available. $–$$$.

ᒼ (ꙩ) **The Irish Cottage** (815-776-0707; www.theirishcottage .com), 9853 U.S. Highway 20, Galena. The owners were inspired to locate the Irish-themed inn here because the Galena landscape reminded them of Ireland.

The dark woods and red walls of the 2-story atrium leave a warm first impression as you walk in the lobby. A wall of windows overlooks an expansive view of the green valley. The library and pub were handcrafted in Ireland, shipped to Galena, and reassembled by the craftsmen. Besides the authentic Irish pub, you will find touches of the Irish throughout the hotel. Each room is marked with a county crest on the door, with details inside about the room's crest. Original prints from Irish artist Roisin O'Shea adorn the guest room walls; above the doorways you'll find St. Bridget's cross, a traditional blessing to a household in Ireland. From the outside, the hotel is designed to look like a streetscape in Ireland. The 75 rooms include a king or two queen beds, TVs, and coffeemakers. The inn also features a fitness center, pool, and spa. $–$$.

(((ŋ))) ✿ **The View Motel** (815-858-2205; www.theviewmotel.net), 2500 US 20 West, Elizabeth. Closed in March. Budget friendly and basic, the motel offers a first-class view. In fact, the motel is located very close to an observation tower built to show off the wonderful view of the valley from this hill. The 11 rooms have a bath and shower, one or two queen beds, flat-screen HDTV, air conditioner, free coffee, and tea. There's a phone and microwave in the lobby and an outdoor fireplace on the grounds. No pets. $.

CAMPING Apple River Canyon State Park (815-745-3302; www.dnr.illinois.gov), 8763 E. Canyon Road, Apple River. Open mid-April through October. This is a great campground to use as a base, as it's not too far a drive from Galena and all the sites. The park has a well-maintained campground called Canyon Ridge, with sites surrounded by dense walls of mature trees. Canyon Ridge backs up to a steep canyon ridge (hence the name), has 49 primitive sites at $8 per night, and one electric site for $18. The park also has a dump station, outhouses, and two sites that are handicap accessible. There are no reservations. Sites are given out on a first-come, first-served basis.

Blanding Landing Recreation Area (877-444-6777 for reservations; www.mvr.usace.army.mil /missriver/default.htm) Open mid-May through October. The campground is located on the river's edge, 8 miles west of Hanover. To get there from Galena, take Blackjack Road south to Blanding Road. Once you are on Blanding, follow signs to Blanding Landing. On the drive, you'll wind through some remote places, with gravel roads that have a European countryside feel. The 37 campsites are right on the river, 30 with electricity. The sites are in an open area, so there aren't really any trees or natural separations for the sites, making it a good option for group camping. The campground also has a playground, flush toilets, shower building, and dump station. Sites: $10–14.

✳ Where to Eat

EATING OUT

Galena

Galena is a great dining destination. I can't possibly list all the options here, so I've included a mix. Note that in the wintertime, when the town is entertaining fewer visitors, some hours may be reduced.

✐ **Durty Gurt's Burger Joynt** (815-776-9990), 235 N. Main Street, Galena. Open 11–8 Sunday through Thursday, 11–9 Friday and Saturday. As a rule, I hate purposeful misspellings, which are found throughout this restaurant, but the burger here did win me over. It's also a good place for kids. Durty Gurt's takes a unique approach to its décor in almost trying to chase the customers away at the doorway with toilets in the foyer. The dining room is designed to look like an old shack or outhouse, with bumper-sticker-like phrases painted on the walls. One example: DINNER CHOICES: #1 TAKE IT. #2 LEAVE IT. The burgers are giant and stuffed with extras so it's hard not to get dirty with them. Some may get frustrated that they're hard to eat with two hands, and have to break down and use a fork. The menu starts with some basic burger options, then moves on to more adventurous choices like the "Greektown," which has feta, gyro meat on top, and Greek tzatziki sauce. The "Obama" features bacon, cheddar, pineapple, and mango mayo. To be fair and balanced in my reporting here, I feel compelled to include that the "Sarah Palin" comes with grilled onions, BBQ ranch, mozzarella and cheddar cheeses, and onion rings. For the really hungry diner, there is the "Woo! Wop! The Bam!" which is four patties of meat. I repeat, *four patties of meat.* Choose from fries that are homemade on site, seasoned fries or sweet potato fries. You can also go for a greener route, with the large Grecian or Mango salads. The menu is rounded out with thick "boozey" shakes such as the "peppermint patty" with peppermint schnapps and chocolate. A decent option for kids, although the portions for them seem overly large as well. $.

The Green Street Tavern (800-343-6562; www.desotohouse.com), 230 S. Main Street, Galena. Open 11–9 Sunday through Thursday, 11–11 Friday and Saturday. Hours reduced in winter. The tavern is one of the restaurants located in the historic DeSoto Hotel. It is going for the bar-and-grill feel in décor and menu. You can have a casual lunch with a Philly beef sandwich or caesar salad. At dinner the choices expand to steaks and seafood dishes. The site, which has been a saloon and a telegraph office at varied points in its history, also has outdoor seating along a prime downtown location. $–$$.

The DeSoto also operates **The Generals' Restaurant**, which is open for dinner 5–9 Saturday and serves specialties like the "drunken soldier," which is chicken marinated in tequila and lemon/lime juice. Other menu selections include Wiener schnitzel, pasta, seafood, and steaks. $$–$$$.

✏ **Procento's Pizzeria** (815-777-1640; www.procentos.com), 105 Franklin Street, Galena. Open 11–10 Wednesday through Monday. The specialty here is the double-decker pizza, which is two thin-crust pizzas layered on top of each other. We enjoyed their traditional thin crust. (Procento's passed my test for pizzerias in that they used fresh mushrooms instead of the rubbery canned kind, a key indicator of whether a place understands what fresh means or not.) The menu also includes decent salads, calzones, pastas, and sandwiches. Like many visitors before him, owner, Jack Edens, was taken with Galena on a vacation, and decided to move his family there. In 2006, he opened the restaurant, transporting his recipes from Double D Pizza in Waukegan to the new location. $.

Boone's Place Restaurant & Pub (815-777-4488; www.boones place.com), 515 S. Main Street, Galena. Open 11–8 Monday through Thursday, 11–10 Friday and Saturday, noon–7 Sunday. Above the Galena Cellars Winery tasting room in the historic downtown, you will find this pub, which has bar seating, booths, and tables inside, or an outdoor deck if the weather is nice. There's a lengthy appetizer menu if you're just grabbing a beer or glass of wine, or a list of entrees ranging from rib eyes to grilled salmon. The stuffed potatoes are a bit unusual in that with the stuffings, they're nearly a meal themselves, as some come filled with ham, veggies, cheese, and bacon. The menu includes vegetarian and children's items. $–$$.

Elizabeth

(((y))) **The Welcome Inn** (815-858-2254; www.elizabethwelcomeinn.com), 102-104 N. Main Street, Elizabeth. Open 11–9 Tuesday through Thursday, 7 AM–10 PM Friday and Saturday, 7 AM–8 PM Sunday. On the main street near the Apple River State Historic Fort, this bar and restaurant has large breakfasts of three-egg omelets or steak and eggs. For lunch, the samplings expand to include burgers, and other hot sandwiches with sides of soup, tossed salad, chips, or fries. Dinner entrees include pork, steak, seafood, and chicken dishes. High-back brown leather booths are dressed up with wine bottles from local vineyards. Portions are large, especially with the sandwiches, I probably had a pound of ham on my lunch sandwich. There's also a salad bar, and an attached bar. $–$$.

E-Town Coffee Co. (815-820-2326; www.etowncoffeeco.com), 141 N. Main Street, Elizabeth. Open 6–6 daily. If you're looking for a caffeine pick-me-up to fuel you through some shopping or a stroll through the nearby state park, this Main Street café in downtown Elizabeth may fit the bill, especially if you're getting an early start, as they open at 6 AM every day. The café also makes paninis, bagels, and breakfast wraps in addition to cappuccinos, lattes, and just plain old coffee. $.

DINING OUT

Galena

111 Main (815-777-8030; www.oneelevenmain.com), 111 N. Main Street, Galena. Open 11–9 Sunday through Thursday, 11–10 Friday and Saturday. The attached lounge is open until 1 AM Friday and Saturday. A wood sign hanging out front says DINE AT GALENA'S TABLE, and the creators of this local-food restaurant have worked hard to create this table. The emphasis on local farmers, produce, and flavors is reflected in the dish descriptions and specials that detail where the apples have been picked or the sausages made. The restaurant also introduces you to these regional food producers through fine black-and-white portraits that adorn the walls of the modern, exposed-brick dining room, showing each person in his or her element. Arnold of Arnold's Farm is holding a pig. Other local products include Iowa beef, Door County cherries, and Galena Cellars mushroom gravy. Share a Galena River Cheese board or Chef Ivo's Five Alarm Wings (using sauce from the Galena Canning Company). The dish presentation and attention to detail definitely adds to the whole experience, even though this is still a place where jeans are fine. Behind the hostess station, you'll find a small gift shop with wine-themed gifts. $–$$$.

Fried Green Tomatoes (815-777-3938; www.friedgreen.com), 213 N. Main Street, Galena. Open 5–9:30 Monday through Thursday, 3–10:30 Friday through Sunday. Of course, there are fried green tomatoes on the menu, lightly breaded with mozzarella cheese and marinara, but there's also escargot, and roasted bulbs of Galena Garlic served with brie. Entrees include espresso-encrusted filets, chicken piccata, Dijon-encrusted snapper, giant crab legs, and spicy spaghetti. The owners sought out a building with historic ties to locate their Italian-themed restaurant and they found it in the stone walls and brick columns here, in the building where Grant's family had their leather store. $$–$$$$.

Vinny Vanucchi's (815-777-8100; www.vinnysgalena.com), 201 S. Main Street, Galena. Open 11–10 daily. I would try to score a seat on the outdoor patio that you'll find tucked halfway up the stairs from Main Street to Bench Street. Known as the "cappuccino garden," it's a lovely place if the weather cooperates. Inside, Vinny's has also created a bistro area and other dining spaces. The menu is straightforward Italian that takes pride in family recipes and lineage. Co-owner, Deb Coulter doubled, and then quadrupled, family recipes to build the menu here, modeled after dishes her "Nana Lu" made on Taylor Street in Chicago's Little Italy neighborhood. The Italian specialties here include baked and stuffed pasta dishes, all named after family members. An excellent wine selection is available as well, along with homemade olive oils and other sauces that you can buy on site. $$–$$$.

 Vines Bar (815-777-4800; www .vinesgalena.com), 216 E. Commerce Street, Galena. Open daily at 4, except for December through April, when it is closed Monday. For martinis or wine flights, head to this wine bar connected to the Flying Horse Restaurant. It's a good choice for dessert too, if chocolate flights assembled by a Galena chocolatier sound good to you. The menu also includes cheese flights, appetizers like crab cakes and bruschetta, sandwiches, burgers, flatbreads, and soups. The martini list stretches on from A to Z and there's an interactive quiz to help you decide between the Appletini or the Zues martini. $–$$.

Fritz and Frites (815-777-2004; www.fritzandfrites.com), 317 N. Main Street, Galena. Open 11:30 until last customer leaves, Tuesday through Sunday. You'll find this French bistro/German restaurant almost near the end of Main Street, under the pretzel logo

sign. As the owners say it's "a little French, a little German, a little bistro." Warm yellow walls and black-and-white tiled floors back up the bistro part of that. The blended menu includes dishes like mussels, escargot, Wiener schnitzel, salmon with lingonberry, and steak frites. $$.

Goldmoor Inn Dining (815-777-3925; www.goldmoor.com), 9001 Sand Hill Road, Galena. Open 11–2 for lunch, 5:30–9 for dinner Thursday through Monday. Similar to the inn, if you'd like a splurge, make a reservation here. If the weather is nice, try for the outdoor patio with stunning views of the Mississippi River, although the views from inside aren't bad either. Start with French onion soup or a Tuscan house salad. Appetizers include a cheese plate or seared ahi tuna served with wasabi aioli and ginger soy sauce. Entrees, which come with a house salad, bread, and seasonal vegetables, include beef Wellington, blackened catfish, or chicken breasts stuffed with spinach, goat cheese, and sun-dried tomatoes. The chef also prepares daily specials. $$–$$$.

Log Cabin Steakhouse (815-777-0393; www.logcabingalena .com), 201 N. Main Street, Galena. Open 4–9:30 daily. The backstory here starts in Greece, where owner, Frank Rigopoulos, was born. He came to Chicago in 1954, working in his uncle's Chicago restaurant as a dishwasher. He eventually opened his own restaurant in DeKalb and moved to Galena in 1975 to open the Log Cabin. The menu includes seafood dishes like Alaskan King Crab, along with Mississippi catfish, pork chops, and aged Angus steaks, which the family is especially proud to serve "charred and bursting with flavor." Of course a few Greek dishes populate the menu, like Greek chicken cooked using a family recipe. Free parking on Commerce Street. $$–$$$$.

✱ Entertainment

BREWERY ❦ Galena Brewing Co. (815-776-9917; www.galena brewery.com), 227 N. Main Street, Galena. Open 11–11 Wednesday through Monday. In the mid 1800s, Galena had nine breweries. Prohibition killed the local brew scene here, but in spring 2009, Warren and Kathy Bell decided to revive the Galena brewery and began making two beers: a hefeweizen called Fevre River Ale and an amber called Miners Treasure. With a new space on Main Street, they expanded their line of beers and profile. The pub has a menu of tapas, soup, salads, and sandwiches. $.

LIVE MUSIC ❦ Frank O'Dowd's Pub (815-776-0707; www.theirishcottage.com), 9853 U.S. Highway 20, Galena. Open 4–1 Monday through Thursday, 11:30 AM–1 AM Friday through Sunday. Part of the Irish Cottage hotel, this pub has a calendar of live music and entertainment including Irish dancing, Celtic music, and other acts. Frank O'Dowd was the hotel owner's Irish grandfather. The mahogany, oak, walnut, and stained-glass pieces were handcrafted in Ireland and shipped to Galena to give it a true authentic feel of a quality Irish pub. The pub has a menu of traditional Irish dishes. Shepherd's Pie, Paddy's stew, and fish and chips are all a good bet here. And of course, there's a good selection of imported beers. $–$$.

✱ Selective Shopping

Main Street Galena offers just about every kind of store. It's the kind of shopping district to wander. Note that during the offseason winter months, many shops reduce their hours.

Poopsie's (815-777-1999; www .poopsies.com), 107 S. Main Street, Galena. Open 10–6 Sunday through Thursday, 10–9 Friday and Saturday. If you're looking for a gift to inspire someone with a phrase, or get a laugh, Poopsie's has many to choose from, along with toys, cards, vases, and unique gifts like hand-painted wine glasses. The key descriptor here is the word fun.

Pollyhops (815-776-9912), 101 S. Main Street, Galena. Open 10–6 Sunday through Thursday, 9–9 Friday and Saturday. Next door, Pollyhops gets slightly more specific, offering unique baby-shower, bachelorette-party, and wedding gifts, along with other general gift items.

& **Galena's Kandy Kitchen**
(815-777-0241), 100 N. Main
Street, Galena. Open 10–9 daily.
Offseason: Open 10–5 weekdays,
10–9 Friday and Saturday, 10–5
Sunday. Grab a bag and fill up on
whatever you'd like. The jellybeans are separated out by flavor
so you can get the perfect mix for
yourself, along with chocolates.
The shop has packaged candies as
well. Usually you will see chocolates, fudge, or toffees being made
on the back counter. The kitchen
was opened in 1974 by George
Paxton, whose family had a tradition of making small batches of
hand-dipped chocolates. George's
father invented the "Chuckles"
jelly candy in the 1920s. Though
George has passed on, the chocolates are still hand dipped according to his philosophies.

**The American Old Fashioned
Ice Cream Parlor** (815-777-
3121), 102 N. Main Street, Galena. Open 11–9 daily. Closed
December through April. Appropriately named, this shop has the
traditional long counter and old
iron ice cream-store chairs. The
parlor also features original cabinets from the 1846 shop, and an
old-fashioned fountain from 1927.

Galena Canning Company
(815-777-2882; www.galenacan
ning.com), 106 S. Main Street,
Galena. Open 8–8 weekdays, 8–10
weekends. Taste buds will be put
to work with the samples in this
crowded but lively shop. Many of
the salsas, sauces, and other good-
ies are made on site with the

owner's recipes. The story goes
that Chef Ivo Puidak moved to
Galena in 1993 and decided to
start bottling his salsas and jams,
just like everyone was asking. He
started out at the farmers' market
at Market House and was selling
out. His line today includes everything from BBQ sauce to fruit
butters and mustards.

Chocolat (815-776-7777; www
.letustemptyouwithchocolat.com),
229 S. Main Street, Galena. Open
10–6 Sunday through Thursday,
10–8 Friday and Saturday. Sleek
and silver, this chocolate shop has
mirrors shining all the light on the
perfect-looking chocolates in the
display case. Here you will find
Valrhona bars, and chocolates
imported from Belgium, Switzer-
land, and Germany. The offerings
also include homemade chocolates, gourmet coffees, and sugar-
free and vegan chocolates.

Galena Candle & Bath Co.
(815-777-3060; www.galena
candle.com), 114 N. Main Street,
Galena. Open 10–6 Sunday
through Thursday, 10–8 Friday,
10–9 Saturday. Create your own
candle, body lotion, or soap here.
For $10.99, use Eco-dots to build
your candle, layering colors in
whatever order you like. The candles are made from all-natural
biodegradable soy wax. You can
then add scents like clean linen or
graham cracker to the candle to
further personalize it. The same
approach is available for bath
products as well.

Vintaj Earth (815-777-3900; www.vintajearth.com), 214 N. Main Street, Galena. Open 10–5:30 Monday through Thursday, 10–6 Friday, 10–7 Saturday. The design of the room aims to take you outdoors, with a side room that looks like a wood cabin, and tree branches artfully placed on the walls. The handmade jewelry featured on the walls and shelves are like pieces of art themselves.

Galena Antique Mall (815-777-3440), 8201 US 20 West, Galena. Open daily 10–5. If you're up for some digging, head west of town to the antique mall to search through jewelry, old toys, and furniture.

ART GALLERIES Brio Art Gallery (815-776-1010; www.brio galena.com), 116 S. Main Street, Galena. Open 10–5 daily. This gallery carries ceramic works, etchings, glass, jewelry, painting, drawings, and sculpture. They also host events throughout the year.

Hello Galena (815-777-1448; www.hellogalena.org), 121 N. Commerce Street, Galena. Open 9–5 Friday through Sunday, 10–2 Monday, Thursday. To get a sense of the local art scene, this store showcases the work of 50 Galena artists in various media: paintings, crafts, pottery, jewelry, stained glass, and photography, among others. Some of the artists may even be there to welcome you.

Stone House Pottery & Gallery (815-777-0354; www.stonehouse potterygalena.com), 418 Spring Street, Galena. Open year-round 10–5 Thursday through Monday and by appointment Tuesday and Wednesday. Artist Charles Fach's works are on display here, as are other local artists, in this very cool old limestone brewery building. Mr. Fach also periodically demonstrates the art of pottery, on the weekends at the Artists' Annex a few buildings down.

West Street Sculpture Park (815-777-9591; www.weststreet sculpturepark.com), 620 S. West

STONE HOUSE GALLERY

Street, Galena. Open dawn to dusk. The gallery here is an outdoor park that is the backdrop for sculptures created by John Martinson, who moved to Galena in 1979 to operate the blacksmith shop and gallery. Free.

✴ Special Events

March: **Wine Lover's Weekend** (815-777-3938; http://wineloversweekend.com) The last weekend in March, the town becomes devoted to wine, with many local restaurants hosting events. Winery tours, a grand wine tasting, and wine dinners are also involved.

May: **Galena Triathlon and Duathlon** (www.galena.org/triathlon) This sprint-distance triathlon and accompanying duathlon takes competitors through Jo Daviess County. The swim is in Apple Canyon Lake and the finish at Eagle Ridge.

June: **Great Galena Balloon Race** (www.greatgalenaballoonrace.com) More than 20 hot air balloons are usually raced in this three-day event. Includes live music, ale festival, and other activities. Hosted at the Eagle Resort & Spa. Free.

September: **Historic Galena Home Tour** (www.galenahistorymuseum.org) Visit five historic homes open to the public for this weekend only.

October: **Galena Oktoberfest** (www.galenaoktoberfest.com) Wiener dog races, live music, polka dancing, German food, and beer celebration the first weekend in October.

November: **Nouveau Wine Festival** (800-397-9463; www.galenacellars.com/nouveau/) An annual celebration of Galena Cellars latest nouveau.

NORTH RIVER ROAD
(SAVANNA TO QUAD CITIES)

T he North River Road that clings to the banks of the Mississippi introduces you to a number of small river towns and the grand Mississippi Palisades. The views from the palisades are inspiring, and the surrounding state park offers great hiking and camping. Nearby you will find the brick streets of historic Mount Carroll, the windmill of Fulton, the ancient mounds of Albany, and the sister cities of Moline and Rock Island.

North of Savanna, start at the Mississippi Palisades State Park. With its great campground and trails, the park could fill your travel itinerary all by itself. Even if you're just driving through, be sure to check out the observation points. The view from these bluffs may divert you for the rest of the day.

As half of the famous "Quad Cities," Moline and Rock Island, like many river cities, are both trying to find a balance between feeding the industry important to the local economy while also embracing the natural recreation possibilities presented by the river. With its John Deere Commons, arena, and Bass Street Landing, Moline replaced a suffering industrial strip with a center for hotels, restaurants, and shops. Rock Island has come quite far in this endeavor as well, unveiling a beautiful, gleaming riverside park in 2010 to complement "the District," a landscaped, pedestrian-friendly area with bars, restaurants, and stores. While they both still have work to do, I've included sites here that are worth seeing.

Both cities' riverfronts include a bike trail that connects with waterfront trails north of the Quad Cities, creating one long path that stretches on for miles and is known as the Great River Trail. Touring by bike is one of the better ways to take in this new riverfront area. The trail allows you to get more intimately acquainted with the shoreline area from Rock Island north to Savanna.

The Mississippi River serves as the border between Illinois and Iowa, separating Rock Island and Moline from the other Quad Cities of Bettendorf and Davenport. Several bridges link them. The 946-acre island in the

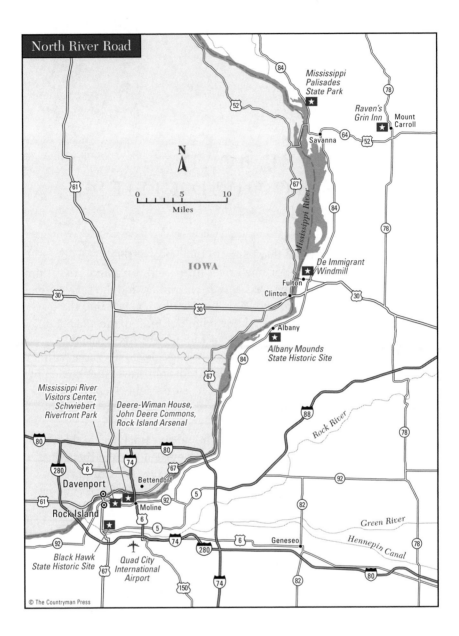

Mississippi
Palisades
State Park

Raven's
Grin Inn · Mount
Carroll

Savanna

IOWA

Miles

0   5   10

N

Mississippi River

De Immigrant
Windmill

Fulton

Clinton

Albany

Albany Mounds
State Historic Site

Mississippi River
Visitors Center,
Schwiebert
Riverfront Park

Deere-Wiman House,
John Deere Commons,
Rock Island Arsenal

Rock River

Davenport

Bettendorf

Moline

Rock Island

Geneseo

Green River

Hennepin Canal

Black Hawk
State Historic Site

Quad City
International
Airport

© The Countryman Press

middle of the Mississippi is home to the Rock Island Arsenal, an active
U.S. Army facility with an intriguing history worth exploring. More than 78
agencies are located on the island and roughly 8,000 people work there.

The area is also bordered by the Rock River, which curves around the
southern border of Moline and Rock Island. While the rivers are beautiful

at points on the landscape, at times the towns must battle the rising waters to protect against flooding.

When it comes to Moline, you cannot understand the city's history without knowing the story of the John Deere Co. Mr. Deere, a blacksmith from Vermont, settled in the western Illinois town of Grand Detour. While there, he invented the self-cleaning steel plow in 1837, which solved a key problem of farming the sticky soil of the Midwest. That sticky soil clung to the cast-iron plows being used at the time, requiring farmers to stop often to clean off the dirt, slowing down the process. In 1848, Mr. Deere moved his company to Moline to be near the Mississippi. Interest in his design exploded as did his empire. He died in 1886, but his heirs led the company for another century. Today more than 50,000 people around the world are employed by the company.

AREA CODES The area codes for this region are 309 and 815. You may also see some numbers with a 563 area code from over the river in Iowa.

GUIDANCE & **Blackhawk Waterways Convention and Visitors Bureau** (815-946-2108; 800-678-2108; www.bwcvb.com), 201 N. Franklin Avenue, Polo. Open 8:30–4 weekdays. This visitors bureau covers communities like Mount Carroll in Carroll County, as well as Whiteside County along the river and neighboring Lee and Ogle counties.

& **Mississippi River Visitor Center** (309-794-5338; www .missriver.org), Arsenal Island, Rock Island. Open 9–5 daily. If you enter the island from the Rock Island side, the visitor center is on the north side of the main road and is a good place to learn how the U.S. Army Corps of Engineers protects river towns from flooding. Exhibits on the locks and dams system explain how the Mississippi River is a "stairway" of water, with

FULTON WINDMILL

29 "steps" from Minneapolis to St. Louis. Boats travel the steps through the lock system. Throughout that distance, the river level falls about 420 feet. The locks, along with Dam 15, were completed here in 1934—the first on the Upper Mississippi—with the aim of controlling the Rock Island rapids, a dangerous section of the river. Then there is the story of the bridges that connect people across the river, like Government Bridge, which has a swing span that turns the bridge 360 degrees. The center also underscores the importance of rivers to commerce and hints to what you may see in the barges traveling down the river. The primary commodities moved on this particular river are gasoline, kerosene, and fuel oil from the oil fields of Texas and Louisiana. Coal is also shipped, along with grains. You'll find a good range of brochures and tourist information and a ranger to answer any questions. From the observation deck, you can watch the boats in action. Note: you must present a photo ID to enter the island. Foreign visitors must register ahead of time by calling 309-782-2686. Tours of the lock and dam depart at 11 and 2 on summer weekends or by appointment. Free.

THE DISTRICT IN ROCK ISLAND

GETTING THERE *By auto:* For a riverfront route from the North, take IL 84, which will take you past Mississippi Palisades State Park and river towns. Mount Carroll is 10 miles east of Savanna on IL 64. I-80 will drop you at the Quad Cities from the east or the west. I-88 (Reagan Memorial Tollway) also is an option if you're coming from Chicago. I-74 will get you to the Quad Cities from the South.

By air: **Quad City International Airport** (309-764-9621; www.qcairport.com), 2200 69th Avenue, Moline. American Eagle, AirTran, Delta, and United Express fly out of this airport, with flights to Chicago O'Hare, Dallas-Fort Worth, Atlanta, Orlando, Detroit, Memphis, Minneapolis, and Denver. Free parking for the first hour.

JOHN DEERE COMMONS

By train: **Amtrak** (800-872-7245; www.amtrak.com) has a station in Moline at 1200 River Drive, and routes that connect Moline with other Illinois cities. Open 24 hours, but there is no ticket office at this location.

GETTING AROUND *By auto:* IL 92 runs close to the river through Moline and Rock Island. I-74 cuts through Moline, offering a good north-south route.

By bus: **The Loop** (563-344-4110; www.qctransit.com) Runs 5 PM–1:30 AM Thursday through Saturday, 11:30 AM–6 PM Sunday. Quad City bus route with stops in Rock Island's District at 18th Street and 2nd Avenue, the Botanical Center and Expo Center; in downtown Moline at 15th Street on 5th Avenue, John Deere Commons and Bass Street Landing. There are stops in downtown Davenport, East Davenport, and Betten-dorf, including the Isle Casino. Buses also have bike racks. Fares: $1 per trip to be paid with exact cash or a token, $3 for unlimited day-use pass.

The Metro also has bus routes through the Rock Island and Moline areas (309-788-3360; www. gogreenmetro.com). Stops marked with blue and green signs. Fares: $1 adults.

MEDICAL EMERGENCIES Trinity Hospital (309-779-5000; www .trinityqc.com), 2701 17th Street, Rock Island. Trinity Regional Health System has four hospitals in the area, including this 338-bed location in

Rock Island, with a Level II trauma center. The system also has a smaller hospital in Moline at 500 John Deere Road, with an emergency room.

✳ Wandering Around

EXPLORING BY CAR Great River Road (877-477-7007; www.great riverroad-illinois.org) This 550-mile route follows the eastern shore of the Mississippi and is a great way to get to know the river towns along it. IL 84 and IL 92 from Savannah to Rock Island comprise the Great River Road for this region.

EXPLORING BY FOOT Schwiebert Riverfront Park Rock Island unveiled this new riverfront park in the summer of 2010, showing off the open-air stages, interactive fountain, dock, rain garden, promenade, bike trail, and green spaces, all with a sweeping view of the Mississippi. The park is near restaurants and shops in The District.

EXPLORING BY BIKE Great River Trail The trail is a 62-mile stretch of bike path from the Quad Cities to Savanna. The trail begins/ends at Sunset Park in Rock Island. Throughout Rock Island and Moline, the path is a bike trail. Elsewhere it may include roads. In Moline, you can take a short side trip to enter Sylvan Island, a former steel-factory site that's been converted to recreational use. You can access the path at Sunset Park, or Ben Butterworth Parkway in Moline.

The Rock Island Arsenal Bike Trail is a 6-mile loop around the island. But this is an active military base, so be careful about not straying off the

THE DISTRICT IN ROCK ISLAND

FULTON RIVERFRONT

trail. On the island, you must use a helmet, as that's part of the regulations here. You can get a bit closer to some of the historic sites than you otherwise may get, such as the 1867 clock tower building, or a pier that was part of the first railroad bridge that stretched across the Mississippi. The bridge was completed on April 21, 1856, and struck by a steamboat two weeks later. The incident resulted in a major legal battle that involved Abraham Lincoln as the counsel for the railroad. The case set legal precedent, giving river traffic the right-of-way over railroads. The bike trail starts at the visitor center, and parking is available there as well.

EXPLORING BY BOAT Channel Cat Water Taxi (309-788-3360; www.qcchannelcat.com), 2501 East River Drive, Moline. Taxis operate Memorial Day through Labor Day 11–7:40 Monday, Tuesday; 11–7:50 Wednesday, Thursday, 9–7:15 Friday through Sunday. During September, it runs 9–7:15 weekends, weather permitting. Taxis depart about every 30 minutes. The water taxis run along a circular route, looping from John Deere Commons Landing to the Ben Butterworth Parkway at Celebration Pier, then on to stops in Bettendorf and East Davenport before returning to Moline. All-day tickets: $6 adults, $3 children.

Celebration River Cruises (309-764-1952; www.celebrationbelle.com), 2501 River Drive, Moline. Ride in the 800-passenger riverboat, the *Celebration Belle*. A 90-minute sightseeing cruise is offered from 2–3:30 on certain dates from May through September, and swings you by Lock and

BASS STREET LANDING IN MOLINE

Dam 15 on the Mississippi River. The captain narrates the ride, sharing some old river lore. Several themed cruises, overnights, daylong, or mealtime cruises are also offered. General tickets: $13 adults, $9 children.

✳ Towns and Villages

MOLINE RIVERFRONT

Mount Carroll Built on a hill, the town of about 1,700 is also the county seat and home of the Campbell Center for Historic Preservation Studies, located on an old college campus with beautiful Georgian brick buildings. The center hosts museum professionals from around the country. A significant portion of the town is a National Historic District. With 100-year-old brick streets, the buildings here draw interest because of their decorative metal facades. There's also a Lorado Taft statue in the courthouse square.

Fulton The first settler, John Baker, was the original namesake for the town, formerly known as Baker's Ferry. In 1859 the name was changed to Fulton, named after the inventor of the steamboat. A port between the upper and lower Mississippi, Fulton hosted a busy lumber industry, and drew many Dutch families, the first one arriving in 1856. In 1965, the town was flooded and became an island, but a levee was built in 1980 and now protects the town. A landscaped hiking and biking trail is also on the riverfront. President Ronald Reagan's parents were born and married here. They lived at 907 12th Avenue. See the family burial plot at Fulton Catholic Cemetery on North 4th Street. Today the city is home to about 3,800 people.

Moline While it presents a good example of how a former industrial strip can be scrubbed up and used for recreation, Moline is still a work in progress with activity along the riverfront in Bass Street Landing. Roughly 43,000 people call it home, just like the John Deere Company does.

ROCK ISLAND ARSENAL MUSEUM

Rock Island With its renewing riverfront, this city of about 40,000 people is home to the Black Hawk State Historic Site, and Augustana College, a 115-acre campus with 2,500 students. The college was founded by Swedish settlers in 1860 and is now affiliated with the Evangelical Lutheran Church. A spin around the Broadway Historic District reveals some of the fantastic architecture of this district. The new riverfront park is definitely worth a visit.

✶ To See

MUSEUMS ⟵ ☂ **Rock Island Arsenal Museum** (309-782-5021; http://riamwr.com/museum.htm), Rock Island Arsenal Island, Rock Island, Building 60. Off Rodman Avenue, turn north onto Gillespie, then right after the first large building. Open 10–4 Tuesday through Friday, noon–4 weekends. Established in 1905, this is the second oldest U.S. Army museum in the country, with a giant collection of guns displayed behind glass walls. To figure out what you're looking at, there are binders of information where you can look up information about the guns displayed. Construction on the manufacturing areas of the island got underway in 1867, and over its lifetime, the arsenal has churned out everything from meat cans to rifles. You can see a couple of the machines used to manufacture rifles and weapons in the earlier part of the 20th century. The museum's collections go way back, though, and include a British field gun surrendered in 1777 by the British Army at the Battle of Saratoga. Another interesting twist in the arsenal's history is that it was used as a Union prison camp during the Civil War. A display, including model of the camp, details the story of the Confederate soldiers held as prisoners here. The kids can get a hands-on experience with Civil War uniforms and period clothing as well as modern-day Army uniforms, which they can also try on. If you are wondering what some of the stately looking mansions on the island are, you can learn the backstory here, including the details about Quarters One—a residence built in 1870, out of Joliet limestone, to serve as a living space for the island's commanding officer and to entertain distinguished visitors. Among the distinguished visitors: Charles Lindbergh (you can see the bed where he slept). The 51-room mansion housed residents until 2008 and is now a garrison building. Free.

HISTORIC SITES Albany Mounds State Historic Site (www.state.il .us/hpa/hs/Albany_mounds.htm), S. Cherry Street and 12th Avenue, Albany. Open dawn to dusk daily, year-round. At least 39 of these prehistoric Native American mounds are still in good condition. Dating back to the Middle Woodland period, these mounds are considered older than the Cahokia Mounds. The site also has walking and bicycle trails. Free.

Black Hawk State Historic Site (309-788-0177; www.blackhawkpark .org), 1510 46th Avenue, Rock Island. Open year-round sunrise–10 PM daily. The site stretches across 208 acres along the Rock River, where the Sauk and Meskwaki lived from 1730 to 1830, and is named after the Native American warrior Black Hawk. A pioneer cemetery is also on the site and you can hike 4 miles of moderately difficult trails. The capital of the Sauk nation—Saukenuk—was next to the site. In 1780, the capital was destroyed by Americans angered because members of the tribe had helped the British during the Revolutionary War. Then in 1804, Indian chiefs signed over 51 million acres of land to the U.S. government. Black Hawk never recognized this as legitimate and fought for the British in the War of 1812. White settlers started moving into the area and the tribes were forced across the Mississippi. Black Hawk stayed put until the governor demanded he and his supporters be removed. Outnumbered by troops, he secretly moved across the river to Iowa but started planning to take back the land. The Black Hawk War, spanning 15 weeks, was the last

Indian war east of the Mississippi River. The Battle of Bad Axe ended the war, and Black Hawk was captured and sent to prison in Missouri. The warriors were released in 1833, but only after a media tour of big cities so people could see the impressive Native American warriors they were reading about in the papers. Black Hawk was returned to Rock Island and died at 71. You can see more of Black Hawk's story at the Hauberg Indian Museum (below).

&. **Hauberg Indian Museum** (309-788-9536; www.blackhawkpark.org), Blackhawk Road, Rock Island. Open 9–5 Wednesday through Sunday. Closed for an hour for lunch between 12–1. Closes an hour earlier November through February. Located in a wonderfully crafted Civilian Conservation Corps building at the Black Hawk State Historic Site, this small museum's collections include Black Hawk's metal-pipe tomahawk and a sculpture of his head, created from a plaster mold made when he was alive. The museum is the collection of Dr. John Hauberg of Rock Island. Life-sized dioramas give a sense of home life for Native Americans during the winter and summer months. The museum is filled with interesting tidbits, such as how Black Hawk had just one wife, although polygamy was not uncommon among the Sauk. You also can see a display about the village of Saukenuk. Suggested donation: $2 adults, $1 children.

Colonel Davenport House (309-786-7336; www.davenporthouse.org), north side of Arsenal Island. Open 11–3 Thursday through Friday, noon–4 weekends, May through October. From the main thoroughfare on Rodman Avenue, turn north on Hillman, head right once you get near the riverfront. George Davenport was the first white settler to make his home here in 1816, with a contract to provide food to soldiers building Fort Armstrong, which served as the military headquarters during the Black Hawk War of 1832. He helped to develop the city of Davenport, Iowa, which bears his name. This home was built in 1833, and he was killed here during a robbery in 1845. A miniature version of the home stands outside. Admission: $5, $10 for family ticket, $3 seniors and students.

Confederate Cemetery Rock Island Arsenal. South of Rodman Avenue, closer to the Moline bridge side. This pastoral field is lined with row upon row of white markers—more than 1,100 in total. From 1863 to 1865, 12,400 prisoners of war were kept here. When the first group arrived they carried with them smallpox, and without a hospital and medicine, the illness spread and wiped out hundreds of men.

&. **Deere-Wiman House** (309-743-2700), 817 11th Avenue, Moline. Tours of the home are only available on Sunday in July and August from 1–4, on the hour. Weekday tours can be arranged by appointment. Now this is a mansion. Positioned up on a hill, the sunny yellow mansion was designed for the youngest son of John Deere, Charles. The family called it "Overlook." Deere family members lived here from 1872 to 1976.

DEERE-WIMAN HOUSE

Changes were made to the house after an 1899 house fire. If you don't make it for the tour, you can always get a sense of the exterior and grounds by walking around the gardens, which are open to the public. Free.

& **Butterworth Center** (309-743-2700), 1105 8th Street, Moline. The center is on the opposite corner from the Deere-Wiman House and guided tours of the lavish 3-story home are also given on the hour, 1–4 Sunday, in July and August. The stately mansion was built in 1892, and presented as a wedding gift to the granddaughter of John Deere, Katherine Deere, and her husband, William Butterworth. Mr. Butterworth served as president and chairman of the board of John Deere Co. Flower gardens are open to the public. Parking is across the street. Free.

CULTURAL SITES & **De Immigrant** (815-589-4545; www.cityoffulton .us), 10th Avenue and 1st Street, Fulton. Open 10–5 Monday through Saturday, 1–5 Sunday, Memorial Day through mid-October. In the fall, weekday hours are reduced. A nod to the town's Dutch-immigrant roots, "De Immigrant" windmill was made in the Netherlands and dedicated on this riverfront site in 2000. It took two Dutch craftsmen 10 months to assemble the windmill. You can walk up to the observation deck out onto the riverfront, where there are benches and landscaping. The bricks in the base of the building are from 150-year-old Dutch buildings. The windmill is fully operational and volunteers mill wheat, rye, and corn. You can buy stone-ground flour at the visitor center across the street. Free. **Windmill**

Cultural Center Across the street from the windmill is this new center that opened in 2010, with models of European windmills, a children's section to teach about windmills, and small exhibits about Dutch immigrants in the town.

✄ ⚲ **Heritage Canyon** (815-589-4545; www.cityoffulton.us), 515 N. 4th Street. Open 9–5 daily mid-April through mid-December, weather permitting. Be sure to drive to North 4th Street. It sort of appears as if you are walking through someone's backyard, but you will be led back to the 1800s village on the site of an old limestone quarry that was abandoned in 1954. Harold and Thelma Wierenga bought the quarry and went to work trying to preserve the Midwestern story of life in the 1800s that they saw in this site. The city took ownership of the canyon in 2005. You can tour the town hall, blacksmith shop, log cabin settlement home, doctor's office, and church, which hosts weddings. Free.

👕 ✄ **John Deere Pavilion** (309-765-1000; www.deere.com/en_US/attractions/index.html), 1400 River Drive, Moline. Open 9–5 weekdays, 10–5 Saturday, noon–4 Sunday. In this light-filled, glass-walled pavilion, you will find early versions of the famous Deere plow, tractors that you can climb on top of, a children's exhibit, and video games that allow you to plow through a field. You can also view historic film clips. Across the way is a John Deere store with toys, clothes, hats, and other collectibles. Free.

✳ To Do

BICYCLING Arnold's Bicycle Repair (815-259-8289; http://arnolds-bikes.com), 831 Main Street, Thomson. During the summer, open 10–6 Monday through Saturday, noon–6 Sunday. Call ahead, hours are reduced in the winter months or if it's slow. Rent bikes or get bike repairs if you're riding the Great River Trail. Rentals: $6 per hour, $24 per day.

RiverStation Visitor Center (309-277-0937), 1601 River Drive, Suite 110, Moline. Open 8:30–5 weekdays. During the summer, also open 10–4 Saturday. Bike rentals on the riverfront bike path from April through November. Rentals: $7 an hour, $28 a day.

FOR FAMILIES Whitewater Junction (309-732-7946), 1601 Longview Drive, Rock Island. Open 11–8 weekdays, 10–6 weekends Memorial Day through mid-August. But if the temperature is below 65 degrees, the park will not be open. Run by the parks department, this water park has pools, body slides, tube slides, tot slides, and spray areas. Kids must be 48 inches tall to use the body slide, or wear a life jacket. Admission: $7 for everyone 3 years and older.

TOURS Learn Great Foods (866-240-1650, 815-244-5602; www.learn greatfoods.com), 203 E. Seminary, Mount Carroll. For a unique dining experience that also provides an up-close look at local farms, try one of these culinary tours through Northern Illinois. Walk an organic farm, talk with the farmer, then create a fantastic meal with the fresh produce from the farm. For $105, you'll visit two organic farms and a couple gourmet food stops. The price also includes the cooking class and dinner. This tour is offered April through November. The list of destinations also takes advantage of some of the talent of local chefs. Reservations required. Tours with meals: $50–225.

& ✿ **Raven's Grin Inn** (815-244-4746; www.hauntedravensgrin.com), 411 N. Carroll Street, Mount Carroll. Open 7–midnight weekdays, 2–5, 7–midnight weekends. The tour is 60 to 90 minutes. October is obviously the busy time for this place, so you may want to make reservations in advance. Inn owner, Jim Warfield, leads most of the tours through this intriguing haunted home filled with hidden doors, secret passages, and a huge subterranean wine cellar. He tries to keep it humorous, this isn't a blood and gore-type haunted house. Admission: $12.

✳ Green Space

Mississippi Palisades State Park (815-273-2731; http://dnr.state.il.us /lands/landmgt/parks/r1/palisade.htm), 16327A IL 84, Savanna. With 15 miles of trails that wind from the riverside up to the palisade's peak, the park offers a great natural experience for any type of effort level you want. The line of steep cliffs along the river present stunning views of the water. For the adventurous, the South Trail system provides quite a challenge along extreme bluff edges that are rated extremely difficult in some places. The trail runs exceptionally close to the edge, so be careful at all times, but especially in wet conditions. The North Trail system takes the effort level down a notch but still has you on a more gradual climb. If you're short on time or feeling a bit tired, you can also drive to various overlooks, like Louis Point. There, you can access a deck that juts out high above the Mississippi River, allowing you to take in miles and miles of the landscape. The park also boasts some unique rock formations, such as the Twin Sisters, which look like human figures on the bluffs.

& ♂ ⊤ **Quad City Botanical Center** (309-794-0991; www.qcgardens .com), 2525 4th Avenue, Rock Island. Open 10–5 Monday through Saturday, noon–5 Sunday. Against the backdrop of industry and railroad tracks, which divide it from the river, the botanical center breathes light and green into the area here. The building has a pitched glass-window ceiling that pulls in light to the tropical atrium of plants below. The Sun Garden boasts 6,444 square feet of beds for the gorgeous and colorful gardens, a waterfall, and a pond stocked with fish. Outside you'll find a butterfly garden, perennials, and wildflowers. Admission: $5 adults, $4 seniors, $3 youth 5 to 12, $1 children 2 to 4.

MISSISSIPPI PALISADES PARK

✳ Lodging

CABINS ♿ **The Nest at Palisades Cabins** (815-273-7824; www.thenestatpalisades.com), Scenic Ridge Road, Savanna. Just north of Savanna and a short walk from the Mississippi Palisades State Park, these cabins nestled in the woods come with a hot tub in the bathroom, shower, deck, grill, gas fireplace, AC, TV, and DVD player. The kitchen area includes dishes, coffeemaker, refrigerator, and microwave oven. You can also take one of the free trail bikes for a spin at the park. Rates: $$.

♿ ✎ 🐾 **Bluff Cabins** (815-238-1080; www.bluffcabins.com), 1000 Calhoun Street, Savanna. These nine cabins are located about 1 mile south of Mississippi Palisades State Park, situated on a bluff. The cabins offer a rustic experience with one main room and a dormitory-style sleeping loft. They can sleep four to six people. Cabins come with cable TV, central air and heat, private bath, deck, and a kitchenette with stove, coffeepot, small refrigerator, and microwave. There's also a fishing pond on site, and fishing in the river across the road. Rates: $$.

♿ (ᵗ⁰) ✎ 🐾 **Timber Lake Resort and Campground** (800-485-0145; www.timberlakeresort.com), 8216 Black Oak Road, Mount Carroll. Campground open April through October. Cabins available year-round. Seven log cabins are available with one or two separate bedrooms, sleeping loft, private bath, kitchenette, air-conditioning, TV, and porch. No pets in the cabins. The 100-site campground is positioned around Timber Lake, with a separate area for tent camping. RV sites have hookups for water, sewer, and electric. There are two bathhouses with shower and laundry for easy cleanup, as well as a recreation building, general store, and outdoor swimming pool. Cabins: $149–179 per night. RV sites: $36–41. Tent sites: $25–33.

HOTELS Two of these entries are chain hotels, but the location makes for a good home base for exploring Moline, so I'm temporarily lifting my rule of not including chains in the listings.

&. (ᵖ) **Stoney Creek Inn** (309-743-0101; www.stoneycreekinn .com), 101 18th Street, Moline. Newer hotel along the riverfront near Bass Street Landing has 140 rooms, 10 suites, and 8 extended-stay cottages. Standard rooms have king or two queen beds, cable TV, bath, refrigerator, and microwave. Like the others, the hotel is designed with a North Woods feel. It features both an indoor and outdoor pool, spa, dry sauna, game room, fitness center, laundry, business center, and a bar. Rates: $$–$$$.

&. (ᵖ) **Radisson on John Deere Commons** (309-764-1000; 800-395-7046 reservations; www .radisson.com/molineil), 1415 River Drive, Moline. This hotel is conveniently located near attractions and restaurants right on the river, and rooms are nicely deco-

rated, with clean white linens and accents of light gold and dark red. The hotel has an indoor pool and fitness center. There is a T.G.I. Fridays in the complex. Rates: $$.

(ᵖ) &. **Jumer's Casino & Hotel** (309-756-4600; www.jumerscasino hotel.com), 777 Jumer Drive, Rock Island. Located off I-280 at the Route 92 exit. The location is not exactly picturesque, off the side of an expressway, but if you're here, you're here to play inside, so it may not matter. The building itself looks straight out of *The Jetsons*. The art-deco look of the interior tries to balance out the bright blinking lights of the machines in the game room. The hotel has 205 guest rooms with 8 junior suites and 3 master suites. Rooms have flat-screen TVs, coffeemakers, and nightly turndown service. Facilities include indoor heated pool, Jacuzzi, fitness center, business center, four restaurants, sports bar, night club, day spa, and valet parking. The game room has 1,100 slot machines, 24 table games, and poker room. $$.

CAMPING Mississippi Palisades State Park (815-273-2731; http://dnr.state.il.us/lands/landmgt /parks/r1/palisade.htm), 16327A IL 84, Savanna. Shower buildings open from May through October. The park has a giant campground with 241 sites, but you can find some nestled into woods or on top of hills. Rates: $18–20 electric sites, $8–10 non-electric sites, $6 primitive walk-in sites.

((•)) 🐾 ✐ ♿ **Geneseo Campground** (309-944-6465; www.campingfriend.com/geneseocampground), 22978 IL 82, Geneseo. Open April through November. About 25 minutes east of the Quad Cities, you'll find this campground directly adjacent to the Hennepin Canal Trail, a 72-mile long hiking and biking trail. The canal also provides canoeing, kayaking, and fishing opportunities, and you can rent boats on site. The campground has 11 tent sites and 63 RV sites with fire rings and picnic tables. If you want to upgrade from a tent, there are also rustic camping cabins available that offer air-conditioning, a double bed and bunk beds, but no baths. The campground also has laundry, store, playground, and dump station. Rates: $22–27 RVs, $20 tents, $45 cabins.

✳ Where to Eat

EATING OUT

Moline

♿ **Dead Poet's Espresso** (309-736-7606), 1525 3rd Avenue A, Moline. Open 6:30 AM–2 PM Monday through Saturday. This café near the riverfront in Moline shares a nice courtyard area with River House Grill. You can grab lattes, cappuccinos, or an Italian soda and relax at one of the outdoor tables, or settle in for a lunch by choosing one of the straightforward sandwiches or wraps. $.

Uncle Pete's Gyros (309-762-6877), 3629 Avenue of the Cities, Moline. Open 11–9 Monday through Saturday. Casual place with take-out and outdoor seating. Many claim they have some of the best gyros around. $.

DEAD POET'S ESPRESSO

&. **Whitey's Ice Cream** (309-762-4335; www.whiteysicecream.com), 1601 Avenue of the Cities, Moline, with locations throughout the Quad Cities area. Open 10–11 daily during the summer, 10–10 Sunday through Thursday, 10–11 Friday and Saturday offseason. Started in 1933 in Moline by Chester "Whitey" Lindgren, who was named so for his white blond hair, the ice cream stores are run today by the family of Whitey's friend, Bob Tunberg. This is the place to indulge in shakes, malts, and sundaes of every flavor, although some are available with fat-free ice cream if you don't want to indulge quite that much. $.

Rock Island
&. **Blue Cat Brew Pub** (309-788-8247; www.bluecatbrewpub.com), 113 18th Street, Rock Island. Open 11 AM–3 AM Monday through Saturday. Sample some of the beers brewed on site, like the Off the Rail Ale, an amber pale ale. The pub is spread over two floors, with a dining room and bar downstairs and bar and games upstairs. The menu has some offbeat offerings like "Duck Drummies," which are served with smoked-cheese sauce. You can choose from a list of burgers (including Black Angus or salmon burgers). Pastas, steaks, and seafood dishes round out the menu. $$–$$$.

&. (ɯ) **Ganson's Neighborhood Bakery & Café** (309-786-6600; www.gansonscafe.com), 3055 38th Street, Rock Island. Open 6 AM–8 PM weekdays; 8–8 Saturday, 10–6 Sunday. Call during the winter because hours may be reduced. Crème brulee-baked oatmeal, anyone? This bakery and restaurant, located in a 1920s farmhouse near the Saukie Golf Course, offers a menu with breakfast pita pockets, and eggs Benedict with olives and jalapenos mixed in. For lunch, there's Chicago-style Italian beef, and paninis served with macaroni-pea salad, cole slaw, or cranberry sauce. Outside, there is one pear tree—original to an orchard that surrounded the property—that still produces pears that the bakery uses to make sauces and desserts. $.

&. **Atlante Trattoria** (309-788-2805), 18th Street and 2nd Avenue, Rock Island. Open 7–2 weekdays, 4–9 Friday, 5–9 Saturday. On a corner near The District, this restaurant with casual ambience has an interesting mix on the menu—New Orleans Muffulettas with a list of pastas. Quad City native and chef, Jerry Bergheger, has a special interest in Italy, that's where he met and fell in love with his wife, who now helps with the family business. Fresh made gelato rounds out the menu. Lunch: $, dinner: $$.

DINING OUT

Moline
&. **River House Bar & Grill** (309-797-1234; www.riverhouse qc.com), 1501 River Drive,

ATLANTE

Moline. Kitchen open 11–10 Sunday through Thursday, 11–11 Friday and Saturday. This Moline restaurant has a great outdoor patio, with an awning overhead in case it rains. The interior is roomy with booths, tables, or bar seating, and a calendar of live music. Salads are huge and come in versions like the BBQ chopped salad with mango salsa and avocado, or the hot fried-chicken salad. You'll also find crab-spinach-artichoke quesadillas or a regular old BLT, as well as entrees like homemade meatloaf served with garlic-mashed potatoes, green beans, and onion rings. $–$$.

&. **La Flama** (309-797-3756; www
.laflamarestaurant.com), 1624 5th
Avenue, Moline. Open 11-9 Monday through Thursday, 11–10 Friday and Saturday, noon–8 Sunday. The Garcia brothers opened their own restaurant in 2004, showcasing their own family recipes from Mexico. You'll find the spicy fajitas and chicken tortilla soup are popular. They also have taken their mom's white rice dish, which they enjoyed as boys, and put their own mark on it. The brothers moved to a modern airy space in downtown Moline in 2010. For those who can't make their final selection to order, you can always select three Mexican classics to make your own combo dish—combining enchiladas, tostadas, sopes, tacos, or a burrito. And of course, you'll find a menu of sangria, margaritas, and Mexican beers. $–$$.

((♥)) **Exotic Thai** (309-797-9998;
www.exoticthaiquadcities.com),
3922 38th Avenue, Moline. Open 11–3 daily for lunch, 5–10 for dinner. In its sleek and sophisticated space, Exotic Thai presents Asian

dishes with healthy portions. The wraps and rolls are particularly good, especially the Vietnamese-inspired fresh roll. You also can find lettuce cups and Thai rolls. Chef Mun Luangruang is from Thailand and has created a menu of fresh salads, curries, noodle dishes, and entrees like dried chili cashew and spicy basil. The restaurant also serves wine and beer. $–$$.

& **Bass Street Chop House** (309-762-4700; www.bassstreet chophouse.com), 1601 River Drive, Moline. Open 5–10 Monday through Saturday, 5–9 Sunday. Located in the RiverStation building in Moline, this restaurant serves up steaks, chops, and seafood. Start out with some lobster corn chowder, or perhaps the char-grilled oysters, although if you're eyeing the 24-ounce porterhouse, maybe you should just get right to business. The menu also includes what they call "jet fresh" seafood that is flown in fresh, not frozen, including Alaskan King Crab Legs, and Chilean sea bass. $$$–$$$$.

Rock Island
& **Le Figaro** (309-786-4944; www.lefigarorestaurant.com), 1708 2nd Avenue, Rock Island. Open 5–10 Tuesday through Saturday. Located in the Rock Island "Dis-

LE FIGARO

trict," the Eiffel Tower on the sign gives a hint of the experience inside. Chef Rachid Bouchareb brings style to signature dishes such as escargot, chateaubriand, duck a l'orange, and frog legs. Filet mignon is prepared with different sauces, and the menu also features seafood, chicken dishes, and dessert offerings that change daily. There's an extensive list of over 90 wines. You also can have a drink and some tapas at the attached Star Bar, where the restaurant menu is available. Reservations recommended. Entrees: $$$.

✳ Entertainment

During the summer, you may find concerts at the **Plaza at Bass Street Landing** in Moline. Located along the riverfront, the outdoor patio area has tables, umbrellas, and a nice outdoor stage. White lights add sparkle to nighttime events. The bike and walking path wind right past it, too. In Rock Island, there's The District, with a covered stage and landscaping throughout. It definitely brings in area college students with beer specials and the like, but there are restaurants, cafes, and a courtyard with mosaic displays and ivy growing on the walls.

LIVE MUSIC Rock Island Brewing Company (309-793-1999; www.ribco.com), 1815 2nd Avenue, Rock Island. Open 5 PM–3 AM Monday through Satur-

day. You can find live music here Thursday through Saturday in all kinds of different forms, from jam bands to bluegrass, country to punk. During the week, you also may find people playing Rock Band on a big screen or singing karaoke. Named after a local brewing company that was shut down during Prohibition, the pub takes their commitment to beer seriously, with more than 100 beers in bottles and 14 on tap. The menu carries hearty pub fare.

& **i wireless Center** (309-764-2000; www.iwirelesscenter.com),

ROCK ISLAND BREWING CO.

1201 River Drive, Moline. This arena pulls in some big name artists and shows. It also hosts sporting events. Purchase tickets through Ticketmaster or at the box office 10–5:30 weekdays, 10–2 Saturday.

MOVIES The Great Escape Theater (309-764-0683; www .greatescapetheaters.com), 4100 38th Street, Moline. This theater with stadium seats carries first-run films. Admission: $9.50 adult, $7 seniors, children, and matinees.

✱ Selective Shopping

& **Great River Road Antiques** (815-589-3355), 23080 Waller Road, Fulton. Open 10–6 daily. If you feel like hunting, this antique mall has more than 80 dealers, and an outdoor flea market every weekend April through October.

Quad City Arts Center (309-793-1213; www.quadcityarts.com), 1715 2nd Avenue, Rock Island. Open 10–5 weekdays, 11–5 Saturday. This storefront site near The District hosts exhibitions, performances, special events, and sells original works of art by regional artists.

Isabel Bloom (309-797-4255; www.ibloom.com), 1505 River Drive, Moline. Open 10–5 weekdays and Saturday, noon–4 Sunday. This shop carries the sculpture work of native Iowan artist Isabel Bloom, who once studied under Grant Wood at the Stone City art colony in central

Iowa. Today Isabel's successor, Donna Young, carries on her work.

& **Watermark Corners** (309-764-0055; www.watermarkcorners .com), 1500 River Drive, Moline. Open 10–6 Monday through Thursday, 10–5 Friday and Saturday. This upscale gift and stationery store is located in an 1860s building near the John Deere Commons, and has a wall of paper, children's books and toys, and jewelry. If you need a Woozie (an insulated sleeve for your wine glass), this is your place.

✎ **Lagomarcino's** (309-764-1814; www.lagomarcinos.com), 1422 5th Avenue, Moline. Open 9–5:30 Monday through Saturday. Angelo Lagomarcino, an immigrant from Northern Italy, founded the ice cream shop in 1908 and it has remained a family operation. The third generation is now running it; the fourth generation working it. Lending to the appeal is the old-fashioned soda fountain and a menu from Way Back When that includes flavored fountain cokes, egg crèmes, and Green River. You can also order sandwiches, and hot fudge that comes in a small pitcher that you drizzle over your ice cream yourself. Pick up a jar of the fudge or the family's home-made chocolates. $.

✸ Special Events

May: **Dutch Days Festival** (www
.cityoffulton.us) Downtown Fulton. The first weekend in May, the
city of Fulton celebrates its Dutch
heritage with dancing, pastries,
crafts, food, parade, music, and
windmill tours.

July: **John Deere Classic** (309-
762-4653; www.johndeereclassic
.com), TPC Deere Run, John
Deere Road and Colona Road,
Silvis. Watch the pros at this PGA
Tour event in nearby Silvis.

September: **Quad City Marathon**
(309-751-9800; www.qcmarathon
.org) The course crosses three
bridges and meanders through all
four cities, before ending in downtown Moline. The course is
Boston-qualifying and if you're not
up for the distance, there's also a
half marathon, 5K, and kids' run
involved.

NAUVOO

Nauvoo is a beautiful, intriguing place with a complicated history. Let's start with the beautiful. As you approach Nauvoo, the Great River Road along the Mississippi whisks you past rocky bluffs, lush farms, and charming towns. The riverfront location, on a bend in the river, is lovely, as is a restored historic area nestled in the lowlands along the river. As you walk along rural roads, through the collection of redbrick buildings and homesteads stretched on large lots, you are in a different world. Blacksmith shops, primitive bakeries, and people in period clothing talking about their trades certainly add to the effect.

If you look away from the river, you'll see a white temple, towering high up on the hill in downtown Nauvoo, symbolic of the church's relationship with this historic district. Nauvoo is an extremely important site to the history of the Church of Jesus Christ of Latter-day Saints and the Community of Christ (formerly known as the Reorganized Church of Jesus Christ of Latter-day Saints) because it was established by Joseph Smith, who founded the church. The historic sites are owned and operated separately by the two religious organizations.

A little background on the church should help explain why church members find Nauvoo so important. The story relayed by Joseph Smith goes like this: He was a 14-year-old in New York trying to decide which church he should join when God and Jesus appeared to him and told him that he should join none of those churches. Smith claimed that God and Jesus had chosen him to restore the true church of Jesus Christ. In 1823, while feeling persecuted for sharing his vision with others, Smith said he was visited by the angel Moroni who told him about a book written on gold tablets that detailed the story of the former peoples of North America, and that two stones would help him translate the story. It turned out the plates were buried in a hill 3 miles southeast of Smith's home in Palmyra, New York. Smith said that he could not show the tablets to anyone, or he would be destroyed. In 1829, Smith started translating the plates into the *Book of Mormon*.

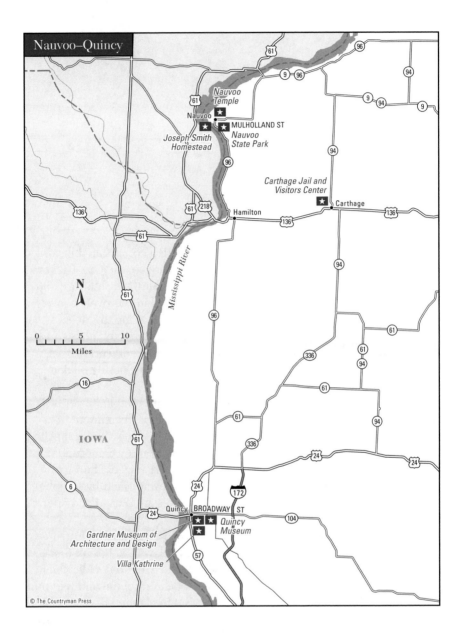

Smith and his followers had communities in Ohio and Missouri, but were forced to leave. In 1839, Smith and his family moved to Nauvoo, and a community grew up around his homestead. But the Mormons' time in Nauvoo came to an end when Joseph and his brother Hyrum were killed at a jail in nearby Carthage in 1844. Smith had ordered the destruction of a press used to print a newspaper critical of the church. His order led to a riot, and Joseph and Hyrum and other church leaders were arrested for instigating the riot. Joseph and Hyrum were also charged with treason for activating the Nauvoo legion. While they were at the jail, a group stormed the jail and shot the Smith brothers.

Shortly after, the church members, led by Brigham Young and other church leaders, basically abandoned Nauvoo to make their mass exodus to Utah. But the town's interesting history does not end there. In 1849, French and German immigrants found their way to Nauvoo, seeing the infrastructure left behind as a good one for housing their utopian communal society. The immigrants called themselves Icarians, pulling the name from a book their leader wrote about a utopian community. The Icarians were led by Etienne Cabet, a political theorist. They believed all property must be held communally. Among other things, the Icarians started the practice of wine making here, and the first vineyard planted in Nauvoo is still growing at the state park. The society ultimately hit a rough patch, and some members left, but the community lasted here until 1860. After that, German immigrants settled in Nauvoo. Today, about 1,100 people make their home here.

NAUVOO

You can explore the Smith homestead, and many of the businesses and church members' homes have been restored. These are religious sites, and the tours do include religious stories, but the site is pretty interesting even for non-members of the church. You could visit and have a completely religious experience, or you could visit and immerse yourself in the history. The women who lead the tours are dressed in period clothing and have name tags with the title "Sister." Up on the hill, the town boasts a few charming shops and restaurants, the state park, and a winery.

GUIDANCE Nauvoo Tourism Office (217-453-6648; 877-628-8661; www.beautifulnauvoo.com), 1295 Mulholland Street, Nauvoo. Open daily but call ahead because they will sometimes be out leading tours. This is the official tourism office for the city of Nauvoo, and you will find friendly staff with extensive knowledge of the area and a large supply of regional and local brochures.

& **Historic Nauvoo Visitors Center** (217-453-2237; www.historicnauvoo .net), 290 N. Main Street, Nauvoo. Summer hours: 9–7 Monday through Saturday, 10:30–5 Sunday, offseason: 9–5 Monday through Saturday, 10:30–5 Sunday, but hours change so call ahead. Here, you will find an exhibit that walks you through the story of Nauvoo and Mormonism. You can view two movies—a short 20-minute film that shares diaries and histories of the people of Nauvoo and a longer 68-minute movie on Joseph Smith. You can pick up tickets for the free wagon or carriage rides here as well.

& **Joseph Smith Visitors Center** (217-453-2246; www.cofchrist.org/js), 865 Water Street, Nauvoo. If you want a guided tour, start at the Joseph Smith Visitors Center near Water and Partridge streets. Open 9–5 Monday through Saturday, 1–5 Sunday from May through October. In November and December, and March and April, the center is open from 10–4 Monday through Saturday. In January and February, hours are 10–4 Friday and Saturday. The 75-minute tour starts with a 12-minute orientation video, then moves through the home of Joseph Smith, where you will see furniture and objects owned by the family. The hour-long tour is aimed at a general audience, so it concentrates on the history of the area. Tour: $3.

GETTING THERE *By auto:* IL 96 is the main artery that will get you to the riverfront town of Nauvoo. From the east or west, take I-80 to I-74 toward Galesburg. From there, take US 34 west to US 61south toward Nauvoo. Cross the bridge on IL 9 and take IL 96 into the town itself.

By air: **Southeast Iowa Regional Airport** (319-754-1414; www.brlair port.com), 2515 Summer Street, Burlington, Iowa. This regional airport is just about a half-hour drive to Nauvoo and has daily flights to and from Chicago and St. Louis via Air Choice One.

By train: **Amtrak** stops in Fort Madison, Iowa, just across the river.

GETTING AROUND *By auto:* Once in the historic area, you can likely park and walk, but you'll need a car to get to some of the other locations in town. IL 96 is the main thoroughfare. The lowland area is where the historic village is located, closest to the river. The Joseph Smith homestead locations are along Water Street. Mulholland Street is the main strip through the retail area of downtown Nauvoo.

MEDICAL EMERGENCIES Carthage Memorial Hospital (217-357-8500; www.mhtlc.com), 1454 N. County Road 2050, Carthage. This new hospital building features a round-the-clock emergency room, birth center, and surgical services.

✳ To See

MUSEUMS ⟁ **Rheinberger Museum** (217-453-6422; www.nauvoo historicalsociety.org), Nauvoo State Park entrance off IL 96. Open 1–4 daily mid-May through mid-October. If you begin to feel like the whole town revolves around Mormonism, you should seek out this museum run by the Nauvoo Historical Society, which dedicates itself to the entire story of Nauvoo. Located in the Nauvoo State Park, the museum rounds out the story of the town of Nauvoo, with displays on the Icarians, Native American tribes, and other peoples who lived here. There are personal stories woven in, such as through the Civil War flag brought home by a local soldier. The collections include quilts, dolls, and military paraphernalia. The museum is named after Alois Rheinberger, who owned the home from about 1850 on. He planted a small vineyard behind this house, one of the first in Nauvoo. You can walk through his arched cavelike wine cellar, wine press room, and see other wine-making equipment. Free.

⟁ **Weld House Museum** (www.nauvoohistoricalsociety.org), 1380 Mulholland Street, Nauvoo. Open 1–4 daily mid-May through mid-October. This museum is also run by the Nauvoo Historical Society and features displays about the businesses that have thrived in Nauvoo, a large collection of arrowheads, farming tools, and the death masks of Joseph and Hyrum Smith. Free.

NAUVOO GUNSMITH

JOSEPH SMITH HOMESTEAD

CULTURAL SITES Some of the historic Nauvoo sites are owned and operated by the Community of Christ and some by the Church of Jesus Christ of Latter-day Saints.

Joseph Smith Homestead On a beautiful bend in the river, this neat log cabin on a slightly sloping green hill is where the Smith family lived upon arriving in Nauvoo. Smith's son, Joseph III, added a 2-story addition on the home and lived there from 1858 through 1866. He was also prophet and president of the reorganized church from 1860 through 1914. You can also see the summer kitchen where Smith's parents lived for a time in Nauvoo. If you want to go inside the home, you'll have to take the guided tour. But if you don't, you can still see the exterior of the home.

HEBER C. KIMBALL'S HOME IN NAUVOO

Smith Family Cemetery Just next to the home is the family cemetery where Joseph Smith, wife Emma, and brother Hyrum are buried, as are Smith's parents and other family members. Joseph and his brother were killed in June 1844 at the Carthage jail. After their deaths, their empty coffins were buried in a Nauvoo cemetery while the bodies were buried secretly in a cellar of an unfinished hotel. The bodies were moved a few times, then in 1928, Smith's grandson ordered the bodies found and moved to this cemetery, where they have remained since.

Just down the street a ways, you'll see the **Red Brick Store**, which served as a general store and a meeting place for the community. Joseph Smith also had his office here. You can purchase some of the same goods that would have been for sale then, like a courting candle.

HISTORIC NAUVOO The collection of buildings near the river have been restored to appear as they did in the 1840s. Buildings are open 9–6 Monday through Saturday, 10:30–5 Sunday from mid-May to Labor Day weekend. Offseason: 11–5 Monday through Saturday, 12:30–5 Sunday. Inside some of the homes, you can see how the pioneers lived. Wander into Heber C. Kimball's home and you'll see the 2-story home arranged like it was back then. Your guide may share stories about his relationship with his wife and church leaders, and how he only lived here for four months with his family before joining the mass exodus from Nauvoo. See the brick home built by Brigham Young, namesake of the Utah university, and the second president of the LDS church. At the **Webb Brothers' Blacksmith Shop**, you can see how wagon wheels were made thanks to

BRIGHAM YOUNG HOME

the blacksmiths working over a forge. This was an important place for the pioneers planning to travel west to Utah. You also can visit the **Scovill Bakery,** and get a taste of the pioneers' gingerbread cookies.

✍ ♿ **Family Living Center** (217-453-6130; www.historicnauvoo.net), Main and White Streets. Greeters in period clothing will answer questions and walk you through the trades that sustained the townsfolk in Nauvoo. See demonstrations of bread making, weaving, and candle making, among other trades highlighted. Kids can learn how to make rope and wooden barrels.

Nauvoo Temple (217-453-6252; www.historicnauvoo.net), 50 N. Wells Street, Nauvoo. The original temple building was dedicated in 1846, a classical Greek-style building that had a zinc domed bell tower. When the Mormons left in 1846, the temple was left empty and destroyed by arson and a tornado. In 1999, efforts commenced to rebuild the temple on the original site in a style similar to the original temple. The new 5-story building was opened in 2002, but the temple is not open to the general public. There is an information center across the street at 1195 Knight Street (217-453-2243), where you can view a film about the reconstruction of the temple, as well as talk to missionaries.

NAUVOO TEMPLE

♿ **Carthage Jail & Visitors Center** (217-357-2989; www .historicnauvoo.net), 310 Buchanan Street, Carthage. Open 9–7 Monday through Saturday, 10:30–6 Sunday during the summer. Hours are reduced in the offseason. About a half-hour drive from Nauvoo is the jail in Carthage where Joseph Smith and his brother were held and later shot. An 18-minute video gives you an introduction to the story, then you take a guided tour through the jail site. Free.

GOLF **Great River Road Golf Club** (800-233-0060; www.golf
nauvoo.com), 771 E. County Road 1850. Open March through October.
This affordable course is carved out of the bluffs of the Mississippi River.
Because of that, the elevation changes 160 feet throughout the course.
Fees: $16–17 for 18 holes, $25 for 18 holes with a cart. $12–13 for 9 holes,
$16–18 with a cart.

TOURS **Wagon Tours of Old Nauvoo** (www.historicnauvoo.net) Pick
up your free tickets at the Historic Nauvoo Visitors Center. Departs from
Partridge and Hubbard Streets. If weather permits, these hour-long
horse-drawn wagon tours leave every half hour from 8–3 Monday through
Saturday during the summer. In the winter they are 9–3 on the hour. You
can also tour the area via carriage, as rides leave every hour at 15 minutes
past the hour from 8:15–3:15 Monday through Saturday during the summer, in the winter it's 9:15–3:15. Free.

WINERY **Baxter's Vineyards and Winery** (217-453-2528; 800-854-1396;
www.nauvoowinery.com), 2010 E. Parley Street, Nauvoo. Open 9–5 Monday
through Saturday, 10–5 Sunday. From January through March, Sunday
hours are reduced to noon–5. Opened by Emile Baxter in 1857, this winery
can claim the title of Illinois' oldest winery. It has been run by the family
since then. Today, Kelly Logan is the fifth generation of the Baxter family to
make wine here. The winery is a complex of white cement-block buildings
where you can sample Nauvoo Red, Icarian Red, and other bottles for free.
The shop also carries supplies for you to make your own wine at home, as
well as T-shirts, gourmet foods, and homemade pies.

✱ Green Space

Nauvoo State Park (217-453-2512; http://dnr.state.il.us/lands/landmgt/parks
/r4/nauvoo.htm), IL 96 on the southern end of Nauvoo. The 148-acre park
has the 13-acre man-made Horton Lake stocked with largemouth bass, catfish, and bluegill. Trails wind around the lake and through the park, which has
a playground. The campground, situated next to the lake, is just a short walk.

✱ Lodging

HOTELS (📶) **Hotel Nauvoo** (217-
453-2211; www.hotelnauvoo.com),
1290 Mulholland Street. Located
right on the main street of downtown Nauvoo, this hotel was built
in 1840 as a Mormon residence,
but an impressive one, with a
porch, veranda, and cupola. The
guest rooms have private baths,
and cable TVs. There is a master
suite that fits four queen beds in
two connecting rooms. Other guest
rooms have a queen or full bed.
The décor is modest and simple,

though it does vary throughout the hotel. $–$$.

CAMPING Nauvoo State Park (217-453-2512; http://dnr.state.il .us/lands/landmgt/parks/r4/nauvoo .htm), off IL 96. The campground is hilly and some of the trees give a Pacific Northwest feel. There are 150 campsites here, near the historic Nauvoo village, with a shower house with bathrooms on site. Fee: $20 electric sites, $10 non-electric.

HOTEL NAUVOO

&. (ꞯ) ✿ **Nauvoo Log Cabins** (217-453-9000; www.nauvoolog cabins.com), 65 N. Winchester Street, Nauvoo. Just off the main street of Mulholland, you'll find these cabins tucked away. To create their getaway, the owners located old pioneer log cabins out West, and dismantled and transported them to Nauvoo, where they were restored. There are a couple new cabins mixed in, and some modern amenities added to the old so that all cabins come with private baths, AC/heat, linens, towels, satellite TVs, microwaves, and refrigerators. Most have full kitchens. You'll also find a booklet detailing the history of the family your cabin is named after. The accommodations range from the modern-but-rustic, four-bedroom, three-bath lodge that sleeps 13, to cozier cabins that sleep just 2. $–$$$$.

✱ **Where to Eat**

EATING OUT Grandpa John's Café and Soda Fountain (217-453-2125; www.grandpajohns cafe.com), 1255 Mulholland Street, Nauvoo. The breakfast buffet is served from 7–10:30 AM and the lunch hot-food bar is open from 11–2. With a country kitchen décor, Grandpa John's café delivers pretty good burgers, sandwiches, fries, and ice cream shakes. Order at the counter then grab a seat. Grandpa John's is named after John A. Kraus, who came to Nauvoo in 1912 and opened Hotel Nauvoo. $.

4:30–8 Tuesday through Thursday, 4:30–8:30 Friday and Saturday, 11 AM–2:30 PM Sunday. For dinner, people come far and wide for the dinner buffet, which includes dishes like Southern fried chicken, roast beef, ham, wild rice dressing, potatoes, homemade bread, and a large salad bar. If you're not up for the buffet, you can order from a menu of steaks and seafood. Hotel Nauvoo also serves wines from the local vineyard, Baxter's. $–$$.

NAUVOO LOG CABINS

Nauvoo Mill and Bakery (888-453-6734), 1530 Mulholland Street, Nauvoo. Open 8–5 Monday through Saturday, 11–4 Sunday. From November through April, closed Sunday. If you're in a hurry, or shopping for a picnic, head here to pick up a deli sandwich on freshly made bread. The staff also makes their own stone-ground flour, then creates 100 percent whole-wheat products from it, such as cinnamon rolls, cookies, and all sorts of bread products. $.

♧ **Hotel Nauvoo** (217- 453-2211; www.hotelnauvoo.com), 1290 Mulholland Street, Nauvoo. Open

✳ **Selective Shopping**

Fudge Factory (217-453-6389; www.nauvoofudge.com), 1215 Mulholland Street, Nauvoo. Open seasonally 10–5 Monday, 10–6 Tuesday through Saturday. Watch how the candy is made before you sample chocolate peanut-butter fudge, candy cane (in December only), vanilla pecan, dark chocolate orange, or just plain old decadent chocolate. Also try the Nauvoo Nutter Cup, a peanut butter cup made with homemade peanut butter.

✳ **Special Events**

September: **Nauvoo Grape Festival** (217-453-2528; www.nauvoo grapefestival.com) Every Labor Day weekend, for 70 plus years, people have gathered in Nauvoo for the annual wine festival, which includes music, food, a grape stomp, wine tasting, and all kinds of other events.

QUINCY

Quincy, named for president John Quincy Adams, is a quintessential industrial river town. The industry is still clustered around the river, save for a riverfront recreation area. Quincy has spectacular mansions in the historic district, especially along Maine Street, with sprawling lots of green along paver-brick boulevards. In Quincy proper, there are about 40,000 people today. The historic downtown area, centered around Washington Square Park, has a Lincoln-Douglas Debate Interpretive Center and a park that focuses on the debate, an important historical moment for the town.

Otherwise, you'll find restaurants and a few shops to peruse. To learn the town's history, head over to the John Wood Mansion. Mr. Wood, who was mayor of Quincy and also governor of Illinois for a time, was the first settler in Quincy, arriving in 1822 and building a log cabin. His career soon demanded larger accommodations, and he started on the construction of the Greek-Revival mansion in 1835, hiring German immigrant craftsmen to build it for him.

Quincy gained official designation as a town in 1834, and apparently had all the resources a thriving town needed at the time, with flour mills and sawmills, healthy rich soil, forests of wood, animals to hunt, and bustling trade system. The abundance of resources gave Quincy the name "Gem city," which you'll still see used today. The town attracted a significant population of German immigrants who arrived in New Orleans and traveled upriver to Quincy. The German heritage is evident in the South Side German historic neighborhood.

Learn more about the architecture you see throughout town at the architecture museum, which is appropriately housed in a very cool limestone Romanesque Revival-style building.

If you time your visit right, you might be able to catch Dr. Eells house when it's open and learn how the town handled the question of slavery, especially when just across the river, Missouri was a slave state. Dr. Eells's home was a stop on the Underground Railroad.

Stephen Douglas lived in Quincy when he became a judge and congressman, and later a senator, so Quincy was his home district. You will see markers discussing Douglas's influence here.

The Mississippi River dominates Quincy's history and landscape, infusing it with life and trade, but also some devastation such as during recent floods. Today, Quincy's economy is still driven by electronics, agribusiness, and industrial machinery.

GUIDANCE & **Villa Kathrine** (217-224-3688; www.villakathrine.org), 532 Gardner Expressway, Quincy. Tour the building 9–5 Monday through Saturday, 1–5 Sunday. Closes at 4 during the winter. This Mediterranean-style mansion is perched above the riverfront, built in 1900 for George Metz, who dreamed up this home based on what he saw of villas throughout the Islamic world. You can pick up brochures and maps here as it is a tourist bureau for Quincy (www.seequincy.com). Admission: $3 adults, $1.50 children 6 and older.

GARDNER MUSEUM

GETTING THERE *By auto:* Quincy sits on the banks of the Mississippi River and is bisected by IL 104, which runs east-west to the river. If you're approaching Quincy from the south and want an expressway route, take IL 100 N to IL 96 N to I-72 and follow that to Quincy. From the north or the south, you can take the Great River Road, which tracks IL 57 south of town. From the north, you might consider IL 96, which will take you to Nauvoo, or US 24, which cuts northeast to Peoria.

By bus: **Greyhound** (217-223-1010; www.greyhound.com) makes stops in Quincy at the America's Best Value Inn, 300 S. 3rd Street.

By air: **Quincy Regional Airport-Baldwin Field** (217-885-3241; www.quincyregionalairport.com), 1645 US 104, Quincy. Cape Air operates flights out of this regional airport (800-352-0714; www.flycapeair.com).

VILLA KATHRINE

By train: **Amtrak** (800-872-7245; www.amtrak.com) has service to Quincy from Chicago, with a station at N. 30th Street and Wisman Lane, Quincy. But the station has odd hours, according to the train schedule, so check before you go.

GETTING AROUND *By auto:* The two bridges that cross the Mississippi are Bayview and Quincy Memorial Bridge. Memorial Bridge carries eastbound traffic from Missouri, while the newer Bayview bridge is for westbound traffic. IL 104, also known as Broadway Street, is a main thoroughfare.

By bus: ♿ **Quincy Transit Lines** (217-228-4550; www.quincyil.gov /Transit/home.htm), 2020 Jennifer Lane, Quincy. Fixed route buses to eight areas of the city Monday through Saturday, and on two routes Sunday. Fares: 50 cents.

MEDICAL EMERGENCIES Blessing Hospital (217-223-1200; www .blessinghospital.org), Broadway Street between 11th Street and 14th Street, Quincy. Largest hospital in the area with a Level II trauma rating from the state, meaning that its staff is ready and able to respond to trauma, stroke, and cardiac problems. It's also certified for emergency pediatric care.

QUINCY RIVERFRONT

✳ To See

MUSEUMS ⊤ ⅙ **Quincy Museum** (217-224-7669; www.thequincy museum.com), 1601 Maine Street, Quincy. Open 1–5 Tuesday through Sunday. The building itself is a living exhibit, a Romanesque Revival mansion built in 1890–91 with fine wood carvings and decorative art glass. On the first floor, you can tour the rooms and see the period furnishings of how people from a different time lived. Upstairs you'll find some exhibits, including an old store front, an Illini Indian longhouse, and a dinosaur room that includes a replica of a T. rex head. Admission: $4 adults, $2 students.

⊤ **Gardner Museum of Architecture and Design** (217-224-6873; www.gardnermuseumarchitecture.org), 332 Maine Street, Quincy. Open 1–4 Thursday through Saturday. The museum is located in an 1888 Romanesque Revival-style limestone building complete with towers. The exhibits focus on Quincy's architectural history, which you can also enjoy by a drive through the historic districts. But there are also exhibits that discuss the architecture of the Mississippi Valley and U.S. From May through October, the museum leads walking tours of historic neighborhoods in Quincy on the first Saturday of every month for $5 per person. A guided tour of the museum is $2.

HISTORIC SITES **Washington Park** (217-223-7703; www.quincypark district.com), between 4th and 5th Streets and Maine and Hampshire

Streets. This park in the center of downtown serves as a town square, and in 1858, hosted one of the Lincoln-Douglas debates. There's a monument marking the occasion when 15,000 people gathered to hear from the two important figures. Mr. Douglas lived in Quincy in the 1840s. To learn more there is the **Lincoln Douglas Debate Interpretive Center** (www.lincolndouglasquincydebate.com) across the street at 128 S. 5th St, with exhibits about abolitionists, the Underground Railroad, and Lincoln's "A House Divided" speech.

John Wood Mansion Log Cabin, and Parsonage (217-222-1835; www.adamscohistory.org), 425 S. 12th Street, Quincy. Open 10–2 Monday through Saturday from April through October. The stately home of John Wood is crisp and clean against the landscape, with bright white pillars and green shutters. Mr. Wood was the first settler in Quincy, building a log cabin in 1822, then this Greek-Revival mansion in 1835. He was mayor of Quincy and lieutenant governor of the state of Illinois. The sitting governor died and Mr. Wood took office, so this mansion became the governor's mansion for a time. The white building next door is the historical society's headquarters and a visitors center. Admission: $3 adults, $1.50 students.

Dr. Richard Eells House (217-223-1800), 415 Jersey Street, Quincy. Open 1–4 Saturday. This historic home is documented as an Underground Railroad site. Built 4 blocks from the river in 1835, the Federal Greek-Revival home has fallen into disrepair. Dr. Eells was an abolitionist whose home was the first Underground Railroad site across the border from

QUINCY MUSEUM

Missouri, which was a slave state. He is credited with helping hundreds of slaves escape their situations. Admission: $3 adults.

CULTURAL SITES ᛏ **Quincy Art Center** (217-223-5900; www.quincy artcenter.org), 1515 Jersey Street, Quincy. Open noon–4 Tuesday through Friday, 1–4 weekends. Exhibits rotate, but feature local and regional artists. The art center offers classes and has a gift shop where you can buy jewelry made by local hands. Admission: $3 adults, $1 students.

✳ To Do

BICYCLING Quincy Bikes/Tour Quincy (217-214-3700; 800-978-4748; www.seequincy.com) This community bike loan program makes refurbished bikes available for check out. You can leave a $10 refundable deposit at one of two locations: Salvation Army at 732 Hampshire Street, or America's Best Value Inn, 300 S. 3rd Street. You also can rent new bikes through Tour Quincy for $8 per hour or $25 per day. A tandem is $10 per hour or $35 per day. Those rentals are available at Villa Kathrine and at the Historic Quincy Business District office on Washington Square.

KAYAKING Kayak Quincy (800-978-4748; 217-214-3700; www.see quincy.com/KayakQuincy.html), Tours depart from All America Park, Front and Cedar streets, in Quincy. On select Saturdays during the summer, you can take a guided tour of the river by kayak. The cost is $40 for a

QUINCY BRIDGES

two-hour tour on the Mississippi, or you also can rent your own kayak for $25. The cost includes all equipment.

TOURS East End Historic District Between 12th and 24th Streets, and Maine and State Streets. Get maps at the Visitors Bureau to start your tour around this neighborhood filled with stately and gorgeous historic homes.

✳ Green Space

Clat Adams Bicentennial Park (www.quincyparkdistrict.com), Front and Hampshire Streets, Quincy. Two acres of riverfront have been transformed into this park, with a view of the bridge, gazebo, boat launch, and rest rooms. It's also home to riverfront festivals.

✳ Lodging

HOTELS & (𝕚) ♪ **Hampton Inn** (217-224-8378; www.hamptoninn .com), 225 S. 4th Street, Quincy. This hotel is a good choice for its location in downtown Quincy, right next to the Hotel Elkton and within walking distance to the downtown square. Rooms are clean and decent and come with TV and coffeemaker. The hotel has a fitness center with pool and a business center. $–$$.

✳ Where to Eat

EATING OUT & 🍴 **Maid Rite** (217-222-9767), 507 N. 12th Street, Quincy. Open 11–7:30 daily. This is a local institution that you may have seen on the Food Network. Opened in 1928, this restaurant offers up the Maid Rite sandwiches of seasoned loose meat. The prices are cheap and the old-school retro feel is fun. $.

Underbrink's Bakery (217-222-1831; www.underbrinks.com), 1627 College Avenue, Quincy.

Open 7–3 Tuesday through Friday, 7–noon Saturday. Claude Underbrink opened this bakery in 1929, and the current owners, LeRoy and Janet Rossmiller, still offer up some of Claude's recipes. The shop also has antique baking tools, original display cases, and gadgets from the 1930s. $.

(𝕚) **Thyme Square Café** (217-224-3515; www.thymesquarecafe.net), 500 Hampshire Avenue, Quincy. Open 7–2 Tuesday through Saturday, 9–1 Sunday. On the square across from Washington Park, this café's focus is on the fresh, seasonal, and local. Soups, salads, and tarts change according to the ingredients available. For breakfast, there's the frittata with farm-fresh eggs, Swiss cheese, and house-made ham or sausage served with potatoes and an English muffin made from scratch. For lunch, there's the house-cured pastrami Reuben. $.

♿ **Fitz's on 4th** (217-223-3489; www.fitzson4th.com), 129 S. 4th Street. Open 11–9:30 Monday through Thursday, 11–10 Friday, 4–10 Saturday. The pizza is cooked in a stone oven so it has a dark, crispy, thin crust. The house combinations include Hawaiian pizza, BBQ chicken, and potato. You can also create your own. On Friday the restaurant hosts an all-you-can-eat fish fry for $10.95. Another specialty is sweet BBQ ribs. $–$$.

((♥)) **Washington Perk Café at the Granite Bank Gallery** (217-224-2233; wwiw.granite-bankgallery.com), 428 Maine Street. Open 7–5 weekdays, 7–3 Saturday. Inside the very cool Granite Bank Gallery building, the smell of the espresso beans, which are roasted in St. Louis, will lead you to this café. You can get fresh-made pastries or order lunch from a menu that includes sweet pea salad, quesadillas, and paninis. While you're here, you can also peruse wine in the gallery building or take in some art. $.

DINING OUT Jorge the Crook's (217-224-9811; www .jorgethecrook.com), 111 Hampshire, Quincy. Open 4:30–10 Monday through Saturday. There is a long story behind the name here, going back to when the owner was in the Marines. A big bar fight broke out, and the bar had to be demolished. The bar owner, "Jorge," claimed it would cost $200,000 to rebuild. It actually cost about $20,000. Because the late 1800s building where the restaurant is located reminded the owner of the bar, it is now called Jorge the Crook's. This menu is extensive, offering everything from surf and turf to basil pesto

THE PIER IN QUINCY

primavera. The wine list is long, too, offering a few by the glass and many by the bottle. $$–$$$$.

&. **The Pier Restaurant** (217-221-0020; www.thepierrestaurant .com), 401 Bayview Drive, Quincy. Open 11–2:30, 5–9 daily. Perched above the Mississippi, this restaurant's tag line is clever: COME DINE WHERE THE ONLY THING WE OVERLOOK IS THE RIVER. The dinner menu offers entree salads like the whiskey-glazed salmon Caesar. Entrees include horseradish catfish and filet mignon. $$–$$$.

&. **Tiramisu** (217-222-9560; www.tiramisuquincy.com), 137 N. 3rd Street, Quincy. Open 11–2 weekdays for lunch, 4:30 until closing for dinner, Monday through Saturday. Roberto and Teresa Stellino promise authentic Italian in this warm stucco-walled room close to the river. Try homemade pastas with seafood, or stuffed with spinach, ham, and ricotta. The restaurant has a pretty good wine list. Usually busy on the weekends so there may be a wait. $$–$$$.

((ɣ)) **The Patio** (217-222-5660; www.patiorestaurant.net), 133 S. 4th Street, Quincy. Open 4–9 Sunday through Thursday and 4–10 Friday and Saturday. With an indoor garden and wall of water, the patio seeks to give you a slightly different dining room experience. The steaks are charcoal broiled. Located in the Hotel Elkton, the restaurant also has a pasta bar a couple times a week, where guests can choose their own pasta ingredients. The menu also includes chicken and seafood entrees. $$–$$$$.

✱ Entertainment

MOVIES AMC Quincy Showplace 6 (217-228-1014; www.amc entertainment.com/Quincy), 300 N. 33rd Street, Quincy. Out near the mall, this movie theater carries first-run features. Tickets: $8 adult, $6 children.

✱ Selective Shopping

&. **Spirit Knob Winery** (217-964-2678; www.spiritknob.com), 2213 E. 640th Place, Ursa. Open 1–5 Wednesday, Thursday, Saturday, Sunday, 1–10 Friday, when they have Wine-down night with live music. Reduced winter hours. Just north of Quincy on Great River Road, you might want to build in a stop at this winery where you can walk the vineyard and sample some of the wines, which are made entirely from Illinois grapes. The vineyard was planted in 1999 and the winery opened in 2002.

✱ Special Events

June: **Midsummer Arts Faire** (www.artsfaire.org), 5th and Maine Street. Juried fine arts festival in Washington Park over three days also includes children's activities, entertainment, and food.

MEETING OF THE GREAT RIVERS (ALTON AND GRAFTON)

Where the Mississippi and Illinois rivers feed into each other, there is a great merging of natural beauty and inviting, fun small towns. I speak of Grafton, which is found along a particularly scenic stretch of the Great River Road, and nestled just south of Pere Marquette State Park, another jewel in the state park system.

Grafton sits at the confluence of the Illinois and Mississippi rivers, and boasts a pretty good group of wineries. You'll also find a public fishing pier, the red-and-white striped lighthouse, and boats along the river. During the winter, eagle watching is a popular attraction.

Founded in 1836, Grafton has a slightly more touristy feel to it than some of its neighbors, with a number of pubs, restaurants, guest houses, and a strip of stores on the riverfront geared toward out-of-towners.

Alton is a nice surprise too, with its main shopping and restaurant district on a hill overlooking the river. The shadow of the world's tallest man can still be seen in the town. The life story of Robert Wadlow, who was 8 feet 11 inches tall when he died, makes for a fascinating exhibit at the local museum. Alton has a nice riverfront park area that almost distracts from the giant ConAgra Mills building that otherwise dominates the riverfront here, but is a necessary part of the city economy.

Alton got its start when Colonel Rufus Easton bought riverside property in 1815 and named the town for his son, Alton. He started a ferry service to bring supplies to settlers in the West. The first steam flour mill opened in 1831 in the same location where ConAgra now operates the giant flour mill. Steamboat traffic fed the local economy, and then the railroad developed rail lines running between Alton and Springfield. The city picked up the nickname of "Pie Town," when soldiers would break near Alton during the Mexican-American War of 1846 and the ladies of Alton would bake them pies. You can see some of the housing from the early days in the Middletown Historic District.

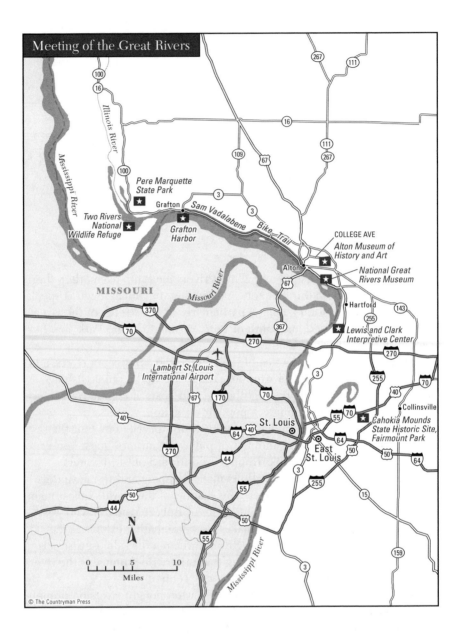

Meeting of the Great Rivers

The final Lincoln-Douglas debate took place in Alton in October 1858. Mary Todd and son, Robert, joined Lincoln for the debate here. Douglas and Lincoln even ate breakfast together at a local hotel. You can see a monument marking the moment overlooking the river at Broadway and Landmarks Boulevard.

Alton is also home to many haunted tours because of a history marked by smallpox, mob killings, and war, all of which you will read about below.

If you're interested in ghosts, see if you can check out the McPike Mansion, which really has a reputation for hosting spirits. Several downtown businesses will share stories about hauntings.

While the river adds to the quality of life in Alton, the flood of 1993 forced the closure of the Great River Road from Alton to Grafton. The lines painted on the ConAgra building and others show how high the water rose during the flood.

You can easily spend a few days taking in Alton and Grafton with some shopping, a meal, boating, fishing, and a drive to take in the cliffs of Pere Marquette State Park. Another great activity is to rent a bike to take on the path between Alton and Grafton, which passes rocky bluffs, parks, Piasa Creek, and of course, the river.

At the south end of this area, I suggest a trip to Cahokia Mounds and the Lewis and Clark Museum, both of which will feed your imagination as you try to sketch out the adventures had here many, many years ago.

GUIDANCE & Alton Regional Convention and Visitors Bureau

(800-258-6645; www.visitalton.com), 200 Piasa Street, Alton. Conveniently located right near the shopping district and close to the riverfront, this visitors bureau has stacks of brochures and maps.

DOWNTOWN ALTON

Grafton Visitor Center (618-786-7000), 950 E. Main Street, Grafton. Open 10–4 Tuesday through Sunday. Right on the river, this visitor center also houses a small exhibit on the town.

GETTING THERE *By auto:* From the Cahokia Mounds in Collinsville, take I-255 north to I-270W towards Kansas City, take the exit for IL-3/Lewis and Clark Blvd toward Alton. From Alton, take IL-100 N/Great River Road to Grafton.

By air: **Lambert-St. Louis International Airport** (314-890-1333; www.lambert-stlouis.com), 10701 Lambert International Boulevard, St. Louis, Missouri. Most of the major carriers fly in and out of here, and it's only 20 miles from Alton.

By train: **Amtrak** has a stop at Upper Alton, 3400 College Avenue (www.amtrak.com).

GETTING AROUND *By auto:* You simply must take IL 100, otherwise known as the Meeting of the Great Rivers Scenic Byway. It's a great drive that will connect you to all the main parts of Alton and Grafton and get you to the state park.

By boat: **Grafton Ferry** (www.graftonferry.com) Located on the riverfront. From Main Street, turn toward the river at Market Street go 1 block to the Grafton Ferry parking lot entrance. Open 6 AM–7 PM weekdays, 10–7 weekends. Closed during ice season. This ferry service operates between Grafton and the Missouri side of the river. The ferry runs nonstop back and forth all day long, so there is not really a set schedule. The ride is about 10 minutes. Cars are $8 one way, $15 round trip. Pedestrians ride for $3, $5 for round trip and cyclists are $4, $7 for round trip.

WORLD'S TALLEST MAN STATUE

ROBERT PERSHING WADLOW
FEBRUARY 22 1918 — JULY 15 1940

MEDICAL EMERGENCIES **Alton Memorial Hospital** (618-463-7474; www.altonmemorialhospital.org), One Memorial Drive, Alton. This 200-bed hospital has a round-the-clock emergency department and is certified to deliver emergency care to children as well.

Saint Louis University Hospital (314-577-8000; www.sluhospital.com), 3635 Vista at Grand Boulevard, St. Louis, Missouri. It is across the river, but it's the closest Level I trauma center in the area, which means it is staffed and equipped to handle the most severely injured and ill patients.

✳ To See

MUSEUMS ↑ ⅇ ✑ **National Great Rivers Museum** (877-462-6979; www.mvs.usace.army.mil/rivers/museum.html), IL 143 at Locks and Dam Way, Alton. Open 9–5 daily. A film will orient you to the story of the power of the river. Discover why the Mississippi is so important to the surrounding land, to the transportation of goods, and to the lore of river towns. The kids may like the exhibit that allows you to steer a barge. Exhibits also walk through the history of the river and its cycles. Free. Also, adjacent to the museum you'll find **Melvin Price Locks and Dam** (877-462-6979) 2 Lock and Dam Way Road, Alton. You can tour the lock at 10, 1, and 3 daily.

↑ ⅇ **Alton Museum of History and Art** (618-462-2763; www.alton museum.com), 2809 College Avenue, Alton. Open 10–4 Wednesday

ALTON

GRAFTON

through Saturday, 1–4 Sunday. You should definitely choose to take the tour at this museum. The objects are not clearly labeled, so if you wander through alone, you may suspect that you're looking at something very cool, but won't have the context or identifiers to help you understand it. You can get more of the background on "Alton's Gentleman Giant," Robert Wadlow, who holds the world record for height. He was normal size when born, maybe a little large at 8 pounds 6 ounces. But a pituitary gland problem fed his growth to an unbelievable size. By eight years old, he was 6 feet 2 inches tall. He struggled with medical problems, including foot infections and broken bones. He apparently did not feel his feet very well and so blisters would form without him knowing. An infection developed and after fighting off high fevers for 10 days, he died. He was 8 feet 11 inches tall and 22 years old. The museum has a room with a pair of his shoes, many photos, and a replica of Wadlow's ring. Admission: $3 adults.

HISTORIC SITES & **Cahokia Mounds State Historic Site and Interpretive Center** (618-346-5160; http://cahokiamounds.org), 30 Ramey Drive, Collinsville. Off the expressway, you'll pass Fairmount Park on your right-hand side, then see a mound on your left and right; turn left into the museum and interpretive site. Center is open 9–5 daily May through October. Closed Monday and Tuesday in the off-season. Grounds are open 8–dusk daily. Cahokia was uncovered in 1811 the largest prehistoric Indian city north of Mexico. There is evidence of very early settlements as far back as 700 A.D. From 800 to 1400 the Mississippian culture developed here, with an agricultural system and complex community. In 1250 A.D. Cahokia was larger than London, and the largest city in the territory that would become the United States—until 1800, when Philadelphia reached 30,000 residents. But at this time, there were as many as 20,000 people here, who built a society and a giant city plaza. Archaeologists have also found evidence of what is called the American Woodhenge, large logs placed in a circle to form a solar horizon calendar. The mounds were built to serve as platforms for important buildings, to bury important people, and to mark areas. You can walk up to the top of the mounds and hike on trails around the site, but use the stairs and don't climb the slopes of the mounds, as it causes damage. The interpretive center is an impressive museum that has a central section of life-sized dioramas showing people in various duties—children playing, men in a sweat lodge, adults working the land. Exhibits detail life on the earth at this time as well as before and after, to show how the site evolved. An exhibit also provides insight into how the archaeologists piece together the story of what happened at this site thousands of years ago. Mound 72, which was discovered between 1967 to 1971, is particularly intriguing. It was not a mound that appeared important in the grand scheme of things, but scientists found evidence of burials that involved elaborate rituals including the sacrifice of young women, grave treasures, and mass human sacrifice. Four male skeletons were found with no heads or hands. No one knows why the Indians abandoned the site. You can watch a 15-minute orientation film "The City of the Sun" at the center or take an iPod or audiotape tour of the site. The iPod tour, which you pick up in the gift shop, is $5. From the

CAHOKIA MOUNDS

center, you can walk out into the grand plaza, the central ceremonial district, and the marketplace. Across the street, you will see Monks Mound, which is thought to be the largest prehistoric earthwork in the Americas. The people built this mound, which is now 100 feet tall, with baskets of earth. Free admission but suggested donation of $4 adults, $2 children.

& **Lewis and Clark Interpretive Center** (618-251-5811; www.state.il .us/hpa/hs/lewis_clark.htm), 1 Lewis and Clark Trail, Hartford. Open 9–5 daily May through Labor Day. Offseason: 9–5 Wednesday through Sunday. Illinois was the point of departure for the Lewis and Clark expedition, as Lewis noted in his journals when they departed in May 1804. This new and bright museum features a replica of the 55-foot-long keelboat the crew took on their voyage. It gives a sense of what life may have been like on the ship, and what you would need to pack for a voyage into the unknown. Outside the museum, wander through a replica of Camp River Dubois, a camp built to house the men from December 12, 1803, until they departed in May 1804. Notice the close quarters of four men in a bunk. The exact location is not known, but historians used journal entries, sketches, and maps to recreate the camp here. You can survey the replica quarters of Captains Meriwether Lewis and William Clark, where they stayed before launching this Corps of Discovery and first diplomatic mission from the U.S. government to the native people of the West. Along the way, they discovered 178 plants and 122 animals, including coyotes, various birds, and mule deer. Clark mapped the trip, and his estimations

LEWIS & CLARK

of the distances traveled turned out to be pretty accurate. After reaching the Oregon coast and establishing Fort Clatsop as winter quarters, they set on their way back and arrived in St. Louis in September 1806. Free.

& **Lewis and Clark Confluence Tower** (618-251-1901; www.confluence tower.com), 435 Confluence Tower Drive, Hartford. Open 9:30–4:30 Monday through Saturday, noon–4:30 Sunday. You must be accompanied by a tour guide. Tours depart on the hour. This new cement tower has three outdoor observation decks at 50, 100, and 150 feet with great views of the confluence of the Mississippi and Missouri Rivers. If the weather is clear, you can see St. Louis's Gateway Arch, which is 19 miles south. Admission: $4 adults, $2 children 12 and under, free children under 2.

Alton Prison (800-258-6645), William Street at Broadway Street, Alton. The first Illinois state prison was in Alton, opened in 1833. It was closed and reopened as a federal prison, but soon became overcrowded; a small-pox epidemic led to the mayor closing all city hospitals and the cemetery to prisoner patients. Sick soldiers were quarantined on an island near the Missouri shore that became known as "Smallpox Island" after more than 260 prisoners died there. The river has washed away the site of the island. But there is a smallpox monument to the soldiers who died there at the Lincoln Shields Recreation Area in West Alton. During the Civil War, the prison was also the home to much more death, as 1,354 Confederate sol-diers, 215 civilians, and 240 Union soldiers and guards died there. You can see ruins at the site today.

& **Lovejoy Monument** (800-258-6645), Alton Cemetery, Monument and 5th Street, Alton. Elijah Lovejoy was a preacher and abolitionist who was driven out of St. Louis because of his anti-slavery writings. In 1836, Love-joy brought his newspaper to Alton after a mob destroyed his printing press in Missouri. He ran the *Alton Observer,* but did not escape his trou-bles by moving across state lines. In November 1837, although 20 Alton men tried to protect him and the building where his presses were, an angry mob set the building on fire. When Lovejoy exited the building, he was shot and died from those wounds. You can see a memorial dedicated to him in the Alton Cemetery. His printing press is at the Chicago History Museum. Mr. Lovejoy was buried in the cemetery at night, in an unmarked spot so the grave would remain untouched. Later he was reburied in a new plot.

CULTURAL SITES **Piasa Bird** (800-258-6645), Piasa Park on IL 100, Alton. In 1673, Louis Joliet and Jacques Marquette moved down the Mis-sissippi in search of a waterway connection to the Pacific, and when they came to the area that is now Alton, Marquette wrote of a large painted image on the bluffs that showed a birdlike monster with horns like a deer. In Marquette's description, it was red-eyed, bearded, scale-bodied, and fish-tailed. The Indians in the area, the Illini, knew the figure as the "Piasa." Native American tribes had legends about this creature going after humans. The original disappeared but a recreation is painted on the wall as you head out of town. It resembles some graphic art you might see on a T-Shirt, but it's not something you see every day.

PIASA BIRD

& **Robert Wadlow Statue** (800-258-6645), 2810 College Avenue, Alton. Photos may suggest just how Robert Wadlow, the world's tallest man, towered over those around him, but standing next to the statue you get a true feel for how tall he was (8 feet 11 inches tall at his death).

✳ To Do

BICYCLING Wild Trak Bikes (618-462-2574; http://wildtrakbikesracing.com), 202 State Street, Alton. Rent a bike for $15 for four hours or $20 for eight hours. The store only has a couple bikes, so if you have a larger group, you may want to check out Grafton Canoe and Kayak, which has a fleet of bikes.

GRAFTON RIVERFRONT

Sam Vadalabene Bike Trail This great 20-mile paved trail runs from Pere Marquette State Park to Piasa Park in Alton, alongside the Meeting of the Great Rivers National Scenic Byway, which has fantastic views of the river.

BOATING Grafton Canoe, Kayak and Boat Rental (618-786-2192; www.graftoncanoeandkayak.com), 12 E. Water Street, Grafton. Open 9–7 daily, weather permitting. Charter a fishing boat with Captain Tom Foster, who has spent 30 years learning the best spots on the confluence. You can also rent a canoe, kayak, waverunner, or pontoon boat to enjoy the river. Mountain bikes are available too: $15 for half-day, $20 for all day. A solo kayak is $25, while a two-person boat is $40.

Grafton Harbor (618-786-7678; www.graftonharbor.net), 215 W. Water Street, Grafton. If you're traveling the river and need an overnight place to dock your boat, you can do so at the harbor for $1.25 per foot, although reservations are encouraged. Daytime dockage is $8 per boat. The marina has a bar and grill, gas, diesel, Laundromat, mechanical services, and bathrooms.

FOR FAMILIES ✍ **Raging Rivers Water Park** (618-786-2345; www .ragingrivers.com), 100 Palisades Parkway, Grafton. Open Memorial Day through Labor Day 10:30–6 daily, although the park stays open an hour later during the core summer period of mid-June through the first week of August. With an excellent hillside location overlooking the river, I would warn families that it will be very difficult to drive past this park and not have to stop. Ride waterslides downhill toward the river, lounge on a raft down the endless river, or take on the wave pools. The toddler set will enjoy Itty Bitty Surf City, with playground equipment, shallow splash pool, and rain tree. There are a couple different cafés where you can get hot dogs, tacos, and other burger-type fare. Tickets: $19.95 adults, $16.95 children age 2 and up. Parking is $5.

✍ **Gypsy Rose Pirate Ship** (314-477-5658; www.gypsyrosepirate ship.com) A pirate ship! If you're driving through town on a summer weekend, you may feel like you've been transported back in time to see this ship sailing down the river. But you can take tours of it from the loading dock of the Grafton Marina. On board, there's treasure,

PIRATE SHIP IN GRAFTON

some skeletons, and a crew dressed as pirates. Tours are $5, and a 45-minute ride is $25 adults, $15 children. You can also rent it for private parties.

HORSEBACK RIDING Pere Marquette Riding Stables (618-786-2156; www.horserentals.com/peremarquettestables.html), 15780 IL 100, Grafton. Open mid-April through October. The stables here offer hay rides, trail rides, and pony rides for kids. Children 8 and older can ride their own horses. Rates start at $35 per hour. Pony rides start at $10.

RACING Fairmount Park (618-345-4300; www.fairmountpark.com), 9301 Collinsville Road, Collinsville. On the way to Cahokia Mounds you will see this 1900s-era track, where you will find live horse races Tuesday, Friday, and Saturday through late spring and summer months. When Fairmount doesn't run their own races, you can see other races simulcast at the park. Admission: $2.50.

TOURS Antoinette's Haunted History Tours (618-462-4009; www.hauntedalton.com) Tours depart from 1513 Washington Avenue, Alton. The owners, who have been leading tours since 1992, claim no gimmicks or tricks. Their trolley tour starts with a Ghosts 101 talk, then they share some of the photos they've taken on their ghost tours. The trolley makes three stops for riders to investigate some of the sites. Tickets: $35–60.

Historic Alton Driving Tour There are three separate driving tours for Alton—of the Middletown District, Christian Hill, and Upper Alton. My preference is Middletown, which gives you a peek into the community built by the town's wealthy residents. Many of the homes are now private residences, so this is a tour where you just enjoy the view from the sidewalk. Middletown is located north of Broadway bounded by US 67 on the west and roughly Pearl Street on the east. Some highlights: The Lyman Trumbull House at 1105 Henry Street, which was built in the 1830s. Senator Lyman Trumbull defeated Stephen Douglas for his seat in 1855, and was a supporter of Lincoln through the Civil War. He was a co-author of the 13th Amendment abolishing slavery. He lived in this home starting in 1849. Just down the street is the Haskell Playhouse, 1211 Henry Street, a Queen Anne-style playhouse built for a 5-year-old girl named Lucy, in the 1880s. Lucy only got to enjoy it for a few years because she died at age 9. Over at 2018 Alby Street, you can find the McPike Mansion, rumored to be haunted, but an overall cool mansion whether or not that's true. This Italianate mansion was built by Henry Guest McPike, a former mayor of the town, in 1869.

WINERIES Aerie's Riverview Winery (618-786-8439; www.aerieswinery.com), 2003 N. Mulberry Street, Grafton. Open noon–7 Monday through Thursday, noon–10 Friday and Saturday, noon–8 Sunday. The bluff-top location offers a nice view to take in from the deck of the winery. In addition to wine, you'll find live music and a menu of cheeses, sausages, pizzas, sandwiches, and soups. Children and pets are not allowed on the deck.

Piasa Winery and Pub (618-786-9463; www.piasawinery.com), 225 W. Main, Grafton. Open 11–6 Monday through Thursday, 11–9 Friday and Saturday, noon–7 Sunday. Open year-round. It's pronounced "pie-a-saw," and the wine is made in nearby Godfrey. You can sit in the small casual indoor room or outside on the deck overlooking the river. Tastings are free. There is a menu with sandwiches and pastas.

Grafton Winery and Brewhaus (618-786-3001; www.TheGrafton Winery.com), 300 W. Main Street, Grafton. With a lofted roof, the winery and brewhaus located on a second floor is light-filled and airy. You can look into the glass-walled production area to see the wine being made. On nice days, you can take your wine out onto a deck that overlooks the river. The wines are made here except for the cabernet and Harbor Red. The beers are handcrafted on site. The menu includes salads, fruit and cheese plates, antipasto with grilled flatbread, and other appetizers. Sandwiches and burgers come with sweet potato fries, French fries, onion rings, potato salad, or a side salad. Entrees include grilled salmon with sweet hickory

GRAFTON WINERY

glaze or a mini London broil. You also may find live music here on the weekends. Tastings free.

Mary Michelle Winery (618-786-2331; www.illinois-wine.com) This winery has a tasting room located at Pere Marquette State Park Lodge in Grafton. They also provide a small menu of appetizers.

✳ Green Space

Two Rivers National Wildlife Refuge (618-883-2524; www.fws.gov /midwest/tworivers), Brussels. On the way out of Grafton, you'll see this wildlife refuge that is a haven for all kinds of birds, including the bald eagle. Roughly 1,000 winter here each year. Trails and observation area are open to the public.

Pere Marquette State Park (618-786-3323; www.dnr.illinois.gov), IL 100 on Great River Road, Grafton. Named after Father Jacques Marquette who, with Louis Joliet, explored Illinois territory in 1673 in this location. The large white cross alongside IL 100 marks the spot where they landed. The park today has a marina, 12 miles of trails, and a scenic drive with several worthwhile overlooks. There is a 2,000-acre hunting area as well.

✳ Lodging

BED AND BREAKFASTS

Alton
  ♿ **Jackson House B&B and Guest House** (800-462-1426; 618-462-1426; www.jacksonbb.com), 1821 Seminary Street, Alton. There are some readers who may be convinced of the need to stay here by the fact that they serve pie for breakfast every day. In the Upper Alton historic district, the white frame house has two guest rooms and traditional bed-and-breakfast décor. The master bedroom has a king bed, and the private bathroom has a claw-foot tub. The fireplace room has a queen bed with a private bath, as well. The "Barn" and the "Cave" are unfortunate names for other

accommodations on site, because the interiors are really designed for comfort. The converted horse barn has a living area, loft sleeping area with exposed wooden beams, king bed, TV, and VCR. The barn also has an enclosed porch. "The cave" is an earth house built like a cave, among trees overlooking a creek. It comes with a king bed, TV, VCR, whirlpool tub, fireplace, mini-refrigerator, and a patio. $$.

INNS AND COTTAGES

Alton
Haagen Haus (618-465-0123; www.haagenhaus.com), 617 State Street, Alton. With three suites in the historic Christian Hill neighborhood, Haagen Haus has created

a space in this Italianate 1870 Victorian for those who want a little room to stretch out. With the décor, fireplace, chandeliers, and other first-class touches, the luxury courtyard suite earns the right to use the word luxury in its title. The suite comes with a king bed, living room, full kitchen, bathroom, and private brick courtyard. The sky view suite is on the second floor and has everything except for the private courtyard. The eagle view suite has two bedrooms on the third floor, in addition to the living room, bathroom, and kitchen. $$.

Grafton
&. **Tara Point Inn and Cottages** (618-786-3555; www.tarapoint .com), One Tara Point, Grafton. Up a steep hill that gives the inn its magnificent view of the river you'll find the inn, with three guest rooms and eight private cottages. Guest rooms have king beds, TVs, and include a continental breakfast. The cottages have private porches, baths, and come with a separate sitting room with a pull-out sofa, wet bar, and woodburning fireplace. $$–$$$.

((•)) &. **Jeni J's Guest Houses** (618-786-2737; www.jenij.com), 210-214 W. Main Street, Grafton. Owners Mike and Nancy Jo Wilson have remodeled these historic buildings inside, creating cute, colorful cottages that provide a nice location and a comfortable place to stay. The properties have living rooms, bathrooms, and

kitchen areas. Choose from one- to three-bedroom cottages. The three-bedroom, two-bath unit has St. Louis Cardinal accents and comes with three queen beds and a full kitchen. $$–$$$.

((•)) ✿ **The Loading Dock Guest House and Cottage** (618-786-3494; www.graftonloading dock.com), 400 Front Street, Grafton. The guest house is decorated in calming yellows and sage green, with built-in white bookcases around the living room, a full kitchen, two TVs, and bedroom with king bed. The kids will love the four bunks close together in a bright room. The house has a side yard and small pets are welcome. The riverside cottage has a back deck facing the river but the Boatworks building is also part of your view. The cottage has a full kitchen, queen bed, and two TVs. $–$$$.

HOTELS

Grafton
&. ✿ **Pere Marquette Lodge** (618-786-2331; www.pmlodge .net), 13653 Lodge Boulevard, Grafton. The stone lodge has a stunning main room with a giant stone fireplace and windows overlooking the park. The lodge has 50 guest rooms, and 22 natural stone cottages nestled into the nearby woods, constructed from limestone from the Grafton rock quarry. The Civilian Conservation Corps constructed the lodge in the 1930s. The rooms have pretty straightforward hotel décor, but

PERE MARQUETTE LODGE

there have been some upgrades made recently that can be seen in the granite countertops in the bathroom. The old-wing rooms boast views of the river. The cabins have three rooms per cabin, so you can either rent out one whole cabin block for a larger group, or just a room for yourself. The cabin rooms are rustic, with knotty pine and stone. Most have two queen beds, some have sofa sleepers too. You still have access to the lodge from the cabins, but you'll have to walk outside to get there. All guest accommodations have private baths, tables and chairs, cable TVs, radios, coffeemakers, and hair dryers. No pets allowed. In addition to the excellent rustic main room to relax in, the lodge also has a hot tub, indoor pool, and small gift shop. $$.

♂ (ᵖ) **Ruebel Hotel** (618-786-2315; www.ruebelhotel.com), 217 E. Main Street, Grafton. The hotel is not shy about advertising that it's haunted. Michael Ruebel built the hotel in 1884, the largest in the county with 32 rooms and a bathhouse. The hotel caught fire in 1912 and was renovated in 1997. Guests claim to have seen and spoken to a little girl ghost named "Abigail." The rooms were renovated in 2008, but still retain that historic country look about them. They come with queen beds, HDTVs, satellite cable, private baths, and most have refrigerators. Some rooms have views of the river. The façade of the hotel still conjures up images of a bustling frontier town. $$.

CAMPING ₺ **Pere Marquette State Park** (618-786-3323; www .dnr.illinois.gov), IL 100 on Great River Road, Grafton. The park has 80 sites with electrical hookups and access to a sanitary dump station, drinking water, shower building, and a playground. There is also a tent camping area that backs up a hill and is nicely wooded. My favorite here is Eagle Overlook campground. Two sites are handicap accessible. You can make reservations at www.reserve america.com. Sites: $10–20.

✳ Where to Eat

EATING OUT

Alton

Y & ✿ Fast Eddie's Bon Air (618-462-5532; www.fasteddies bonair.com), 1530 E. Fourth Street, Alton. Open 1–11 Monday through Thursday, 11–11 Friday through Sunday. Bar is open later. You must be 21 to enter. My last visit, the line wound through the

bar, the place was so slammed with people. But they know how to handle it, moving people through pretty quickly to sample the short menu. The outdoor bar area is huge and they also bring in live bands. The building was constructed in the 1920s by Anheuser-Busch as a drinking establishment, but they had to sell it because breweries were prohibited by law from owning bars. In 1981, Eddie Sholar (the namesake Fast Eddie) bought the place and started serving up beer. The food has gained attention from the Food Network's Alton Brown as a roadhouse that prides itself on quality food at a low price. Try the $2.99 Big Elwood on a stick, which is a marinated tenderloin with green peppers grilled on a stick. Just 99 cents will get you a half-pound burger, while 29 cents

HOTEL RUEBEL

FAST EDDIE'S

gets you a peel-and-eat shrimp. No carry outs. $.

Grafton
O'Jan's Fish Stand (618-786-2229) 101 W. Main Street, Grafton. Hot fish sandwiches right on the river, everything is deep-fried and served open face on bread. The buffalo catfish is $4.25, or try the frog legs for $3.25. Your meal will be served in a cardboard box and you can take it over to the wooden deck and camp out at a picnic table to watch the river, where some of the catch may be swimming. You can buy fresh fish in Ready's Fish Market, attached.

DINING OUT

Alton
🍸 ♿ **Chez Marilyn** (618-465-8071), 119 W. 3rd Street, Alton.

Open 10:30–2 Tuesday and Wednesday, 10:30–4 Thursday through Saturday for lunch. Dinner: 4–9 Sunday through Thursday, 4–10 Friday, Saturday. Bar open later. Slowly Marilyn has converted her beauty shop (it's still there in the back) into a bar, martini lounge, and restaurant area with an excellent outdoor patio. The bar ceiling is illuminated with bright blue lights, and the room next door goes for a totally different look with exposed brick, and old movie posters. She has a martini named after each movie referenced on the wall. Like the *Gone with the Wind,* which blends peach vodka, peach schnapps, orange juice, and grenadine for a Southern-inspired cocktail. For dinner, you can order from a tapas-inspired menu, such as the crostini trio of goat-cheese dip, fresh pesto, and bruschetta. Tapas entrees include Sicilian steak skewers or pesto-encrusted chicken. On the weekends you may find live music out on the patio, just next to the landscaped waterfall out front. For the lunch crowd, there's a decent special that will fill you up; you choose any two of the following—soup, small salad, or half-sandwich. But all are pretty hearty portions. $.

Grafton
The Fin Inn (618-786-2030; www.fininn.com), 1500 W. Main Street, Grafton. Open 11–9 daily during the summer, 11–8 during winter. Your experience with this restaurant may depend on how

you feel about staring at some of the creatures in the 8,000 gallons of aquariums found here, which feature many types of fish from the Mississippi, as well as turtles. The rock-fronted restaurant is tucked back off Main Street. Some tables are bordered by windows looking into the aquarium. But the menu has some interesting dishes, and includes turtle soup, fried catfish fillet sandwiches, alongside a menu of burgers and the like. $–$$.

&. **Ruebel on Main** (618-786-2315; www.ruebelhotel.com), 217 E. Main Street, Grafton. Open 4–9 weekdays, 8–10 AM for breakfast, 11–9 Saturday and Sunday. The bar and restaurant connected to the Ruebel Hotel boasts a walnut bar that was part of the Bavarian Exhibit at the 1904 World's Fair in St Louis. Otherwise the room is casual, with a dark pink carpet and wood furniture. On the menu, you'll find the Ruebel Angus burger, and a whole list of sandwiches and pizza. Entrees range from mostaccioli to filet mignon with herb butter. $–$$.

&. **The Loading Dock** (618-786-3494; www.graftonloadingdock .com), 400 Front Street, Grafton. Open 11–9 weekdays, 11–10 weekends May through September. Open weekends only October through April. Right before they opened, the owners (who thought the view from the old Boatworks machine shop should be shown off to the world) had 8 feet of water in the restaurant, which ruined their

plans of opening. That was during the great flood of 1993. They opened later, but a fire destroyed the building in 1999. The owners opened a new building in 2001 built to combat flooding, with walls made of steel garage doors with glass panes. The doors are raised to let water flow through and to welcome guests and river air. The Loading Dock has decks with tables for outdoor seating. The restaurant serves sandwiches, wraps, and hand-pattied burgers. $.

&. **Pere Marquette Lodge Restaurant** (618-786-2331; www .pmlodge.net), 13653 Lodge Boulevard, Grafton. Open 7 AM–8 PM Sunday through Thursday, 7 AM–9 PM Friday and Saturday. Enjoy the rich dark woods in the ceilings and beams, and the stone walls that show off the craftsmanship of the Civilian Conservation Corps that constructed the lodge in the 1930s. The menu is casual, home-style Midwestern food—family-style fried catfish or fried chicken. $–$$$.

✳ **Entertainment**

During select weekends, the city of Alton has a block party downtown, with kids' activities early in the evening, then live music, food, and drink later.

Riverfront Park and Amphitheater (618-463-3580; www.riverfrontamphitheater.com), Riverfront Drive, Alton. The city has a schedule of live outdoor concerts at this cool venue right on the riverfront.

& **Argosy Casino** (800-711-4263; www.argosy.com/stlouis/), Alton riverfront. Open 8 AM–6 AM daily. The bright lights against the river-front are that of this casino, with more than 1,000 slot and video poker machines. The table games include blackjack, roulette, and poker.

✳ Selective Shopping

& **State Street Market** (618-462-8800), 208 S. State Street, Alton. This charming market has wines, gourmet foods, produce, and gifts. There's also a wall of windows on the back wall that looks onto a sweet brick courtyard that evokes images of Europe.

& **Mississippi Mud Pottery** (618-462-7573; http://mississippi mudpottery.biz), 310 E. Broadway, Alton. Open 10–5 Monday through Saturday, noon–4 Sunday. Watch the artisans at work in the studio at this handmade pottery shop as they make dinnerware and gift items.

Jeni J's Gift Shop (618-786-2737; www.jenij.com), 210-214 W. Main Street, Grafton. Located on the main street in Grafton up on a stone terrace overlooking the river, this cute shop has wine-themed gifts, candles, bottles of wine for sale, baby onesies, and other gifts. Through the gift shop, you'll find the Grafton IceHouse Winery, which offers Illinois wines and some made by the shop owners themselves. Free samples offered.

& **Grafton Riverside Flea Market** (618-786-8210), 400 Front Street, Grafton. On the fourth weekend of the month from April through October in the Boatworks building on the river-front, vendors show off all kinds of crafts, jewelry, and finds. The market is open from 9–5.

✳ Special Events

May: **Wood River Rendezvous** Near the intersection of IL 3 and 143, Wood River. Meet artisans and traders, watch battles, and interact with Lewis and Clark re-enactors at this historical celebration of frontier life and the fur-trade era.

June: **Great Rivers Towboat Festival** (618-786-7000), Grafton riverfront. Along with towboat tours, there's music, BBQ, kids' activities, and historical displays at this annual festival.

The Heart
of Illinois

4

FIVE·DOLLARS·FINE·FOR·DRIVING·MORE·THAN·TWE
AT·ONE·TIME·OR·FOR·LEADING·ANY·BEAST
ON·OR·ACROSS·THIS·BR

STARVED ROCK

BISHOP HILL

PEORIA

COLLEGE TOWNS (BLOOMINGTON-
NORMAL/CHAMPAIGN-URBANA)

STARVED ROCK

A trip to Starved Rock promises adventure. The canyons and falls deliver on that promise. Breathe in the landscape, hide behind waterfalls, hike up rocks, and get acquainted with these forests. Starved Rock State Park, and for that matter, the nearby Matthiessen State Park, are great day-trips from Chicago (just about an hour away), or even better, overnight trips, in a tent or at the artfully crafted park lodge.

On your way to Starved Rock, you may pass through Ottawa, a small but engaging city where the Fox and Illinois Rivers meet. The larger Illinois River winds east-west through this part of the state before rounding a big curve toward Peoria, just south of Princeton. Ottawa and its 19,000 or so residents can be a good host for the visit to Starved Rock, a great place to stop for coffee or breakfast before a day of hiking at the park, or if you want to extend your visit in town, add the historic town square where Abraham Lincoln and Stephen Douglas held one of their famous debates. Nearby you'll find the Reddick Mansion and a decent downtown area with restaurants, coffee shops, and stores. It also could be a good place to bring your tired legs for dinner after exploring the parks.

The name of Ottawa comes from the Algonquin word "Adawe" which translates into "trading place." The history of Ottawa, and of this greater region, is wrapped up in that of the I & M Canal (Illinois and Michigan) built to improve transportation throughout the area. Construction started in 1836, and when the canal opened in 1848, it helped connect Lake Michigan to the Mississippi River via the Illinois River, which ultimately helped link the east coast to the Gulf of Mexico through these waterways. The canal started at the south branch of the Chicago River at Bridgeport and stretched for 96 miles to the Illinois River at La Salle. More than 2,000 men, mostly Irish but also Germans and Swedes, lived in shanty-towns and were paid partially with whiskey for the hard work of digging the canal by hand. Aqueducts were also constructed that carried the canal over other waterways like the Fox River. Once open, the canal brought vital supplies to the towns along the path and gave them a new way to get

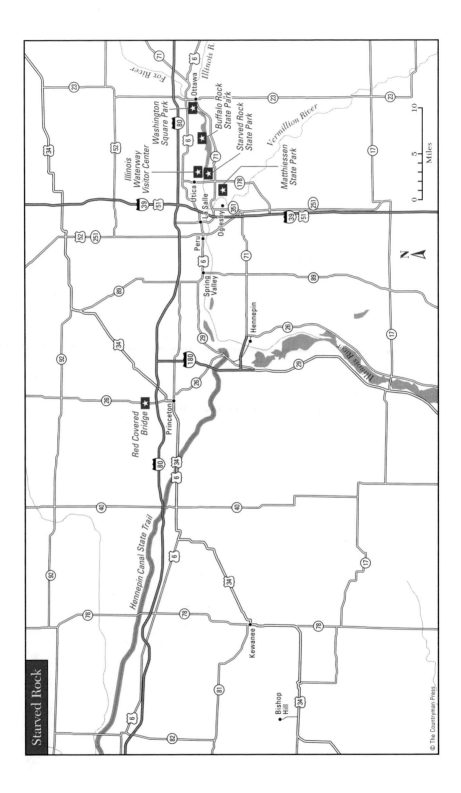

Starved Rock

Fox River

Illinois R.

Ottawa

Buffalo Rock State Park

Starved Rock State Park

Washington Square Park

Vermillion River

Illinois Waterway Visitor Center

Matthiessen State Park

Utica

La Salle

Peru

Oglesby

Spring Valley

Hennepin

Illinois River

Red Covered Bridge

Princeton

Hennepin Canal State Trail

Kewanee

Bishop Hill

N

Miles

© The Countryman Press

their goods out into the world. The barges were pulled through the canal by mules or horses walking the towpaths. People could go from Chicago to LaSalle in a day instead of the weeks it usually took by canoe and foot, or days by wagon and stagecoach. The canal closed in 1933 after the completion of the Illinois Waterway, which included the Sanitary and Shipping Canal.

For Ottawa, the canal enabled the town to move sand, gravel, and clay that were mined in the area. Today, you can still see the Fox River aqueduct and the canal tollhouse in Ottawa. In Chicago, the canal is buried under the Stevenson expressway.

While you're in town, you also may notice some mentions of the Boy Scouts, at the Ottawa Scouting Museum and elsewhere. Ottawa native William D. Boyce founded the Boy Scouts of America after a scout in London helped him find his way when he was lost, but declined the compensation Boyce offered. A Boy Scout statue watches over the Boyce family grave at the Ottawa Avenue Cemetery.

Just west of Ottawa, you'll find the tiny town of Utica, also worth a visit for its shops, wineries, and outdoor recreation activities. It too is home to restaurants that you might want to try if you're spending a few days in the state parks.

Starved Rock State Park itself has a pretty good restaurant and lodge, and the cabins are a good option for people who want the experience of camping but may have some members who aren't completely committed to the idea. The area here offers great hiking, canoeing, and fishing, and like I said, plenty of adventure.

GUIDANCE From I-80, exit IL 23 to get to Ottawa, but don't be discouraged by the chain places surrounding the expressway, there's a character-filled downtown and much green to see if you keep driving toward the Illinois River. Just 1.5 miles later, as you reach the visitors center, the whole look of the town changes.

Stop in the **Ottawa Visitors Center** ♿ (815-434-2737; www .experienceottawa.com), 100 W. Lafayette Street, Ottawa. Open

VIEW FROM ATOP STARVED ROCK

9–5 weekdays, 9–4 Saturday, 10–2 Sunday. Nestled behind the stately Reddick Mansion, the staff can offer friendly advice and information on the region and other state destinations as well.

Heritage Corridor Convention and Visitors Bureau (800-926-2262, 815-667-4356; www.heritagecorridorcvb.com), 801 E. US 6, Utica. Open 9–4 daily. The heritage corridor encompasses a broad area, but the bureau has a visitor center in Utica.

Illinois Waterway Visitor Center (815-667-4054), 950 N. 27th Road, Ottawa. Open daily 9–5. Watch the operation of the Starved Rock lock and dam and learn more about the waterway's use. The location of this U.S. Army Corps of Engineers site provides a great view of Starved Rock itself. With exhibits and a theater, the center also has park rangers available to answer questions and give tours. During the winter, see the bald eagles in action.

Starved Rock State Park Visitors Center (815-667-4726; www.starved rockstatepark.org), Utica. Open 9–6 daily. The center has exhibits that detail the legends of the park and the land's history. But the most important part is the desk staffed by helpful volunteers and workers who can recommend the best hikes for the type of adventure you seek. You'll have a number of stairs to climb to reach the top of Starved Rock from here, but it's definitely worth it.

GETTING THERE *By auto:* I-80 is the main thoroughfare from Chicago, cutting straight across the state. I-39 runs north and south just west of Ottawa and Starved Rock. IL 178 south from I-80 will get you to Utica and Starved Rock.

By bus: **Greyhound** has service to Peru with a station at 3130 May Road (815-224-1065; www.greyhound.com). Station open 8–5 weekdays, 8 AM–midnight Saturday.

By train: **Amtrak** (800-872-7245; www.amtrak.com), 107 Bicentennial Drive, Princeton. This station is open 8–8 daily and has an enclosed waiting area but no ticket office. Princeton is a stop on the Southwest Chief, the California Zephyr, and Illinois Service routes.

MEDICAL EMERGENCIES Illinois Valley Community Hospital (815-223-3300; www.ivch.org), 925 West Street, Peru. A 72-bed acute-care hospital with 24-hour emergency room.

Community Hospital of Ottawa (815-433-3100; www.chottawa.org), 1100 E. Norris Drive, Ottawa. The hospital has a round-the-clock emergency room and is certified for pediatric emergency services. There is also a birth center on site.

EXPLORING BY CAR **Illinois River Road National Scenic Byway** (309-495-5909; www.illinoisriverroad.org) This road starts in Ottawa and follows the curves of the Illinois River for 140 miles, with plenty of stops for exploration at state parks, wetlands, and small towns. Some parts are more picturesque than others, but definitely more scenic and intimate than the interstates.

EXPLORING BY FOOT **Old Town Ottawa** Start at Washington Square Park, which puts you close to Reddick Mansion with Ottawa's visitors center behind it. The park has nice gardens and statues memorializing the Lincoln-Douglas debate site. From the park, head across the street, down LaSalle Street toward the old downtown area, with its coffee shops, stores, and restaurants. The river cuts through the town, and has nice walking paths to explore as well. If you're interested in architecture, pick up a map of the architectural walking tour for downtown Ottawa.

EXPLORING BY BIKE **Illinois and Michigan Canal Towpath** (815-220-1848; www.canalcor.org), 754 First Street, LaSalle. Cyclists will enjoy the 96-mile state trail with exhibits and waysides along the way. The path is located north of the Illinois River in downtown Ottawa between Michigan and Superior Streets. It also runs through downtown Utica.

Hennepin Canal State Trail (815-454-2328; www.dnr.illinois.gov) Locally, access this trail at Bureau Junction south of Princeton on the river. Altogether, there are 85 bridges along the route where you can access the trail. The sister canal to the I & M, the Hennepin is now surfaced from the Illinois River to the Rock River, making for a great 104-mile bike and hiking trail. Only three areas along the stretch have water, so be sure to bring some along, and look out for horses.

EXPLORING BY BOAT **Starved Rock Marina** (815-433-4218; www.starvedrockmarina.com), 1 Dee Bennett Road, Ottawa. Located 5 miles east of IL 178. Open 9–5 weekdays, 9–4 weekends. With more than 200 boat slips, the marina has a boat launch and overnight docking as well. The launch ramp fee is $10 per launch. Mechanics, fuel, waste pump-out station, and a bar and grill are also on site.

EXPLORING BY TROLLEY & **Starved Rock Trolley** (815-220-7386; www.starvedrocklodge.com) The tours depart from the Starved Rock Lodge. Depending on the season, these trolleys take you closer to the canyons to see fall colors and bald eagles, or to learn about the region's history. Tickets: $24–$35 adults, $5 off for children.

✳ Towns and Villages

Ottawa Charming and walkable, and also the county seat of LaSalle County, roughly 19,000 people now call Ottawa home. In 1858, Ottawa hosted the first of the famous debates between Abraham Lincoln and Stephen Douglas.

Utica A devastating tornado ripped through the downtown of this tiny town of 970 people on April 20, 2004, killing 8. Physical repairs have been made, and the people here have worked hard to rebuild and attract visitors back to their town, with a 2-block strip that includes comfortable pubs, a gourmet-food store, and a sophisticated winery. It bills itself as the gateway to Starved Rock. The I & M canal winds through the town near the historical society's museum.

Princeton Settled in 1831, Princeton today is known for its much-photographed red covered bridge, two downtown strips, and historic homes. The town of about 7,500 was also the home of abolitionist Reverend Owen Lovejoy, who helped many African Americans on the Underground Railroad to Canada.

✳ To See

MUSEUMS ⅃ ⛱ **LaSalle County Historical Society and Museum** (815-667-4861; www.lasallecountymuseum.org), 101 E. Canal Street, Utica. Open 10–4 Wednesday through Sunday. Open noon–4 Friday through Sunday during winter. Near the bridge over the I & M canal you will find this small museum. One interesting piece: a carriage that brought Lincoln from the rail station in Ottawa to the debate site in Washington Square Park, where he would spar with Douglas in 1858. Displays tell the history of the town's employers, and the wars that its men left to fight. A Civil War sword and other war memorabilia are worth a look. Across the street near Duffy's, you can visit the blacksmith shop.

HISTORIC SITES ⛱ ⅃ **Reddick Mansion** (815-433-6100; www.reddick mansion.com), Columbus and Lafayette Streets, Ottawa. Call for tour times. Built in 1855 by Irishman William Reddick, this landmark in downtown Ottawa was said to be one of the most expensive residences ever built in the Midwest during this time period. The Italianate building constructed of Lemont limestone and red brick was the town's library until 1975, and now is being restored. A supporter of Stephen Douglas, Mr. Reddick served in the Illinois Senate, operated a general store in Ottawa, and made lucrative real estate investments that supported his lifestyle. Inside, appreciate the wood finishes and ornate crown molding seen throughout the 22 rooms of the home. Period costumes, hats, books, and other antiques lend to the authentic feel of the mansion. But in the bedroom, don't be jarred by the headless mannequin in black clothing!

Ottawa Murals (866-687-2571; www.ottawaillinoismurals.com), downtown Ottawa. The town has taken to the walls to tell its story, with eight
painted murals. If you come upon one of the murals and want to hear the
backstory, call the number listed above. Actors and actresses from the
town will take you back to the time depicted. You'll pick up interesting
details that you otherwise may miss, such as pointing out a city mayor as a
little boy sitting atop his father's shoulders in the *Streetscape Reflections*
mural. In the *Jefferson School* mural, you'll see the familiar face of Bob
McGrath, an area native who starred in *Sesame Street*.

Red Covered Bridge (www.visitprinceton-il.com) Just north of I-80, off
IL 26. Look for signs; the bridge is one of only six remaining in a state
that was once covered with them. Built in 1863, the bridge crosses Big
Bureau Creek and has a park next to it. Princeton also has the Captain
Swift covered bridge, a modern bridge built in 2007 that even semi trucks
can fit through today. The structure is constructed entirely of wood.

Washington Square Park (888-688-2924; www.experienceottawa.com),
Lafayette and Jackson Streets, Ottawa. This historic park is one of those
green spaces that gives a town a sense of community, with towering trees
forming green ceilings above the square. In 1858, more than 10,000 people gathered here for the first senatorial debate between Abraham Lincoln and Stephen Douglas. Mr. Lincoln argued that the phrase ALL MEN
ARE CREATED EQUAL obviously applied to African Americans and that slavery should be abolished. Mr. Douglas declared it a state's right to determine whether or not it wanted slavery within its borders. A boulder, a
plaque, and a fountain topped by bronze statues of the two influential
men mark the historic moment in Ottawa. Lincoln also practiced law at
the courthouses in downtown Ottawa. The park also features monuments
for war veterans, one so old, the stone carvings of the names have been
worn down.

✳ To Do

BOATING C & M Canoe Rental (815-434-6690; www.cmcanoerental
.com), 3401 E. 2062nd Road, Ottawa. Open spring through fall. Canoe the
Fox River with day-trips that have you paddling 7 or 12 miles on the lower
Fox River, a Class 1 river with no dangerous currents but lovely scenery.
Rental rates include use of a 17-foot river canoe, paddles, life jackets, and
transportation to the launch spot. All trips begin and end at Chet's Fox
River Tavern. You must book in advance. Cost: $45, a two-day trip is
$80–85.

Vermillion White Water Rafting (815-667-5242; www.vermillionriver
rafting.com), 781 N. 2249th Road, Oglesby. The trips depart between
9:30–2 daily May through mid-July. The 50-mile Vermillion River has a 9-

mile stretch where you can experience some rapids. Altogether there are about 14 sets of rapids, most classified 1 and 2 out of the 6 classes, but with a few 3s. The trips run about three to four hours. The company also shuttles your vehicle out to the endpoint so it's waiting for you when you finish the trip. Cost: $25 adults, $20 children under 16, which includes rafts, paddles, and life vests. Credit cards not accepted.

Belle of the Rock (815-434-9200; www.belleoftherock.com) For a different vantage point to view Starved Rock, these paddlewheel boat tours depart from the state park and travel on the river for a 45-minute cruise. Cost: $14 adults, $12 seniors, $8 children. Canoes and kayaks are also available for rent.

GOLF Pine Hills Golf Club (815-434-3985;www.ottawapinehillsgolfclub .com, 1665 N. 2501st Road, Ottawa. Located 1.5 miles south of town off IL 23, the course was designed by Thomas Bendelow, who was behind the Medinah Country Club and other well-known courses, and is carved out of some lovely canyons. Fees: $10–15 for 9 holes, $15–25 for 18 holes. Carts: $8–16.

HORSEBACK RIDING ✐ Cedar Creek Ranch (815-481-3337; www .ccrstables.com), 249 E. IL 71, Cedar Point. Open 11–5 weekdays, 10–4 weekends. Trail rides depart every 90 minutes. The hour-long ride winds through 3 miles of hills, water, and timber on the ranch. Guides will point out the two historic sites on the property: a Civil War cemetery, and an old coal-mine site. The cost is $25 per rider. Children ages 7 to 10 can ride the trail as long as a parent is on a separate horse. Those 6 and younger can take a motorized route alongside, or have a guide lead a controlled ride for $15. There is a 260-pound weight limit, and you must have a reservation.

Starved Rock Stables (815-667-3026) Located 1 mile west of Starved Rock State Park on IL 71. Rides depart at 10, 12, 2, and 4 Wednesday through Sunday. The guides here offer a one-hour trail ride through the nature preserves surrounding Starved Rock, and through two canyons. You must be at least 10 years of age to ride, and there is a 225-pound weight limit. Cost: $25 per person, but they only accept cash, so plan ahead.

SKYDIVING Skydive Chicago (815-433-0000; www.skydivechicago .com), 3215 E. 1969th Road, Ottawa. Open 9–5 weekdays, 8–sunset weekends. Closed December through mid-March. If this is your first time skydiving, you'll sit through a 20-minute class before loading into a plane that will take you up to 13,500 feet. And then, you will jump out of a plane! (Just making sure you realize this part of it.) You will freefall for 60 seconds before the parachute deploys for a 5 to 7 minute canopy flight. If the

exclamation point above signaled some anxiety on my part, you are right in
guessing I did not try this myself. But I'm all for adventures and if this is
your thing, hey, don't let me rain on your skydiving. First-timers will make
their dive harnessed to a professional instructor. The cost is $209. Skydive
Chicago is located on a 220-acre resort with canoeing, volleyball, camping,
a bar, and café.

TOURS & **LaSalle Canal Boat** (815-220-1848; www.lasallecanalboat
.org), 754 1st Street, LaSalle. Trips depart Tuesday through Saturday at
10:30, 1, and 2:30 from May through October. With guides in period costumes, this one-hour voyage on a replica 19th century canal boat pulled by
mules will transport you back to life on the historic I & M canal, a hand-
dug waterway that pioneers used to travel from Chicago to LaSalle. The
canal was part of a waterway linking Lake Michigan with the Mississippi
River, and ultimately, the East Coast with the Gulf of Mexico. Tickets are
available at the Lock 16 Visitor Center and cost $14 adults, $8 youth, $12
seniors.

Starved Rock Adventures (815-434-9200; www.srarock.com) Located
inside the Starved Rock Marina on Dee Bennett Road. Open 9–5 weekdays, 9–6 weekends from April through October. Rent pontoon boats, jet
skis, speed boats, and fishing boats. If you want a different lodging experience, you can also rent houseboats. Fishing boats run between $75–95.
Speed boats will cost more—up to $330 for the day.

WINERIES & **Illinois River Winery** (815-667-4012; www.illinoisriver
winery.com), 723 S. Clark Street, Utica. Open 10–5 daily. Known for their
fruit wines, this winery is located in a strip of country-themed stores. In
the tasting shop, you can also get coffee, antipasti, and bread sticks.
Exceptionally popular is the Hollowine, a spiced-apple wine served warm
with cinnamon, clove, and nutmeg. Tastings free.

& **August Hill Winery** (815-667-5211; www.augusthillwinery.com), 106
Mill Street, Utica. Open 10–5 Monday through Thursday, 10–8 Friday and
Saturday, 11–5 Sunday. After inheriting the family farm in Peru, Mark
Wenzel made it his mission to care for the land in the same way as his
grandfather Augie (the August in the name). He started studying winemaking, and today, there is a vineyard and winery on the property south of
the Illinois River. The motto for the winery: FROM THE HEART TO THE
HAND. In Utica, this tasting room is a sleek, gray-and-white, modern room
serving wine in special Riedel stemware. Taste six wines for $3.

✳ Green Space

✐ **Starved Rock State Park** (815-667-4726; www.starvedrockstatepark
.org), 2568 E. 950th Road, Oglesby. Park open from 5 AM–9 PM, with trails

open from dawn to dusk. The waterfalls and the canyons are the draw at Starved Rock, calling to an estimated 2 million people a year. A personal favorite, Starved Rock and its 13 miles of trails offer up a great blend of views: rivers, rock formations, waterfalls, forest seen from the top of a cliff or from the bottom of a canyon. You'll have to put in some effort because the destinations are either at the river level or up on a cliff, meaning you'll have inclines and stairs to conquer, but it's worth it. Helpful volunteers at the visitors center can recommend the best hikes depending on what you seek. In the spring you'll find about 18 waterfalls. Wildcat is the tallest at 70 feet. You can walk behind the waterfall at LaSalle Canyon, and St. Louis Canyon is good for kids because of the sandy area provided by a collapse of sandstone. For a longer, less-populated hike, try LaSalle Canyon. But if you don't want to walk the 2 miles from the visitors center, you can park at Parkman's Plain and walk just 20 minutes or so to the canyon. You should return for the other seasons because in the fall, you'll find colorful carpets of orange, red, and yellow on the canyon grounds. In the winter, the waterfalls are crystallized into gorgeous ice falls. During the winter months you can also find bald eagles fishing near the Starved Rock Lock and Dam. They congregate near the dam, where the water remains unfrozen and they can fish. Near Leopold and Plum Islands, you'll find them roosting in the winter. The months of December, January, and February are the best time to catch the eagles, and the best view is from the top of Starved Rock. You can borrow binoculars at the visitor center. Ice climbing is allowed in certain canyons, but you must sign in at

STARVED ROCK STATE PARK

the park office. But note that rock climbing is not allowed. You can fish for walleye, white bass, carp, and catfish on the north side of the main riverside parking lot, and in the river from a boat. So many visitors have walked on the top of Starved Rock that between the time the state took over the park in 1911 and 1981, rangers noted that 18 inches of the ground had been worn down by all those footsteps. The name of the park actually has a tragic backstory, rooted in the Native American legend of Pontiac, a chief of the Ottawa tribe slain by a member of the Illiniwek tribe while attending a tribal council in the 1760s. A battle ensued and eventually a group of Illiniwek became surrounded at the rock and died of starvation.

✍ **Matthiessen State Park** (815-667-4868; http://dnr.state.il.us/lands /landmgt/parks/r1/mttindex.htm) From I-80, take exit 81 to Utica. Travel 5 miles south on IL 178 to the park entrance. This geological wonder has stunning rock formations and mineral springs. The park has 5 miles of marked, surfaced hiking trails running along steep cliffs and into deep canyons. During the winter, the park has 6 miles of cross-country ski trails and ski rental available as well. Waterfalls can be found in the spring at Matthiessen Lake Falls and Cascade Falls. To start out, you'll have to navigate the stairs down to Cascade Falls, where the canyon drops 45 feet to the start of the Lower Dell. You can walk among peaceful pools of water at the canyon bottom, listening to the rush of the fall nearby. On the rock walls surrounding you, notice the marks of the minerals that color the rock. The park is named after a prominent industrialist and philanthropist from LaSalle, Frederick Matthiessen, who developed the land as a 176-acre private park. After its donation to the state, it grew to 1,938 acres. No camping is allowed. If you're bringing kids, build in some time for them to play in the restored fort at the trailhead. The

CASCADE FALLS IN MATTHIESSEN STATE PARK

log structure is modeled after the fortifications the French built in the Midwest in the 1600s and 1700s.

Buffalo Rock State Park (815-433-2224; http://dnr.state.il.us/lands /landmgt/parks/i&m/east/buffalo/home.htm), 1300 N. 27th Road, Ottawa. West of Ottawa 3 miles, this bluff was once an island in the Illinois River. Now the 298-acre park offers some impressive views of the Illinois River. From the trails high above, view the *Effigy Tumuli*, inspired by Native American burial grounds. Artist Michael Heizer has created this "earth art," which involves sculptures of a snake, turtle, catfish, frog, and water strider. It is best viewed from a distance. The park has picnic areas, and hosts two bison who have made a home there. There are three primitive camping areas on the trail between Buffalo Rock and Utica, but no water or rest room facilities. You must bike or walk in. Permits are required. Across the street from the park, you can access the Illinois and Michigan Canal Trail.

✳ Lodging

A number of chain hotels are available in Ottawa near I-80.

BED AND BREAKFASTS (ᵎ)

Brightwood Inn (888-667-0600; www.brightwoodinn.com), 2407 IL 178, Oglesby. Near both Starved Rock and Matthiessen State Parks, the owners of this newer bed and breakfast (built in 1996) aim to help you get lost in the peace and quiet on their 14 acres. The eight guest rooms have TV, DVD, seasonal fireplace, and private bath. Some rooms have large two-person Jacuzzi tubs. Full breakfast comes with the room, with dishes that focus on fresh organic herbs and vegetables grown on the grounds. $$–$$$.

Fox River Bed and Breakfast (815-431-9257; www.foxriverbnb .com), 3367 E. 2072nd Road, Ottawa. This bed and breakfast is located 8 miles north of downtown on a 17-acre spread in the country.

Word is Charles Lindbergh once stayed in this Victorian farmhouse, built in 1901, and one of the rooms is named after Mr. Lindbergh, who reportedly slept in the room when his mail plane went down on the property. The home overlooks the Fox River Valley and is now run by Charlotte Beach, a registered nurse who bought the place in 2007 and is dedicated to preserving the history of the home and farm. Rooms include satellite TV, CD/DVD player, microwave, and refrigerator. The tribal room, decked out with Native American, African, and Aboriginal art, also features a Kanga drum for you to play. Primitive tent camping is also available on the grounds, $20 per two-person tent. Each additional person is $10. The camping area is located in the woods, with two large fire pits, a grill available, games, and access to the home's bathroom. $–$$.

Landers House (815-667-5170; www.landershouse.com), 115 E. Church Street, Utica. Just around the corner from the main strip of shops and restaurants in downtown Utica, Landers House has four cottages—all designed around a theme—such as the Caribou cottage or the La Noche cottage. The cottages feature two-person whirlpools, fireplaces, two-person showers, sky lights, cable TV/VCR, CD players, and wet bars. Breakfasts may include blueberry blintz soufflé, lobster quesadillas with poached eggs, or apple bacon cheddar bake. $$–$$.

(ᵗᵖ) **Madison Street Living** (815-434-1500; madisonstreetliving .com), 224 W. Madison Street, Ottawa. Rent a small apartment in this historic 1888 building in downtown Ottawa. The apartments come with a full kitchen with granite countertops and new appliances, a washer and dryer, flat-screen TV, and a king bed. $$.

Foster Suite (815-667-4717; www.fostersuite.com), 155 ½ Mill Street, Utica. For an apartment-like stay in downtown Utica, Foster Suite can accommodate four people. You can have the refrigerator stocked with your favorite beverages or the wine rack filled from the local winery for your arrival. The suite includes gas-burning fireplace, flat-screen TV, whirlpool Jacuzzi tub, and room service available from nearby Skoog's Pub and Grill. $$–$$$.

HOTELS & (ᵗᵖ) ✎ ♋ **Starved Rock Lodge** (800-868-7625, 815-

667-4211; www.starvedrocklodge .com), IL 178 and IL 71, Utica. You can stay in the lodge or cabins. The pioneer family cabins sleep five and have two king beds, and a pull-out sleeper chair. You won't find TVs, the cabin focus is on being close to nature, with exposed log interiors and modest decor. The cabins are heated and have air-conditioning, so they are available year-round. In the lodge, which was built by the Civilian Conservation Corps in the 1930s, there are a range of room styles from the knotty pine east wing rooms to the more recently updated west wing rooms that come with flat-screen TVs. The resort features an indoor pool, gated children's pool, hot tub, sauna, restaurant, and bar. There's also the great room centered around the stone fireplace. $$–$$$.

& **Starved Rock Inn** (815-667-4211; www.starvedrocklodge.com), IL 178 and IL 6, Utica. For a more economical choice, there's this eight-room motel that offers rooms 3 miles north of the park, from April through November. Because of its affiliation with the lodge, guests can use the lodge pool and other pluses. Rooms come with private baths and satellite TVs. $.

(ᵗᵖ) & ♨ **The Willows Hotel** (815-667-3400; www.thewillowshotel .net), 325 Clark Street, Utica. Fronted by two stories of porches, this white building looks like it belongs on the oceanfront. Inside, there's a coffee bar and an art gallery run by North Central Illinois

Artworks. Standard rooms are on the first floor and have either two queen beds or a sofa sleeper and queen bed, small refrigerator, microwave, coffeemaker, toaster, iron, and bath. Junior suites have a separate bedroom and a kitchen. $$.

CAMPING �& ✍ **Starved Rock State Park Campground** (815-667-4726; www.starvedrockstate park.org), 2570 E. 950th Road, Oglesby. This popular campground is usually full from May through October, so book early if you plan to reserve a site. The park keeps 30 of the 133 sites available for a first-come, first-served basis, but those fill up every weekend. Each site has electricity, a parking space, picnic table, and grill. The campgrounds have showers and flush toilets. There is a $5 reservation fee, plus $25 per site camping fee; reservations can be made online at www .reserveamerica.com.

((•)) ✍ **LaSalle Peru KOA Kampground** (815-667-4988), 756 N. 3150th Road, Utica. Camp in a tent, cabin, or RV at this campground north of Starved Rock. With 85 sites, you'll also be happy to find modern bathrooms and free hot showers. The campground has a heated swimming pool, playground, small store, and propane and laundry facilities. It also has electrical, water, and sewer hookups. Tent sites are $25–30. Cabins run $50–100 depending on the size.

((•)) ✍ **Hickory Hollow Campground** (815-667-4996; www .hickoryhollowcg.com), 757 N. 3029th Road, Utica. Located near Starved Rock, this campground offers wooded tent sites with picnic tables, grills, and fire rings. There is a store, rec room, showers, laundry, heated swimming pool, playground, and dump station on site. If you'd like a little more shelter, you can also rent a small rustic log cabin or a condo. You must bring bedding and dishes for the cabins. The small condos sleep four to six people and come with a full bathroom. The larger version sleeps up to eight, with two bathrooms and a full kitchen. RV sites with full hookups are $34. Tent sites with water and electric are $32, while the plain tent sites are $25. Cabins: $, Condos: $–$$.

RESORTS ✍ ((•)) �& **Grizzly Jack's Grand Bear Resort & Indoor Waterpark** (866-399-3866; www.grizzlyjacksresort.com), IL 178, Utica. This 60-acre North Woods-themed resort (with the Moose Crossing and Honey Pot snack area) is geared toward families—on school breaks, for large reunions, or other group events. Its location just across the street from Starved Rock State Park makes it a great starting point for families who may have little ones who can't hike all day long. The main building has a year-round indoor water park, with a wave pool, waterslide, lazy river, and kiddie pool. An arcade, pizza place, and bar will also help round out your itinerary. Across the parking lot, a hulking warehouse of a building houses an indoor amusement park with nine full-sized amusement park rides. But call ahead to make sure everything will be open when you're planning a trip. If school is in session and there are not many guests, they sometimes shut down certain features until it gets busy again. The guest rooms attempt a woodsy feel with furniture made to look as if it was constructed out of logs. But otherwise, the rooms are relatively modern with TVs, microwaves, coffeemakers, and refrigerators. The standard family suites come with two queen beds and a sofa sleeper. The lodge also has king suites, kid cabin suites that come with twin bunk beds, or deluxe family suites that have a private bedroom and a living room. Your pass to the parks is included in any booking. If you need a little more room for your family, try the 2-story, 1,800-square-foot vacation villas that accommodate up to nine people, with extras like a kitchen and washer and dryer that can be good when traveling with a family. The 3-story luxury cabins can fit up to 18 people. Both the villas and cabins feature fireplaces, kitchens, living rooms, washers and dryers, two-person Jacuzzis, patios, and balconies. $$–$$$.

✳ Where to Eat

EATING OUT (ᚖ) **Starved Rock Café** (815-667-4211; www.starved rocklodge.com) Open 6:30–5 Monday through Thursday, 6:30 AM–8 PM Saturday, 6:30–6 Friday, Sunday. Located in the lobby of the lodge, this very casual café/store offers free wine tasting from 4–5 Saturday. You'll also find a few tables where you can snack on homemade fudge, ice cream, sandwiches, coffees, and other treats. $.

DOWNTOWN OTTAWA

((ŋ)) & **Jeremiah Joe Coffee** (815-566-3507; www.jeremiahjoecoffee .com), 807 LaSalle Street, Ottawa. Open 6 AM–8 PM Monday, 6 AM–9 PM Tuesday through Thursday, 6–10 Friday, Saturday, 8–5 Sunday. One unique extra that you'll find here: From the coffee shop, there's a window that gives you a view of coffee beans being roasted at the LaSalle Street Roasting Co., which is housed in the same building. Comfy leather chairs and warm burnt orange walls invite you in. The espresso bar kicks out lattes, mochas, and cappuccinos, iced or not. You can also choose from baked goods and just regular good old coffee. If the weather is nice, there's a wonderful large outdoor patio that looks onto LaSalle Street, but is set back and covered from the sun. $.

& **Skoog's Pub & Grill** (815-667-5800; www.skoogspubandgrill .com), 155 Mill Street, Utica. Lunch: 11–2 weekdays, 11–4 Saturday, 11–7 Sunday. Dinner: 5–9 Thursday through Saturday. On Monday through Wednesday, choose from a smaller menu of wings, sandwiches, and appetizers. Skoog's was one of the downtown businesses that survived the 2004 tornado, and their thankfulness is reflected in a plaque above the entrance commemorating the tornado. Utica native, Andy Skoog, opened the restaurant in 2000 in a former closed tavern. The menu specializes in ribs, pastas, and steaks, but also includes the massive Skoog burger, sandwiches, and homemade soups. $–$$.

& **The Cheese Shop** (815-433-0478; www.thecheeseshop.biz), 1219 Fulton Street, Ottawa. Open 8–7 Monday through Saturday. The Ruhlands have been making cheese in this area since the 1940s, and elsewhere before that. Current owner, Marty, has converted the old family cheese-factory building into this deli, adding meats, chili, salads, and soups to the offerings, although it's clear from the milk bottles, creamers, and other antiques that the cheese still plays a big role. Also check out the other antiques Marty has collected over the years. $.

& **Bee Hive Restaurant** (815-433-5640; www.beehiverestaurant .us), 701 LaSalle Street, Ottawa. Open 6–3 daily. This corner diner across from the county courthouse serves up breakfast all day long with a country flair. Think skillets packed with breakfast meats, potatoes, and eggs. You also can get crepes and pancakes. The rest of the menu is filled with traditional diner offerings—burgers, croissant sandwiches, chef's salad, and melts. $.

& **Cajun Connection** (815-667-9855; www.ronscajunconnection .com), 897 East US 6, Utica. Open 4–9 PM Thursday through Saturday, noon–6 PM Sunday. Louisianan Ron McFarlain is your chef and guide to Cajun cuisine in this neck of the woods. His specialties include fresh-battered Louisiana alligator, gumbo, jambalaya, and roasted pecan pie. You'll also find a selection of Cajun beers. $–$$.

DINING OUT The Main Dining Room at Starved Rock State Park (815-220-7321; www.starved rocklodge.com) Open at 8 for breakfast. Dinner: 5–8 weekdays, 5–9 weekends. Brunch: 10:30–2 Sunday. The dining room fireplace invites tired hikers to relax. The menu offers comfort as well—with dinner offerings like pot roast, classic fried chicken, and meat loaf. If you visit during the spring or summer, the veranda may be open for meals, as well. $$–$$$.

Canal Port Bar & Grill (815-667-3010; www.canalport.com), 148 Mill Street, Utica. Open 11–9 Tuesday through Thursday, 11–9:30 Friday and Saturday, 11–8 Sunday. With tin ceilings and a beautiful wood bar and stone fireplace, Canal Port's dining room and bar is a versatile place where you can sit at the bar and have a burger or take a seat in the dining room for a different dining experience (without having to change out of your jeans). You'll find New York strip in a Jack Daniels sauce, prime rib, or surf and turf. The seafood offerings include salmon, orange roughy, and fried walleye. The burgers and sandwiches are creative, with some unique ingredients—like the chipotle crab-cake sub, or the Swiss and portobello turkey burger. I must say the fries are cooked exceptionally well here. $–$$$$.

& **Hank's Farm** (815-433-2540), 2973 N. IL 71, Ottawa. Open 4:30–9 Monday through Thursday, 4:30–10 Friday, Saturday, 3:30–9

Sunday. Brunch runs from 11–2 Sunday. Inside the large white barn on 20 acres, you'll find this Italian American restaurant with traditional dishes like fettuccini alfredo and baked rigatoni. There's also a lengthy seafood menu of shrimp dishes, baked cod, and frog legs. In addition, the place is known for its fried chicken and ribs. Children's menu also available. $$–$$$$.

✳ Entertainment

LIVE MUSIC ⵆ **Tracy's Row House** (815-434-3171; www.tracys rowhouse.net), 728 Columbus Street, Ottawa. Open 5–10 Friday, Saturday, and from 5–9 Sunday. Lunch: 11–5 daily. An 1880s row house makes for an intimate, warm setting for this martini bar that also books live music and has quite a wine list. The quaint patio with paver bricks and iron furniture is a nice setting for a drink. For martinis, you'll find no fewer than 72 kinds here. Dinner includes comfort dishes like meat loaf and chicken pot pie. $–$$.

MOVIES & **Roxy 6** (815-433-8303; www.21stcinemas.com/Roxy .htm), 827 LaSalle Street, Ottawa. This old-time-looking theater in downtown Ottawa features first-run films. Admission: $7.25 adults, $6 children 12 years and under.

THEATER Follies Theatre (815-667-7008; www.folliestheatre .com), 122 Mill Street, Utica. Performances are generally at 8 PM

Tuesday through Sunday. This live entertainment hall boasts of booking Branson, Missouri–style acts with casts who also perform there.

✳ Selective Shopping

&. **Cattails Gifts & Wine Tasting Room** (815-667-4550; www .shopcattails.com), IL 178 and IL 6, Utica. Open 10–5 Monday, Thursday through Saturday, and noon–5 Sunday. A short drive out of town, this corner where two highways meet has been prettied up by this gift shop and Starved Rock Inn, which sits behind the gift shop. Stop by the wine-tasting room for wines by the glass. The stone-paved wine patio is a nice place to relax after a day of hiking, or before dinner. A range of foodie gifts, including homemade fudge, flowers, crafts, and local history books await in the gift shop. The Cottage Boutique offers footwear, handbags, and hats.

&. **Starved Rock Hot Glass** (815-313-5445; www.starvedrockhot glass.com), 700 W. Main Street, Ottawa. Open 10–6 Tuesday through Friday, 11–5 Saturday. See glass artist Laura Johnson create beautiful jewelry and art glass in her studio. Demonstrations are given daily. You can schedule a class to learn how to do it yourself, or pick up one of Johnson's brightly colored vases, paperweights, or other pieces.

Ottawa Antiques 200 block of West Main Street, Ottawa. Peruse through antiques, collectibles, and crafts at several stores on this block of Main, which is home to Rural America, Main Street Antiques, and Grandma's Attic.

Main Street Princeton (www .visitprinceton-il.com) You'll find pleasing strips of shops in two sections of Main in Princeton—North and South. There are antique stores, bead shops, handmade pottery stores, galleries, cafes, candy shops, wine stores, and gift shops.

✳ Special Events

June: **Festival 56** (815-879-5656; www.festival56.com) Box office is located at 316 S. Main Street, Princeton. This large summer theater festival is held in Princeton each year, drawing professionals from across the country for six weeks of creative collaboration. They put on Shakespeare shows in the park, or perform musicals and classics elsewhere in town.

September: **Vintage Illinois Wine Festival** (www.vintage illinois.com) Held at Matthiessen State Park, this festival brings together more than 20 Illinois wineries to showcase what these grapes can do. A $15 entry fee gets you five tasting tickets and a wine glass.

October: **Burgoo Festival** (815-667-4861; www.lasallecounty museum.org) For more than 40 years, on the second Sunday in October in downtown Utica, the LaSalle County Historical Society has put on this festival. What is burgoo exactly? Well the burgoomeister may not tell you exactly what's in it, but it's a traditional pioneer stew. It used to be made with wild game such as venison or squirrel and what the pioneers had from the garden, but state health laws prohibit selling soup made from game. So today this burgoo blends beef, carrots, potatoes, hominy, celery, tomatoes, cabbage, onions, peppers, and other vegetables with spices and herbs. It's cooked outdoors for 12–18 hours over a wood fire. Locals work around the clock the night before, chopping vegetables, and the burgoomeisters guard the pot and their exact spice and herb recipes. The festival has a flea market and music, and you'll also find demonstrations by basket weavers and blacksmiths.

BISHOP HILL

Valkommen! You will see this greeting throughout the small historic town that emerges out of farm fields in eastern Illinois. Bishop Hill is worth a day at least, with its inviting, friendly shops, and interesting museums about a people who wanted to create a utopian community on the prairie.

A little background will help you to better understand the story: In the mid 1800s, the population exploded in Sweden, which meant there was not enough land for everyone to farm and make a proper living. People started heading to America. Meanwhile, the Swedish government became focused on preserving the Lutheran state religion. Those who disagreed faced persecution. Eric Janson was one such person, feeling the heat because of his religious beliefs that diverged from the state-sponsored view of religion. Having built a group of followers, in 1846 he led a group from Sweden to this spot in the Illinois prairie to create a community where they could worship their own way. "Jansonism" was a return to the simple, basic tenets of Christianity. Janson, who rejected the Lutheran theologians, claimed that God spoke to him.

The followers pooled together their resources and traveled to the United States, walking 160 miles to this site from Chicago. During the first winter, 96 people died in the makeshift shelters they built. But the colonists rebounded. They built 20 large commercial buildings and started farming. They were able to produce just about everything they needed and even had enough to sell elsewhere. But in 1850, Janson was murdered in a disagreement involving his cousin, Charlotta. Charlotta accompanied the colonists to Bishop Hill, and Janson, being her oldest male relative in the area, became her guardian of sorts. Charlotta married a man named John Root, who was a new arrival in Bishop Hill. They married with the agreement that if Root ever wanted to leave the colony, Charlotta would remain in Bishop Hill. After about a year, Root decided he had had enough and wanted to leave. He left and later sent some men to get Charlotta and their son. Janson then retrieved his relatives, fanning the flames.

In May 1850, Janson was in Cambridge taking care of colony business at the courthouse when Root found him and shot him.

A decade later, the colony was dissolved amid disagreements about the financial management. Property was divided among the members in 1861. Some people left, some stayed, and the town continued to prosper. After World War II, the community struggled and more people moved away. In 1946 the community gave some of the buildings to the state.

It took until the 1960s for the real preservation effort to awaken. One of the historic buildings, a brewery, was torn down, and in response the Bishop Hill Heritage Association formed. The state became more active and the village was made a National Historic Landmark in 1984.

Today, about 120 people live in Bishop Hill, and by local count, roughly 20 percent are descendants of the colonists. Artisans and all kinds of crafty people have set up shop here, opening up quaint country gift shops or offering demonstrations of the trades and crafts the colonists would have used. The town slogan is UTOPIA ON THE PRAIRIE—THEN AND NOW. You can walk to and from most of the sites, as the town is set up around a central park.

BISHOP HILL

GUIDANCE When you get to town, you can start at the **Bishop Hill Museum**, which has a short orientation film about the village (see To See). You can also pick up brochures. For more help, there's www.bishophill.com, which provides village information, and the **Bishop Hill Arts Council** (www.bishophill artscouncil.com), an organization with a pretty thorough Web site.

GETTING THERE *By auto:* Bishop Hill is about 30 miles northeast of Galesburg, and 40 miles southeast of Moline, on County Highway 39, which is north of US 34. If you approach from the south end, the museum will be on your left side as you come into town. Continue north to reach the main town square.

COLONY CHURCH

MEDICAL EMERGENCIES **OSF St. Mary Medical Center** (309-344-3161; www.osfstmary.org), 3333 N. Seminary Street, Galesburg. This acute-care hospital in nearby Galesburg has 99 beds, a 24-hour emergency department, and advanced pediatric center.

✳ To See

MUSEUMS For all sites, please call to check hours if you want to visit during the winter, as travel can be difficult in the rough winter months. The Bishop Hill Museum, Bjorklund Hotel, and Colony Church are operated by the state and the following contact information and hours apply to all three: (309-927-3345; www.state.il.us/hpa/hs/bishop_hill.htm), open 9–5 Wednesday through Sunday, March through October, 9–4 Wednesday through Sunday, November through February. Suggested donation: $4, $10 for families.

&. **Bishop Hill Museum** Off Bishop Hill Road (County Road 39) at the south end of town. This museum will introduce you to Bishop Hill and the colonists through a short film. There is a small display of photos and paintings depicting the story of the settlers. The work of folk artist Olof Krans is also on display. His family joined the colony in 1850, when he was 12, and later in his life he painted his memories of the colony.

Bjorklund Hotel West Main and Park. The state bought this stucco building in 1968 and has been restoring it, with two floors set up to appear as they would have back during the colonists' times.

&. **Colony Church** Bishop Hill Street and Maiden Lane. Barnlike in appearance, the main floor of this 1848 building is a series of rooms outfitted with exhibits about the people who came here and the trades that allowed the community to exist. Settlers in Bishop Hill rented these rooms, sometimes combining an upstairs and downstairs room into a family home, like a condo. In some rooms, the walls are stripped away so you can see the innards of the historic building. Upstairs is the main church area, a stripped-down sanctuary of plain creamy white walls and dark wooden pews, illustrative of the colonists' beliefs about religion. The room is dressed up by some grand chandeliers.

Steeple Building Museum (309-927-3899; www.bishophill.com), 103 N. Bishop Hill Street. The Bishop Hill Heritage Association, which raises money for preservation efforts, operates this museum, along with other historic buildings. Open 10–5 Monday through Saturday, noon–5 Sunday, April through October. Offseason hours: 10–4 Monday through Saturday, noon–4 Sunday. The idea was for this 3-story brick Greek Revival–style building to serve as a hotel when it was built in 1854, but the townspeople instead lived in it, educated their children here, and used it as a bank. The clock tower on the building still has the original clock made by the colonists. The exhibits here give the background of life in Sweden, why the Swedes would want to leave, how they traveled by ship, and what they brought with them. It also provides context about the religious persecution they battled, while outlining the biography of colony leader Eric Janson. Different rooms of the old hotel display period farming equipment and other items that helped the colonists with their trades and crafts. Some rooms are set up as they would have been used by the colonists. The museum also hosts rotating exhibits, such as one we caught on weddings.

Henry County Museum (309-927-3528), Knox and Park Streets. Open daily 10–4, May through October. With large displays showing the setup of a general store, a blacksmith shop, a country school, and early home scenes, the museum rounds out the tale of life on the prairie. You'll learn why Henry County is known as the Hog Capital of the World, and can see a windmill in operation outside.

HISTORIC SITES Around the town, you can see more of the historic buildings, which are used as businesses. Some are private homes. The **Boys Dormitory** and the **Dairy Building** are not open, but you can see the exteriors. Pick up a map for a walking tour.

✳ Lodging

BED AND BREAKFASTS ((¡))
**The Colony Hospital Bed and
Breakfast** (309-927-3506; www
.bishophilllodging.com), 110 N.
Olson Street, Bishop Hill. This
sunny building was built in 1855
to serve as the colony hospital and
is now a National Historic Landmark. The rooms are pretty
simple, with quilts and straightforward furnishings, and are
named after colony doctors and
leaders. A portico is outfitted with
rockers to allow for guests to hang
out with wine or coffee. There are
three rooms, two of them suites
with kitchenettes, one with a private screened-in porch. All come
with private baths, queen beds,
dining tables, chairs, coffeemakers, refrigerators, microwaves, and
TVs. You also will receive a breakfast basket with fresh muffins,
scones, hard-boiled eggs, fresh
fruit, and yogurt. On weekends,
you get a breakfast at the Filling
Station diner. No children under
10 unless you are booking all
three rooms as a family. No pets.
$$.

HOTELS AND INNS **The Bish-
op Hill Gallery Inn** (309-927-
3080; www.bishophillgalleryinn
.com), 109 W. Main Street. The
recently restored 1856 Colony
Administration building faces the
park, and has three nice guest
rooms with private, modern baths.
The original use for the building
was to house the offices of the
colony trustees on the second

floor, and family apartments on
the third floor. The owners reno-
vated the second floor to serve as
the inn, with their Bishop Hill
Gallery on the main floor. The inn
has a large sitting room and a
small kitchenette with refrigerator,
ice, sink, and microwave. Rooms
come with coffeemaker, TV with
Dish network, AC. Groups can
rent the entire floor to fit six to
eight people. No pets. $–$$.

CAMPING ((¡)) ✿ ✿ **The Old
Timber Campground** (309-937-
2314; www.theoldtimber.com),
10768 E. 1600th Street, Cambridge. Located about 10 minutes
away from Bishop Hill, this campground has about 100 sites and a
lake for fishing that also has a
roped-off swimming area. Old
Timber has a store, game room,
volleyball pit, and playground.
Besides sites for RVs or tents, they
have a few tipis for rent. Fees:
$15–23.

✳ Where to Eat

EATING OUT **Bishop Hill
Colony Bakery** (309-927-3042;
www.bishophillcolonybakery.com),
103 S. Bishop Hill Street. Open
9–5 Wednesday through Saturday,
11–5 Sunday. Located in Mrs.
Smith's Boarding House, as the
sign says outside, this colorful yellow house is surrounded by gardens populated by sweet
wildflowers. The smell is sweet
inside as well, with breads and
cinnamon rolls, muffins, and other
pastries. There's a small counter

BISHOP HILL BAKERY

area with glass cases of the baked goods, a small dining area, and the outdoor picnic area in the garden. The bakery also serves sandwiches

THE RED OAK IN BISHOP HILL

and soups. There's a shop inside, **The Mustard Cupboard,** filled with lots of homemade aprons, candles, linens, and gifts. $.

&. ♪ **The Red Oak Comfort Food & Pie Company** (309-927-3539; www.theredoak.com), 106 Bishop Hill Street. Open 11–2 Tuesday through Sunday. Depending on the weather, the restaurant is only open on weekends in January and February. This friendly looking restaurant has brightly painted walls of orange, apple green, red, and yellow, and plates that feature Swedish American food cooked from scratch. That means Swedish meatballs, of course, but there's also beef cabbage rolls, open-faced Scandinavian sandwiches, American sandwiches, and salads served with homemade Swedish rye bread. You can also pick up home-baked pies and hand-churned ice cream. Food is also shipped or home-delivered. $.

✷ Selective Shopping

There are a number of residents carrying on the crafts of the colonists, from woodworkers and furniture makers to quilters. I've listed a few shops here, but if you wander you'll find more artisans at work.

Bishop Hill Gallery (309-927-3080; www.thebishophillgallery.com), 109 W. Main Street. The gallery is located in the Colony Administration building. Open 10–4 Wednesday through Saturday, noon–4 Sunday. Closed mid-December through January. During February and March, open 11–3 weekends. The gallery walls have a distinct focus on Swedish artists, colonist Olof Krans, and American artists like Grant Wood and Winslow Homer. It also has original local art on consignment in a variety of mediums such as photography, watercolors, and collage.

Bishop Hill Colony Store (309-927-3596), 101 W. Main Street. Open 10–5 daily, April through December, 10–4 January through March. An 1853 general store with fudge, candies, coffees, books, and ornaments, this is the place to pick up key Swedish dishes and ingredients such as Swedish meatballs, lingonberries, and Swedish herring. You can also pick up a cookbook with local recipes. And note,

all proceeds go to the continued restoration of buildings in the area.

& **Prairie Arts Center** (309-927-3008), 203 Bishop Hill Street. Open 10–5 Monday through Saturday, noon–5 Sunday. Hours reduced January through March. This basic redbrick building features the handiwork of local artisans. The building was the blacksmith shop in 1857, but today is the "colony potter" with a network of artists showing their work for sale. You may walk in to find a fiber arts, weaving, broom-

PRAIRIE ARTS CENTER

making, or pottery demonstration. Among the items you can buy: handmade rugs, hats, and ornaments. The resident potter also works out of the center. Be sure to go upstairs to the gallery, which features fine art.

Sweet Annie's Primitives (309-927-3037), 201 W. Main Street. Open seasonally 11–4 Wednesday through Sunday. This shop focuses on "primitive" cupboards, folk art, textiles, and pottery, which means antique furniture with old paint and original surfaces.

Village Smithy (309-927-3851; www.villagesmithyquilts.com), 309 N. Bishop Hill Street. Open Monday through Saturday 10–5, noon–5 Sunday. Reduced winter hours. See quilting demonstrations at the Village Smithy, where the craft has been taught from generation to generation going back to the Swedish ancestors. You can purchase quilts and quilting supplies, hand-woven rugs, and table runners.

✳ Special Events

September: **Jordbruksdagarna Agriculture Days** Celebrate the fall harvest 19th century style at this annual festival. There's live music and vintage baseball. The colonists also serve up their special stew.

December: **Lucia Nights** Annual festival of lights through town. The festival includes musical performances.

PEORIA

Explore the riverfront district, ride up Grandview Drive for stunning views of the river, and visit Wildlife Prairie State Park. That would be Day 1 in Peoria, a metropolis of 115,000 on the Illinois River. And while past generations may not have fully embraced the riverfront location, handing it over to industry, current Peoria residents seem intent on seizing the river for its recreational opportunities. They've done a pretty good job too, through the RiverFront district, which basically is a long park that lines the river with fountains, restaurants, stages, parks, and bars. A new museum is underway as well.

Peoria's backstory includes French explorers Marquette and Joliet, who in 1673 came across the Peoria tribe of the Illiniwek Indians. Fort Creve Coeur was constructed on the east side of the river in 1680. In 1691, Fort St. Louis was built on the city's North Side by Henri de Tonti and French marines, creating the first European settlement in Illinois territory. Peoria was officially incorporated as a city in 1845.

Today it is the home of Caterpillar and Bradley University, as well as the place where politicians think they can measure the pulse of everyday Americans. The question, "Will it play in Peoria?" dates back to vaudeville, when the question was asked to see whether mainstream America would take to a particular play. Now, it's used constantly by talking heads during election season.

Across the river you'll find East Peoria and a riverboat casino, but quite frankly the destinations seem to be concentrated on the Peoria side of the river. If you head outside the city limits, you'll come across some interesting small towns like Edwards and Kickapoo. And in the other direction, Eureka, home of Eureka College, with a museum on its famous graduate, President Ronald Reagan.

GUIDANCE & **RiverFront Visitors Center** (309-672-2860; www.peoria riverfront.com), 110 NE Water Street. Open 9–5 weekdays, 9–4 Saturday. Pick up any type of brochure or maps for Peoria. Located in the Powell

GRANDVIEW DRIVE

Press building, which was moved here from Washington Street in 1997, the building has been a saloon, toy factory, soda parlor, church, print house, and now a visitors center. It's the only pre–Civil War commercial structure still standing in Peoria, built in 1852 as the John Schwab Grocery and Beer Saloon.

GETTING THERE *By auto:* I-74 will get you here from the southeast or northwest. From Chicago, settle in for an approximate three-hour drive down I-55 until it connects with I-74, then take that into the city. From the southern end of the state, you can take I-55 north to I-155.

By air: 📶 **General Wayne A. Downing International Airport** (309-697-8272; www.flypia.com), 6100 W. Everett McKinley Dirksen Parkway. Several airlines fly in and out of this airport on the southwest side of the city, including Allegiant Air, American Eagle, Delta, and United Express. There's free long-term parking as well.

GETTING AROUND *By auto:* The riverfront area is walkable, but to get to other attractions, a car may be the best bet. US 24 crosses the river from East Peoria and runs southwest along the river. Parking can be a bit challenging during events on the riverfront. Just west of downtown is Bradley University, near Main and University Streets. I-74 cuts through downtown and also crosses the river. I-474 wraps around the edge of the city and hooks up with IL 6.

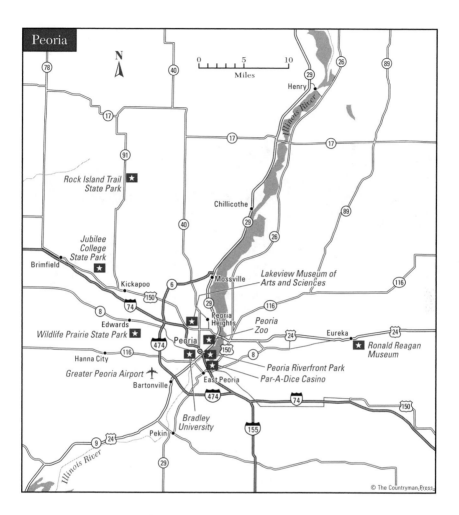

By bus: **Citylink** (309-676-4040; www.ridecitylink.org) Transit center is at 407 SW Adams Street. This public transit system has 23 bus routes that fan out throughout the city, and also connects riders to Pekin and East Peoria. Fares: $1 adult, $5 for weekend bus pass. Seniors ride free.

MEDICAL EMERGENCIES OSF Saint Francis Medical Center (309-655-2000; www.osfsaintfrancis.org), 530 NE Glen Oak Avenue, Peoria. A level I trauma center, St. Francis has 800 doctors and 616 patient beds, making it the fourth-largest medical center in the state. It is also a major teaching affiliate of the University of Illinois College of Medicine at Peoria.

PEORIA RIVERFRONT PATH

Methodist Medical Center (309-672-5522; www.mymethodist.net), 221 NE Glen Avenue, Peoria. Located downtown with 353 beds, and 586 physicians, Methodist is rated a level II trauma center with an emergency room staffed round-the-clock.

✷ Wandering Around

EXPLORING BY CAR Illinois River Road National Scenic Byway (309-495-5909; www.illinoisriverroad.org), 100 SW Water Street, Peoria. This byway starts in the Ottawa area but meanders through Peoria on a scenic road along the Illinois River. You can ride the byway along IL 29 on the west side of the river and IL 26 on the east side. Heading south from downtown, follow US 24 southwest to IL 97 to Havana.

Grandview Drive Access off IL 29, Peoria. Head up past the wooded entryway and as you climb the hill, you'll see some truly gorgeous mansions and estates perched on this hill that offers amazing views of the river and surrounding countryside. Teddy Roosevelt called this strip the "world's most beautiful drive," when he visited in 1910, and it's still worthy of that title today. There are a few observations points that allow you to pull over and enjoy views of the river, and the homes. Grandview Park also has hiking trails and picnic areas. Keep an eye out for the castle.

EXPLORING BY FOOT Peoria RiverFront District (309-671-5555; www.peoriariverfront.com) From the visitors center, wander either direction and you're bound to find some festival or event. There are plenty of places to park yourself and relax, and also restaurants, a marina, a fountain, walking paths, and shops. North of the Riverplex, find the walking and biking trail that leads to the historic Springdale Cemetery.

EXPLORING BY TROLLEY **Peoria Historical Tours** (www.peoria historicalsociety.org) Tours depart from Kelleher's on the riverfront, 619 SW Water Street, Peoria, or from the Harp & Thistle, 4605 N. Prospect Road, Peoria Heights. They are given Thursday through Saturday from June through October and last about 90 minutes. The schedule of tours varies by the day. Certified guides from the historical society will share stories about Peoria's connections to famous events and people, and show off some of the most scenic areas. The society leads tours of Grandview Drive and Springdale Cemetery. The "River City" tour covers Grandview Drive and the downtown area, while the "Old Peoria and the Judge" tour tells about the city's founding father and includes a tour of the Flanagan House Museum. The "All American City" tour delves into gangster stories and leads you through downtown, while the "Abraham Lincoln and the Civil War in Peoria" tour details Lincoln's visits to Peoria. Tickets: $9 plus $1 for the trolley.

✳ To See

MUSEUMS ✄ ⊤ ઙ **Lakeview Museum of Arts & Sciences** (309-686-7000; www.lakeview-museum.org), 1125 W. Lake Avenue, Peoria. Open 10–4 Tuesday through Saturday, noon–4 Sunday. This museum nestled in

REAGAN STATUE AT EUREKA COLLEGE

a park north of downtown has a small exhibition space, but one that really focuses on kids. The children's discovery center has some fun stations on creating tornadoes or clouds, a mineral room, and other activities. Adults can learn about a site located on a bluff of the Illinois River in southeast Fulton County, one that proved especially fruitful when archaeologists in the early 20th century uncovered an extensive collection of artifacts indicating that the area was a temple town or a regional center around 1350–1450. You can also walk through the folk art gallery and see the straw art, as well as pieces of Anna Pottery. Not surprisingly, the museum's permanent collection emphasizes Illinois or Midwest connections, such as the Illinois River wildfowl decoy collection, and features paintings, sculpture, and decorative arts. There are usually rotating temporary exhibits on site as well. The kids will also love a show at the planetarium, where they can tour the skies. The planetarium offers several sky shows throughout the day. You can also go on a driving tour of the community solar system, with buildings throughout town representing different planets. Ask for a map if you're interested. Museum tickets: $6 adults, $5 seniors, $4 for kids 3 to 17 years. Planetarium show tickets: $4 adults, $3.50 kids 3 to 17 years. Combo ticket for the museum and planetarium: $8 adults, $6 kids. Laser light shows: $5.

☂ & **John C. Flanagan House Museum** (309-674-1921; www.peoria historicalsociety.org/flanagan.html), 942 NE Glen Oak Avenue, Peoria. Tours are given 1–3 Saturday from March through May and September through November. The oldest standing house in Peoria was built by Judge Flanagan in 1837. The American Federalist–style home shows off river views and features a collection of antiques. Admission: $5 adults, $2 children.

Dickson Mounds State Museum (309-547-3721; http://www.museum .state.il.us/ismsites/dickson/), 10956 N. Dickson Mounds Road, Lewistown. Open 8:30–5 daily. Located 45 miles south of Peoria, the exhibitions at this archeological museum will take you through 12,000 years of Native American life in the Illinois River valley. In "Reflections on Three Worlds" learn about the Mississippian people whose sites surround the museum, then walk outside where you will find three preserved Native American buildings in the Eveland Village. Free.

✐ ☂ **Wheels O' Time Museum** (309-243-9020; www.wheelsotime.org), 11923 N. Knoxville Avenue, Peoria. Open noon–5 Wednesday through Sunday from May through October. Vintage cars, tractors, trains, and trucks are a big part of the experience here, with Model Ts and other cars built as early as 1915. But the owners also attempt to take you back to life a couple generations ago. You'll hear a barbershop quartet and see a 1940s radio station. The museum has fire trucks, farm tractors, and Caterpillar machinery. Admission: $6 adults, $3.50 children, free for children under 3.

REAGAN SIDETRIP

You can also see Reagan's boyhood home in Dixon, about 90 miles north of Peoria. **Ronald Reagan Boyhood Home & Visitors Center** (815-288-5176; www.ronaldreaganhome.com), 816 S. Hennepin Avenue, Dixon. Open 10–4 Monday through Saturday, 1–4 Sunday from April through mid-November. You can tour this unassuming white house in Dixon where the future president lived with his parents and brother from 1920–23. He was born in Tampico, which is about half an hour southwest of Dixon. His family moved here in 1920, and resided in Dixon until 1933. A young Reagan left Dixon to attend Eureka College. Besides the tour, there's a statue of the president, gift shop, and a short film. Admission: $5.

RONALD REAGAN BOYHOOD HOME IN DIXON

⬆ **Ronald Reagan Museum at Eureka College** (309-467-6407; www.eureka.edu/campus/museum.htm), Donald Cerf Center, 300 East College, Eureka. Open 8–8 weekdays, 10–6 Saturday, noon–8 Sunday during the school year. Summer hours: 8–4 weekdays and 10–2 Saturday. Located about 20 miles outside of Peoria, the Eureka College campus is home to the largest collection of Reagan materials outside of his presidential library in California. The collection traces his student days on campus, his movie career, and political career. Nearby, the garden on the small but picturesque campus has a friendly looking statue of the former president and a piece of the Berlin Wall. Free.

CULTURAL SITES & **Contemporary Art Center of Peoria** (309-674-6822; www.peoriacac.org), 305 SW Water Street, Peoria. Open 11–5 Tuesday through Saturday. This cultural center on the riverfront spotlights the local art scene. Peruse the exhibitions or check out the studios, art classes, yoga, and music performances. You'll find free two-hour parking across the street.

CONTEMPORARY ART CENTER

✳ To Do

BICYCLING The paths along the riverfront are easily explored by bike. If you don't have your own, you can rent a slightly more unusual cycle from **World On Wheels** (309-453-0916; www.worldonwheelspeoria.com). Summer hours: 9–9 Monday through Saturday, 4–7 Sunday. Spring and fall hours: 9–5 Monday through Saturday and 2–5 Sunday. Rent a quadracycle or take a tour on a Segway. Adults can take a 30-minute spin on a quadracycle for $8, children $4. Segway tours range from $25–65 per person depending on the time.

BOATING *Spirit of Peoria* (800-676-8988; www.spiritofpeoria.com), 100 Water Street, Peoria. This crew has bragging rights for being the only authentic paddlewheel-driven boat to offer overnight trips in the U.S. But for a shorter excursion, try the 90-minute sightseeing cruise down the Illinois River, which runs Wednesday, Friday through Sunday from June through September. Buy your tickets at the dock on the riverfront. Boarding

THE SPIRIT OF PEORIA

starts at 12:45 PM. Tickets: $15 adults, $13 seniors, $9 kids 5 to 15 years. The *Spirit* also makes one-day cruises to Starved Rock. Cruises feature live entertainment and buffet meals. Look for special "themed" cruises like a murder mystery tour or fall foliage tour.

FOR FAMILIES ✔ ♿ **Apple Blossom Farm** (309-243-5757; www.apple blossomfarm.com), 9809 IL 91, Peoria. Open August through December, 10–5 Monday through Saturday, 11–5 Sunday. Located just northwest of Peoria, this farm hosts a number of farm-related activities for families, like a petting zoo with rabbits and goats, a 10-acre corn maze, a train barrel ride, playground with a giant slide, and apple and pumpkin picking. The gift shop and produce market offer honey, apples, apple-cider donuts, jams, and jellies for sale. The kids can also race at the peddle cart track. On the weekends, you can ride a monster truck. Corn maze admission fee: $5 adults, $3 kids under 12.

GOLF Coyote Creek Golf Club (309-633-0911; www.golfcoyotecreek .com), 8201 W. Lancaster Road, Bartonville. Designed by the late Bruce Borland, senior designer for Jack Nicklaus, this 18-hole course winds around lakes, trails, and stone bridges. Fee: $33–53 for 18 holes, depending on the day and time.

Detweiller Golf Course (309-692-7518; www.peoriaparks.org), 8412 N. Galena Road, Peoria. A 9-hole municipal course with views of the river. Fee: $11.

Donovan Golf Course (309-691-8361; www.peoriaparks.org), 5805 N. Knoxville Avenue, Peoria. Another course operated by the Peoria Park District, Donovan also has a putting green, practice area, pro shop, and snack bar. Fee: $20 for 18 holes, $15 for 9.

♂ **Weaver Ridge Golf Course** (309-691-3344; www.weaverridge.com), 5100 Weaver Ridge Boulevard, Peoria. This championship golf course, which has been rated the No. 2 public course in Illinois by *Golf Digest*, promises a challenge. No jeans permitted, only collared shirts, and slacks or Bermuda shorts. Fee: $63 Monday through Wednesday, $73 Thursday through Sunday. Carts: $20 per person.

WINERIES ♂ **Kickapoo Creek Winery** (309-495-9463; www.kickapoo creekwinery.com), 6605 N. Smith Road, Edwards. Open 11–5 Tuesday through Saturday, noon–5 Sunday. About 10 minutes west of Peoria, this vineyard has taken advantage of the property's "timber soil," which is not well suited for corn, but great for grapes. Sample local wines in the tasting room or stop for lunch. For $1, you'll get three tastings. The wines are mostly made from grapes grown on site, or from Illinois grapes. Kickapoo Creek also has local cheese for sale, a grape train, and a vineyard you can wander, as well as beautiful gardens, seeing that the site is also a nursery.

ZOOS ✍ ♂ ♿ **Peoria Zoo** (309-686-3365; www.peoriazoo.org), 2218 N. Prospect Road, Peoria. Open 10–5 daily. Watch the seals sun themselves and feed, chat with zoo keepers, and meet some of the 100 species of animals who make their home at this zoo on the north side of the city. The Africa exhibit takes visitors through the Zambezi River Village. Barriers are invisible to the public, so you'll have great views of the white rhino, giraffes, and lions. The temperature drops as you enter the forest area, where you'll see Red River Hogs and mandrills. The Asia exhibit houses Amur tigers and binturongs, while the Australia area has wallabies and emus. You can take a guided zoo tour for an extra fee, and there are programs for kids throughout the year. Admission: $8.50 adults, $4.75 children 3 to 12 years, $7.50 seniors, free for children under 2.

✍ ♿ **Wildlife Prairie State Park** (309-676-0998; www.wildlifeprairie statepark.org), 3826 N. Taylor Road, Hanna City. From Memorial Day through Labor Day weekend, open daily 9–6:30. In spring and late fall, the park closes at 4:30. In the 1960s, founder William Rutherford heard that the Brookfield Zoo in Chicago's suburbs was looking for an area to raise exotic, endangered animals and he thought his family's foundation could use its land to help out. The two groups started planning for the park, but Brookfield Zoo ultimately went with another plan. Rutherford's foundation decided to go ahead with the project, opening the park in 1978. Its 2,000 acres are focused on the animal species that are native to

PEORIA ZOO

Illinois, particularly at the pioneer farmstead that features animals the settlers likely brought with them when they moved west toward Illinois,
including sheep, cattle, goats, and miniature donkey. Altogether, there are
150 animals—wolves, bison, elk, cougar, black bear, bald eagle, and otter,
among others. You can hike 10 miles of trails, or for $2, take a train ride
through a covered bridge, past a lake, and through the park. Anglers can
fish from Caboose Lake, Deep Lake, Beaver Lake, and Horseshoe Lake.
A "Snakes 'n More" exhibit will introduce you to snakes, turtles, salaman-
ders, and toads. If you get hungry, there's a snack shop, ice cream, and
vending. Another plus for families: the park has playgrounds and a 58-foot
slide. A Frisbee golf course and mountain bike trails have recently been
added to the park, and if you want to stay nearby, there are cabins for
rent. (See Lodging.) Admission: $6.50 adults, $4.50 children, free for children under 3. Save a dollar off admission during March, November, and
December. On "carload" day (Wednesday) the whole car can enter the
park for $18.

✴ Green Space

& **Forest Park Nature Center** (309-686-3360; http://www.peoriaparks
.org/forest-park-nature-center), 5809 N. Forest Park Drive, Peoria. Center
is open 9–5 Monday through Saturday and 1–5 Sunday. Trails are open
daily, dawn to dusk. In forested bluffs above the river, this 540-acre site

WILDLIFE PRAIRIE STATE PARK

offers 7 miles of hiking trails through prairies, forests, and a natural history museum with bird-viewing rooms.

Rock Island Trail State Park (309-695-2228; http://dnr.state.il.us /lands/landmgt/parks/r1/rockisle.htm) From I-74 on the northwest side of Peoria, take IL 6 to Chillicothe exit, exit Allen Road. Turn left on Allen Road, and follow it around as it curves left. After the curve, you'll find the Rock Island Trail parking lot about 0.75-mile later on the right side of Alta Road. Prairie grass and wildflowers have grown over the rail corridor itself, but you still can see signs of rail travel at the Chicago Burlington & Quincy train depot in Wyoming. The state created the trail on the rail right-of-way in 1989, opening the 26 miles for hiking, biking, and cross-country skiing. Parking, water, and toilets are located at the access areas. The Wyoming depot has a visitor center and railroad museum. Primitive camping sites are available and accessible only by trail.

& ♂ **Luthy Botanical Garden** (309-686-3362; www.peoriaparks.org /luthy-botanical-garden), 2218 N. Prospect Road, Peoria. Open 10–5 Tuesday through Saturday, noon–5 Sunday. From Memorial Day through Labor Day, the garden is open until 7 Tuesday through Saturday. A quiet place next to the chaos that can be the zoo, Luthy has 5 acres of land-scaped gardens. With the All-Season garden producing flowers all year long, pick up new ideas for your home garden. Crab Apple Cove showcases flowering fruit trees, while the herb garden aims to awaken your sense of smell. The park also has a children's garden and a conservatory. Admission: $2 adults, free for children under 12.

✳ Lodging

BED AND BREAKFASTS (ᵚ)

Mission Oak Inn (309-370-4083; www.missionoakinn.com), 1108 County Road 930E, Henry. Luxury is apparent but understated in this two-room inn where you can see the craftsmanship of innkeeper Denny Reed throughout. He's the chef, while wife Jan handles the books and most other things. This inn is located on 120 acres near a 7-acre private lake with deer, fox, and wild turkey roaming. Suites have fireplaces, whirlpools, satellite TVs, DVDs, private baths, and private porches. Breakfast is served in the dining room overlooking the lake. A homemade dessert and use of a canoe comes with the room. $$.

(ᵚ) **Old Church House Inn** (309-579-2300; www.oldchurchhouseinn.com), 1416 E. Mossville Road, Mossville. The name says it all. This brick inn was originally built as a church in 1869 and served as one until the 1960s. The building was renovated in 2008, and features a cool "library loft," with ladder. The suite features an antique headboard carved of walnut, with luxury linens in the bedroom. The sitting room has a flat-screen TV, DVD, desk, sofa, refrigerator, microwave, and coffeemaker. They promise orange juice that is freshly squeezed, not frozen, and fresh-baked muffins or pastries in the morning, among other dishes. No pets, but children who are "well behaved" can stay with special arrangements. $$.

RESORTS ✐ Wildlife Prairie State Park

(309-676-0998; www.wildlifeprairiestatepark.org), 3826 N. Taylor Road, Hanna City. The park has several different options for your stay. The Cabin on the hill is a single-room rustic log cabin that sleeps four or more and comes with a porch swing, small refrigerator, coffeemaker, microwave, and playhouse for the kids. Cottages by the lake include a kitchenette and of course, a lake view. The single cottages sleep three while the double cottage sleeps eight. The train cabooses are actual train cars that have been converted into barebones sleeping rooms, with bunk beds that sleep four. The prairie stable looks like a horse barn from the outside but has the comforts of modern life inside. You receive two days park admission, linens, bathrooms with showers, TVs, grills, and picnic tables with each rental. $–$$.

HOTELS ♿ (ᵚ) Hotel Pere Marquette

(800-447-1676; www.hotelperemarquette.com), 501 Main Street, Peoria. In downtown Peoria, this hotel's motto is that the Pere Marquette is where HISTORY LIVES AND SERVICE IS STILL IN STYLE. The grand entryway with murals and chandeliers helps you imagine some of that history, which starts with the opening of the hotel in 1927 and includes hosting five sitting presidents and first ladies. The rooms have been recently renovated, with dark wood furniture and a rich, regal color palette. Pets are allowed. Rooms come with flat-screen TV, free parking, coffeemaker, iron, telephone with voice mail, and hairdryer. Suites have extras like sofa beds, wet bars, and refrigerators. $$.

& (((o))) **Mark Twain Hotel** (866-325-6351; www.marktwainhotel.com), 225 NE Adams Street, Peoria. A lot of thought has gone into creating a literary-looking world. The biggest contributor to

HOTEL PERE MARQUETTE

that feel is the writer's library that you see when you first enter the hotel, complete with carved wood ceilings, leather furnishings, and books everywhere. The guest rooms are decorated in a soothing sage, with clean white linens and light wood furnishings. Many rooms have views of the river. All rooms have a microwave, refrigerator, coffeemaker, modern bathroom, and hair dryer. Guests can work out in the fitness room onsite or make use of the hotel shuttle and the free day-pass to the RiverPlex, a giant workout facility on the riverfront. $$.

& (((o))) **Par-A-Dice Hotel Casino** (800-547-0711; www.paradice casino.com), 21 Blackjack Boulevard, East Peoria. The casino and hotel are located across the river from downtown Peoria, with 202 rooms and suites. It is not a very Vegas-y location but the rooms are neat and simple, with flat-screen TVs, coffeemakers, refrigerators, irons, and safes. $$.

CAMPING & **Jubilee College State Park** (309-243-9489; http://www.dnr.state.il.us/lands/land mgt/parks/r1/jubilee.htm), 11817 Jubilee College Road, Brimfield. Campground open mid-April through October. Great campground if you are in the Peoria area. The grounds have a shower building with flush toilets, a trailer dump station, graveled pads, grills, water hydrants, and some primitive toilets. The Coyote Cove campground mostly hosts RVs on its big sprawling site, but it is in close proximity to the trail that goes to the fishing pond. There's also a playground and handicap-accessible sites. Most of the sites are grouped together in a large field, but you will find some more private spots around the edge of the woods. Possum Bend generally has more tent campers while the Woodchuck Ridge campground has slightly more wooded sites. An equestrian camping area is also available. During the winter, the Coyote Cove loop is open. At that time, the park has electricity, but no running water available. Permits can be obtained from the site staff. No reservations are required. Fees: $8 for tent sites, $18–25 for sites with utilities.

✳ Where to Eat

EATING OUT ♿ ♈ **Kelleher's Irish Pub & Eatery** (309-673-6000; www.kellehersirishpub.com), 619 SW Water Street, Peoria. Open 11 AM–midnight Monday through Wednesday, 11 AM–2 AM Thursday through Saturday. This traditional Irish pub is located in an old warehouse building constructed in the late 1800s, and is part of the revitalized riverfront. It offers a few options for seating—at the bar, staring at paintings of the Irish countryside, in booths, which are separated by old windows, or on a brick patio that overlooks the riverfront. If the weather is bad, you can still feel like you're sitting outside by grabbing a table on the indoor patio, which has a glass window ceiling.

But what you really probably care about is the beer list here—18 microbrews and imports on tap, and 90 different kinds of bottled beers. The Irish influence also is seen in the menu. You can start off with corned beef on rye wedges with Swiss cheese as an appetizer, move on to an Irish potato and leek soup, or a Guinness beef sandwich. The pub also hosts live music. $–$$.

Ludy's Kickapoo Creek Saloon (309-692-6446), 9828 US 150, Edwards. Open 11–2, 5–10 Monday through Thursday, 11–10 Friday and Saturday, noon–8 Sunday. Bar open later. Reduced hours during winter. This place is dive-y but popular. The burger is the draw here. Inside, the bar, located in a former house, is segmented into different rooms with tables and video games. You can also order pizza (but why would you with this burger?) and there is outdoor seating. $

((ψ)) **One World** (309-672-1522; www.oneworld-cafe.com), Main and University Streets, Peoria. Open 7 AM–11 PM weekdays, 8–11 weekends. Located near Bradley University, the café celebrates diversity and the arts while embracing the local flavor. Opened in 1993 by the Eid brothers as a one-room coffee shop, One World helped transform the neighborhood nearby and has expanded greatly. In 2007, they opened the Green Dragon lounge. The café has menu options for vegetarian, vegans, and carnivores alike. The menu does travel the globe. You'll find Cuban pork, a tilapia sandwich with basil-pesto aioli, gyros, falafel, pizza, and Cajun shrimp. All sandwiches come with a choice of a side of kettle chips, soup, pesto potato salad, seasoned fries, or sun-dried tomato pasta salad. $–$$.

DINING OUT Two25 (309-282-7777; www.two25peoria.com), 225 NE Adams Street, Peoria. Open 11–2 for lunch weekdays. Dinner: 4:30–9 Monday through Thursday, 4:30–10 Friday and Saturday. Located on the ground floor of the Mark Twain Hotel, this restaurant goes for "fine dining without the pretense." Though you don't need to put on your best suit, maybe get out an iron and press that button-down; you will be spending some money if you come

here. The menu is a mix of pizzas, pastas, steak, seafood, and chicken. Bison is on the list as well, but you can get a number of different cuts of steak here. The designers of the restaurant have made use of a little pocket of space between the road and the building to create a concrete patio that's sunken in next to the street, if you'd like to dine outdoors. Lunch includes wraps, burgers, and sandwiches. In addition to bottles, you can also order wine flights. Lunch: $–$$. Dinner: $$$–$$$$.

(((•))) & **Seven on Prospect** (309-682-7007; www.7onprospect.com), 4609 N. Prospect Road, Peoria Heights. Bar opens at 4. Open 5–9 Monday through Thursday, 5–10 Friday and Saturday. Seven bills itself as a cosmopolitan grill, and the room and patio are a good place to relax for a nicer dining

TWO25 IN PEORIA

experience. The appetizer menu includes Asian tuna tartare, crab cakes, and pulled-pork quesadillas. For entrees, you have the Cuban pork chop or the "magnificent Seven" dish, which includes prawns, scallops, lump crab, calamari, clams, mussels, and lobster meat simmered in tomato broth and served over pasta. $$$.

June (877-682-5863; www.june restaurant.com), 4450 N. Prospect Road, Peoria Heights. Open 5–close Tuesday through Saturday. Chef/owner and Peoria native, Josh Adams, decided to leave the family business and become a chef after eating at the world famous Charlie Trotter's in Chicago. After culinary school, he worked at Alinea in Chicago and Vie in the Chicago area, which is focused on farm-fresh ingredients. Adams decided to transport that farm-fresh approach to his hometown, showing off organic produce from local farms through some fancy cooking methods. Adams has networked with area farmers and has 80 acres of certified organic land growing produce for the restaurant. What does all that mean for the menu? Well, first course options include a dish combining a farm-fresh egg, house-made pancetta, coffee-smoked shitake mushrooms, brioche, and hollandaise. For the entrees, how about Berkshire pork belly, rice, wild ramps, wood sorrel, and mustard-beet emulsion? You can bring in wine but there is an $18 corkage fee. June, which is in a small strip mall off Prospect Road, has an extensive wine list for wines by the glass or bottle, and a mixed drink menu. $$$–$$$$.

✳ Entertainment

The "Old Quarters" area of the Peoria riverfront (around the 600 block of Water Street) is blocked off periodically throughout the year for dancing, art shows, live music, and games.

LIVE MUSIC CEFCU Center Stage at the Landing (309-689-3019; www.peoriariverfront.com)

JUNE RESTAURANT

Located right on the river, this stage hosts jazz, rock, and cultural festivals throughout the year. Check the calendar before you plan your trip.

Rhythm Kitchen Music Café (309-676-9668; www.rhythm kitchenmusiccafe.biz), 305 SW Water Street, Peoria. Open 11–2, 5–10 Wednesday and Thursday; 11–2, 5–midnight Friday; 8–2, 5–midnight Saturday; occasional Sunday brunches. Appropriately placed in the Contemporary Art Center, this artsy café brings in live bands every weekend. To find it, walk past the windows of the Academy of Fretted Instruments, into a hallway with elevators leading up to some of the exhibit space. In the corner, you'll find the lively Rhythm Kitchen. When you walk in, you are immediately greeted by an old piano. The stage is to your right, outfitted with an old beat-up rug that lends to the sense that this is a great place to discover something genuine. Art is apparent everywhere, from the painted bench of a reclining lady to the black-and-white photographs on the wall. Colored lights add to the festive feel. On the weekends you'll find live jazz and blues. Oh, and they have food too. Appetizers like crudités with hummus, or a fruit and brie platter. The salads are especially good. There's the Brazilian chicken or Mexican chicken. Entrees include grilled tuna, meatloaf, and seafood skewer. Breakfast is also served, along with coffee drinks. $–$$.

Par-A-Dice Casino (800-727-2342; www.paradicecasino.com), East Peoria. If the slots are calling you, there are 1,100 slot, keno, and video poker machines here. You'll also find table games like blackjack and roulette.

Ⓨ **Martinis on Water** (309-655-5003; www.martinisonwater.com), 212 SW Water Street, Peoria. Open 4–1 Monday through Wednesday, 4–2 Thursday through Saturday, 4–12 Sunday. This is a cool place for a drink, in the historic Rock Island train depot building, built in 1891. If you can, score a seat on the patio. On a slightly colder evening, the fireplaces and pits will warm you up, along with the vodka or gin in your martini. Speaking of which, they have more than 100 martini recipes to choose from. But the inside also has towering ceilings, warm walls, leather couches, stained-glass windows, and other touches. The bar brings in live music several times a week, as well.

Ⓨ **Rhodell Brewery** (309-674-7267; www.rhodells.com), 619A Water Street, Peoria. Open 3–10 Tuesday through Thursday, 3–midnight Friday, 2–midnight Saturday. You can make your own beer here, although you'd have to come back to bottle it. But you can also sit back and enjoy what they've already brewed for you. The brewery is intent on the idea that beer should have flavor. You can sit in the red pub area or the brick patio next to Kelleher's.

MOVIES Apollo Theatre (309-673-4343; www.apolloinpeoria .com), 311 S. Main Street Peoria. The historic theater shows classics and some recent films. Admission: $5 adults, $4 seniors, students.

Peoria Theater (309-202-2278; www.peoriatheater.com), 3225 N. Dries Lane, Peoria. Open Tuesday through Sunday. For lesser-known and independent films, this is your place. The theater has a schedule filled with documentaries, foreign films, and film festival-type movies as well as pizza and a full bar, so you'll need ID to get in. Admission: $6 adults, $5 seniors, students.

SPORTS Peoria Chiefs (309-680-4000; www.peoriachiefs.com), O'Brien Field, 730 SW Jefferson Street, Peoria. For minor league baseball in these parts, Peoria offers up the Chiefs, who have an affiliation with the Chicago Cubs. Some noted alum include: Greg Maddux, Rafael Palmeiro, Mark Grace, and Albert Pujols.

THEATER Corn Stock Theatre (309-676-2196; www.cornstock theatre.org), 1700 N. Park Road, Peoria. The performances are at Upper Bradley Park during the summer. This outdoor community theatre group stages several shows under the park tent. The main stage season runs during the summer. During the fall and winter, catch shows at the group's theater center in Bradley Park. Tickets: $12–18 adults, $10–12 students.

Ġ **Peoria Civic Center** (309-673-3200; www.peoriaciviccenter.com), 201 SW Jefferson Street, Peoria. Box office is open 10–5:30 weekdays, 10–2 Saturday. You'll find Broadway musicals, comedians, live music, ballet, hockey, and college basketball at the civic center.

✳ Selective Shopping

Ġ **Illinois Antique Center** (309-673-3354; www.peoriariverfront .com), 311 SW Water Street, Peoria, Open 9–5 Monday through Saturday, 11–5 Sunday. On the main floor of Waterfront Place, this antique center is housed in a renovated old industrial building with features such as exposed brick arches and duct work. The center has 100 dealers, and is clean and more organized than a lot of antique malls. You'll find furniture, jewelry, gumball machines, books, magazines, and signs. You can park free for two hours in the city lot across the street during the weekday and after 5 PM on weekends and holidays.

Gallery Store of the Peoria Art Guild (309-637-2787; www.peoria artguild.com), 203 Harrison Street, Peoria. Open 10–6 Monday through Thursday, 10–5 Friday and Saturday. Peruse the handiwork of local artists on display at the art guild's store. The pickings include jewelry pieces, ceramics, paintings, glass, photography, and other gifts.

Toraason Hand Blown Glass (309-495-0919; www.toraason

glass.com), 506 Evans Street, Peoria. Open 9–5 weekdays. Artist Hiram Toraason demonstrates the art of glassblowing in his studio and gallery, the result being gorgeous and colorful creations. Classes offered. Appointments preferred.

RiverFront Market (www.peoria riverfront.com) Open 8–noon Saturday from June through September. Every Saturday through the summer, find local produce, fresh flowers, jewelry, crafts, and other items on display under white tents along the riverfront at Liberty Park.

North Prospect in Peoria Heights has a nice strip of interesting shops, like **I Know You Like A Book** (309-685-2665; www.likeabook.net), 4707 N. Prospect Road, Peoria Heights. Open 10–6 Monday through Saturday, with extended hours Thursday and Friday for the wine bar. This bookstore offers new and used books for sale. Tables are set up outside and there's also a small bar where you can have a glass of wine.

✳ Special Events

June: **Steamboat Festival and Classic Sports Festival** (www .peoriaevents.com, www.steam boatclassic.org) Every June, Peoria welcomes athletes from around the world for the Steamboat Classic running race and the Proctor Cycling Classic. The Steamboat Festival includes live music, stunt shows, and a carnival.

July: **Prairie Air Show** (309-661-6546; www.prairieair.org) Catch military and civilian pilots doing their best to thrill the crowds at the Peoria International Airport each year.

September: **Illinois Blues Festival** (www.illinoisbluesfestival.com) Two days of blues on the riverfront, with multiple stages of blues performers, food, and other vendors.

Morton Pumpkin Festival (www .pumpkincapital.com) Downtown Morton. The town claims that 80 percent of the world's canned pumpkin is processed at a plant here, a number celebrated with this festival around the pumpkin-canning season. There's a parade, live music, carnival, arts and crafts, and lots of food.

November/December: **East Peoria Festival of Lights** (800-365-3743; www.peoria.org) includes a glowing winter wonderland park and a parade of illuminated floats that brighten the winter streets in East Peoria in late November, to kick off the holiday season.

COLLEGE TOWNS

The draws to the Champaign-Urbana and Bloomington-Normal areas are the universities. The state's flagship university, the University of Illinois, is centered in Champaign and Urbana. Illinois State University and Illinois Wesleyan University call the Bloomington-Normal area home. So if you're beckoned to the university for a college visit, conference, or performance, I've included some restaurants, parks, and museums that might help fill out your itinerary. The two hyphenated areas are roughly an hour's drive from each other, separated by green space and farmland.

The twin cities of Bloomington and Normal are linked in many ways, most scenically through the Constitution Trail, which offers miles of paths for biking or walking. But there are distinctions and slightly different flavors: Bloomington is larger than Normal, with about 74,000 people compared to roughly 52,000 people. Bloomington has downtown; Normal has what it now calls Uptown. Bloomington's downtown retail and nightlife district has bars, restaurants, coffeehouses, and a historic courthouse square with some interesting architecture around it, such as the art deco of the Ensenberger building. The city is also home to the picturesque campus of Illinois Wesleyan University, a liberal arts university with about 2,100 students on an 80-acre campus.

Normal has its recently renovated Uptown, which has tried to reverse the trend of shopping malls sucking all the life out of the traditional town centers. A number of projects have breathed life into the area, with new streets and sidewalks creating a clean-looking shopping and entertainment district around Uptown circle. Besides finding a number of restaurants, you'll also find a children's museum, a 1937 movie theater, and Illinois State University, the state's first public university, founded in 1857. The campus is spread across 350 acres and enrolls about 20,000 students.

Outside of Bloomington, you may be intrigued by the giant wind turbines of the Twin Groves Wind Farms, which include 240 turbines, enough to power about 118,000 homes. Construction on the wind farm started in 2007 and has expanded since then.

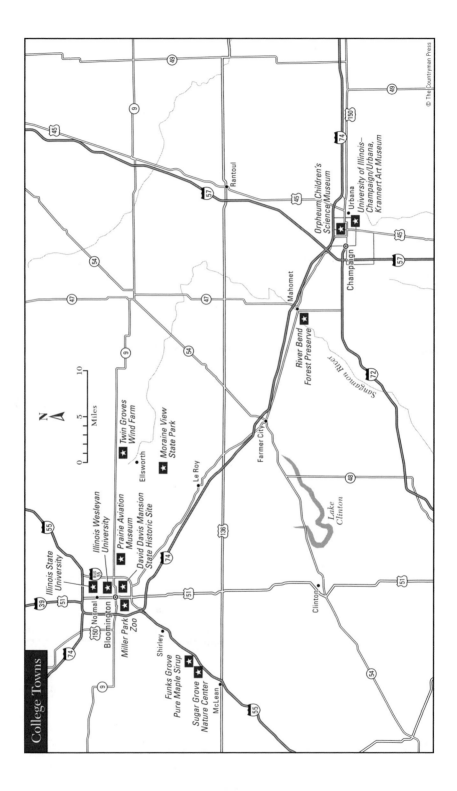

College Towns

© The Countryman Press

Southwest of the Bloomington-Normal area is Champaign-Urbana, with 80,000 people in Champaign and about 40,000 in Urbana. The grand star of the region is the University of Illinois, with its renowned research facilities and 40,000 students. Urbana has some lovely historic neighborhoods with paver-brick streets and canopies of green trees. Champaign has some activity in its downtown area, with newer restaurants and buildings taking shape. With a campus filled with many techies, Champaign has free WiFi throughout the downtown district.

GUIDANCE Bloomington-Normal Area Convention and Visitors Bureau (800-433-8226; bloomingtonnormalcvb.org), 3201 CIRA Drive, Suite 201, Bloomington. Open 8:30–5 weekdays. The CVB is not the most convenient site, unless you're coming in to the airport. But you can find maps and other brochures in this office located on the second floor of the airport.

Champaign County Convention and Visitors Bureau (800-369-6151; www.visitchampaigncounty.org).

GETTING THERE *By auto:* From Chicago, you take I-57 and a slight jog on I-74 to get to Champaign. I-55 will get you to Bloomington-Normal. I-74 links the two cities and can connect you to Indiana and Peoria.

By bus: (ᵍ) & **Megabus** (877-462-6342; www.megabus.com) This bus carrier has routes that stop in Champaign and Normal. The fares vary according to demand on the Internet.

Greyhound (www.greyhound.com) Buses stop in Champaign and Bloomington. In Champaign the line stops at 45 E. University Avenue (217-352-4150). In Bloomington, the stop is at 527 Brock Drive (309-827-5599).

By air: **Central Illinois Regional Airport** (309-663-7383; www.cira.com), 3201 CIRA Drive, Bloomington. AirTran Airways, American Eagle, and Delta fly in

URBANA

and out of this regional airport. Free parking and parking shuttle service available.

Willard Airport at the University of Illinois (www.flycmi.com) Located off US 45 just north of Monticello Road and east of I-57. American Eagle and Delta have flights to and from Chicago, Detroit, and Dallas from this regional airport.

By train: **Amtrak** (800-872-7245; Amtrak.com), 100 E. Parkinson Street, Normal. It's a two-hour ride from the Normal station to Chicago or St. Louis. There is also a station in Champaign at 45 E. University Avenue (217-352-5905).

GETTING AROUND *By bus:* **Bloomington-Normal Public Transit System** (309-828-9833; bnpts.com) This bus system that connects the two cities offers fairly regular service. Fare: $1 adults.

&. **Champaign-Urbana Mass Transit District** (217-384-8188; www .cumtd.com), 1101 E. University Avenue, Urbana. The transit district provides bus service on fixed routes throughout the two cities. You can board at any street corner along a route, where you can do so safely, except through campus, which has designated stops. Note that "hopper" buses only serve portions of a certain line during peak times, so if you're going farther, pay attention to those signs. Fares: $1 adults.

MEDICAL EMERGENCIES OSF St. Joseph Medical Center (309-662-3311; www.osfstjoseph.org), 2200 E. Washington Street, Bloomington. In the Bloomington-Normal area, this is a Level II trauma center with 157 beds.

Carle Foundation Hospital (217-383-3311; www.carle.org), 611 W. Park Street, Urbana. For the Urbana-Champaign region, Carle is a 325-bed Level I trauma center and a teaching hospital.

✳ Wandering Around

EXPLORING BY BIKE Constitution Trail Bloomington and Normal used old railroad right-of-way to create this path, which covers 24-plus miles through Normal and Bloomington and winds past gardens. There are picnic areas, rest rooms, and benches along the way.

✳ To See

MUSEUMS

Bloomington-Normal
&. ✝ **McLean County Museum of History** (309-827-0428; www.mc history.org), 200 N. Main Street, Bloomington, Open 10–5 Monday,

Wednesday through Saturday, 10–9 Tuesday. In the traditional county courthouse spot in the middle of the town square, you will find this interesting museum in the former court building. The building has wonderful features such as an artfully laid mosaic tile floor and a painted rotunda. The exhibits are impressive for a county museum. Each office of the old county building focuses on the people, the politics, the work, or the farming of the people of Central Illinois (the county claims to lead the nation in corn and soybean production). In the work section, you'll learn about State Farm Insurance, which was founded in the city and continues to be one of the area's largest employers. The museum tells the story of the Native Americans, African Americans, Irish, and Germans who settled here, and you hear the tales told in those voices through recordings. The exhibits reveal tidbits such as that Normal was founded as an alcohol-free community for the new state teacher's college. They tell of the political importance of some of the region's notable characters, like Adlai E. Stevenson II. A re-created log cabin offers kids a hands-on look at pioneer life. Upstairs, you can check out an old courtroom or one of the temporary, rotating exhibits. Admission: $5 adults, $4 seniors, free for children.

MCLEAN COUNTY MUSEUM OF HISTORY

Prairie Aviation Museum (309-663-7632; www.prairieaviation museum.org), 2929 E. Empire Street, Bloomington. Open 11–4 Thursday, Saturday, noon–4 Sunday. Located just outside the Central Illinois Regional Airport, this museum's main attractions are in the outdoor airpark, where you can get a closer look at a number of military aircraft, including an F-14D Tomcat from the U.S. Navy, an AH-1J Sea Cobra helicopter, and other aircraft. Inside, peruse the rest of the museum's collections, and maybe try out the flight simulator. Admission: $5 adults, $2 children.

Champaign-Urbana
⅄ ⊤ **Krannert Art Museum**
(217-333-1861; www.kam.uiuc

PRAIRIE AVIATION MUSEUM

.edu), 500 E. Peabody Drive, Champaign. Open 9–5 Tuesday through Saturday, with extended hours until 9 on Thursday, 2–5 Sunday. This museum is tucked away among academic buildings, but the sculptures in front and the decorative golden ironworks around the window whisper that this building, with its glass atrium hallway, might be a little different. As the state's second largest art museum, the Krannert has 10 permanent galleries, and changing exhibitions throughout the year. It also hosts film screenings, performances, and speakers. Suggested donation: $3.

DAVID DAVIS HOME

& ↑ **Spurlock Museum** (217-333-2360; www.spurlock.uiuc.edu), 600 S. Gregory, Urbana. Open noon–5 Tuesday, 9–5 Wednesday through Friday, 10–4 Saturday, noon–4 Sunday. The University of Illinois museum explores ancient cultures of the world, from

Mesopotamia to Oceania and Ancient Rome. Its 40,000 items include one of the most complete casts of the Parthenon Frieze, which you can see on display in the feature galleries. Changing exhibits bring new stories into the museum. Suggested donation: $3.

HISTORIC SITES & **David Davis Mansion State Historic Site** (309-828-1084; www.daviddavismansion.org), 1000 E. Monroe Drive, Bloomington. Guides conduct 45-minute tours every half hour between 9:30–4 Wednesday through Sunday. Judge David Davis was a slightly connected individual who was a friend to President Abraham Lincoln and served as a U.S. Supreme Court justice. His mansion, built in 1872, offers a peek into the world of the wealthy and politically powerful of that era. You can see the stable where Lincoln kept his horse when he arrived for visits. Mrs. Davis created lovely gardens that live on today. Suggested donation: $4 adult, $2 child.

CULTURAL SITES

Bloomington-Normal

& ↑ **Illinois State University Planetarium** (309-438-5007; www.phy .ilstu.edu/~trw/planetfiles/public.html), College Avenue and School Street, Normal. The planetarium projector of the white-domed building can illuminate 2,354 stars along with the Milky Way. Tickets can be purchased 20 minutes before each show at the planetarium gift shop. Cost: $4 adults, $3 seniors, students, and children 5 to 12 years, $2 preschoolers.

Champaign-Urbana

& ↑ **William M. Staerkel Planetarium** (217-351-2568; www2.parkland .edu/planetarium), 2400 W. Bradley Avenue, Champaign. Open August through May with shows Friday and Saturday at 7, 8 PM. The planetarium machine projects about 7,600 simulated stars, the sun, moon, and five planets on the 50-foot domed screen. Admission: $5 adults, $4 children, seniors, and students.

✳ To Do

FOR FAMILIES

Bloomington-Normal

& & ↑ **Children's Discovery Museum** (309-433-3444; www.childrens discoverymuseum.net), 101 E. Beaufort Street, Normal. Open 9–5 Tuesday, Wednesday, Saturday; 9–8 Thursday, Friday, 1–5 Sunday. An anchor in Uptown Normal with its curved glass front, this children's museum provides three floors of play and exploration, from exhibits about healthy eating to those on trains, bodies, and clocks. There are also art activities, a

SCI-FI MOVIE SET?

Giant wind turbines rising out of the farmland can be a little unnerving the first time you come across them. They're just so large and imposing. You'll see plenty outside of Bloomington-Normal. If you want to find out more about how the wind farm works, head to the lookout platform for **Twin Groves Wind Farm** (309-724-8278; www.horizonwind.com), 13682 N. 2900 East Road, Ellsworth. The platform is a sidewalk laid out the size of a turbine, with storyboards that will walk you through the process of how the 240 wind turbines generate enough electricity for about 118,000 average Illinois homes. Groups of 10 or more can schedule guided tours that depart from the lookout platform, but they must be prearranged.

WIND FARMS OUTSIDE BLOOMINGTON

toddler playground area, play medical center, and a place for children to create their own city. And no children's museum would be complete without a place to splash around in the waterplay center. Admission: $6 for ages 2 and over. Children under 2 free.

🖉 ♿ **Miller Park Zoo** (309-434-2250; www.cityblm.org/parks/Miller-Park -Zoo/about-the-zoo.htm), 1020 S. Morris Avenue, Bloomington. Open

daily 9:30–4:30. This small city zoo is a great choice for families, as it still
has enough exotic animals to intrigue the kids. See daily feedings of sea
lions or river otters. The zoo's family includes sun bears, Sumatran tigers,
red pandas, and leopards, who live in various indoor and outdoor exhibits,
including the Tropical America Rainforest and Children's Zoo. Admission:
$5 adults, $3.50 for youth and seniors. Children under 3 free. Free parking.

Champaign-Urbana
♪ ↑ **Orpheum Children's Science Museum** (217-352-5895; www
.orpheumkids.com), 346 N. Neil Street, Champaign. Open 10–4 Tuesday
through Friday, 1–5 weekends. The focus here is fun too, but with an
emphasis on science, through a dino dig exhibit in the outdoor courtyard,
a veterinary clinic, waterworks area, and a castle that gets kids into an
engineering state of mind. The museum is housed in the old Orpheum
Theatre, which opened in 1914. Admission: $4 adults, $3 for children age
2 and up.

GOLF

Bloomington-Normal
♂ **The Den at Fox Creek** (309-434-2300; www.thedengc.com), 3002
Fox Creek Road, Bloomington. An Arnold Palmer course that offers 18
holes of golf laid out Scottish links style, the Den has sand traps and a
number of lakes and streams that wind through the course. Carts come
with GPS. Fees: $31–41 for 18 holes, $22 after 4:30. Carts: $15 per per-
son.

Ironwood Golf Course (309-454-9620; www.golfironwood.org/), 1901 N.
Towanda, Normal. This par-72 championship course gives golfers four sets
of tees with play that stretches 5,400 to 6,900 yards. The links design has
water play and an island green on one hole. Fees: $18–22 for 18 holes,
$15 after 3 PM. Carts: $13 for 18 holes.

Champaign-Urbana
Stone Creek Golf Course (217-367-3000; www.stonecreekgolfclub
.com), 2600 S. Stone Creek Boulevard, Urbana. An 18-hole public championship course with many stone creeks, thus the name. Fees: $45–49 for
18 holes, $30–34 for 9. Carts: $15–20.

✳ Green Space

Bloomington-Normal Area
♂ **Ewing Cultural Center at Illinois State University** (309-829-6333;
www.ewingmanor.ilstu.edu), 48 Sunset Road, Bloomington. Open daily

8–dusk. The gardens around Ewing Manor are worth a stroll, as the original layout was designed by landscape architect Jens Jensen in 1927. The 6-acre estate also has a Japanese garden and sensory garden. No pets.

Moraine View State Park (309-724-8032; www.dnr.state.il.us/lands /landmgt/PARKS/R3/Moraine.htm), 27374 Moraine View Park Road, LeRoy. Just southeast of Bloomington-Normal, you'll find this state park, which offers great camping, hiking, fishing, and a beach swimming area on a 158-acre lake. The moraine here is an irregular crest that sweeps across the land from Peoria to Indiana. The park spreads across 1,600 acres. The lake has largemouth bass, bluegill, crappie, perch, and northern pike and can be fished from the shoreline, boat, or the fishing pier.

✿ **Sugar Grove Nature Center** (309-874-2174; www.sugargrovenature center.org), 4532 N. 725 E. Road, McLean. Open 9–5 Tuesday through Friday, 10–3 Saturday from April through October. For the winter months, the center is open from 10–3 Tuesday through Saturday. Trails open from dusk to dawn. Just south of Bloomington and Normal in Funks Grove, you'll find more than 1,000 acres of the largest remaining intact prairie grove in the state. Portions are designated a national natural landmark. Get lost in the 5 miles of maintained trails, and wind your way past the Funks Grove church, cemetery, and chapel. Imagination Grove invites kids of all ages to search for fossils, climb trees, and explore. You'll also find an astronomy observatory, blacksmith forge, and other gardens. Free. Pets allowed on leashes.

MORAINE VIEW STATE PARK

Champaign-Urbana Area
University of Illinois Arboretum (217-333-7579; www.arboretum .illinois.edu), Lincoln Avenue Florida Avenue, Urbana. Open daily sunrise to sunset. This is still a work in progress, but the university has several gardens here, such

as the selections garden and the welcome garden. The "idea" garden spotlights what's hot in plantings, and includes a section just for kids. Free.

River Bend Forest Preserve (217-586-3360; http://www.ccfpd.org /attractions/river_bend.html), 1602 W. Mid America Road, Mahomet. Open 7 AM–9 PM daily April through August, 7–7 September and October, 7–5 November through March. This 275-acre preserve near the Sangamon River features two lakes, Sunset Lake and Shadow Lake, as well as hiking and nature trails. There's a boat ramp on Sunset Lake, rest rooms, and shelter, but boats with gasoline motors are not allowed as they're intent on keeping invasive species out of the clear, clear lakes here.

✳ Lodging

BED AND BREAKFASTS

Bloomington-Normal

((ᵠ)) ♂ **Vrooman Mansion Bed & Breakfast** (877-346-6488; www .vroomanmansion.com), 701 E. Taylor Street, Bloomington. In a residential section of Bloomington, not far from the downtown, this 1869 Victorian historic home has gorgeous woodwork, stained-glass windows, built-in cabinets, high ceilings, and gardens. The owners are renovating a nearby carriage house to add more rooms. If you want more than a room, there is the three-room suite, with a light-filled bathroom and claw-foot tub. The house is named after Carl and Julia Vrooman; Julia's aunt was married to Adlai Stevenson I, whose family was important in Illinois politics. Carl also was a politician; Julia Vrooman lived here until she was 104 years old. The house has many cool features, like the still-used English lift to transport items from the ground level to upper levels. There's also a circular carved-wood dining room table that is original to the home.

VROOMAN MANSION

You won't find TVs or phones in your rooms, but a guest area has a TV, desk, and drinks. All rooms have fireplaces and come with gourmet breakfast, robes, free soft drinks, water, and snacks. Each suite is decorated in a theme to represent the family who lived in the gorgeous home. $$.

Champaign-Urbana
((ʸᵖ)) **Sylvia's Irish Inn** (217-384-4800; www.sylviasirishinn.com), 312 W. Green Street, Urbana. This renovated Queen Anne bed and breakfast is just a few blocks from the shops, restaurants, and the campus. Built in 1895, this was the home of Dr. Austin Lindley, who used the first floor for his office. The Victorian home has three suites with one suite in the attic. Rooms come with robes, TV/VCRs, AC, and breakfast. $–$$.

HOTELS

Bloomington-Normal
& ♂ ((ʸᵖ)) **The Chateau** (309-662-2020; www.chateauhotel.biz), 1601 Jumer Drive, Bloomington. These are pretty standard hotel rooms, with a little more masculine décor of dark blues. The exterior of this hotel near I-55 looks like a chateau, with a fountain in front, and a restaurant and lounge inside. The hotel also has an indoor pool, fitness center, business center, and free parking. Rates: $–$$.

Champaign-Urbana
& ((ʸᵖ)) **I Hotel and Conference Center** (217-819-5000; www.stay atthei.com),1900 S. First Street, Champaign. Located conveniently close to campus, this newer building, with a Houlihan's Restaurant and Bar in the lobby, has a sleek reception area. Rooms have queen or king beds, iPod clock radios, flat-screen HDTVs, granite bathroom countertops, designer spa products, robes, and artwork by local artists. There's also a business center, a fitness center, and shuttles to and from campus. Rates: $$–$$$.

CAMPING Moraine View State Park (309-724-8032; www.dnr .state.il.us/lands/landmgt/PARKS /R3/Moraine.htm), 27374 Moraine View Park Road, LeRoy. You can camp just steps away from a lake, on nice tree-covered spots, or backpack to a campsite at Tall Timber. The park also has a larger campground that is a good option for RVs. In fact the park has 137 Class-A campsites with electricity, and a sanitary station. Open year-round but shower buildings are closed November through April. Book at www.reserveamerica.com. Fee: $6 for primitive sites. $20–30 for others.

✳ Where to Eat

There are many chain restaurants in these parts, in fact Steak 'n Shake was founded in Normal in 1934. I've focused here on more locally owned establishments. Also, Uptown Normal has a strip of restaurants in the newly renovated area.

EATING OUT

Bloomington-Normal

((•)) & **Kelly's Bakery & Café**
(309-820-1200; www.kellysbakery
andcafe.com) 113 N. Center
Street, Bloomington. Open 7
AM–6 PM weekdays, 7–2 Saturday.
Fourth-grade teacher Kelly found
herself making hundreds of
dozens of cookies in her home
kitchen during a holiday season,
and decided to open this restaurant off the square in downtown
Bloomington, offering a European
café-style menu, and of course,
her famous butter cookies as well
as other baked goods. For breakfast try one of the daily quiches,
made with free-range organic
eggs, or pick from the sandwich
menu, which includes mozzarella-
tomato-basil or portobello ciabat-
ta. The bakery serves coffee
roasted in Bloomington. $

& ((•)) **Coffee Hound** (309-827-
7575; www.coffeehound.net), 407
W. Main Street, Bloomington.
Open 6:30 AM–6 PM Monday
through Saturday, 8–5 Sunday.
Also a location in Normal. The red
tin ceiling, yellow walls, and mis-
matched worn tables scream out
café, as do the authentic espresso
drinks and fresh roasted coffee.
(You can check out a roaster
machine in the back of the shop.)
Outdoor seating as well. $.

& **Lucca Grill** (309-828-7521;
www.luccagrill.com), 116 E. Market Street, Bloomington. Open 11
AM–1 AM Monday through Saturday, 3–10 Sunday. Started in 1936
by the Baldini brothers, who grew

up in Lucca, Italy. Locals talk up
the thin-crust pizza here, although
the menu covers the traditional
pastas and sandwiches too. $–$$.

Champaign-Urbana

& ((•)) **Café Kopi** (217-359-4266),
109 N. Walnut, Champaign. Open
7 AM–midnight daily. This is the
kind of place where you settle in
for hours, especially if the weather
is nice and you can snag a table on
the sidewalk patio. Menu includes
soups, sandwiches, in addition to
coffees, fresh juice, and smoothies.

& Y **Black Dog Smoke and Ale
House** (217-344-9334), 201 N.
Broadway, Urbana. Open 11
AM–10 Monday through Thursday,
11–11 Friday and Saturday, 11–9
Sunday. Choose your sauce—the
hot and smoky chipotle or the
sweet Georgia Peach for brisket,
pulled chicken, or pulled pork.
Then there's the "burnt ends,"
brisket smoked on a wood-fired
pit for 12 hours, dry-rubbed again,
and smoked again. $–$$.

DINING OUT

Bloomington-Normal

Y **Reality Bites** (309-828-1300;
www.realitybitesinc.com), 414 N.
Main Street, Bloomington. Open
11–9 Tuesday and Wednesday,
11–10 Thursday through Saturday.
Bar is open until 11 weekdays, 2
AM weekends. For a more upscale
lunch, this restaurant offers a couple different seating options—outdoors on a patio fronting the
building, inside, on the main floor,

or walk up a few steps to a higher dining room. The menu is tapas, such as small plates of bacon-wrapped dates, or tuna tartare. You can also order risotto, tacos, and a Kobe beef burger. They offer flights of wine, beer, and martinis. $$–$$$.

&. **Lancaster's Fine Dining** (309-827-3333; www.lancasters restaurant.com), 513 N. Main Street, Bloomington. Open at 5 daily. This steaks and chops restaurant in historic Bloomington also offers pasta, fish, and veal entrees. Appetizers include seared tuna on a green onion and ginger pancake with wasabi mayonnaise, or baked goat cheese with marinara. Steaks are served with roasted garlic-mashed potatoes. The restaurant also carries an extensive selection of wines from around the world. $$–$$$.

Medici (309-452-6334; www .medicinormal.com), 120 North Street, Normal. Open 11–9 Sunday and Monday, 11–10 Tuesday through Thursday, 11–11 Friday and Saturday. This is from the same people who head up Medici in Hyde Park, Chicago. Here the restaurant offers up a menu of salads, pizza, entrees like chicken marsala and beef stroganoff, pastas, coffee drinks, and shakes. The bar has 32 taps with microbrews and imports as well as some classics. The interior is pretty cool as well, with a giant mulberry tree stretching up through the 2-story atrium, and slices of trees visible in the bar and tables. There's also a bakery and an upstairs patio. $$–$$$.

Champaign-Urbana
&. **Jim Gould** (217-531-1177; www.jimgoulddining.com) Neil and Main, Champaign. Open 11–10 weekdays, 7 AM–11 PM Saturday. On Sunday, brunch is 10–2, dinner 5–9. Jim Gould offers a lengthy menu of seafood dishes, steaks, chops, salads, and duck. They also serve breakfast, and for lunch, paninis, sandwiches, and burgers. Breakfast: $; lunch: $–$$; dinner: $$–$$$$.

&. **Ko Fusion** (217-531-1166; www.kofusion.com), One East Main Street, Champaign. Lunch: 11–4 daily. Dinner 4–10 Sunday, Tuesday through Thursday, 4–11 Monday, Friday, and Saturday. Ko Fusion serves natural meats, wild-caught seafood, and local produce on a menu that fuses sushi and contemporary American cuisine with Asian dishes. The result may be a meal where you start out with sushi for appetizers, then move on to an entree of rib eye with organic shitake mushrooms, carrots, spinach sauté, chive-potato puree, and soy-sake butter sauce. The restaurant has small plates and you can order sushi in the restaurant or in the bar. There's also a nice wine list and outdoor seating. Lunch: $–$$; dinner: $$–$$$.

✷ Entertainment

BARS/BREWERIES

Bloomington-Normal

Υ **A Renee Wine Café** (309-827-3524; www.arenee.com), 306 N. Center Street, Bloomington. Open 11–9 Tuesday through Thursday, 11–10 Friday, 9 AM–10 PM Saturday. Stop in for a glass of wine, craft beer, limoncello, or port. The café on a downtown corner has plates with local cheeses, fruit and bread, and also desserts like truffles. An attached wine shop carries gourmet spreads, other foods, candles, and gifts, in addition to wine glasses and wines by the bottle. The shop is open 11–6 Tuesday through Friday, 10–5 Saturday.

Champaign-Urbana

Υ ♿ **The Blind Pig Co.** (217-398-1532; www.blindpigco.com), 120 N. Walnut Street, Champaign.

Open 3–2 daily. Brewery in walkable area of Champaign that makes its own beers, as well as offering a whole long list of others.

Υ ♿ **Cowboy Monkey** (217-398-2688; www.cowboy-monkey.com), 6 Taylor Street, Champaign. Bar and patio open 4–2 daily. Kitchen open 4–9 Sunday through Tuesday, 4–11 Wednesday through Saturday. Late-night appetizers served until 1 on certain nights. The menu is Mexican, with Baja steak tacos, or Chihuahua zucchini tacos. An extensive drink menu and a schedule of open mic nights, dance lessons, and live music make this a good late-night spot. $.

♿ Υ **Seven Saints** (217-351-7775; www.sevensaintsbar.com), 32 E. Chester Street, Champaign. Open 11 AM–2 AM Monday through Saturday, noon to midnight Sunday. Seven Saints has a lengthy beer

THE BLIND PIG CO. IN CHAMPAIGN

list, and wine, but really shows its muscle when it comes to whiskey, with over 250 bottles. They also have a good menu, with a focus on sliders, although it's a bit more creative than the traditional slider. For example, the "tropical stack" slider has grilled pineapple and spicy peanut sauce. Or how about a salmon slider? There are also more sandwiches, soups, and a menu of salads. $.

MOVIES

Bloomington-Normal
The Normal Theater (309-454-9722; www.normaltheater.com), 209 North Street, Normal. Opened in 1937, this art deco theater has been restored and is now open as a film center showcasing classic and independent film. Tickets: $6 adults, $5 children.

Champaign-Urbana
Y **The Art Theatre** (217-355-0068; www.thecuart.com), 126 W. Church Street, Champaign. This historic 1913 theater focuses on independent and art-house films. Wine, beer, and liquor served during the film as well. Tickets: $9 adult, $7.50 students, $6 seniors, children, $5 for late-night movies.

PERFORMING ARTS

Bloomington-Normal
& **Bloomington Center for the Performing Arts** (866-686-9541; www.cityblm.org/bcd), 600 N. East Street, Bloomington. Box office is open 10–5 weekdays and 10–curtain on show days. Built in

1921, the building opened as the Bloomington Scottish Rite Temple. The 1,320-seat theater was the largest stage west of New York. Duke Ellington, Beverly Sills, and Pablo Casals are among the artists who appeared on stage here. Renovations started in 2000 and the building reopened in 2006 as the center for performing arts. The theater now offers a calendar of well-known musicians, plays, comedians, dance groups, and authors.

& **Braden Auditorium** (309-438-5444; www.bsc.ilstu.edu/events/braden/) Located in the Bone Student Center, 100 N. University Street, Normal. A 3,450-seat space at Illinois State University in Normal, this auditorium welcomes Broadway musicals, speakers, and other entertainers throughout the year. Tickets can be purchased at the Braden Box Office or through Ticketmaster.

Champaign-Urbana
& **Assembly Hall** (217-333-5000; www.uofiassemblyhall.com), 1800 S. First Street, Champaign. This 17,000-seat white-domed hall welcomes a Broadway series, concerts, U of I basketball, and other sporting events.

& **Krannert Center for the Performing Arts** (217-333-6280; www.krannertcenter.com), 500 S. Goodwin, Urbana. You can find everything from unplugged performances to symphony orchestras and other arts events at the many performing arts spaces here.

❋ Selective Shopping

Bloomington-Normal Area
Uptown Normal (www.uptown normal.com)You'll find it in the area around North Street and Beaufort Street. More is planned for this area, but you'll find a record store, book store, and other retail shops.

Downtown Bloomington (www .downtownbloomington.org) has some interesting shops to check out, including the **Chocolatier,** which has glass jars filled with colorful mixes of gumdrops and jellybeans and of course, chocolate. There's the nonprofit fair-trade shop called **Crossroads** as well as an antique shop and bead store.

For more of a traditional mall, you can head to the **Shoppes at College Hills** (www.theshoppesat collegehills.com) on North Veterans Parkway.

Funks Grove Pure Maple Sirup (309-874-3360; www.funks maplesirup.com), 5257 Old Route 66, Shirley. Having established the farm here in 1824, the Funk family has been making maple syrup forever. Correction: sirup. They prefer the original Webster's spelling of sirup, not syrup. Stop in off historic Route 66 and get some maple sirup or candy. Call ahead for store hours as sirup is only available March through August.

Champaign-Urbana
Downtown Champaign has some interesting shops including

B. Lime (217-359-5741; www .blimegreen.com), 12 E. Washington Street. Open 10–5 Tuesday through Saturday, noon–4 Sunday. A green store, you can see the commitment to earth-friendly products throughout the shelves of clothes, housewares, cloth diapers, and other items that will help to turn your own home more eco-friendly.

❋ Special Events

April: **EbertFest** (www.ebertfest .com) Film critic Roger Ebert hosts an annual film festival in Champaign.

June through August: **Illinois Shakespeare Festival** (309-438-2535; thefestival.org) Every summer Illinois State University puts together this festival devoted to the Bard, with performances held at Ewing Manor, 48 Sunset Road, Bloomington. Tickets: $22–42.

July: **Sugar Creek Arts Festival** (309-829-0011; www.mcac.org /festivals.htm) Uptown Normal invites artists and art lovers to this annual festival that also features music, and of course, festival food. Free.

August: **Urbana Sweetcorn Festival** (www.urbanabusiness .com/downtown/sweetcorn.html) For more than three decades, downtown Urbana has hosted this celebration of corn on the cob. Also includes bands, arts, crafts, and other food.

There's also the **Sweet Corn Blues Festival** (www.normal.org /uptown/cornfest.asp) in Uptown

Normal. After the harvesting of the corn from area farmers, everyone comes out for a taste. There's plenty here—at least 50,000 ears of it. Free.

October: **Homecoming** at Illinois Wesleyan University and Illinois State University.

Land of Lincoln

5

SPRINGFIELD

SPRINGFIELD

Illinois is nicknamed the Land of Lincoln, and Springfield is the center of that land, with an impressive and worthwhile new Abraham Lincoln Presidential Museum and numerous other historic sites that enable you to become intimately acquainted with the story of our 16th president.

As the capital city, Springfield is home to the sprawling campus of state buildings and the legislature, although a lot of business is also conducted in Chicago. Springfield has its ebbs and flows. When the legislature is in session, powerbrokers pack the bars and restaurants and parking lots around the capitol.

Springfield can play host for one of my family's favorite type of travel days—one in which we become obsessed with one particular story (such as Lincoln), and spend the day soaking up every detail. We take breaks at great restaurants, where we can all share our observations. To achieve a day like that in Springfield, spend a few hours inside the fantastic presidential museum, or at the Lincoln Home Historic Site. Stop for lunch in the historic square. Many of the restaurants there are only open for lunch, so take advantage of it. In the afternoon, head to whichever attraction you missed—the museum? Law offices? Capitol? The Lincoln Home Historic Site is very cool, with park rangers brimming with all kinds of fun facts about the president, his family, and neighbors. There is something very special about walking around the neighborhood as it looked back during his time. There are plenty of historic sites here to fill out your itinerary, and overflow into another day. You will also want to make the drive to the Lincoln New Salem site, which is probably at least a half-day experience when you figure in the drive. Once you close out the first day though, head to some of the fun restaurants—you can go for casual and seek out the famous Horseshoe, or mix it up with a vibrant restaurant in the downtown area.

Founded in 1821, Springfield had a relatively quick growth spurt at the beginning. It started its association with the young Abraham Lincoln when he moved from New Salem in 1837, and started practicing law. He

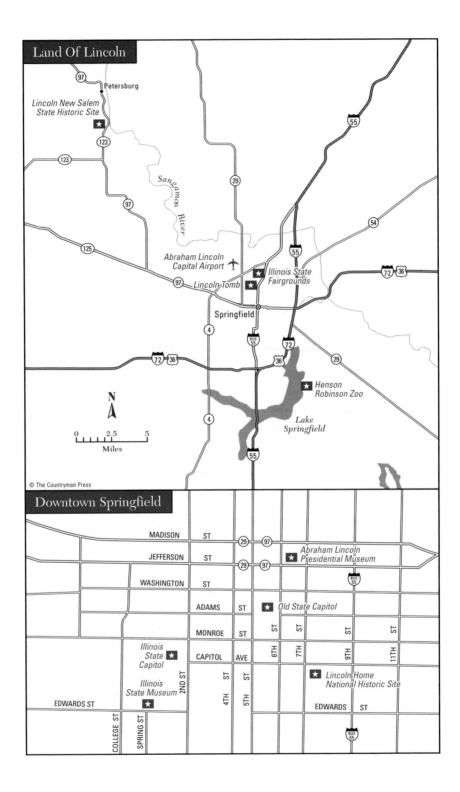

Land Of Lincoln

Petersburg

Lincoln New Salem
State Historic Site

Sangamon River

Abraham Lincoln
Capital Airport

Illinois State
Fairgrounds

Lincoln Tomb

Springfield

Henson
Robinson Zoo

Lake
Springfield

N

0   2.5   5
Miles

© The Countryman Press

Downtown Springfield

MADISON ST

JEFFERSON ST

Abraham Lincoln
Presidential Museum

WASHINGTON ST

ADAMS ST

Old State Capitol

MONROE ST

Illinois
State
Capitol

CAPITOL AVE

Illinois
State Museum

Lincoln Home
National Historic Site

EDWARDS ST

EDWARDS ST

COLLEGE ST

SPRING ST

2ND ST

4TH ST

5TH ST

6TH ST

7TH ST

9TH ST

11TH ST

practiced on the Eighth Judicial Circuit, traveling around central Illinois, which is why in your travels you'll see a lot of places claiming that "Lincoln slept here," and whatnot. He met Mary Todd and they were married in 1842. Robert Todd Lincoln was born in 1843, while they lived at the Globe Tavern. A short time later, Lincoln bought the Springfield home at 8th and Jackson that you can walk through today.

By 1837, Springfield took on the role of Illinois' state capital, when Lincoln and a group of other tall legislators (seriously, they were all at least 6 feet tall, so they were known as the "long nine") urged a move of the capital from Vandalia to Springfield. They obviously were successful, as you can see two capitol buildings in the city today. Lincoln lived in Springfield until he departed for Washington, D.C. in 1861 to take on the office of president.

During the Civil War, Springfield's Camp Butler housed Confederate prisoners and also trained Illinois soldiers. The first casualty of the Civil War was a Springfield native. Another important historic moment for the country happened here. In the 1900s, a race riot in Springfield led to the founding of the National Association for the Advancement of Colored People (NAACP). A gruesome historic note: The Donner party is said to have started their trip in Springfield, a moment marked by a plaque downtown.

The city's political importance did not end with Lincoln, as Barack Obama spent time here as a state senator. As a U.S. senator, he announced his candidacy from the Old State Capitol in 2007, with all the world watching. Today Springfield has a population of just under 115,000.

GUIDANCE All addresses in this section are in Springfield unless otherwise indicated.

Union Station Tourist Information Center (217-557-4588), 500 E. Madison Street. Open 9–5 daily. In 2007, the city renovated Union Station, shining up a jewel of a building originally constructed in 1898 by the Illinois Central Railroad. To find it, look for the clock tower. Inside, the giant halls are warmed by golden color on the walls and by the original woodwork seen in the benches, trim, and exterior doors. The floors are replica. You can purchase tickets to the Abraham Lincoln Presidential Museum from the help at the front desk. Outside, there's a park, and statues of Lincoln stand in front.

&. **Capitol Complex Visitors Center** (217-524-6620), 425 S. College Street. Open 8–4:30 weekdays. Get your bearings with a 20-minute video presentation and brochures about the state government buildings and historic sites.

Lincoln Home Visitor Center (217-492-4241 ext 221; www.nps.gov /liho), 426 S. 7th Street. Open 8:30–5 daily. This is your starting point to take in the historic site of Lincoln's Home and neighborhood. Inside the center, there's a model of the city that gives a bird's-eye view of Springfield at the time of Lincoln. Small exhibits provide more context to give you a better understanding of what you're about to see. National Park Service rangers lead tours of Lincoln's home and the neighborhood. The tours depart frequently but you will need a ticket, which you can pick up at the desk. They're free. Tour groups are kept small so that everyone can fit into the rooms in the Lincoln Home.

✐ ☀ ♿ **Lincoln's New Salem Visitors Center** (217-632-4000; www .lincolnsnewsalem.com), 15588 History Lane, Petersburg. Located off IL 97, 20 miles northwest of Springfield. Open 8–4 Wednesday through Sunday from November through February. Spring and summer hours: 9–5. Learn all about the 1830s village where Lincoln lived and worked. A 17-minute movie introduces you to the story of New Salem. Volunteers can outfit you with trail maps and brochures with descriptions of the buildings you'll see in the village.

Looking for Lincoln Cell Phone Audio Tour (217-213-3003) For background information on nine major sites in town, dial the audio tour number and punch in the code of the building. If you don't know the code, enter "11" to hear a list of options.

GETTING THERE *By auto:* From the north or south, I-55 provides access to Springfield. The city is 200 miles from Chicago, and about 100 miles from St. Louis. I-72 is the route to take from the east or west.

By bus: **Greyhound Bus Depot** (800-231-2222; www.greyhound.com), 2351 S. Dirksen Parkway.

By air: ((♠)) **Abraham Lincoln Capital Airport** (217-788-1060; www.fly spi.com), 1200 Capital Airport Drive. United Airlines and American Airlines currently fly out of this airport to Chicago's O'Hare. Direct Air also operates a route to Myrtle Beach.

By train: **Amtrak** (800-USA-RAIL; www.amtrak.com), Washington and Third Streets. Open 6 AM–11 PM daily. The Texas Eagle route stops in Springfield on its way from Chicago to St. Louis, as do Amtrak's Illinois Service trains, which connect several downstate cities. The station has an enclosed waiting area and rest rooms.

GETTING AROUND *By auto:* Streets are one-way through the heart of downtown. The capitol complex is on the west end of downtown, a giant square of government buildings bordered by Monroe, College, Edwards, and 2nd Streets. Most of the parking surrounding the complex is for state employees. Many of the restaurants and shops are closer to the Old Capitol building at 6th and Adams. You can park in the lot beneath the Old

State Capitol, and at the Abraham Lincoln Presidential Library. There is street parking, but depending on the season and legislative schedule, it may or may not be available.

By bus: ἀ **Springfield Mass Transit District Historic Sites Bus** (217-522-5531; www.smtd.org) This local bus line runs through the historic district sites, with stops every 30 minutes from 8:15–6 PM mid-April through Labor Day. Service is hourly during the offseason. The bus line doesn't operate on Sundays. The rest of the year, the bus runs hourly. The bus line also has routes through other areas of the city. Fares: $3 all-day pass, $1 for one ride. You must have exact fare.

By trolley: **Springfield Trolley** (217-528-4100), 522 E. Monroe Street, Suite 300. During summer this open-air trolley has stops at all the major sites. Tickets sold at downtown locations.

MEDICAL EMERGENCIES Memorial Medical Center (217-788-3000; www.memorialmedical.com), 701 North 1st Street. This regional medical center has emergency, heart, vascular, and transplant services. The hospital also has a maternity center and is the regional burn center for the area. St. John's, Memorial Medical Center, and Southern Illinois University School of Medicine have joined together to form a Level I trauma center that rotates between the two hospitals.

St. John's Hospital (217-544-6464; www.st-johns.org), 800 E. Carpenter. With 539 beds, this Catholic hospital is the largest in downstate Illinois. It has an emergency room, birth center, children's hospital, and is a teaching hospital for Southern Illinois University.

✳ Wandering Around

EXPLORING BY CAR IL 97 will take you west and north to Lincoln's New Salem Historic Site near Petersburg. Explore the area around Lake Springfield by taking I-55 south to East Lake Shore Drive.

EXPLORING BY FOOT Most of the historic sites in downtown Springfield are walkable, and best seen this way so you're not growing more and more frustrated trying to find parking. Start out at the Abraham Lincoln Presidential Museum on the north side of the city, and work your way down through the downtown sites to Lincoln's neighborhood. The state capitol building and historic homes line the route. You also can take the 1908 Race Riot Walking Tour, which takes you through the story of the events that led to the founding of the NAACP in 1909. The self-guided tour starts at the corner of Seventh and Jefferson Streets. You can pick up a map at the Springfield Convention & Visitors Bureau sites (see above).

LINCOLN'S NEIGHBORHOOD

EXPLORING BY BIKE Interurban Trail (www.springfieldparks.org /bicycletrails/interurbantrail.asp) Access this bicycle and running trail at Wabash Avenue and MacArthur Boulevard, then head south along an old railway line. The path does run along an active rail line as well, and connects with the Lick Creek bike trail that runs around Lake Springfield. You also can access the Wabash Trail at the same trailhead. The Wabash Trail is 3 miles long along a railroad right-of-way on the city's southwest side and isn't quite as scenic, running through industrial and commercial property as well as residential. The 5-mile Lost Bridge trail starts on the city's east side, and does pass under I-55, but otherwise crosses creeks and borders the lake. You can access it near the Illinois Department of Transportation building at 2300 S. Dirksen Parkway.

EXPLORING BY HORSE Springfield Carriage Company (217-299-0959; www.springfieldcarriage.com) Board the carriage at the Old State Capitol Plaza on the 6th Street side. The horses are generally out there in the evening from 6–9 PM Friday and Saturday, depending on the weather. If you want to experience modern Springfield like Lincoln and his contemporaries did, perhaps try a horse-drawn carriage ride through town, to all the Lincoln sites. Cost: $25 per couple, $5 for each additional person.

MUSEUMS ✐ ♿ ✟ **Abraham Lincoln Presidential Museum** (800-610-2094; www.presidentlincoln.org), 212 N. Sixth Street. Open daily 9–5. A great first stop to get your bearings, this impressive museum, opened in 2005, gives you the complete story of Lincoln, supplementing the facts with some emotional displays and insight into the shaping of this important American leader. After meeting the president, Mary Todd Lincoln, and sons, Robert, Eddie, Willie, and Tad here, the other sites have a little more meaning. When you walk into the light-filled central hall, choose to enter the White House, or the log cabin where Lincoln spent his early years. In the White House, exhibits feature the dresses that Mrs. Lincoln and the Washington social set wore at the time, and explain how the press and critics discussed Lincoln's policies. A four-minute interactive display underscores in a very powerful way the progression of battles and the large numbers of lives lost in the Civil War. Key moments in the president's life are depicted with lifelike mannequins, including one melancholy scene in which the president and Mrs. Lincoln have left a White House party to check on young son Willie, who has taken a turn for the worse. Mr. Lincoln looks on darkly as he clutches Willie's doll in one hand. Actors dressed from the period may greet you at some of the displays, asking questions or pointing out interesting details about the scene. In the log cabin, learn about Lincoln's family, his modest upbringing, the events that influenced his life, and helped him form the set of principles that he lived by. Another exhibit showcases "treasures" from the collection, including white gloves the president always carried with him to shake hands in crowds. The gloves in the exhibit are blood-stained from the tragic night at Ford's Theatre. A stovepipe hat shows two marks on the brim, which the president wore into the fabric by tipping his hat to those passing by. The Holavision Theater's "Ghosts of the Library" wows the crowds with some tricks. I don't want to ruin it so I'll leave it at that. A children's museum rounds out the tour. Plan a few hours to take in this interesting collection. Tickets: $12 adults, $9 seniors, students, $6 for children 5 to 15 years. Some special exhibits have extra fees.

((ᵞ)) ♿ **Abraham Lincoln Presidential Library** (217-558-8844, www.presidentlincoln.org), 112 N. Sixth Street. Building open 9–5 daily. Research center open 9–4:30 weekdays. The library is located across the street from the museum, and is open to the public, with small exhibits on the first and second floors of the atrium halls. Generally, it is visited by those who come with a purpose of researching Lincoln, Illinois history, and genealogy. Free.

♿ ✟ **Korean War National Museum** (888-295-7212; www.kwnm.org), 9 South Old State Capitol Plaza. Open 10–5 Tuesday through Saturday. Still a work in progress, parts of this new museum for veterans of the Korean

LINCOLN PRESIDENTIAL LIBRARY

War are open after a rather rough start. The Denis J. Healy Freedom Center opened in 2009 with 3-D interactive exhibit, a canteen, and a center for veterans to record their personal experiences. Plans eventually call for a 50,000-square foot museum.

&. ↑ **Illinois State Museum** (217-782-7386; www.museum.state.il.us), 502 S. Spring Street, south of the state capitol building. Open 8:30–5 Monday through Saturday, noon–5 Sunday. The focus here is on the land, life, people, and art of Illinois. The "Changes" exhibit focuses on the environmental changes and geology. With life-sized dioramas and pieces from the collection, the "Peoples from the Past" area reveals the story of the Native Americans who first called Illinois home. In 2010, the museum replaced its children's museum with a play museum designed for children ages 3 to 10 years. The exhibits aim to make children feel like scientists. They'll be able to crawl through caves, excavate a mastodon skeleton, collect minerals, and load a Jeep to go on a scientific expedition. The museum also showcases art and temporary exhibitions. Note: If you can find a spot, you can park for free in the state capitol complex visitor center lot 1 block west of the museum. Free.

LINCOLN SITES &. **Lincoln Family Pew** (217-528-4311; http://lincolnschurch.org), First Presbyterian Church, 321 S. Seventh Street. Tours offered 10–4 weekdays from June through September. It's pew No. 20 that's of particular interest in this historic church located near the site of

Lincoln's old neighborhood. Lincoln rented the spot for his family so they could attend services, although he himself was not a regular attendee. Mrs. Lincoln turned to the church after the death of their second son, Eddie. For the tours, enter the First Presbyterian Church through the two arched red doors on Seventh Street. At other times of the year, call ahead to arrange a visit or you'll not be able to find the pew. Free.

& **Lincoln-Herndon Law Office** (217-785-7289; www.state.il.us/hpa /hs/lincoln_herndon.htm) Northeast corner of the square around the Old State Capitol. Open 9–5 daily mid-May through Labor Day. Open 9–5 Tuesday through Saturday during the offseason. A tour will take you through the disorderly offices of Lincoln and his law partner, William Herndon, and give you insight into how the future president worked. Mr. Lincoln moved into the existing building in 1843, which also housed the federal courts for a time. On the first floor of the building, visitors can learn about Lincoln's work and see photos of Lincoln through the years (note how drastically he ages during the Civil War). During Lincoln's time, a post office was also located in the building, and that is represented on the first floor as well. Tinsley Dry Goods Gift Shop on the first floor offers many Lincoln-themed souvenirs. Suggested donation: $4.

LINCOLN-HERNDON LAW OFFICE

& **Lincoln Home National Historic Site** (217-492-4241 ext. 221; www.nps.gov/liho), 8th and Jackson Streets. Open 8:30–5 daily. The tours are free, but you must pick up a ticket at the visitor center information desk. If you only have a short time here, be sure to include this on your itinerary. Four blocks in the middle of Springfield are impressively preserved as they were in Lincoln's time. Lincoln's brown 2-story home with hunter green shutters sits in the middle. The only home he ever owned, he bought it from the minister who married him to Mary Todd. Notice that the Lincolns' sidewalk is made of brick, as compared to the plank boardwalks that surround the area. Park rangers lead tours of Mr. Lincoln's house, pointing out original pieces like the sofas and chairs upholstered with black horsehair, and sharing stories about the family's life here. The handrails are the same that Mr. Lincoln gripped while walking up the stairs. Other original items: a stove that the family installed just before moving to D.C., a toy that belonged to the Lincoln boys, and a desk and other bedroom furniture in Lincoln's bedroom. The wallpaper in his room is an exact replica of the pattern on the walls when the Lincolns lived here. Be sure to stay on the blue carpet during the tour through the house, or you'll set off alarms. Outside you can see the outhouse, and view the neighborhood as the Lincolns did. Across the street is the Charles Arnold house, which had been rebuilt over the years but now has been returned to the look and style it had when Mr. Arnold was a neighbor of the Lincolns. Inside his home is a museum that discusses how archaeologists and researchers piece together the history of a home and reconstruct it. The Harriet Dean house, also across the street from Lincoln's home, has been converted to an interesting museum that tells the story of the Lincolns' home life, from the courtship of Mary and Abe to their departure for D.C. Learn how Mr. Lincoln's frequent trips away from home to practice law on the circuit left Mary alone for months at a time, and how the family home evolved over time with a number of additions. A garden in the back shows how yards of that time period looked, probably much different than those of today, with families keeping animals and having many more outdoor chores to do. Meander through the rest of the 4-block area, which is closed to vehicular traffic, and learn about the Lincolns' neighbors through signs that detail how they interact-

LINCOLN HOME

ed with the Lincolns and what the inhabitants did for a living. Though the buildings are used as offices for the park staff, the exterior of the homes look as they did back then. You can also use your cell phone to dial the numbers listed on many of the signs to hear a more extensive story about the property.

Lincoln Ledger (217-527-3860), 6th and Washington Streets. The bank is open from 9–5:30 weekdays, 8–noon Saturday. The original Lincoln family account ledger is kept in a glass case in the center of the lobby of what is currently Chase Bank. Walk right into the center of the bank as if you were going to get in line to cash a check and you will see a small glass table. Inside are the yellowed, faded pages listing actions on the president's account, which he opened at the Springfield Marine and Fire Insurance Company in 1853 with $310 that he kept there until his death in 1865. The entries reveal some details about the president's life, such as that his income as an attorney averaged about $3,000 a year. Free.

&. ♂ **Edwards Place** (217-523-2631; www.springfieldart.org), 700 N. 4th Street. Tours given on the hour 11–2 Tuesday through Saturday. To complete the story of the Lincolns' life in Springfield, you won't want to miss the "Lincoln Courting Couch" now located in this historic home, once the center of the social scene in Springfield. The couch was taken from the parlor of the home where Lincoln and Mary Todd were married. As you tour the home, you'll learn more about the important people who were entertained here by Benjamin and Helen Edwards, who lived here from 1843 to 1909. It is the oldest home in Springfield that sits on the original foundation. The home is also the headquarters of the Springfield Art Association. Suggested donation: $3.

&. **Lincoln Tomb** (217-782-2717; www.state.il.us/hpa/hs/lincoln_tomb .htm), Oak Ridge Cemetery, 1500 Monument Avenue. The cemetery is a short drive north of downtown. Open 9–5 daily May through Labor Day, closed Sunday, Monday from September through November and March through April. The hours are reduced to 9–4 Tuesday through Saturday during the winter from December through February. The monument sits high up on a hill, with a dramatic statue of Lincoln and bronze sculptures of Civil War infantry, artillery, cavalry, and navy on the corners. The tomb was dedicated in 1874 and stands 117 feet tall. A bust of Lincoln greets visitors, a bronze replica of the marble head of Lincoln located in the U.S. Capitol in Washington D.C. Visitors have worn the coating off his nose by rubbing it for good luck. Inside, follow a circular marble hallway lined with statues of key moments in Lincoln's life. You'll reach the back room with a monument marking the spot where Lincoln's remains lie, 10 feet below the ground. Mary and Abe visited the cemetery while he lived in the city so Mrs. Lincoln decided to have him buried here after his assassination. Opposite from him, the remains of Mary, Eddie, Willie, and Tad lie behind stone markers. Robert Todd Lincoln, the only son to live into adulthood, is buried in Arlington National Cemetery, but there is a marker here for him as well.

✎ **Lincoln's New Salem State Historic Site** (217-632-4000; www .lincolnsnewsalem.com) 15588 History Lane, Petersburg. The village is located about 20 miles northwest of Springfield. Open 9–5 daily, spring and summer. Otherwise hours reduced. From November through February, open 8–4 Wednesday through Sunday. The village of New Salem sprouted up around the Sangamon River with hopes that it would turn into a commercial center. Lincoln was drawn here as a young man after passing by on a flatboat down to New Orleans. He returned and made himself part of the community. Despite the hopes of the founders, steamboats could not fit on the river, and eventually the town disappeared. Lucky for us, historians have pieced together what the town looked like, using information upturned during archaeological digs and other research. New Salem has been fully re-created on this 700-acre state historic site. As you wander the site, you can picture life here, especially with volunteers dressed in period clothing doing chores in the garden or working in their shops. Talk to the blacksmith about his work and his friends. See the mill that led to the creation of the town, the blacksmith shop, the cooper shop, the store run by Lincoln and William Berry, and the log cabins they filled with family and belongings, turning them into homes. Stop in the visitor center first to get your bearings, and pick up a map of the trail around New Salem that includes descriptions of all the buildings. For

LINCOLN'S STORE IN NEW SALEM

MORE LINCOLN?

If you want more of the Lincoln story, plan a side trip to Vandalia, about 75 miles southeast of Springfield. ♿ **Vandalia State House Historic Site** (618-283-1161; www.state.il.us/hpa/hs/vandalia_statehouse.htm), 315 W. Gallatin Street, Vandalia. Open 9–5 daily May through Labor Day. Hours reduced to 9–4 Tuesday through Saturday otherwise. This state house served as the capitol from 1836–39. The building includes the original floors that Lincoln himself walked on. This building was constructed to keep the state capitol located in Vandalia. Pick up all kinds of fun facts from the knowledgeable guides, such as how the legislators and officials needed to burn the beef-fat candles that illuminated the building right away, so they would not start to smell. There's another fascinating story about Lincoln that you can pick up in the small park across the street. Apparently young Lincoln accidentally became engaged during a conversation he considered just lighthearted joking. Admission: $4 adults, $10 families.

VANDALIA STATE HOUSE

each building, you can read the story of the people who lived there during Lincoln's time, from the Trent Brothers to the Millers. You might want to pack a picnic lunch. The store next to the visitor center has a gift shop and the New Salem Diner, which has a limited menu of cheeseburgers, hot dogs, fries, and nachos. Suggested donation: $4 adults, $2 children, $10 family.

HISTORIC SITES & ↑ **Illinois State Capitol** (217-782-2099), 2nd and Capitol Avenue. Open 8–4:30 weekdays, 9–3:30 weekends. Walk the vast marble-lined hallways that stretch on in both directions, with giant doors opening to state offices. At the center of the building, look straight up to the striking dome with its colorful stained-glass center. All four floors of the 1886 revival building are open to the public (after you walk through metal detectors). The outer walls are made of limestone from Joliet and Lemont. When the legislature is in session, visitors can watch the action (or inaction as is often the case in Illinois politics) from the fourth-floor galleries. Unfortunately, the story of Illinois politicians of late has not been fitting of such a gorgeous setting, with two recent governors charged with corruption. On the grounds outside are statues of Illinois' famous statesmen. For a tour, contact the convention and visitors bureau in advance at 800-545-7300. Tours depart from the information desk in the rotunda of the first floor. To enter the capitol, you may need to show ID. Free.

ILLINOIS STATE CAPITOL

& ↑ **Old State Capitol** (217-785-9363; www.illinoishistory.gov), 6th and Adams Streets. Open 9–5 daily mid-May through Labor Day. Closed Sunday and Monday at other times of the year. On the Springfield cityscape, this maroon dome marks the spot of the stately building where Stephen Douglas and Abraham Lincoln worked for

OLD STATE CAPITOL

20 years. The fifth capitol in Illinois, this building was constructed in 1839 and served as the hub of the state's business until 1876. The offices are set up as they were back then, with original pieces like an auditor desk from the 1860s. A Lincoln campaign sign hangs from the walls. The cream walls and columns are set off by dark wood railings and floors. The rotunda is sometimes tinted gold by the light coming through. Take a walk through Representative Hall where Lincoln gave his famous "House Divided" speech, and the state supreme court where he presented cases. The building also has an original senator's desk on the upper level in the senate chamber. Notice the spittoons under the desks of the "statesmen." Guides know plenty about the history that played out here so be sure to ask if you have any questions.

& **Camp Butler National Cemetery** (217-492-4070; www.cem.va.gov /cems/nchp/campbutler.asp), 5063 Camp Butler Road. Open from 8–sunset daily. When the Civil War broke out, General William Tecumseh Sherman was sent to find a site for a military training camp for Union troops. He settled on a plot 6 miles northeast of Springfield. As the fighting escalated, Confederate prisoners of war were also sent here. In 1862, a smallpox epidemic wiped out 700 POWs. About 1,600 Union and Confederate soldiers are buried at Camp Butler, which is now a national cemetery. Notable military personnel buried here include Colonel Otis B. Duncan, a Springfield man who was the highest-ranking African American officer during World War I. Free.

CULTURAL SITES & **Executive Mansion** (217-782-2525; www.illinois .gov/mansiontour.cfm), 410 E. Jackson Street. Tours are given 9:30–11 AM, 2–3:30 PM Tuesday and Thursday, and 9:30–11 Saturday. Visitors can tour three levels and see the ballroom, dining room, and the Lincoln bedroom. Illinois governors have been living here since 1855, although not all of them have lived here, most notably former Governor Rod Blagojevich, who kept his home in Chicago. Free.

↑ **Dana-Thomas House** (217-782-6776; www.dana-thomas.org), 301 E. Lawrence Avenue. Tours operate from 9–4 Wednesday through Sunday. Frank Lloyd Wright was commissioned in 1902 to remake the Lawrence family home, an Italianate-style Victorian. What he produced illustrates the unique style of the Prairie School of Architecture. Suggested donation: $5 adults, $3 children.

Shea's Gas Station Museum (217-522-0475), 2075 Peoria Road. Open 8–4 Tuesday through Friday, 8–noon Saturday. Bill Shea ran a gas station for many years along Route 66 and shares his story through his collection of service-station memorabilia including oil cans, fuel pumps, and the like. Admission: $2 adults, $1 children.

✳ To Do

FOR FAMILIES & ♦ **Knight's Action Park** (217-546-8881; www .knightsactionpark.com), I-72 and Chatham Road (Exit 96). Open 9 AM— 11 PM daily mid-May through Labor Day, 9–9 daily in September, 9–6 in October, 9–dusk in November and December. The action park includes a driving range, miniature golf, go-karts, batting cages, Ferris wheel, and a game room. The water park, **Caribbean Water Adventure**, is open 10–6 from mid-May through Labor Day. It features a wave pool, waterslides, bumper boats, and children's area. Admission: $26 adults, $20 children, $4 toddlers under 2 years. A package deal for $30 per person gets you a water park pass and unlimited use of areas of the action park.

GOLF ♂ **The Rail Golf Course** (217-525-0365; www.railgolf.com), 1400 S. Club House Drive. Located north of the city off I-55. Depending on what kind of game you're looking for, the Rail may or may not be for you. It hosted the LPGA State Farm Classic for three decades and includes 82 sand bunkers and five lakes. It earns 4 stars from *Golf Digest* magazine. Fees: $31–39 for 18 holes, $21–25 for 9 holes. Carts: $10–15.

♂ **Piper Glen Golf Club** (217-483-6537; www.piperglen.com), 7112 Piper Glen Drive. Located southeast of the city, this course is a great option for those looking for value. Fees: $34 for 18 holes. $16–19 for 9 holes. Carts: $15 for 18 holes, $9 for 9 holes.

TOURS Springfield Walks Tours and Guide Services (217-502-8687; www.springfieldwalks.com), 113 6th Street. Tours depart from the Union Station Visitors Center at 7:30 Tuesday through Saturday from March through October. A new way to see the Lincoln sites, the Lincoln's Ghost Walk tour investigates the stories about Lincoln's ghost at the White House, Mary Lincoln's insanity trial, and the legends of his tomb. Tickets: $12 adults, $10 seniors, $8 kids 11 to 17 years. A Scandalous Springfield walk takes groups through the true-crime history of this Midwestern city. Tickets for that tour are $10.

ZOOS ⅙ ∅ **Henson Robinson Zoo** (217-753-6217; www.hensonrobin sonzoo.org), 1100 East Lake Drive. Open 10–5 weekdays, 9–6 weekends from March through October. During the summer, the park has extended hours until 8 PM on Wednesday. During the winter, the zoo is open daily 10–4. On the sprawling park grounds surrounding Lake Springfield, this zoo operated by the Springfield Park District offers a close-up look at bears, bobcats, cougars, gibbons, marmosets, and penguins. Exhibits include a barnyard and a butterfly garden. Through the admission house, you'll walk out to find a pool of water that streams around the park, and a great playground area. The zoo also fills the calendar with programming for kids. Admission: $4.50 adults, $3 seniors, $2.75 for children 3 to 12 years, free for children under 2.

Thomas Rees Memorial Carillon (217-753-6219; www.carillon-rees .org), on Fayette Avenue, east of Chatham Road in Washington Park. Open noon–dusk Wednesday through Sunday during the summer. During spring and fall, the carillon is only open on weekends. The world's fifth largest bell tower has three observation decks from which you can view greater Springfield. Thomas Rees, publisher of the *State Journal Register* from 1881–1933 donated the money for the carillon after developing an interest in carillons during his travels. Inside the tower, there are 67 bells that are played like a musical instrument. Concerts are given on Sunday afternoons in the summer.

✳ Green Space

Lake Springfield (217-757-8660 ext. 1011; www.cwlp.com/lake_spring field/lake_springfield.htm) The area is best accessed by car from Adlai Stevenson Drive. Located southeast of downtown, the Henson Robinson Zoo, and parks all line this 4,200-acre reservoir. It's the source of drinking water for the city, but also adds to the local scenery. The lake has public boat launches, including one off I-55 at exit 88 at the Lake Springfield Marina.

⅙ **Lincoln Memorial Garden & Nature Center** (217-529-1111; www .lincolnmemorialgarden.org), 2301 East Lake Drive. Garden open daily sunrise–sunset. Nature center open 10–4 Tuesday through Saturday, 1–4 Sunday. Designed to approximate what the landscape looked like at the time of Abraham Lincoln, this living memorial offers 6 miles of trails for walking. It's covered with plants from Illinois, Indiana, and Kentucky, where the former president lived. Benches are inscribed with Lincoln quotes. Landscape architect Jens Jensen, a leader of the Prairie School of landscape architecture, designed the garden in the 1930s. No bikes or pets allowed. Free.

✳ Lodging

BED AND BREAKFASTS ((ᵖ)) ♂
Pasfield House Inn (217-525-3663; www.pasfieldhouse.com),

PASFIELD HOUSE INN

525 S. Pasfield Street. Innkeeper Tony Leone has stayed in hotels and inns throughout the country and determined what travelers want. He kept that in mind when designing his Pasfield House Inn. Leone, a former clerk for the Illinois general assembly, bought the building in 1996 and started renovating it into a bed and breakfast. As he went to work on the building, he uncovered more and more of the history of the Pasfields, a prominent Springfield family, and if you want an interesting story, ask Tony to show you some of the maps and photos he's found. As for the building, the foyer is impressive, with a gorgeous wooden staircase. A chef's kitchen downstairs is used for cooking classes. The inn was also host to a gingerbread throwdown on the Food Network for *Throwdown with Bobby Flay.* Located west of the capitol, the home has a "French quarter" patio and a gazebo. There's a library sitting room for guests, and a large dining room for special events. The six guest rooms all do have a little something extra to them, and it's not as heavy on the antiques as many bed and breakfasts. My

favorite room is the "Frank Lloyd Wright" suite. Rooms include a kitchenette with stocked refrigerator and granite countertop, flat-screen TV, and DVD player. Suites have sitting rooms, some with fireplaces, and roomy bathrooms. There's also an exercise room, and DVD library with more than 500 films. $$.

((ᵖ)) ♂ **The Rippon-Kinsella House** (217-241-3367; www.ripponkinsella.com), 1317 N. Third Street. To learn the details of this 1871 Italianate mansion, start out with a tour led by the owners. The inn is located on the north side of Springfield, within walking distance to the Oak Ridge Cemetery. Rooms have TVs and private baths. No pets. $–$$.

HOTELS �& ☀ **Carpenter Street Hotel** (217-789-9100; www.carpenterstreethotel.com), 525 N. 6th Street. For a no-frills option, but one that is clean, try this independently run hotel north of downtown, just a few blocks from the Lincoln Museum and Library. The owners recently completed a remodel of the interior. $.

�& ((ᵖ)) **Hilton Springfield** (217-789-1530), 700 E. Adams Street, Springfield. On the Springfield cityscape, this hulking concrete tower hovers above the city. Inside, guests benefit from that vantage point, with 360 rooms that all have a city view. A pool, fitness center, Bennigan's, and a Starbucks are also located in the hotel. Rooms include flat-screen HDTVs

and coffeemakers. Self parking is $8 a day, valet is $15. $$.

�& ☀ **Mansion View Inn & Suites** (800-252-1083; www.mansionview.com), 529 S. 4th Street, Springfield. Directly across from the Governor's Mansion, this stately looking hotel draws many state legislators and government officials. It offers 98 guest rooms and several suites, some with Jacuzzi tubs. Rooms include coffeemaker, cable TV, and alarm clock. $–$$.

((ᵖ)) �& **President Abraham Lincoln Hotel & Conference Center** (866-788-1860, 217-544-8800; www.presidentabrahamlincolnhotel.com), 701 E. Adams Street. This redbrick hotel has 316 guest rooms that include coffeemaker, TV, and alarm clock. It has an indoor pool, fitness room, sauna, and is home to the Globe Tavern. There's a $7 daily fee for parking. $–$$.

((ᵖ)) �& ☀ ♂ **The Statehouse Inn** (217-528-5100; www.thestatehouseinn.com), 101 E. Adams Street. Good location if you want to be near the Capitol, which makes it a prime spot for legislators and lobbyists who are called to town for the legislative sessions. If you're there when the legislature is working, you'll see deals being made in the hallways and the bar downstairs. This historic hotel is 1960s all the way. Inside, the retro design continues but in a hip way, especially in the lobby with its swanky red furniture and grand piano. The rooms are kind of plain canvases with accents of bright oranges. The bathrooms are outfitted with granite counters, cool tiles, and upscale bath products. Rooms come with TVs, and breakfast buffet. The hotel also has a fitness center, business center, and cocktail lounge. $$.

CAMPING Lincoln's New Salem State Historic Site (217-632-4003; www.lincolnsnewsalem .com), 15588 History Lane, Petersburg. Open year-round, but no water or showers from December through mid-March. The historic grounds have 200 campsites, including 100 electric sites, and two shower houses. There are no water or sewer hookups, just hydrants for campers to fill their storage tanks, and faucets throughout the park. There is a sewage and gray-water dump station. Reservations not accepted. Sites are $20 for electric sites and $10 for non-electric sites.

LODGES & (ᵞ) ☕ **RiverBank Lodge** (217-632-0202; www.river banklodge.com), 522 S. 6th Street, Petersburg. If you want to stay outside of town, near Lincoln's New Salem, another option is this lodge in Petersburg. Rooms and suites come with flat-screen TVs, and some suites have Jacuzzi tubs and fireplaces. Rooms are decorated differently but all keep to the Northwoods lodge theme. Some rooms have views overlooking the Sangamon River, so be sure to ask for one of these rooms. The lodge also has a lounge that serves drinks and food. $–$$.

✳ Where to Eat

Springfield has many restaurants that serve lunch only, catering to the downtown workforce and tourists. Sixth Street in particular has a college-town feel, with a number of restaurant, bar, and café options.

EATING OUT & **The Feed Store** (217-528-3355), 516 E. Adams. Open 11–3 weekdays. March right to the counter at the back and order yourself some homemade soup (the offerings change daily), a sandwich, or

THE GARDEN OF EAT'N IN SPRINGFIELD

salad, then take a number and sit down. The staff will deliver your food at modest wooden tables. The décor is hotel-like inside this building right off the capitol, with hunter green carpet and pink-and-green flowered wallpaper, but the soups are the draw, with between 150 to 250 quarts served daily. The family that has run it for the past 30-plus years boasts of recipes made with fresh vegetables, extra virgin olive oil, unsalted butter, and real dairy products. In the summer, try one of the chilled soups—cucumber mint or the popular strawberry soup. $.

Charlie Parker's Diner (217-241-2104; www.charlieparkers diner.net), 700 North Street. Open 6–2 Monday through Saturday, 7–2 Sunday. This diner in an old Army Quonset hut is focused on breakfast all day, but also is known for its Horseshoe, a Springfield original dish that calls for a layer of toast, followed by meat (usually hamburger, but here they also do it with ham, bacon, turkey, and pork tenderloin, among other items). Then the plate is doused in cheese sauce and topped off with French fries. Portions here are giant. Breakfast is served all day and the staff throws down a daily challenge: Eat the four-stack of Charlie's giant 16-inch pancakes and it's free. Good place for kids, but hard to find. North Street is off Stanford Avenue. $.

The Garden of Eat'n (217-544-5446; www.gardeneatn.com), 115 N. Sixth Street. Open 11–3 week-days, 5–9 Friday dinner, 12–3 Saturday. This charming, clean lunch restaurant near the Lincoln Museum specializes in healthier fare in the form of fresh salads and wraps with a Persian influence. You can even design your own salad. $.

&. **Cozy Dog Drive In** (217-525-1992; www.cozydogdrivein.com), 2935 S. Sixth Street. Open 8–8 Monday through Saturday. People come here for the famous "cozy dog," a corndog on a stick, created by Ed Waldmire in 1946. Located on Route 66, the inside is filled with Route 66 memorabilia and the Waldmire family still runs it. $.

&. **Trout Lily Café** (217-391-0101; www.troutlilycafe.com), 218 S. Sixth Street. Open 7–3:30 weekdays, 9–2 Saturday. For a break, try this café where it would not be unusual to find a trio of musicians playing while diners sip coffee. Dishes incorporate local produce when possible and sandwiches come on multigrain bread made by a local baker. You'll also find quiche, homemade cookies, muffins, and scones, and a long list of coffee drinks. $.

DINING OUT &. Y **D'Arcy's Pint** (217-492-8800; www.darcys pintonline.com), 661 W. Stanford Avenue, Springfield. The kitchen is open 11 AM–10 PM Monday through Thursday, 11–11PM Friday and Saturday. The bar is open until 1 AM. The Horseshoe at this Irish pub often makes it onto "best of" lists, so if you're looking for a good one, this is a good bet, with specialty "shoes" like the chili cheeseburger, or the supreme with seasoned ground beef, spicy cheese sauce, tomatoes, bacon, and scallions. You can also order from a menu with more traditional pub food like burgers and sandwiches. Irish dishes include the Irish-style oak-smoked salmon, the Irish boxty (potato cakes with jalapenos drizzled in cheese sauce), and corned beef and cabbage. The beer garden is open year-round, weather permitting. $–$$.

& **Caitie Girl's** 400 E. Jefferson Street. Open 11–9:30 Tuesday through Thursday, 11–10:30 Friday, 5–10:30 Saturday, 4–9 Sunday. The design here is festive— brightly colored walls with a rainbow of bright plastic chairs at each table, and paper lanterns hanging from above. As they say here, the food is gourmet, but jeans are appropriate. Prepare for giant portions of comfort food (even the salad I had to start was huge). The chef offers a twist on some classics—like the sweet tea-brined fried chicken that has a good amount of spice, served with charred corn on the cob, mac and cheese, and more. $$–$$$.

& **Maldaner's Restaurant** (217-522-4313; www.maldaners.com), 222 S. Sixth Street. Open for lunch 11–2:30 weekdays. Dinner: 5–9 Tuesday through Thursday, 5–10 Friday, Saturday. Established in 1884, this white-tablecloth restaurant uses local produce to create a menu that has Mediterranean influences. Dinner entrees include seared tuna loin, chicken two ways, and quail stuffed with sausage. You'll also find the specialty, beef Wellington. Lunchtime menus cover a variety of sandwiches and of course, the Horseshoe. Lunch: $–$$, dinner: $$–$$$.

✳ Entertainment

MOVIES Route 66 Twin Drive-In (217-546-8881; www.route66 -drivein.com) From I-72, exit Route 4 and head south toward Chatham. Don't take the first Recreation Drive you see. Keep going past the golf course and turn east on Woodside Road. Turn left on Old Chatham Road, then right on Recreation Drive. The double screens offer nightly double features of first run films from Memorial Day through Labor Day. Admission is $6, $4 for children 12 and under, although under 3 are free.

PERFORMING ARTS & **Hoogland Center for the Arts** (217-523-2787; www.scfta.org), 420 S. Sixth Street. You may find a production of *Grease,* a concert, or film festival at this hub for cultural activities in downtown Springfield. Initially constructed as a Masonic temple in the early 1900s, the center now houses a 500-seat theater, two smaller theaters, an art gallery, and other gathering areas.

Springfield Ballet Co. (217-544-1967; www.springfieldballetco.org)

The company has three major performances each season. Performances are at the Hoogland Center for the Arts and the Sangamon Auditorium of the University of Illinois-Springfield.

ᵴ **The Muni** (217-793-6864; www.themuni.org), 815 E. Lake Drive. Each summer the large community theater group puts on four musicals at this outdoor amphitheater near Lake Springfield. Tickets: $8–12 adults, $5 children 3 to 12 years.

✳ Selective Shopping

Pease's Fine Candies & Salted Nuts (217-241-3091; www.peasescandy.com), 6th and Washington. Open 9–6 weekdays, 9–5 Saturday. Take a step into this pink-walled world and you will be overwhelmed by the scent of caramels being cooled, or popcorn being popped. How about a Lincoln penny made out of chocolate? Or a milk chocolate state of Illinois? This is the place. The Pease family has been making candies in Illinois forever. Youngest son, Martin Pease Jr., opened the first Pease's shop in Springfield in 1930 and the operation has continued to expand, to five locations in Springfield. The original candy recipes created by Martin Pease Sr. are still used.

✳ Special Events

August: **Illinois State Fair** (www .agr.state.il.us/isf/index.php), 1101 Sangamon Avenue. For about a week or so in August, you'll find livestock competitions, horseshoes, horse racing, carnival rides, big-name concerts, and tons of food. Each day also has a special event, like Governor's day, or Republican day, so check the schedule.

September: **International Route 66 Mother Road Festival** (www .route66fest.com) Get a look at classic cars and a new appreciation for Route 66 at this annual festival in downtown Springfield.

The Shawnee 6
Forest

WESTERN REGION

EASTERN REGION

INTRODUCTION

P arts of this rugged expanse of green have fittingly earned the title "The Garden of the Gods." Throughout the Southern tip of the state, it's easy to see the almost spiritual connection that locals develop with the Shawnee National Forest, with the peace that can be found under awnings of leaves, the stories whispered from the cool air of mysterious caves, the sweeping vantage points, and rock formations that reveal the greater history of the land. This is one of my favorite places to send people in Illinois because it erases stereotypes of Midwest landscapes as boring plains of farmland. Cliffs in Illinois? Yes, indeed.

The southernmost region of Illinois between the Ohio and Mississippi Rivers stands apart from the rest of the state, on maps and from the car window. As you make your way south, the landscape evolves from flat prairies to green hills that nurture peach and apple orchards, vineyards, and vegetable farms. The geological backstory behind the creation of this natural wonder is that millions of years ago most of the state was a large inland sea. The sandy shores of that sea were gradually compressed into the sandstone rock formations that now appear to have been carved out of the land. This area is part of the "unglaciated" section of the U.S., which basically means, well, something geological that is beautiful to see.

Native Americans made their homes here as far back as 11,500 years ago. European settlers arrived near the Ohio River in the late 1700s. Pioneers heading out to the great western borders of the young democracy liked what they found in these Illinois Ozarks. The forest provided wood for their houses and fuel for the winter, and, once cleared, farmable tracts. But unfortunately, the new residents worked the land a little too much. By the 1930s, they couldn't get the land to grow the potatoes, corn, wheat, and oats they depended on. Local citizens asked the government to help revive the overwrought property. In 1933, the Forest Service, Civil Works Administration, and Civilian Conservation Corps went to work rejuvenating the land, building roads, and planting trees.

Decades later, the forest that has taken root provides an extraordinary

GARDEN OF THE GODS

landscape for hiking, horseback riding, bird watching, rock climbing, hunting, swimming, boating, and fishing. As generation upon generation makes trips to visit "Old Stone Face" or "Camel Rock," these stone formations have developed into local characters all their own. Other local characters include wild creatures that are sure to add some excitement to your adventure. In one recent trip to the eastern part of the forest, I was a bit, umm . . . surprised? (maybe some would call it scared to death?) when some rattlesnakes slithered across the road before me. Then, there was the bobcat who sauntered near our cabin as if he were just out on a stroll and thought he'd say hello. (Not really accustomed to seeing wild bobcats just a few yards away, I couldn't identify the creature at first. "Is that a giant weird cat?" I asked my helpful guide, Mike Tipsord, owner of the Cedar Hill River Resort. "Hell no! That's a bobcat!" he exclaimed excitedly, then jumped into his four-wheeler to see where the thing was headed.) Beyond these two incidents, we also encountered wild turkey on the side of the road and numerous species of birds so vibrantly colored I wished I had a bird book along to identify the various winged residents here.

The natural beauty (and excitement) does not end at the borders of the national forest. The state has a few parks in this region that should not be missed. Giant City, for one. The state park lodges, private cabins, and resorts offer a great home base for your explorations. As one who has daydreams of someday moving to a serene, quiet farm like the ones found here, I am sold on all the outdoor offerings in this region. And while I love trying new restaurants, the dining scene is not why we're here. We come here to sleep on the ground and cook dinner over a fire. There are definitely some restaurants you should add to your Southern Illinois itinerary, like the 17th Street Bar & Grill in Murphysboro. But you also might want to pack some provisions and book a cabin with a kitchenette, or be ready to use your campsite grill.

In addition to the outdoors, another reason to visit these parts is the young but impressive Shawnee Hills Wine Trail. Over the past couple decades, farmers have transformed hilly fields into vineyards. Yes, fruit and sweet wines are big here, but the region produces some nice dry varieties as well.

As you travel the area, two national scenic byways on either edge of the forest escort you through lines of small river towns. Some towns are just a short strip of shops and a smattering of homes. But there are also places like Makanda, which looks like a movie set randomly placed in the middle of the forest. A few towns are worth a drive through, but may not have all the essentials. That's why you might have to stock up on camping items and the like while you're in some of the larger towns like Jonesboro, Anna, Harrisburg, or Carbondale.

With approximately 280,000 acres, the forest is divided into two ranger districts—the Mississippi Bluffs office manages the Western section of the park out of Jonesboro and the Hidden Springs ranger district oversees the Eastern region out of Vienna. To get you started on your exploration, I've divided this chapter into an Eastern and Western section as well to make it easier for you to navigate.

VIEW FROM CEDAR HILL RIVER RESORT

THE SHAWNEE FOREST: WESTERN REGION

The blend of experiences is what's great about this region of the state. You can tire yourself out with a hike at Giant City State Park or Little Grand Canyon in the national forest, then reward yourself with a visit to a couple nearby wineries. A trip here must include stops at "the Streets" of Giant City, several natural attractions in the forest, and the Shawnee Hills Wine Trail.

Carbondale is a good home base from which to explore the Southwest part of the state. Home to Southern Illinois University, this college town has the requisite cafes, bars, restaurants, and shops to round out your visit. It also draws some national acts to the university arena and auditorium. The whole area carries the nickname of "Little Egypt," a title thought to have been assigned during an 1830s drought, when northern settlers headed south for food. The nickname is carried through in other ways, like the Southern Illinois University "Salukis." A saluki is a thin, swift dog first bred in Egypt.

Besides being home to Southern Illinois University, Carbondale is also considered the birthplace of Memorial Day. In April 1866, the city honored lost soldiers during a ceremony at Woodlawn Cemetery, the first memorial service of its type. The event is credited with giving rise to the national holiday that we celebrate each May.

The development of the Shawnee Hills Wine Trail has also fanned the growth of bed and breakfasts, restaurants, bars, and shops in this area, a good thing as far as travelers are concerned. It's also simply a great place for a drive, as the roads are bounded by orchards, vineyards, farms, and scenic woods.

GUIDANCE The place to get your start in Carbondale is the **Old Illinois Central Railroad Depot** (618-529-8040; www.carbondalemainstreet .com), 121 S. Illinois Avenue, Carbondale. The Carbondale Main Street

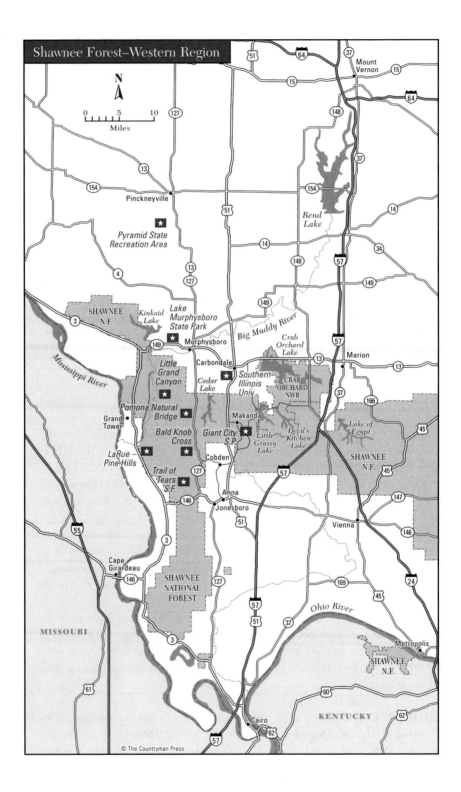

organization, which is dedicated to the downtown district, has its offices here. The staff will arm you with a stack of maps and brochures about the area. The depot also has train memorabilia from the Illinois Central Railroad. Outside the depot, climb aboard a little red caboose or see a 1950s diesel engine. Pick up maps for a historic walking tour of the downtown area here.

The **Carbondale Convention and Tourism Bureau** (800-526-1500; www.cctb.org), 1185 E. Main Street, Carbondale, is located out at the University Mall shopping center near the Macy's.

Shawnee National Forest-Mississippi Bluffs Ranger District (618-833-8576), 521 N. Main Street, Jonesboro. Open 8–4:30 weekdays. For trail maps, forest background, and trip suggestions, stop in and talk with the rangers about this side of the forest.

GETTING THERE *By auto:* I-57 cuts north-south through this area. For Carbondale, exit I-57 at IL13 and head west, this will take you right through downtown Carbondale, toward the Mississippi River.

By air: The nearest major airport is Lambert-St. Louis International Airport, which is then a two- to three-hour drive from the Carbondale area. But it does feature major carriers. Another option is the small **Williamson County Regional Airport** (618-993-3353; www.wilcoairport.com), 10400 Terminal Drive, Marion. This regional airport offers daily flights to St. Louis via Cape Air.

By train: An **Amtrak** (800-872-7245; www.amtrak.com) station with waiting room and rest rooms is located at 401 S. Illinois Street in Carbondale. Trains run daily between Chicago and Carbondale.

GETTING AROUND *By auto:* If you enter Carbondale on IL 13, you'll drive through the newer

THE STREETS AT GIANT CITY

commercial district, with a shopping mall, chain restaurants, and big-box stores. Keep going and you'll find the original downtown area. A few one-way streets run downtown, so be sure to think about that when planning your routes. Southern Illinois University is off US 51 just south of the main downtown area. The 1,100-acre main campus stretches pretty far west and if you wind your way through, you will eventually discover a lake and the farms that are part of the agricultural program. US 51 is a quick way to get north or south in this area, but IL 127 is more scenic and has a number of wine trail stops and parks along the way. It's not all that slow either. To get to the Mississippi, take IL 13 west to Murphysboro and follow it until it changes into IL 149. Hop on IL 3 for access to the natural areas and to the river.

By bus: **Saluki Express** (618-453-5749; http://siustudentcenter.net/saluki express) Southern Illinois University operates a bus line on several routes through Carbondale when school is in session. The general public can ride for $1, but have exact change if you plan to board.

MEDICAL EMERGENCIES If you find yourself in need of medical services near Carbondale, go to **Memorial Hospital of Carbondale** (618-549-0721; www.memorialhospitalofcarbondale.org), 405 W. Jackson Street. This regional medical center has 132 beds, cardiac services, and the only pediatric unit in Southern Illinois. The parent company, Southern Illinois Healthcare, also operates **St. Joseph Memorial Hospital** (618-684-3156; www.stjosephmemorialhospital.org), 2 South Hospital Drive, Murphysboro. The hospital offers 25 beds and is a critical access hospital. A little farther south, there is **Union County Hospital** (618-833-4511; www .unioncountyhospital.com), 517 N. Main Street, Anna. The 25-bed critical access hospital offers cardiac services and has a 24-hour emergency department, with rapid transport of patients via helicopter available when needed.

✴ Wandering Around

EXPLORING BY CAR IL 127 quickly became my favorite road down here, because of the scenic backdrop. Winding through pretty country-side, it also provides access to the Trail of Tears State Park, Bald Knob area, Pomona, and Little Grand Canyon. The Shawnee Hills Wine Trail follows some of IL 127, even if you're not into wine, the drive itself is worth it. Plus, it passes near key parts of the forest. From Carbondale, head west on IL 13 toward Murphysboro, then hop on IL 127 South. Wine trail signs are posted along the route to nudge you in the right direction. Von Jakob, Alto, Hedman, and Inheritance Valley are located off 127. Cut over to US 51 by heading east on Aldridge Road and you'll pass through Cobden, which has a gas station should you need it. If you're interested in a few more great wineries, continue along Water Valley Road off US 51 east of Cobden and follow the signs to Owl Creek and Blue Sky. To get back to Carbondale, head up US 51, with one last stop at Rustle Hill Winery off US 51. Besides wineries, the trail takes you through several small towns with character, such as Makanda.

EXPLORING BY FOOT The natural areas definitely provide ample opportunities to give your legs a workout, but Carbondale also offers a walking tour. Start at the old train depot in Carbondale and pick up a brochure for a self-guided tour of the historic town square that highlights architectural details and stories about the structures that stand there today. There are a few little strips of shops and restaurants worth a detour, such as Jackson Street.

✳ Towns and Villages

Carbondale calls itself the capital of Southern Illinois and that certainly feels true. The city's story is intertwined with that of the Illinois Central railroad. Two men from nearby Murphysboro were looking for a place to build a new town along the path of the railroad and chose a wooded, unsettled parcel. Founder Daniel Harmon Brush named the town for the Mt. Carbon coalfields near Murphysboro and thoughtfully created a public square in the center of town. He also apparently had some strong feelings against drinking, as the sale of liquor was prohibited in town (not sure how today's college students would have dealt with that if it wasn't voted out in the 1890s.)

MAKANDA BOARDWALK

At the peak of the railroad age, about 50 trains a day stopped in Carbondale, giving quite a boost to the local economy. The railroad centralized its operations here. The town's forefathers also set their minds to establishing a state college in Carbondale. To help with their cause, they went through the trouble to fix up the public square into a park. (Legend has it that the fountain in the square held a few alligators at one time.) In 1869, the school was chartered, and ground was broken on the first building of the Southern Illinois University campus. In 1874, SIU started molding minds through its teacher training institution. Today the campus has about 20,000 students and is the driver of the local economy. Strips of inviting restaurants, cafés, and stores dot downtown Carbondale, but in a disconnected way. Not to say it isn't worth visiting. You'll find some great places here, and it's a logical home base when exploring the wonderful parks nearby.

Makanda Reminiscent of a Western town from yesteryear, Makanda's boardwalk is literally just a few storefronts, but not of typical findings. The scent of coffee beans welcomes you into the Makanda Country Store, which sells ice cream and sandwiches. An art gallery filled with offerings from local artists is next door. Enter the hallway to see bulletin boards with community events, and places to stay and eat. Down the hall a ways you'll see other shops tucked in back. Across the railroad tracks are the remnants of a shuttered wood-plank building that only lends to that Western town feel. About 400 people call this unique town home.

Cobden Originally called South Pass, the townspeople agreed to change the name of the town after a particularly successful visit in the 1850s by a British statesmen named Sir Richard Cobden. (Now can you get any nicer than that? You seem like a pretty nice guy, let's rename the town after you!) Today, Cobden has a few more businesses and restaurants than Makanda, and importantly if you're on the wine trail, a gas station. The train tracks run through the middle of town, with the main strip of businesses on either side. The Yellow Moon Café, Palace Pizzeria, and a couple of other shops are worth a stop. Cobden is home base to a number of bed and breakfasts. Peaches are still an important part of the local culture, with the town gathering for an annual Peach Festival every summer.

Anna is a relatively larger town with about 4,800 people, and has the chain stores and restaurants if you need a quick meal or to pick up some supplies that might be harder to find at a small country store. The town is also home to the Anna Quarry, which has long produced crushed rock and lime.

Murphysboro is proud of Civil War General John Logan, a local hero. You'll hear lots about him if you stop here on your way to Kinkaid Lake or other parks. Close to Carbondale, the town has cute residential areas with paver-brick streets. Its location makes it a good stopping point for a bite to

KINKAID LAKE

eat, perhaps some barbecue at the 17th Street Bar & Grill? But I wouldn't plan on a lot of time here, as the beauty lies outside of town, such as in the hilly orchards on the outskirts.

Grand Tower Along the Mississippi River, this small town is named for a rocky island on the Missouri side of the Mississippi River, long a navigational reference point for explorers such as Lewis and Clark. The town itself is mostly residential, with a tiny strip of places along the Mississippi River. If you're in the area, consider camping at Devil's Backbone campground on the river's edge.

✶ To See

MUSEUMS General John A Logan Museum (618-684-3455; www .loganmuseum.org), 1613 Edith Street, Murphysboro. Open 1–4 Tuesday through Sunday from September through May. From June through August, open 10–4 Tuesday through Saturday, 1–4 Sunday. Mr. Logan definitely left an imprint around these parts. The politician and native Illinoisan joined the Union as a colonel in the Civil War. By the end of the war, he commanded the Army of the Tennessee. After the war, despite starting out as a pro-Southern Democrat, Mr. Logan found himself fighting for African American rights as a Republican. He ran for vice president in 1884 and lost in a close race. The small Logan museum is located in the

VIEW FROM BALD KNOB

Christopher C. Bullar house in a quiet residential section of Murphysboro, his hometown. It shares the story of Logan's life through photos, maps, family antiques, and Civil War weapons. Donation: $2 adults, $1 children.

&. **University Museum at Southern Illinois University** (618-453-5388; www.museum.siu.edu), 1000 Faner Drive, Carbondale. Open 10–4 Tuesday through Friday, 1–4 Saturday. But note the museum closes when the university is not in session. This squat, blocky concrete building designed in the "brutalism" architectural style houses the university's art collection, and prehistoric and scientific objects. The museum has a number of changing exhibits, created both from its own collections and brought in from other institutions. The permanent collections include 2,500 objects in fine and decorative arts, thousands of geological specimens, and archeological artifacts from Southern Illinois. Free. If you go, the English castle-like building across the way that's calling out for a photo to be taken? That's **Altgeld Hall**, 1000 S. Normal Avenue. The campus's oldest building, it was constructed in 1896.

HISTORIC SITES Woodlawn Cemetery 405 E. Main Street, Carbondale. On a hill overlooking Main Street, with traffic passing on either side, is a quiet patch of green of historical significance. Here, among the graves of Confederate and Union soldiers, the first memorial service for Civil War veterans was organized in April 1866. About 200 veterans met at the old blue church on East Jackson Street then walked to Woodlawn Cemetery. General John A. Logan, who helped lead the procession that day, became the commander of the Grand Army of the Republic after the war. The memorial service inspired him to establish a national Memorial Day on May 30, 1868. There are some mysteries here too, such as the one about the sarcophagus in the center of the cemetery—does it hold the remains of a Mississippi woman who did not want to be buried in Yankee soil so she was buried above ground? Or does it hold a Union colonel whose family had him placed in the aboveground stone coffin so he would not share ground with a Confederate soldier? There is also a marker to honor 30 freed slaves buried in an unmarked area of the cemetery.

CULTURAL SITES & **Bald Knob Cross** (www.baldknobcross.com), 3630 Bald Knob Road, Alto Pass. Open year-round dawn to dusk. Bald Knob is part of the Illinois Ozark Mountains, and sits 1,000 feet above sea level. So if you construct a 111-foot tall white cross on top of that mound, it makes quite a statement. Word is you can see four states from the top of the mound and that the cross can be seen for 7,500 square miles. I could not verify that, but the vista is tremendous. After years of hosting Easter services on the hill, local community members purchased the hill and started raising funds to build the cross. They broke ground in 1959, and by 1963 had a completed white structure constructed with 900 bright white steel panels. With the addition of lights, the Bald Knob Cross could even be seen at night. The past decade has been difficult as the site was locked down during a prolonged legal battle involving the board, and the cross fell into disrepair. Since 2009, a transitional board has been restoring

SOUTHERN ILLINOIS UNIVERSITY

the monument. You'll likely notice the cross from other sites throughout the region, but to get to the top from IL 127, take the pretty 5 to 6 mile drive up Bald Knob. Once you drive to the top of the hill, there is a small visitors center. You can walk up another hill to the cross itself. There also is a trail about three-fourths of the way up the hill, on the right hand side. Donations accepted, but otherwise free.

✳ To Do

FOR FAMILIES Rend Lake (618-724-2493; www.mvs.usace.army.mil /rend/) Located off I-57 at Exit 77. About an hour north of Carbondale is this 18,900-acre man-made lake, originally built to solve decades of problems stemming from a lack of water in the area. You see, the region's clay ground could not soak in rain, putting groundwater in high demand. The Army Corps of Engineers finished building the lake in 1973. Today, waterskiers and others have discovered the great recreation opportunities here. Fishermen will find largemouth bass, crappie, catfish, and bluegill. South Sandusky Beach offers a swim area, shower house, picnic shelter, and sand for the kids to play in. You can rent fishing and pontoon boats at the marina on Rend City Road (618-724-7651). A 19.2-mile bike trail winds through forest, fields, and wetlands. The 0.75-mile Blackberry Nature Trail is an easy hike that should take about 30 minutes or so. A $3 day fee is charged at the boat ramps, and adults may be charged a fee at the swimming beach.

BALD KNOB CROSS

GOLF Rend Lake Golf Course (618-629-2353; www.rendlake.org) Off I-57, head west on IL154, look for the giant towering golf ball and you're close. Turn left at Golf Course Drive, and right at Golf Course Road. Rated one of the best public courses in the Midwest, the 27-hole course with vast greens was designed by Chicago architect Lawrence Packard and overlooks Rend Lake at points. Five sets of tees for golfers of all levels. The course has a pro shop and driving range with raised target greens. Fees: $46–51 for 18 holes, $25–30 for 9 holes with a cart.

Hickory Ridge Golf Course (618-529-4386; www.cpkd.org), 2727 Glenn Road, Carbondale. This 18-hole championship public golf course operated by the Carbondale Park District features long fairways and is designed for all skill levels. The Southern Illinois University Women's Golf Team calls this municipal course home. Fees: $30 for 18 holes, $19 for 9. Carts: $10–15.

Stone Creek Golf Club (618-351-4653; www.stonecreekgolf.com), 503 Stone Creek Drive, Makanda. Spectacular views are promised for those up for the challenge at Stone Creek. Fees: $22–27 for 18 holes, $15–22 for 9 holes. Carts: $9–15.

TOURS Shawnee Adventure Guides (888-588-9724; www.shawnee adventureguides.com), 550 S. Rocky Comfort Road, Makanda. Head out with professional guides who love and know this forest well. They'll share their expertise on half-day trips to places like the Pomona Natural Bridge, or on daylong trips to remote sections of wilderness deep into the Shawnee. In addition to hikes, the service offers overnight backpacking, rock climbing, and paddling trips. The guides advise you to wear hiking boots or comfortable, worn-in athletic shoes, and to dress for the weather; they'll take care of the other gear. Fees range from $35 for a half-day hike to $175 for an adventure weekend.

WINERIES Shawnee Hills Wine Trail (www.shawneewinetrail.com) The first vineyard on the Southern Illinois map was Alto Vineyards, founded in 1984. After Alto's first release of wine in 1987, interest grew and ground was broken on the Pomona Winery, which specializes in wines created from apples and local fruits. In 1995, the owners of Alto convened with the owners of Pomona Winery and Owl Creek Vineyard to create the wine trail. Now many shops and bed and breakfasts have built up around it. In 2006, the Shawnee Hills region was designated an American Viticultural Area, so wines that are made with 85 percent or more of grapes grown within the region can stamp the bottle with the Shawnee Hills name. The primary varieties grown are Chambourcin, Chardonel, Vignoles, Norton, and Cabernet Franc. Sweet wines are pretty popular down here, but there are a surprising number of nice, dry reds and whites to please all palates. Today, the trail has 12 wineries. Pick up a wine trail map at one of the wineries for an adventure in enology. The wineries are open year-round, although many reduce their schedule in the winter.

Kite Hill Vineyards (618-684-5072; www.kitehillvineyards.com), 83 Kite Hill Road, Carbondale. Open noon–5 Sunday through Thursday, noon–7 Friday, 10–7 Saturday. From November through March, the vineyard is closed except for the weekends. Off IL 127, look for the signs for Kite Hill, and a gravel road will take you past the vineyard to a cheerful house perched high above a pond. Inside the house, you'll find the tasting room, where you can sample all the wines. There is a small fee for tastings. You can unwind on the big deck that overlooks the lake. On Fridays, check out "Wine Down Friday," which includes appetizers.

Hickory Ridge Vineyard and Winery (618-893-1700; www.shawnee winetrail.com/UCW/hickoryridge.html), 1598 Hickory Ridge Road, Pomona. Family-owned and operated, Hickory Ridge grows all its own grapes for its wines. The tasting room, housed in a cabin-like building, is open noon–6 Thursday through Sunday, March through December.

Pomona Winery (618-893-2623; www.pomonawinery.com), 2865 Hickory Ridge Road, Pomona. Open 10–5 Monday through Saturday, noon–5 Sunday. From January through March, the winery is closed Tuesday through Thursday. The focus here is on fruit wines made from locally grown fruits other than grapes. Think wines made from Golden Delicious apples, black currants, peaches, strawberries, or blueberries. The owners, Jane Payne and George Majka, had been making wines for about 10 years when they started the winery in 1991, making it the second in the area.

Von Jakob Vineyard (618-893-4500; www.vonjakobvineyard.com), 1309 Sadler Road, Pomona. Open 10–5 Monday through Saturday, noon–5 Sunday. Open until 6 during the summer. Calling itself "Little Germany" in the Illinois Ozarks, the original vineyard of Dr. Paul and Rhoda Jacobs is in Pomona, with a deck where you can enjoy wine or a bite to eat. The second location is farther down IL 127 in Alto Pass, with indoor and outdoor fireplaces, a new microbrewery, and live music. The tasting room offers more than 20 varieties of wine. They are known for the honey blush wine, which blends raw honey mead and concord grapes to produce a semisweet blush wine. Their white oak port has been a winner at competitions in California.

Alto Vineyards (618-893-4898; www.altovineyards.net), IL 127, Alto Pass. Open 10–5 Monday through Saturday, noon–5 Sunday. The first winery on the trail, Alto released its first Illinois wine in 1988, which was the culmination of a dream for owner, Guy Renzaglia. Over the years, production has increased from 8,000 gallons to 25,000 gallons to meet demand. The third generation of the Renzaglia family is now involved in the business. The wine list is filled with everything from the Villard Blanc, a dry white with lemon flavors, to a sweet rosé called Heartland Blush. The dry Norton red will please those who like French Bordeaux.

Hedman Orchards & Vineyards (618-893-4923; www.peachbarn.com), 560 Chestnut Street, Alto Pass. Anders Hedman, a native of Sweden, bought this farm to keep himself busy after his wife got a job in

ILLINOIS WINE

The state's roots in winemaking go back to 1857 when Emile Baxter founded Baxter's Vineyards, which the family still operates in Nauvoo. But the cold climate here has not been exactly nurturing to the famous European grapes. As Bill Shoemaker, a University of Illinois research specialist who works with growers, told me: "People think if it can grow in Germany, it can grow here, and that's not true." But research in recent years has produced new breeds of grapes, opening up new opportunities for Illinois winemakers with the development of cold-resistant hybrid grapes that blend European fruit qualities and North American plant qualities. With the introduction of those heartier grapes, grape growing has exploded in Illinois. The majority of Illinois vineyards have opened in the past decade. Families have transformed their farms into vineyards, dropping corn for Chambourcin. Still, the grape names in some of the wines sold in Illinois are not as universally recognized. Instead of Chardonnay and Merlot, we have Vignoles and Chambourcin. (That Chambourcin grape sure won me over.) As the winemaking industry grew, wine trails started developing as well. The Shawnee Hills wine trail was the original, but Illinois now has six wine trails throughout the state.

BLUE SKY VINEYARD

Carbondale. But he claims boredom set in, so he threw himself into converting the property into a vineyard. The grapes for his wines are all grown on site. The wine offerings include the sweet wines loved by Illinoisans, but the owner's European experience can be seen in some of the dry ones. The winery is in a blue barn-like building overlooking a hill and pond. A restaurant inside the winery is open Wednesday through Sunday, starting in May. Of course, the menu features Swedish specialties, but you'll also find plates such as beef tenderloin on a cedar plank. Bottles also can be purchased in stores around Carbondale.

& **Inheritance Valley Vineyards** (618-893-6141; www.inheritancevalley .com), 5490 IL 127 North, Cobden. Open noon–5 Wednesday through Friday, Sunday, 10–5 Saturday. Tim and Kendall Waller borrowed money from her parents to buy the land for the vineyard and luckily, their venture paid off, as they were able to repay the loan to her parents. "So, we're back in the will," Tim says, thus the name "Inheritance Valley" for their vineyard. The Wallers started selling grapes to Alto Vineyards in 2001. But Tim had been making his own beer and wine for years and eventually in 2003, the couple decided to open their own winery, the fifth one to join the wine trail. A popular bottle is the Cobden Cream Sherry, which is bottled three times a year, and always has a waiting list. There's no charge for tastings and you can also buy a glass to drink in the covered gazebo overlooking the vineyard.

& **Owl Creek Vineyard** (618-893-2557; www.owlcreekvineyard.com), 2655 Water Valley Road, Cobden. Open noon–5 Monday through Thursday, noon–6 Friday, Sunday, 10–6 Saturday. Reduced hours January and February. The winery's ChardonOwl, a Chardonel, was served at President Barack Obama's inaugural festivities in D.C. in 2009. The winery was originally built in 1995 by Ted Wichmann, the first commercial winemaker in the region. The Genung Family took over in 2005, with the mission of further showing off the region's varietals. The second-floor tasting room is light and airy, a great place to study up on wine with the knowledgeable staff. A self-guided walking tour will bring you closer to the grapes. Staff will encourage you to take a glass of wine or picnic along for your journey. During the summer and fall, musicians add a backdrop of music to the café on Saturday afternoons. Tastings are $5 and include a wine glass.

& ♂ ((ŋ)) **Blue Sky Vineyard** (618-995-9463; www.blueskyvineyard.com), 3150 S. Rocky Comfort Road, Makanda. Open 10–6:30 Monday through Thursday, 10–sunset Friday, 10–7:30 Saturday, noon–7 Sunday. A Tuscan villa is not what you may expect to find here, but it seems perfect in its location. The warmth of the orange stucco and craftsmanship of the giant wooden doors show the level of detail given to the place, which was modeled after a 400-year-old Italian villa. The grounds showcase giant, modern metal sculptures that conjure up images of birds. Inside windmill-like fans

hang from the high ceilings. Windows open up to views of the patios overlooking the vineyard. Tastings are free on weekdays, the cost is $1 for five
on the weekends. A menu of sandwiches, pizza, and appetizers is also
offered.

Orlandini Vineyard (618-995-2307; www.orlandinivineyard.com), 410
Thorn Lane, Makanda. Open noon–5 Wednesday through Friday, 10–6
Saturday, noon–6 Sunday. The vines were first planted here in 1988, at
this site on one of the region's highest ridge tops. In 2001, the family
began putting out the wines it had been carefully experimenting with.
Tastings are free.

♂ **StarView Vineyards** (618-893-9463; www.starviewvineyards.com),
5100 Winghill Road, Cobden. Open noon–5 Sunday through Friday,
noon–6 Saturday. Scott Sensmeier and his wife, Kate, opened the vineyard
in 2006. Family-operated, the wines are made on site. At the tasting room
café grab a salad, croissant sandwich, pulled pork, and other snacks to take
on a picnic.

Rustle Hill Winery (618-893-2700; www.rustlehillwinery.com), 8595 US
51, Cobden. Open 11–6 Monday through Thursday, 10–9 Friday through
Sunday. This former family farm was opened as a vineyard by the Russell
family in 2008, and they've been
ambitious in their attempts to give
you a relaxing and picturesque surrounding to enjoy a glass of wine.
There are a few patios and decks
overlooking a pond, and an
amphitheater. From a table on a
slope between the pond and the
winery, you can enjoy music and
order food or wine. The tasting
room has a menu with soups,
sandwiches, and appetizers. Tastings are free.

✳ Green Space

Shawnee National Forest
(618-833-8576; www.fs.usda.gov
/shawnee) The Mississippi Bluffs
section of the forest has many
treasures, such as **Little Grand
Canyon**. Open 6 AM–10 PM. You'll
find this rugged but gorgeous
piece of the park 7 miles south of

LITTLE GRAND CANYON TRAIL

Murphysboro. Signage is sketchy, but here's how I got there: Take IL 127 south to Etherton Road and take a right. Look for handmade signs that point you in the direction of Little Grand Canyon. When you come to a brown-and-white sign that says "351" take a right, and that takes you up to the trailhead. (It's the third turnoff.) Parking, rest rooms, and a picnic area are available. The road is a roller-coaster ride. At points, you can't see what lies ahead of you as you near the top of a steep hill or enter a sharp curve. Don't be surprised to see wild turkey on the road. This deep box canyon was carved by powerful waters heading down to meet with the Big Muddy River. The stream there today drops 350 feet, and is still carving the area. A 2.9-mile long trail traverses down to the forest floor then up into the bluff, with views of the Mississippi River floodplain and Big Muddy River. The trail is rated moderately difficult, so you'll get a work-out. With a number of slopes and a bit of climbing along the way, the trail may take three to four hours. If you don't want to head all the way down into the canyon (and back up), you can plan a trip that follows shorter paths to scenic overlooks. At the bottom of the canyon floor, you'll discover waterfalls and migratory songbirds. Bobcat, mink, fox, and deer make their home here, as do copperheads and timber rattlesnakes. Flash floods do occur in the canyon so pay attention to developing weather.

POMONA NATURAL BRIDGE

BALANCED ROCK AT GIANT CITY

Pomona Natural Bridge Near Pomona, this site features one of a handful of natural bridges in the U.S. To find it, take IL 127 to Pomona Road, head west a mile to the three-way stop. Turn right, at the Y in the road, veer right onto Natural Bridge Road. The trailhead is at the end of the road. Created by millions of years of erosion, the star here is a 90-foot sandstone bridge that stretches above the forest floor. A 0.3-mile loop trail descends through the forest to the creek bottom, so you can view the bridge from a few different vantage points. The hike definitely will work the glutes, but is worth the effort.

Giant City State Park (618-457-4836; www.dnr.illinois.gov), 235 Giant City Road, Makanda. One of my favorite state parks, the unique cool canyons and rock formations will likely give you pause and can be explored along the park's miles of hiking trails. Giant City earns its name from the popular "Giant City Streets," which are towering slabs of rock that form giant walled passageways in the woods. You'll find the Streets on the Giant City Nature Trail. Don't follow the lead of those who have traveled before you by chiseling your name into the precious formations of the streets, but it is interesting to study the graffiti left behind. Search out the names of Albert S. and T. W. Thompson, February 22, 1862. The brothers were home for a visit during the Civil War and carved their names on the rock where they used to play as boys. Rumor has it that during the Civil War, deserters camped out in these canyons and are responsible for some of the writing that dates back to that era. Inside the rocky

SNAKE MIGRATION AT LARUE PINE HILLS

Every spring and fall, snakes take over a 2.5-mile section of LaRue Road near the Mississippi River.

The road is shut down for the biannual snake migration, in which thousands of reptiles and amphibians move to their summer or winter habitats. If you're feeling adventurous (or crazy?) and want to get up close and personal with 35 different species of snakes, you can take a hike along this stretch of slithering road. Wildlife biologist Chad Deaton says the middle of each closing period is the best time to visit. But if you come up on a snake, take a step back. Walk slowly and keep your eyes open. Three poisonous breeds make their home here: Timber rattlesnakes, Copperheads, and Cottonmouth Water Moccasins. In the spring, the snakes are moving from winter denning sites, found in the crevices of the limestone bluffs on the east side of the road, to the swamps on the west side. In the fall, they're headed back underground. Rangers first closed the road in 1972 after finding far too much roadkill on that stretch every year. If you can take your eyes off the road for a moment, you are also likely to be impressed by the 150-foot limestone bluffs that were once the deepest part of the inland sea that covered the state millions of years ago. The road is closed mid-March through mid-May and September through October. To get there from Carbondale/Murphysboro, take IL 149 to IL 3, head south 14 miles on IL 3 to Big Muddy Levee Road. Drive 3 miles east to LaRue Road. Turn into Winters Pond parking lot.

passageways, you're also likely to notice the cool air that, even on a hot summer day, makes it feel as if someone has switched on the AC. If you continue on the nature trail, you'll walk under "balanced rock," a hulking boulder sitting atop a much smaller rock that looks as though it might slip off at any moment. Geologists think it's been there for thousands of years. Wooden walkways and steps take you through some of the 1-mile nature trail, but you do have to do some climbing. Don't be surprised to see local college kids climbing the rocks. Elsewhere in the park, experienced hikers may be drawn to the 12-mile Red Cedar Hiking Trail. The 0.3-mile Post Oak Trail is wheelchair and stroller accessible. The park has a 12-mile loop horse trail, and guided horseback rides are offered by Giant City Stables (618-529-4110) from March 15 through October. Keep an eye out for the rock shelters created by sandstone shelves that were used as temporary housing by people long ago. In some areas, you may see evidence of their habitations in ceilings colored black from the fires they built in the shelters. Near the lodge, an 82-foot water tower features an observation deck where you can get a big-picture view of the park from above. Fishing is allowed from the bank of the ponds, but only with a state fishing license. Rock climbing and rappelling are allowed at Devil's Standtable bluff and the 100-foot high bluff behind Shelter No. 1.

Trail of Tears State Forest (618-833-4910; www.dnr.illinois.gov), 3240 State Forest Road, Jonesboro. Located 5 miles northwest of Jonesboro, this 6,000-acre state forest in the southern Ozark Hills memorializes a heartbreaking event in the nation's history. The name dates back to 1838 when the U.S. Army forced the Cherokee, Creek, and Chickasaw nations to make way for settlers by moving them to reservations in the Oklahoma Territory. On land 2 miles south of the forest, an early, devastating winter hit the group, some of whom were barefoot, and hundreds succumbed to the cold and lack of food. Now, as part of the permanently protected Ozark Hills Nature Preserve, the forest appears as it must have to the first non-Native American settlers. The forest features hiking trails, horseback riding, picnic sites, hunting, tent camping, and backpack camping. The plantings and trees you'll see in parts of the forest are part of the state nursery on site.

Crab Orchard National Wildlife Refuge (618-997-3344; www.fws.gov/midwest/Crab Orchard), 8588 IL 148, Marion. Just east of Carbondale, you'll find this collection of lakes and wildlife sanctuary. Every Sunday in October, you can drive through sections normally closed to the public to see wild turkeys, coyotes, foxes, and bobcats. The 44,000 acres of land are located near the midpoint

THE STREETS AT GIANT CITY

of the Mississippi Flyway, so the refuge gives Canada geese a winter stopover place. By December, there may be as many as 180,000 birds hanging out in these parts. Three active bald eagle nests also call the park home. In the 1930s, after the land had been eroded by constant farming and logging, the federal government took control of the area along Crab Orchard Creek, intending to create three recreational lakes. In World War II, this became the Illinois Ordnance Plant, one of the largest producers of ammunition during the war. Finally in 1947, the area was designated as the Crab Orchard National Wildlife Refuge. Be aware that you must pay a $2 daily user fee for all vehicles and boats.

Pyramid State Recreation Area (618-357-2574; http://dnr.state.il.us /lands/landmgt/parks/r5/pyramid.htm), 1562 Pyramid Park Road, Pinckneyville. Many of the lakes here can only be reached by foot, so if you want to fish alone or get away from the crowds, this is a good spot. Visitors with canoes also may find the rough terrain to their liking. The park has 16.5 miles of trails for hikers, horseback riders, and mountain bikers.

LAKES Poplar Camp Beach (618-549-8441) From Carbondale, take US 51 south to Old US 51. Follow it about 2 miles to Cedar Creek Road, head west on Cedar Creek until you see the signs for the beach and boat dock. Open 9:30–5:30 weekdays, 9:30–7 on weekends and holidays. Located on Cedar Lake, this sandy waterfront has a swim and play area, a lap lane, and certified lifeguards. You'll also find rest rooms, picnic tables, and a concession stand. Admission: $2, children under 4 free.

Cedar Lake (618-549-8441), Cedar Creek Road, Carbondale. Located in the western portion of the Shawnee National Forest, this 1,750-acre lake is 6 miles south of Carbondale between US 51 and IL 127. The shore stretches for 40 miles, and the lake floor drops 60 feet, and is home to largemouth bass, sunfish, crappie, channel catfish, and more.

Crab Orchard Lake (618-997-3344; www.fws.gov/midwest/CrabOrchard), IL 13 east of Carbondale. Largemouth bass, bluegill, catfish, bullheads, and carp can be found in the almost 7,000 acres of water that make up this lake. The area has two marinas where you can start your fishing trip. Car decals are required; pay your fee at the visitors center on IL 148. **Little Grassy Lake** (618-457-6655), is also located in the Crab Orchard National Wildlife Refuge, south on Giant City Road, east on Grassy Road. This 1,000-acre lake has 29 miles of shoreline and goes 100 feet deep. Find black and white crappie and walleye, in addition to largemouth bass, bluegill, and carp.

Devil's Kitchen Lake South on Giant City Road, east on Grassy Road, Carbondale. This 810-acre lake is stocked with rainbow and brown trout, along with bass, sunfish, crappie, and bullheads. No swimming or camping is allowed, but you can hike the trails around the lake.

KINKAID LAKE SPILLWAY

Kinkaid Lake (618-684-2867) Located off of IL 149 about 5 miles north-west of Murphysboro. Here is one of the few area lakes where you'll find muskie. At the Spillway Recreation Area near Crisenberry Dam, you can set up near the end of the three-tiered waterfall created by the spillway and enjoy the views and sound of the water rushing by. A swimming beach is located at the Johnson Creek Recreation Area off Gum Ridge Road. No lifeguards are on site. Open daily 6 AM to dusk May through September.

Lake Murphysboro (618-684-2867) Located off IL 149 west past Mur-physboro. This man-made lake was built in 1950 and sprawls across 144 acres of Lake Murphysboro State Park. Anglers seem to like taking advan-tage of the tree-shaded shores to do their fishing on this picturesque body of water.

✳ Lodging

BED AND BREAKFASTS (📶)
Blue Sky Vineyard (618-995-9463; www.blueskyvineyard.com), 3150 S. Rocky Comfort Road, Makanda. The Italian villa-esque winery has two guest suites in the bed and breakfast located upstairs from the tasting room. Furnished with taste-ful antiques, each room has a pri-

vate bath, phone, microwave, mini refrigerator, satellite TV, and DVD. $–$$.

Shawnee Hill Bed &Breakfast (618-893-2211; www.shawneehill bb.com), 290 Water Valley Road, Cobden. Deep in the woods, off a long gravel road, this house and cottage seek to create a peaceful base for you to enjoy the mature tree-lined property around you. Each room has an outdoor patio. The luxury suite combines high ceilings, wooden walls, fireplace, whirlpool tub, and wraparound deck, with a fire pit and hot tub on the deck. The deck overlooks a red barn and quiet grounds that include trails, a pond with a boat for fishing, and a cave. The other two rooms in the cottage have queen beds, a couch, fireplace, tables, and roomy bathrooms. The décor there runs more country cottage. $–$$.

⟨ᵥ⟩ Von Jakob Vineyard Cottage Suites (618-893-4500; www.von jakobvineyard.com), 1309 Sadler Road, Pomona. The vineyard's five suites have king beds, Jacuzzi tubs, refrigerators, and private decks overlooking the vineyard. A nice extra touch: a complimentary bottle of wine. No pets. $–$$.

⟨ᵥ⟩ Kite Hill Vineyards Bed & Breakfast (618-684-5072; www .kitehillvineyards.com), 83 Kite Hill Road, Carbondale. Two rooms are available at this lovely site. There's Chambourcin, which overlooks the lake and is named after a fine red wine produced by the winery. The lighter Chardonel room faces the front 6 acres of the property, sometimes giving a peek at the deer, at dusk and dawn. Both rooms have a queen bed, private bath, TV, DVD, and VCR. A three-course breakfast is included. $$.

♂ ⟨ᵥ⟩ Historic Bell Hill Bed & Breakfast (618-697-0326; www .historicbellhill.com) Bell Hill Road, Cobden. Bell Hill is no small hill, and this bed and breakfast that sits atop that hill offers a truly grand view. The five guest rooms here have different personalities, from the romantic red of the "Metiney Room" to the British colonial style of "Todd's Room." The Ball Room Suite, a loftlike room with wooden walls that was the former ballroom of the estate, offers a bit more room to stretch. History buffs may enjoy the story of the property, which was originally owned by James Bell, who made his fortune in the timber industry in the 1800s. Some rooms have whirlpool tubs and a private balcony; all come with private baths. Free bottled water, cookies, chips, and chocolates in every room. At least one suite can accommodate families with children. $$.

⟨ᵥ⟩ Barton House Bed & Breakfast (618-457-7717; www.barton housebedandbreakfast.com), 1655 N. Reed Station Road, Carbondale. With the forest bordering one side of the property and wheat fields the other, the brick house does give a sense of peace and privacy, but from the outside, it has the look of someone's suburban house rather than a bed and breakfast. Still the rooms offer a step up from the usual hotel experience, with breakfasts that include homemade Belgian waffles or quiche. And it is close to downtown Carbondale. A gazebo in front dresses up the grounds. There are three rooms with private baths, saunas, and whirlpools. $–$$.

 Makanda Inn (618-697-7929; http://makandainn.com), 855 Old Lower Cobden Road, Makanda. The Makanda Inn draws its inspiration from the beautiful grounds, and has an eco-friendly design with repurposed and sustainable products used throughout. The building sits on a bend in the road, hidden behind trees. Greg Wellman searched from Belize to Wisconsin for the perfect property for his family's inn. Then he discovered this green spot on 18 acres just outside Makanda. Daughter Janelle Weber, moved from Chicago to run the inn. Guests are greeted in a light-filled foyer, with natural wood stairs that look like slices of logs that have been sanded down perfectly. Downstairs, a large stone fireplace invites you into the common area, decorated in a sophisticated yet minimalist way. The dining area opens into the kitchen, with modern appliances and tons of natural light. This is a great home base for hiking, visiting Giant City, or the wine trail. Outside, a creek winding through the property provides a pleasant backdrop. There is also a wrap-around porch where you can park yourself with a coffee and a book. The four guest rooms have a balcony, sitting area, TV, DVD, iPod stereo, king bed, toiletries, private bath, and shower. Breakfasts fea-

MAKANDA INN

ture local organic and sustainable produce. $$.

 Train Inn Bed & Breakfast (618-549-1717; www.train-inn .com), 406 E. Stoker Street, Carbondale. The Train Inn is located in a charming yellow Arts and Crafts bungalow close to campus. The accommodations themselves are modern and nice, but the location is close to some busy roads, near campus and apartments, overlooking a childcare center. But if you want to be in the city, the inn offers four rooms with king or queen beds, an outdoor hot tub, walking tours with audio guide, cable TV, DVD, private bathrooms, and a full breakfast with cappuccino. A kitchen is available for those guests who want to prepare their own dinner. No children or pets allowed. $$.

CABINS/RESORTS & **Giant City Lodge** (618-457-4921; www .giantcitylodge.com), 460 Giant City Lodge Road, Makanda. The lodge cabins and restaurant open the first Friday in February through mid-December. During the Great Depression, one of the ways President Franklin D. Roosevelt got people back to work was through the Civilian Conservation Corps. Three units of the CCC constructed the roads, cabins, and lodge in the park, and they did so with great respect for the local land. Native building materials were used wherever possible and the lodge was designed to disturb as few trees as possible. The location also takes advantage of the surrounding countryside, providing excellent views from the high point of the lodge. The building is impressive, bearing the look of the

GIANT CITY LODGE

GIANT CITY CABINS

1930s era in which it was constructed. Inside, the exposed logs, stone walls, wooden furniture, and large inviting fireplace add to the national park lodge feel. The lodge also features second-story balconies, wireless Internet, historic lounge, bar, and gift shop. As for your stay, the actual guest rooms are in cabins surrounding the lodge. There are one-room "Historic" cabins with two double beds. The 18 "Prairie" cabins come with a queen bed in the bedroom, a full Murphy bed in the living room, a small refrigerator, satellite TV, and coffeemaker. The four "Bluff" cabins are a step up, with a deck overlooking serene woods. They have two queen beds, an electric fireplace, wet bar, refrigerator, and coffeemaker. There is a winding ramp down to the four cabins, which feature high ceilings and a large bedroom. $–$$.

✎ **Rustle Hill Winery Cabins** (618-893-2700; www.rustlehill winery.com), 8595 US 51, Cobden. Across the pond from the winery, the family has built several new wooden cabins, which are cozy but nicely done, with high ceilings to make the space feel a bit bigger. The small kitchen includes the essentials, with stainless steel appliances elevating the look a notch. The master bedroom has a king bed, and steep stairs lead up to the loft where kids can stay. All have a wooden deck that wraps around the outside. TVs, central air, and fireplaces also included. $$.

Rend Lake Resort (618-629-2211; www.rendlakeresort.com),

11712 East Windy Lane, Whittington. Just off exit 77 on I-57. The resort has traditional hotel rooms, cabins, and "boatels," which are the bright blue rooftops lining the coast of Rend Lake. A "boatel" is a hotel room that gets you as close as possible to the waterfront. Choose from the downstairs boatel rooms with two queen beds or the loft room with a queen upstairs and a daybed downstairs. At the Flagship boatel, you get a Jacuzzi and a gas fireplace in the living area. Cabins located near the pool have a private bedroom, a futon, wet bar, and a private deck. There are also traditional hotel rooms in the main building. The resort complex also includes the Blue Heron Café & Gift Shop and the Blue Heron General Store, which offers bike and boat rentals. $–$$.

((ψ)) **Seasons Lodge at Rend Lake** (618-629-2600; www.rend lake.org), 12575 Golf Course Road, Whittington. Located on the golf course, the design of the building is more traditional, with its large country porch and tones of tan and hunter green. The lodge has an outdoor spa located under a gazebo, free bicycles, and an outdoor pool. Suites are available with spas and fireplaces. $–$$.

& **Green Retreat** (618-687-1717; www.greenretreat.com), 6096 Chautauqua Road, Murphysboro. A sprawling green retreat it is, with a 97-acre working farm, ponds, and horses. The new five-bedroom Victorian bed and breakfast opened in 2010. Three studio cabins sleep two, and come with kitchenette, bath, and shower. The 3-story cedar tree house has a loft

REND LAKE

WOODLAND CABINS IN CARBONDALE

bedroom, full kitchen, two queen beds, 1.5 baths, a wraparound porch, and a private pond. The house boasts a wall of windows from which you can take in the peaceful view outside. The garden cottage sleeps eight, with three bedrooms and 2.5 baths. RV slots also available for $35 a night. $–$$$.

Stone Creek Cabins (618-351-4653; www.stonecreekgolf.com), 503 Stone Creek Drive, Makanda. Located on the Stone Creek Golf Course, these one and two-bedroom cabins are just 0.5-mile from the clubhouse. The cabins feature microwave, TV, VCR, AC, gas fireplace, toaster, coffeemaker, and small refrigerator. No pets. $–$$.

Woodland Cabins (618-457-7400; www.woodlandcabins.net), off Kennedy Road, Carbondale.

It's amazing how close this property is to downtown Carbondale, but how remote it feels. Off a rustic narrow road with extreme hills, you find the gravel road that leads to the resort. The cabins are located back past the open fields and horse stables. The cabins are roomy and comfortable and have great places to relax outdoors. My favorite cabin, Woodsong, has a multilevel deck overlooking a small pond, with an outdoor fireplace, hot tub, and a very popular bird feeder that attracts colorful creatures and chipmunks. At dusk, you can watch the deer congregate in the fields nearby, then take a walk up to the barn to see the horses. Inside, the cabins are quite modern with a great room, fireplace, and laundry. The full kitchens are outfitted with stainless steel appliances and most of the hardware you would need to cook a feast. The living area and bedroom have sliding glass doors leading out to the deck. Cabins include charcoal grill, TV, DVD, CD player, towels/linens, coffee, central heat and air, and paddle boat. No pets. $$.

CAMPING Giant City State Park (618-457-4836; http://dnr .state.il.us/lands/landmgt/parks/r5/ gc.htm), 235 Giant City Road, Makanda. The park offers a family campground with 85 sites outfitted with electricity, water, and a sewage dump station. A horse campground has 25 sites with hitching posts, electricity, and water. (The fee for both is $20 per night/$30 on holiday weekends.) For tent campers, there are 14 sites at the south end of the family campground with access to water for $8 per night. All campgrounds have access to a shower house, and campsites have picnic tables, fire pits, and charcoal grills.

Crab Orchard Campground 10067 Campground Drive, Carbondale. Having recently undergone a renovation, the campground features lakefront sites with full service for RVs. Hot showers, flush toilets, and a country store are also on the campgrounds. $25 for a full hookup site, $20 for electric and water, $10 for non-electric.

Devil's Backbone Park (618-684-6192) West of Grand Tower on the Mississippi River. From

Murphysboro, take IL 149 west to IL 3, head south and look for signs. Named for the rock ridge known as the Devil's Backbone that runs along the Mississippi, this park has camping right on the river's edge from March through November. Picnic tables, grills, flush toilets, a shower house, concessions, and playgrounds are also on site. The park has year-round horse trails and 10 horse-camping sites with water and electricity. Sites are $17 a day.

Kinkaid Village Marina (618-687-4914) A year-round campground at Kinkaid Lake with 8 tent sites and 28 RV sites. The tent sites have a fire pit, grill, and picnic table, and can accommodate up to two large tents. One site is especially close to the water. The RV sites come with water and electric hookup. The campground also has shower houses, Laundromat, dump station, and bait and tackle shop with ice, drinks, and other items. A restaurant is attached. Sites are $15–$25.

&. **Lake Murphysboro State Park** (618-684-2867) Located off IL 149 about 1 mile west of Murphysboro. The star-shaped lake has 54 trailer sites with electricity and 20 tent sites surrounding it, including 4 handicapped-accessible sites. The Water Lily and Shady Rest tent campgrounds are peaceful lakeside retreats. Some sites even have water on both sides and are close to docks for fishing. The 145-acre lake with tree-lined shores was built in

1950. There is a concession stand near the boat dock area and a 3-mile hiking trail. Sites are $10–20.

✳ Where to Eat

EATING OUT Quatro's Pizza (618-549-5326; www.quatros.com), 218 W. Freeman Street, Carbondale. Open 11 AM–midnight Sunday through Thursday, 11 AM–1 AM Friday and Saturday. This Carbondale institution is located near the entrance of Southern Illinois University. The look of the dining room is a little *Three's Company,* with white-painted walls, dark brown trim, red leather booths, and gold, orange, and red stained-glass lamps. A casual place for families of students and students themselves, seat yourself before ordering one of their deep pan pizzas. With its flavorful tomato sauce and browned cheese, this pan pleased even skeptical Chicagoans. Salads are very large, and arrive with a side bowl of croutons and cheddar cheese. Menu also includes sandwiches, pastas, and subs. $.

Harbaugh's Café (618-351-9897), 901 B South Illinois Avenue, Carbondale. Open 7–2 Monday through Saturday, 8–2 Sunday. For breakfast or lunch close to the university campus, Harbaugh's offers omelets, frittatas, breakfast burritos, pancakes, French toast, salads, and an inventive line of sandwiches. One that comes to mind: "Sweet Sensation," which blends turkey breast,

Swiss cheese, and apples on sweet raisin bread. $.

Longbranch Coffeehouse and Vegetarian Café (618-529-4488; http://lbchouse.com), 100 E. Jackson Street, Carbondale. Open 7:30 AM–9 PM Sunday through Friday, 7:30–midnight Saturday. On one of those cute Carbondale shopping strips with a paver-brick street outside, Longbranch serves up some great food with their philosophy about life built into the menu. The focus here is vegetarian. They serve only free-range eggs and use organic flour in their homemade breads. The organic, fair-trade coffees come from small independent regional roasters. Local art fancies up the walls. Virtually everything is made on premises. The bright yellow walls and retro red sparkling vinyl chairs add a friendly feel to the place. A back room hosts poetry readings, bands, and other community events, while an outdoor garden patio offers more places for conversation and coffee. A steady stream of locals files in during the morning to pick up a coffee. But you can stay and get a meal. For breakfast, choose from breakfast burritos that have quite the kick, and a range of other dishes. For dinner there are europizzas, which are baked on hot stones, paninis, and vegetarian specials such as Thai curry or spinach lasagna. $.

Giant City Lodge (618-457-4921; www.giantcitylodge.com), 460 Giant City Lodge Road,

LONGBRANCH COFFEEHOUSE

Makanda. The lodge's season runs from the first Friday in February through mid-December. Open 8–8:30 Monday through Saturday, 8–8 Sunday. On Sunday afternoons (11:30–4), a family-style chicken dinner is served exclusively. This being Giant City, the restaurant in the lodge has kept with the theme by offering rather giant portions of food, from Grandma's breakfast, which includes just about every breakfast item imaginable, to the all-you-can-eat fried chicken dinner served family style. The menu also includes bison, seafood, and steaks, with your choice of three sides. The dining room overlooks the stone patios, offering nice views of the nearby forest and cabins. $–$$.

Thai Taste (618-457-6900), 100 S. Illinois Avenue, Carbondale. Open 11–3, 5–9 Monday through Thursday, 11–3, 5–10 Friday, 5–10 Saturday, 5–9 Sunday. This downtown Carbondale restaurant presents authentic Thai food with a menu of the basic Thai classics, such as Pad Thai or Laad Nar, as well as curries, salads, and soups. Try the lunch special, which allows you to choose from nine entrees and also comes with egg roll, soup, and iced tea. $–$$.

Yellow Moon Café (618-893-2233; www.yellowmooncafe.com), 110 N. Front Street, Cobden. Open 8 AM–2 PM Tuesday through Friday; 7 PM–10 PM Friday, 9 AM–midnight Saturday. The philosophy here is to buy locally whenever possible, meaning local organic produce and local grass-fed beef with no antibiotics, hormones, or pesticides. Yellow Moon has a breakfast menu of granola, Italian strata of the day (a baked egg dish served with fresh fruit and toast), a lunch menu of soups, salads, and sandwiches, and occasional dinners to complement the lineup of independent music acts that the owner books. The menu features local wines and beers, including those from Big Muddy Brewery and the nearby Shawnee Hills Wine Trail. $.

17th Street Bar & Grill (618-684-3722; www.17thstreetbarbecue.com), 17th Street, Murphysboro. Open 10–10 Monday through Saturday. Featured on the Food Network, this barbecue haven is run by legendary pit master Mike Mills and has drawn quite a bit of foodie attention. The menu features wings, Southern-fried dill pickles, and ribs that have been named the best in America by *Bon Appétit*. The ribs are sprinkled with what they call Magic Dust and slowly cooked in the barbecue pit with apple and cherry woods for five to seven hours. You may also know Mr. Mills as author of the cookbook *Peace Love and Barbecue*. Other entrees include steaks, seafood, and pork. $$–$$$.

Italian Village (618-457-6559; www.italianvillagecarbondale.com), 405 S. Washington Street, Carbondale. Open 11–10 Sunday through Thursday, 11–11 Friday and Saturday. The dark wood walls have layers of greetings scrawled by guests who have enjoyed the casual atmosphere and hearty portions here. Once you walk in, order your dishes up at the cashier, then grab a table. The menu allows you to build your own pasta dishes and pizza, and during lunch you can order a slice. If you don't want to dine inside, there is drive-up window service as well, but then you miss out on the salad bar that sits on top of a wooden boat. The game room will keep the kids (or some adults) busy while you wait for your food. $.

DINING OUT The Newell House (618-549-6400; http://the-newellhouse.com), 201 E. Main Street, Carbondale. Open 11–9 Monday through Thursday, 11–10 Friday, 4:30–10 Saturday. The gold lettering and black-and-white striped awning lend a more stately look to the restaurant. This bistro in the downtown district specializes in Italian American food, with an extensive wine list and more than 30 specialty martinis. Lunch offerings include chicken, asparagus and mushrooms baked in an herb crust, Cobb salad, Italian pizza burger, seafood ravioli, and a crab cake BLT. The dinner menu adds pizzettes, steaks, and seafood. Lunch: $, dinner $$–$$$.

Windows at Rend Lake Resort (618-629-2211; www.rendlakeresort.com) Open 7 AM–9 PM Sunday through Thursday, 7 AM–10 PM Friday and Saturday. Located near the boatels on Rend Lake.

On a nice summer day, snag a table on the white patio at Windows Restaurant for a most pleasing view of the activity on the lake. The restaurant has a breakfast menu of pancakes, croissant French toast, and breakfast sandwich. For lunch, choose from burgers, sandwiches, and salads. The dinner menu is expanded to include lobster, filets, and pork chops. Lunch $, dinner $$–$$$$.

✳ Entertainment

Check the calendar for campus events, as the university brings in well-known comedians, traveling theater productions, and musicians to **Shryock Auditorium at Southern Illinois University** (www.siu.edu/~shryock), 1050 S. Normal Avenue, Carbondale. There's also the **SIUC Arena** in Carbondale. With 10,000 seats, the arena welcomes nationally touring music acts, theater groups, circuses, and sporting events.

LIVE MUSIC As a college town, Carbondale has its selection of bars with cheap beer specials. But that means they also attract some live acts. During the summer, the university and city put on the Sunset Concert Series held near the steps of the Shryock Auditorium that features some notable performers.

In Cobden, also check the calendar for the **Yellow Moon Café**, which books independent acts. (618-893-CAFÉ; www.yellow

mooncafe.com) 110 N. Front Street, Cobden.

Tres Hombres (618-457-3308; www.trescarbondale.com), 119 N. Washington Street, Carbondale. Open 11 AM–2 AM daily. It is a Mexican restaurant, but the bar also books a range of bands that bring everything from blues to jazz and funk. The outdoor patio is also a nice place to have a drink on a summer night.

✳ Selective Shopping

Town Square Market (618-529-2312), 106 E. Jackson Street, Carbondale. Organic, free-range, or just old-fashioned good is the motto in this natural foods store in the historic town square. Open 10–7 weekdays, 9–7 Saturday, noon–6 Sunday.

Makanda Board Walk (618-549-5523), 530 Makanda Road, Makanda. This block of storefronts dating to the 1890s now features space for local artists and craftspeople. You'll find ice cream, coffee, sandwiches, and more in this tiny district.

Anthill Gallery & Vintage Curiosities (www.anthillgallery .com), 102 N. Front Street, Cobden. Open noon–6 Thursday through Sunday. Reduced winter hours. This studio features the art of Bob Hageman, whose color photographs offer a fresh take on some seemingly mundane objects, and Linda Austin, who creates stained-glass work.

Flamm Orchards (618-893-4241; www.flammorchards.com), 8760 Old Highway 51 North, Cobden. Open 9–6 daily. Pick up whatever is in season in its most basic fresh form—whether that is strawberries, apples, or peaches. Or, you can pick it up wrapped in butter and sugar in the form of homemade pies, shortcakes, cobblers, and dumplings.

Rendleman Orchard (618-893-2771; www.rendlemanorchards .com), 9860 IL 127 North, Alto Pass. The farm market is open 9–5 Monday through Saturday, noon–5 Sunday from July through December. This orchard has been in business since 1873, sharing peaches, apples, and nectarines with the world. The orchard is actually designated an Illinois Centennial Farm, after marking 137 years of family farming.

Southern Illinois Art & Artisans Center Rend Lake (618-629-2220; www.museum.state.il.us /artisans), Exit 77 off I-57, 14967 Gun Creek Trail, Whittington. Open 9–5 daily. The center near Rend Lake has galleries displaying the work of more than 850 Illinois artisans as well as arts and crafts for purchase.

✳ Special Events

April: **Southern Illinois Irish Festival** (618-549-3090; www.sil irishfest.org) The festival celebrates "the music, the spirit and the traditions of Celtic peoples."

All you need to know is that means good music and dancing. The main fest is usually held the last week of April, but the organizers also host concerts and other events throughout the year.

May: **HerrinFesta Italiana** (800-483-3782; www.herrinfesta.com) Held between 16th and 17th Streets and Harrison and Walnut Streets in Herrin. This lively festival celebrates the Italian heritage of Herrin with food, car show, parade, carnival, music, art show, athletic events, and a bocce tournament. Show off your Italian roots in the pasta sauce contest, or maybe the pasta eating contest, depending on where your talent lies. Then there's the "Bigga Nose" contest in which contestants compete to be crowned Mr. or Mrs. Bigga Nose and win the $100 prize. Contestants are asked to clean their nose beforehand. Usually held on Memorial Day weekend.

Downtown Art & Wine Fair (618-529-8040; www.carbondale mainstreet.com), N. Washington and Jackson Street, Carbondale. Twice a year, local winemakers and artists gather downtown to share their creations. You'll also find live music and dishes from local restaurants. The entry fee of $10 buys you tastings, but wines are also sold by the glass. If you're not drinking there is a $2 cover charge for the music. This is held in May and again in October.

June: **Southern Illinois Music Festival** (618-453-6000; www
.sifest.com) Hosted by Southern Illinois University, the festival venues are scattered throughout Southern Illinois to attract musicians from throughout the world to the region. The lineup includes orchestral and chamber music, jazz, ballet, opera, and new music. Most performances are free, but check in advance because some do require tickets.

December: **Lights Fantastic** (618-529-8040; www.carbondale mainstreet.com) This holiday tradition is held the first weekend of December in downtown Carbondale, attracting more than 10,000 people for the illuminated floats parading through the downtown district.

THE SHAWNEE FOREST:
EASTERN REGION

For this leg of the journey, get ready to become even better acquainted with the Shawnee. The forest is the main draw here. This is a land to hike, bike, canoe, fish, camp, and climb. And while you're taking a break on top of a bluff, relaxing under a tree, or floating on a raft, you'll find yourself disconnecting from regular life, a necessary occurrence in my opinion. Nothing greater than when you can let go enough to let the images of a grand landscape push those to-do lists out of your mind. Then you know you have achieved a vacation state of mind.

You do not need to be a triathlete to get to the sites I'm talking about here. Sure, you can craft a challenging itinerary that will leave you exhausted by the end of the day, but if you just want a taste of the land, you will still be able to see some pretty awesome natural sites. This Eastern region of the forest is defined by the Ohio River and stretches west to about I-57, which roughly cuts down the middle of the state. Even if you have an address for some of the locations here, you might still need a local to give you directions to your cabin, so unmarked (and off the grid) are some of these roads.

The bigger towns are Harrisburg and Metropolis, and that's where you should head if you need a grocery store with more than one brand of soup. We always try to plan meals ahead of time here, so we're not about to eat our arms off only to realize that the local market only carries soda and chips, not the ingredients we were hoping to grill for dinner at our campsite. And if you're planning to go out to eat, check the hours. Some dining establishments are only open for lunch or during the weekend. We want to help you avoid having to cobble together a dinner from a vending machine.

This region is really a collection of small river towns. And some are proud of their small town feel. As I sit in city traffic, I often daydream of a place where I would never be stuck at a stoplight again, and I'm here to

DEVIL'S BACKBONE PARK

tell you they do exist. Golconda has zero traffic lights and only one four-way stop.

Settlers started arriving here along the Ohio River during the late 1700s. Elizabethtown was known as McFarlan's Ferry, after the founder, James McFarlan. As the years progressed, pirates, yes, river pirates, hid out at Cave-In-Rock. Golconda grew into an important port for shipping local timber and produce out into the world. The discovery and mining of the region's natural resources—lead ore and fluorspar—fed the local economy for many decades. While you still will see many a barge heading down the Ohio River, the river economy is not what it was when these river towns flourished.

Many of the towns are worthy of a quick spin, or a lunch. Cave-In-Rock, Golconda, and Elizabethtown all have walkable areas. But the main attraction is always the natural features of the forest close by.

GUIDANCE & **Shawnee National Forest Ranger Station—Hidden Springs** (618-658-2111; www.fs.usda.gov/shawnee), 602 N. First Street/ US 45 North, Vienna. Open 8–4:30 weekdays. With gray wooden siding and stone features, this new welcome center is reminiscent of the national park lodges of the 1930s era. It also is home to friendly rangers who will help determine which trails might fit your trip itinerary best. They are in charge of about 157,000 acres of the forest and have come to know them well.

Hardin County Tourism (www.hardincountyil.org) This Web site will set you up with the basics. Request a brochure, which will be addressed by

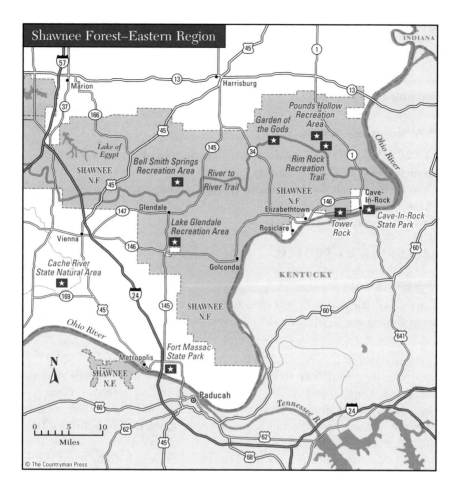

Shawnee Forest–Eastern Region

hand and sent off to you promptly, a signal of the more casual, informal
but entirely friendly attitude of the people you'll encounter here.

GETTING THERE *By auto:* From I-57, head east toward the Ohio River
along IL 146, which will take you to the southern attractions. IL 13 follows the northern border of this region of the forest, while IL 1 and 145
run north and south.

GETTING AROUND *By auto:* The roads here are narrow, winding, and
often give you no sense of what lies ahead, but that's part of the fun. IL
146 escorts you near many of the park entrances or river towns in this
area. Where it doesn't, IL 147, 145, 34, and 1 are the main roads for the
northern section of the forest.

MEDICAL EMERGENCIES Harrisburg Medical Center (618-253-7671; www.harrisburgmedicalcenter.com), 100 Dr. Warren Tuttle Drive, Harrisburg. One of the larger health facilities in this region, this hospital has 45 physicians, 86 beds, and a surgery center. The emergency medicine department is staffed 24 hours a day.

✳ Wandering Around

EXPLORING BY CAR Ohio River Scenic Byway (www.ohioriver scenicbyway.com) This road hugs the Ohio River and takes you through Cave-In-Rock, Elizabethtown, and Golconda along the easternmost edge of the forest. The byway cuts through three states, and Illinois is the host for 188 miles of the road.

EXPLORING BY FOOT All of the recreation areas in this beautiful swath of country are worth a hike. And you'll find trails for whatever kind of hike you seek. If you're pressed for time, definitely don't miss the **Garden of the Gods** observation trail. This popular trail winds past many impressive sights and will take less than an hour. But the park also has longer, less explored, and amazing paths through the forest.

If you are ambitious and want to be even closer to the natural wonder here, consider the **River to River Trail** (800-699-6637; www.rivertoriver trail.com). The 160-mile hiking and equestrian trail runs from Battery Rock on the Ohio River to Devil's Backbone Park in Grand Tower on the Mississippi, traversing through some of the best features in Southern Illinois, such as the wilderness of the Shawnee National Forest, Giant City State Park, and small towns of the wine trail. The whole thing would take you about two to three weeks, if you're up for the adventure. Following old pioneer roads, Native American trails, and horse trails, you'll hike across dirt roads, rocky stretches, pavement, gravel, and grass. You can access the trail from several points, at Garden of the Gods, One Horse Gap Area, and Giant City State Park. To access the beginning of the trail at Battery Rock, from Highway 1, turn east on Lambs Road. About a mile past the point where the pavement turns into gravel, you will find the trailhead parking lot. Bring a compass and maps and be sure to have planned out your food for the trip in advance.

EXPLORING BY BIKE Tunnel Hill State Trail (618-658-2168) is 45 miles of crushed limestone that stretches from Harrisburg to Karnak along an old railroad right-of-way. Completed in 2001, the trail is a tour through shifting scenery—wetlands, swamps, river bluffs, and smooth plains of farmland. Despite the change in the landscape, it's a pretty easy ride, as the grade increases by no more than 2 to 3 percent along the trail. There are some hills, but they're gradual. When the rail line was being constructed, designers decided to cut a tunnel through this hill rather than go all the way around it, thus the name Tunnel Hill. The tunnel, part of which collapsed in 1929, now stretches 543 feet and is found at the halfway point. You can access the trail at many different points and will find basic toilets and drinking water along the way. If the water fountains aren't working, there are parking areas at each of the towns where you can veer off to grab something to drink or eat. You can travel the whole trail in a day, but if you're on foot, there are no camping facilities on the trail. You'd have to travel to the forest for that.

EXPLORING BY BOAT & *Shawnee Queen* **River Taxi** (877-667-6119; www.ridesmtd.com) Board the taxi in Golconda, Rosiclare, Elizabethtown, and Cave-In-Rock. Runs from mid-May through October. Does not run Sunday and Monday. A different kind of river road, this cruise along the Ohio River offers views of historic homes, caves, and wildlife. It also gives a new perspective of the Cave-In-Rock cave. The river taxi also serves as public mass transit, with scheduled trips between the river communities. Fares: $1 to $10 for one-way trips depending on the distance traveled. Children under 11 pay half price. Longer round-trip rides range from $10–20 per person.

✳ Towns and Villages

Golconda If nothing else, this river community is likable for the story of its founder, Sarah Lusk, who is immortalized in a plaque in the town square as a brave pioneer woman who always had a rifle at hand to protect passengers traveling along the river. She established the first ferry across the Ohio River. That's why, in 1800, this town was known as Sarahville. Today Golconda has a sparse main business strip with a couple shops, restaurants, and a courthouse. Near the courthouse, you will find the historic Buel House and a log cabin that has been moved to the site. The main strip is right off the river. Golconda also boasts a marina with 200 boat slips.

Elizabethtown Up the river from Golconda is this even smaller town of 350 situated on a couple of hills along the river. Today, Elizabethtown boasts a scenic riverfront with a few restaurants, shops, and bed and breakfasts, most notably the historic Rose Hotel. With its sprawling porches and gazebo, the Rose Hotel offers an impressive view of the Ohio. As for restaurants, locals always recommend the "floating restaurant," which is indeed just that, because sometimes you can't get to it if the river level is too high.

Cave-In-Rock This town is named for a large riverfront cave with quite the scandalous past that is now part of Cave-In-Rock State Park. You see, pirates and other criminal elements used to hide out in the cave and have greatly added to the local lore. There still is an element of outlaw to be found in the town, with the old town jail that sits unattended and just a little bit creepy on East Clay Street. There are a couple of diner-like restaurants here, with barebones décor and menus written on whiteboards.

Vienna Centrally located in the southernmost region of the state, Vienna is large enough to have a little more to offer than the small riverfront towns, in the way of restaurants and shops. So this is the place to head for supplies, stock up on food, or grab a bite to eat. Don't forget to stop into the ranger station for maps and the like. And remember, it's Vy-enna here, not Vee-ena like the Italian city.

Metropolis South of the forest on the southern border of the state is Metropolis, a town that existed long before Superman, but only rather recently embraced the connection to this hero of millions. In the 1970s, a Kentucky man moved to Metropolis and was shocked to see the town had not yet done this. He was key to making it happen, and Metropolis formally adopted Superman in 1972. The local newspaper embraced the change by changing its name to the Metropolis Planet. When the *Superman* movies came out in 1979, the town initiated its annual festival devoted to Clark Kent's alter ego. In Superman Square, you can find a giant 15-foot bronze statue of the superhero. A recent addition is a statue of the actress Noel Neill as Lois Lane.

✳ To See

MUSEUMS Saline Creek Pioneer Village & Museum (618-253-7342), 1600 S. Feazel Street, Harrisburg. Tours Tuesday through Saturday from 2–4. This 1877 Victorian farm is now a museum with several log homes, a barn, old Quaker church, a jail, and a school.

HISTORIC SITES Buel House and Davidson Cabin (618-683-9702), 328 S. Columbus Street, Golconda. Located just across from the courthouse, the light yellow Buel House looks rough around the edges, the victim of state budget woes. The local historical society has stopped giving tours of the property because of the sad state of it. But if you're downtown, you can take a stroll around to get a look at the log cabin that is the John Thomas Davidson Cabin. The cabin was moved from a farm in Azotus in 1993 to a lot next door to the Buel House.

CULTURAL SITES ⚓ **The Super Museum** (618-524-5518; www.super museum.com), 517 Market Street, Metropolis. Open 9–5 daily. Take note: You must walk through the souvenir shop to reach the museum, which is from the private collection of Jim Hambrick, who has more than 100,000 Superman items. His featured collection includes props from the movies, toys, original costumes, and special effects devices used in the 1950s TV show. Admission: $5, children under 5 free.

✴ To Do

BOATING ♿ **Golconda Marina** (618-683-5875; www.golcondamarina .com) Located at 1 Marina Lane on the waterfront in Golconda. With 200 boat slips, the marina provides access to the Smithland Pool, a 23,000-acre area of Ohio River tributaries. Smithland Pool was formed in 1980, stretching from the Smithland Lock on the Ohio River 72 miles down to the Uniontown Lock. It's a popular destination for boaters and fishermen. The site has gas for purchase, mechanic services, food, and showers. The marina also has boat rentals, a campground, picnic sites, and two hiking trails on a bluff overlooking the river.

DIVING **Mermet Springs Diving** (618-527-3483; www.mermetsprings .com) West Side of US 45, just south of IL 169 (Karnak Road). From May through December, open 9–6 Monday, Tuesday, and Thursday; 9 AM–10 PM Friday; 8 AM–10 PM Saturday; 8–5 Sunday. In the winter, opens an hour later and is also closed on Sunday. A recreational diver discovered this abandoned quarry lake and started plans to turn it into a clean, clear haven for scuba divers. He upped the intrigue of the diving experience by adding things like the fuselage from a Boeing 727 that was crashed for a scene in the Tommy Lee Jones film *U.S. Marshals*. The lake also has 100-foot underwater cliffs, sunken wrecks, and fish. Divers pay a $20 entry fee, $5 for non-divers. Equipment is available for rental.

WINERIES **Southern Illinois Wine Trail** (www.southernillinoiswine trail.net) The Southern Illinois Wine Trail is less established than the Shawnee Hills Wine Trail, but still has some local vineyards worth a stop.

♿ ♂ **Bella Terra Winery** (618-658-8882; www.bellaterrawinery.com), 755 Parker City Road, Creal Springs. Open 11–6 daily. Owner, Edward Russell, has transformed a hayfield into a lovely vineyard in Creal Springs. With a bocce court, horseshoes, fishing pond for the kids, and a hitching post for those riding in on horseback, the Bella Terra Winery grounds certainly encourage you to settle in and relax a bit. Mr. Russell planted the grapes about 10 years ago, after learning how to make wine. About three years ago the winery opened, showcasing the Chambourcin reds and dry Vignoles whites made from his grapes. Besides the free tastings, you can buy wine by the glass, beer, mixed drinks, and three different kinds of sangria. The menu includes Italian beef, and chicken-salad sandwiches, pizzas, and panini.

ও **Cache River Basin Vineyard & Winery** (618-658-2274; www.crb winery.com), 315 Forman Lane, Belknap. Open 10–6 Monday through Saturday, 1–5 Sunday. Owner, Jack Dunker, opened this winery in December 2001. After retiring as a school superintendent, Mr. Dunker immersed himself into the study of winemaking. He found an old farm and transformed it into a vineyard. He makes all the wines himself, which he finds similar to cooking ("A lot of trial and error.") But it seems he's worked out the kinks and has had fun assigning names to his various creations, like the semisweet "Swamp Water." No charge for tastings. On the weekends, you can also check out the restaurant, Wineaux's.

✷ Green Space

Shawnee National Forest (618-658-2111; www.fs.usda.gov/shawnee) A high priority on any itinerary should be the **Garden of the Gods.** From IL 34, head east on Karbers Ridge Road for 2.5 miles to Garden of the Gods Road, turn north and the entrance is 1.5 miles. From the heights of cliffs formed 320 million years ago, you will take in the "garden of the gods" in the greenscape below. There are 5.5 miles of trails to explore. The shorter flagstone observation trail is just 0.25 mile, but it's a favorite for views that challenge anyone to say the Midwest landscape is boring. The position of the rock formations creates some interesting surprise views, as you emerge from the wooded parts of the trail to find yourself on a cliff. Looking across, you may see other visitors standing on a rock that seems to be floating like an island in a sea of treetops. When you move back into the trail and take a closer look at the rock formations, they reveal details about the chemical mix in the water that originally carved the stone here, as minerals mixed in the water were pressed into layers of reds and oranges. The observation trail takes about 45 minutes and includes steps. Outhouses are located at the parking area. No rock climbing allowed. **Pounds Hollow Recreational Area** features a lake that was built in the 1940s and attracts swimmers, boaters, and hikers. A fishing pier on the 25-acre lake gives anglers a shot at some largemouth bass, channel catfish, and sunfish. The swimming area, which is open from dawn to dusk, has a shower area and a picnic area with grills. The entrance is located off Karbers Ridge Road, about 9 miles east of IL 34 and 2 miles west of IL 1. **Rim Rock Recreation Trail** To take in the beauty of the Pounds Hollow area, this 0.5-mile trail runs along the rim of a rock cliff. The upper trail is paved, the lower trail has dirt, rock formations, and a cave worth checking out. Located off Karbers Ridge Road, just west of the entrance for Pounds Hollow Recreational Area. **Bell Smith Springs Recreation Area** has been designated as a National Natural Landmark because of its geological wonders and diversity of plant life. The views from the 8 miles of trails will impress, with extraordinary overlooks, unique rock formations, rocky streams, canyons, and cliffs. Because the trails are interconnected, you can hike for a couple hours or cover the whole trail system over a couple days. It's rated moderate to difficult because you have to climb down stone steps to reach the canyon bottom. Rest rooms and parking on site. To access from Vienna, take IL 45 north to Ozark and follow the signs to the entrance.

Cave-In-Rock State Park (618-289-4325; www.dnr.illinois.gov) Located on the banks of the Ohio River east of IL 1. Once you get to Main Street, turn left and look for signs for Cave-In-Rock State Park. Once there, head to the riverfront where you will find the path that takes you to the 55-foot wide cave on the north bank of the Ohio River. The cave sheltered Native Americans and French explorers, but then river pirates and other unsavory characters discovered the advantage the cave presented as a hideout and place to launch attacks on unsuspecting river travelers. Take Samuel Mason, an officer in George Washington's Revolutionary Army, who made a tavern in the cave in 1797. He sent his men to "help" travelers on the river, but instead instructed them to rob the commuters when they got close to the river. After the Mason Gang, the Harpe Brothers made their home here, somehow escaping their execution date for murder in Kentucky. They used the cave as their hideout to commit more crimes, until they were killed. In other less notorious claims to fame, Walt Disney filmed some of the Davy Crockett movies near the cave. But when the river is high, sometimes the path floods, and you cannot access the path to the cave, so you may want to call ahead if the waters are high. If you climb the hill above the cave, you'll notice a large grate-covered hole. Put your

CAVE-IN-ROCK STATE PARK

hand over it and feel the cool cave air coming out of what served as a makeshift chimney. You can also get a peek at the cave from the river if you take a boat ride. The park also has boating, fishing, hiking, and camping. (See Lodging.)

&. **Cache River State Natural Area** (618-634-9678; www.dnr.illinois .gov), 930 Sunflower Lane, Belknap. In these 13,000 acres around the Cache River, you will get acquainted with some old characters—the giant 1,000-year-old cypress trees with bases of 40 feet in circumference or more. The forested swamp that is known as Heron Pond is a good place to start, with an easy 1.5-mile trail that will take you to the floating boardwalk in the middle of the pond. Canoers will enjoy the Lower Cache River trail, where you can paddle through a cypress-tupelo swamp. Start at the Lower Cache River access area, and follow the arrows or yellow stripes on trees to find your way. The park also has 21 miles of hiking trails.

Fort Massac State Park (618-524-4712), 1308 E. 5th Street, Metropolis. On the banks of the Ohio River, Fort Massac became Illinois' first state park in 1908, but its history dates back to the 1750s, when the French built their first fort here. You can still see the outline of that fort. (A reconstructed version, modeled after an 1802 version, stands next to the original fort site.) In the 18th century, a fort on site was burned to the ground by Chickasaws, who found it abandoned by the French. George Washington ordered it rebuilt in 1794. The fort was used during the War of 1812, and as a training camp for a short time during the Civil War, but abandoned after a measles outbreak swept through the camp. A half-mile trail leads through the woods near the fort. The park also features a boat launch into the river, picnic areas, 50 campsites, disposal station, shower building, and tent camping.

✳ Lodging

BED AND BREAKFASTS &.
Historic Rose Hotel (618-287-2872; www.therosehotelbb.com), 92 Main Street, Elizabethtown. This hotel claims the title of the oldest operating hotel in Illinois. It was built in 1812, and it's obvious why it's not been allowed to close: unparalleled views of the Ohio River. The white porches that stretch across the front of the 2-story mansion overlook green gardens, a white gazebo perched on a rocky cliff, and the river itself. In the gift shop, peruse a photo album of moments captured at the hotel, from a snapshot of the namesake Rose herself, to pictures from the floods of 1913 and 1937, when the waters reached nearly to the top of the gazebo. Now a bed and breakfast with tours offered by appointment, the hotel has five sizable guest rooms that mix antiques, floral patterns, and regal pieces of furniture. All rooms have private bath, refrigerator, microwave, coffeepot, clock radio, and cable TV

HISTORIC ROSE HOTEL

with DVD/VCR. Country breakfast in the dining area on the first floor, served by the owner, who dresses in 1800s period clothing. $$.

River Rose Inn (618-287-8811; www.riveroseinn.com), 1 Main Street, Elizabethtown. With views of the Ohio River, this Greek-Revival mansion built in 1914 is located across from the Rose Hotel. The hotel overlooks the Ohio River, and opens into a foyer with a grand staircase lined with books and movies. And what's that at the top of the stairs—an extensive collection of Elvis memorabilia. Catch a view of the river from the outdoor Jacuzzi spa or the mosaic-tiled porch. The rooms in the main house have river views, cable TV/VCRs, queen beds, private baths and showers, some with

two-person whirlpool tubs and private balconies. The hotel has an outdoor pool as well. There also is a cottage available with a gas log fireplace, microwave, refrigerator, coffeemaker, cable TV/VCR, and private porch. $–$$.

RESORTS/CABINS ✐ **Cedar Hill River Resort** (217-652-4257; www.cedarhillriverresort.com) Tower Rock Road, Elizabethtown. Something about driving down a gravel road for a while makes you feel like you're really getting *away*. At the end of a gravel road outside of Elizabethtown, the Tipsords, Mike and Carol, have enhanced that feeling with the design of the one- and two-bedroom cabins that blend into the wooded acres lining the Ohio River. The cabins are up on stilts,

RIVER ROSE INN

which provide a nice perch from which to watch the boats passing by or to stare out at the water. Each cedar cabin is surrounded by trees to give a little privacy, and each has a deck with hot tub. Inside, the cabins are all pine, with a corner fireplace and furnishings to give it a clean, modern look. They also have kitchens. The most important thing for a vacation rental is that it has a dishwasher, because as Mr. Tipsord says, "Who wants to do dishes on vacation?" The one bedrooms have a queen bed in the main bedroom and two full beds in a loft above the living area. The two bedrooms have two baths, with doors that section the areas off into two separate suites. Deposits must be mailed ahead of time. $$.

& ✿ ✐ **Rim Rock's Dogwood Cabins** (618-264-6036; www

.rimrocksdogwoodcabins.com) Located east of Karbers Ridge, Elizabethtown. These rustic cabins would make a good home base for a family or larger group, as they sleep four to nine people. In their design, the owners have brought some of the outdoors inside, with touches like railings made of tree limbs. Some cabins have sleeping lofts, and all come with air-conditioning, heat, stove, refrigerator, microwave, coffeemaker, toaster, bathroom, screened-in porch, electric fireplace, satellite TV, DVD, linens, cookware, grill, and a picnic table. But note: You will need detailed directions from the owner to find the cabins, which seems like a selling point all by itself. $$.

Williams Hill Pass (618-252-6978; www.williamshillpass.com), 1935 Peak Road, Harrisburg. If off-roading is your thing, then definitely check out Williams Hill Pass, which offers opportunities for all levels. And for a pretty economical stay, the bunkhouse cabins accommodate four for $50 per night, with a full bed and bunk beds. The welcome center has a shower house.

♿ **Cave-In-Rock State Park Lodge** (618-289-4545; www.cave inrockkaylors.com), New State Park Road, Cave-in-Rock. These four duplex cabins are perched 80 feet above the Ohio River on Pirate's Bluff. The eight suites are nothing fancy, but can accommodate up to four people. All are outfitted with a kitchenette, dining area, two queen beds, satellite TV, private balcony overlooking the river, tub, and shower. A restaurant on site serves breakfast, lunch, and dinner. $.

Golconda Lock and Dam Homes (618-683-6702; www .golcondalockmasterhomes.com) These four homes were built in the 1920s to house U.S. Army Corps of Engineers employees who were working as lockkeepers along the Ohio River. But the construction of the Smithland Lock and Dam downriver meant the Dam 51 near Golconda wasn't needed, and the corps abandoned the property. The town of Golconda restored the homes and now offers them for vacation rentals. One nice extra is a screened-in porch with a hot tub overlooking the river. The homes have fireplaces, living rooms, and kitchens. Depending on your group size, there are two 3-bedroom homes, which fit up to eight people, and two 1-bedrooms, which can fit up to four adults. $$.

CEDAR HILL RIVER RESORT

CAMPING The Shawnee National Forest (618-658-2111; www.fs.usda.gov/shawnee) has several campgrounds, but does not accept reservations. All campsites are doled out on a first-come, first-served basis. Primitive camping is allowed except within designated natural areas or research natural areas.

The forest's **Camp Cadiz Campground** is located off IL 1, east of Karbers Ridge. Open year-round, this campground can accommodate trailers or tent camping. Camp Cadiz was an old work camp for the Civilian Conservation Corps, whose handiwork can be seen all around these parts. But the only thing left from the original camp are two large fireplaces. The 11 sites come with tables, fire pits, and lantern poles. Drinking water and rest rooms are also located on site. The park itself has hiking and equestrian trails. $10 per site.

Oak Point Campground Just east of IL 145, south of the town of Glendale, you will find this popular campground in the Shawnee's Lake Glendale Recreation Area. Its popularity has something to do with the fact that it's the only campground in the forest with electric sites and showers. With 31 electric sites, and 26 non-electric, campers will also find drinking water, rest rooms, dumping stations, hiking, and fishing. The campground is open all year and the charge is $10–14 per site. Another reason for its draw is

the beach, which has a lifeguard on duty and a bathhouse. The beach is open from 10–dusk, Memorial Day through Labor Day. Admission: $3 adults, $1.50 children under 6. Paddleboat and canoes also can be rented.

& **Pharaoh Campground** For camping in the Garden of the Gods Recreation Area, these 12 campsites are available in the forest year-round. Much like the "garden" itself, the campground offers nice tree cover and views. Each site has a picnic table, fire pit, and grill. There are also things like drinking water and rest rooms on site that make your stay a bit less of a struggle. The cost is $10 per night.

Tower Rock Campground Off IL 146, Elizabethtown. For riverfront camping, these 25 sites offer a scenic base for anglers who might want to take advantage of the boat launch. Outhouses and drinking water are located on site. There's also a trailhead leading up Tower Rock.

& **Cave-In-Rock State Park** (618-289-4325) Off IL 1, Cave-In-Rock. Another option near the Ohio River is this state campground, with 34 electric sites and 25 tent sites. You can choose a site in an open area or one surrounded by mature trees, depending on what type of camping experience you're after. Showers, rest rooms, and a dump station are also available. As far as activities to keep you busy during the day, there's fishing, boating, and hiking. Sites are $10–30 per night.

✳ Where to Eat

There are slim pickings when it comes to restaurants in these parts. When you ask for suggestions in just about every town, you get the same two or three restaurants. As you get closer to the regional centers like Harrisburg, you can find some chain restaurants and a few additional options.

EATING OUT **Kaylors' Cave-In-Rock Restaurant** (618-289-4545; www.caveinrockkaylors.com) Open 8–7 Sunday through Thursday, 8–8 Friday and Saturday. Cave-In-Rock State Park. This restaurant, with its large stone fireplace and window-lined dining room is operated by Anne and Marty Kaylor. They offer decent food with a menu that ranges from $3 burgers to charbroiled pork tenderloin, tilapia, or butterfly shrimp. Entrees come with your choice of three sides. If you're there on the weekend, you might want to check out one of the "all you can eat" catfish or fried chicken deals. The deck is a great place to relax after checking out the park. A small gift shop is attached, behind the cash register. $.

E'Town River Restaurant (618-287-2333) Elizabethtown riverfront. Open seasonally 11–7 Sunday through Thursday, 11–8 Friday and Saturday. I'm not sure if people really know this is the name of this place, as everyone recommended it to me as the "floating restaurant." You walk up a plank ramp to the boat of a restaurant, which specializes in frying up fresh catfish. And that's what you should order, because it doesn't get any fresher than this. Be aware that sometimes if the river is high, you can't get up to the door, as happened to us on one visit. $.

The Riverport (618-683-2602) 319 E. Main Street, Golconda. Open 11–1:30 weekdays. Catfish sandwich anyone? If not, this main street Golconda restaurant serves chicken salad, burgers, and paninis. The salads are served with dressings homemade on site. $.

DINING OUT **Wineaux's Restaurant** (618-658-2274; www.crbwinery.com), 315 Forman Lane, Belknap. Open 4:30–9 Friday, noon–9 Saturday, noon–5 Sunday. On the weekends, you can head to this spot at the Cache River Basin Winery for a nice meal with a view of the vineyard. The menu runs the gamut from surf and turf to a lighter mahi mahi glazed in tarragon butter. Burgers, pasta, and chicken dishes fill out the menu. The lunchtime menu features a line of salads and sandwiches. $$–$$$.

✳ Selective Shopping

&. **The Chocolate Factory** (877-949-3829; www.thechocolate factory.net), IL 146, Golconda. Open 9–5 Monday through Saturday. All kinds of crèmes and clusters and chocolate heavenly goodness to be found here. The gourmet chocolates also come in sugar-free versions.

Riverport Antique and Gifts (618-683-2002) 301 Main Street, Golconda. Open 10–5 Friday and Saturday. If you find yourself in historic downtown Golconda, stop in to browse the antiques or get a few gift ideas from the other items for sale.

✳ Special Events

April: **Illinois River to River Relay** (http://rrr.olm.net) The race starts on McGee Hill in LaRue Pine Hills, south of Grand Tower on the Mississippi River, and ends at the river in Golconda. To give you a sense of the popularity of this annual race across the southern end of the state: When registration opens in October, slots are booked up in just minutes. Working in teams of eight, runners complete three sections of 2.5 to 4 miles across gravel and country roads through the Shawnee National Forest. Together, the team has the challenge of an entire 80-mile course that starts on a bluff overlooking the Mississippi and follows country and gravel roads to the Ohio River in Golconda.

June: **Superman Celebration** (800-949-5740; www.superman celebration.net), Metropolis. For this four-day annual celebration, it's not unusual to see people walking down the street in super-hero costumes. The Illinois town that adopted Superman as its hometown son celebrates the superhero with film screenings, appearances by celebrities who have starred in Superman movies or TV shows, costume parades, road races, music, and other events.

September: **Shrimp Fest** (www .mainstreetgolconda.org) With its location on the banks of the Ohio River, Golconda celebrates the harvest of Illinois freshwater shrimp with a day-long festival. You'll also find helicopter, carriage and river-taxi rides, beer, wine, music and of course, shrimp, shrimp, and more shrimp.

October: **Fort Massac Encampment** (618-524-4712; www.dnr .illinois.gov), Fort Massac State Park. If you're in these parts in the fall, it would definitely be a good time to get a unique look at Fort Massac State Park. During this two-day annual festival, you can see mock battles, tactical demonstrations, and all kinds of activities dedicated to re-creating life in the late 1700s. From Metropolis, follow the signs to the fort.

INDEX